NAKED

Also by Susan Zakin

Coyotes and Town Dogs: Earth First! and the Environmental Movement

Naked

Writers Uncover the Way We Live on Earth

EDITED BY SUSAN ZAKIN

Four Walls Eight Windows
New York/London

Published in the United States by
Four Walls Eight Windows
39 West 14th Street
New York, NY 10011
http://www.4w8w.com

First printing March 2004
Printed on 100 percent old-growth-forest free, recycled paper.

Cataloging-in-Publication Data for this book
has been filed with the Library of Congress

ISBN: 1-56858-294-3

Text composition by Ink, Inc., New York.
Printed in Canada

10 9 8 7 6 5 4 3 2 1

TABLE OF CONTENTS

ACKNOWLEDGEMENTS

Unpublished letters by Edward Abbey copyright © the estate of Edward Abbey.
    Reprinted by permission of Clarke Abbey.
"Searching for Mr. Watson" by Bill Belleville, copyright © 2003 by Bill Belleville.
    Reprinted by permission of the author.
"Gunnison Beach" by Rita Welty Bourke, copyright © 2003 by Rita Welty Bourke.
    Reprinted by permission of the author.
"Blue" from *Blue Desert*, by Charles Bowden. © 1986 The Arizona Board of Regents.
    Reprinted by permission of the University of Arizona Press.
"Dogology" by T. C. Boyle. Copyright © 2002 by T. C. Boyle. Reprinted by
    permission of Georges Borchardt, Inc. for the author.
"Audubon's Inquiry," from *Audubon's Watch: A Novel* by John Gregory Brown.
    Copyright © 2001 John Gregory Brown. Reprinted by permission of
    Houghton Mifflin Company. All rights reserved.
Reprinted with permission of Simon & Schuster Adult Publishing Group from *Last
    Car to Elysian Fields* by James Lee Burke. Copyright © 2003 by James Lee Burke.
From *The Songlines* by Bruce Chatwin, copyright © 1987 by Bruce Chatwin. Used by
    permission of Viking Penguin, a division of Penguin Group (USA) Inc.
"Chicken 81" by Sarah L. Courteau, copyright © 2003 by Sarah L. Courteau.
    Reprinted by permission of the author.
"Wet" by Joe Donnelly, copyright © 2003 by Joe Donnelly. Reprinted by permission
    of the author.
From *Don't Let's Go to the Dogs Tonight* by Alexandra Fuller, copyright © 2001 by
    Alexandra Fuller. Used by permission of Random House, Inc.
From *Team Rodent: How Disney Devours the World* by Carl Hiaasen, copyright © 1998 by
    Carl Hiaasen. Used by permission of Ballantine Books, a division of Random
    House, Inc.
"Island of the Damned" by Jack Hitt, copyright © 2003 by Jack Hitt. Reprinted by
    permission of the author.
From the book *Ark Baby* by Liz Jensen, copyright © 1998 by Liz Jensen, reprinted by
    permission of The Overlook Press.

From *The Shadow of the Sun* by Ryszard Kapuściński, translated by Klara Glowczewska, copyright © 2001 by Klara Glowczewska. Used by permission of Alfred A. Knopf, a division of Random House, Inc.

From *On Bullfighting* by A. L. Kennedy, copyright © 1999 by A. L. Kennedy. Used by permission of Random House, Inc.

From *Kinski Uncut* by Klaus Kinski, translated by Joachim Neugroschel, copyright © 1996 by Joachim Neugroschel. Copyright © 1996 by Genevieve and Nanhoi Nakszynski, for the Estate of Klaus Kinski. Used by permission of Viking Penguin, a division of Penguin Group (USA) Inc.

From *In an Arid Land* by Paul Scott Malone, copyright © 1995 by Paul Scott Malone. Reprinted by permission of TCU Press.

"Blood Lust: Why I Kill" by Thomas McIntyre, copyright © 2003 by Thomas McIntyre. Reprinted by permission of the author.

"Die, Baby Harp Seal!" by Lydia Millet, copyright © 2003 by Lydia Millet. Reprinted by permission of the author.

Reprinted by permission of Farrar, Straus and Giroux, LLC: Excerpt from *Easy Travel to Other Planets* by Ted Mooney. Copyright © 1981 by Ted Mooney.

Reprinted by permission of Farrar, Straus and Giroux, LLC: Excerpt from *Catfish and Mandala* by Andrew X. Pham, copyright © 1999 by Andrew X. Pham.

Beyond the Last Village: A Journey of Discovery in Asia's Forbidden Wilderness, by Alan Rabinowitz. Copyright © 2001 Alan Rabinowitz. Reprinted by permission of Island Press/Shearwater Books, Washington, D.C. and Covelo, California.

"Habits and Habitat of the Southwestern Bad Boy" by Stacey Richter, first appeared in *Hayden's Ferry Review*. Copyright © 2003 by Stacey Richter. Reprinted by permission of the author.

"Me Jane, You're Kidding" by Elizabeth Royte, copyright © 2003 by Elizabeth Royte. Reprinted by permission of the author.

From *The Hidden West* by Rob Schultheis, copyright © 1978, 1979, 1980 by Rob Schultheis. Reprinted by permission of North Point Press.

From *The Snakebite Survivors' Club*, copyright © by Jeremy Seal 1999, reprinted by permission of Harcourt, Inc. First published in England in 1999 by Picador.

"The Luckiest Horse in Reno" by Deanne Stillman, copyright © 2003 by Deanne Stillman. Reprinted by permission of the author.

"Save the Whales, Screw the Shrimp," from *Ill Nature: Rants and Reflections on Humanity and Other Animals* by Joy Williams, reprinted by permission of International Creative Management, Inc. Copyright © 2001 by Joy Williams.

Introduction and an excerpt from *Tierra Incognita* by Suzan Zakin, copyright © Susan Zakin, reprinted by permission of the author.

O N A SNOWLESS CHRISTMAS DAY, I helped my father move into an apartment just off Beekman Place in Manhattan. Dad was on his second divorce and he wasn't feeling particularly festive. He also wasn't sympathetic when his teenage slacker daughter went on strike a few minutes after we started. I dropped a cardboard box on the floor of the building's lobby and whined: "Can't we eat something first?"

"Susie," my father said. "You're so ... *basic.*" A mordant exhale.

Basic? I was talking about food, yet Dad seemed horrified by my very connectedness to some revolting biological urge, as if responding to hunger were a sort of abject surrender. Obviously, Dad was on a mission that day, and any interruption could lead to thoughts of a painful variety. But I wonder, too, if good old Dad was, like most of his generation, unconsciously prey to the idea that Nature and Culture are two opposing forces, that Homo Sapiens is engaged in a zero-sum game with its own habitat.

When genes became the hot new metaphor among the science crowd, one of the first things we learned was that our DNA differs from a chimp's by a measly .05 percent. We weren't creatures endowed with a separate "human nature" but animals very much dominated by Nature itself. Our impulsive, chimplike behavior was not some remnant of the natural world, but what we are.

This provides small comfort, since our chimpster actions—I want that banana *now!*—may soon be the last goofy remnant of the natural world. Yet as our influence grows, the outlines of nature take on bizarre and interesting shapes. In the past, writing about Nature echoed my father's idea that the environment is locked in a Manichean battle with an implacable enemy (Man, extraction industries, angry ranchers, municipal governments, snow-mobilers, Forest Service bureaucrats, aging Communist regimes, or Disney-World—depending on where you live.)

Now, maybe, we're beginning to see that it's not so simple. We want to feel close to Nature so we buy tiger cubs and boa constrictors and lock them in our apartments. Environmentalists labor mightily to stop logging in a national forest in Oregon, causing a logging company to amp up operations in Borneo, where a rare ape dies. If we are at war with anything, it is with our own natures.

All this is disturbing, to say the least, but excellent fodder for art.

This anthology maps a subtle terrain rife with conflicting impulses and seemingly irrational but all too human behavior. It is also, quite consciously, an attempt to haul a decrepit genre out of its self-imposed ghetto of boundless purity and bloodless prose.

It's easy to understand why it all went south. As Joy Williams points out in one of this book's essays, the nomenclature itself is problematic: How can you fall in love with the word *environment*? At best, it has a sterile, technical sound, calling to mind a dustless laboratory where a race of genetically engineered actors is spawned. At worst it evokes: "Eat your edamame beans, Summer," and "Hey, honey, take it easy on the organic Chardonnay, would you *please*?" A word once synonymous with hipness and a very elemental kind of excitement can't shake its current association with people who've sworn off deodorant or humor, or both.

Mindful that repulsion is the inevitable result of earnestness, New York publishers, who have little or no contact with nature anyway, shy away from publishing books or articles on the subject especially if they contain the merest hint that something could be intrinsically wrong with the way we do business. So what if our hairy cousins are on a bullet train to extinction? If you want to read about it, don't scan the regular pages of any major magazine. Check out the Kenneth Cole ad. Odds are, you won't find it anywhere else.

Writers who manage to eke a living out of the green ghetto tend to be well-intentioned, contemplative, and downright inspirational. Men sport the inevitable beard and speak in a considered, responsible manner. Women intone sentimental aphorisms revealing a certain mystical streak. They drive Volvos. They drink uncaffeinated tea. They meditate. None of them have messy lives that are the stuff of good writing—or maybe they just don't admit it. For at least a decade, these navel-gazing purveyors of lapidary prose have dominated environmental literature. Their books about rare animals or exotic places aim at a niche market of upscale Baby Boomers. Darwin's finches masquerade as toys on the shelves of the Nature Company store at the mall. Frankly, I'd rather look at the Kenneth Cole ad. It's more honest, more entertaining, and a whole lot better looking.

Still, there are writers with a different take on things. Their stories contain all the elements missing from endless reveries upon a rock: drama, wit, and actual characters. Their passion is unmistakable, whether expressed by a hardboiled detective at his wife's gravesite in a Louisiana bayou, a decadent actor's brief spell of happiness in the Amazon, or a weird tale of a Bible-thumping snake handler gone very, very wrong.

These are the writers in this anthology. They are linked not only by a considerable level of accomplishment, but also by a certain sensibility. For instance, T. Coraghessan Boyle and Joy Williams are recognized solely for their literary gifts, yet they are longtime workers on the underground railroad of smart environmental writing. Boyle and Williams eschew sentimentality—in fact, they often parody it—but place no limits on passionate engagement. As more writers join their ranks, a clandestine literary movement threatens to erupt into outright rebellion, skewering sincerity with a jagged postmodern flourishing of obscure and not-so-obscure novels, of disturbing short stories, of essays that smack of truth. The iconoclasts include Generation X writers with a penchant for the grotesque like Lydia Millet and Stacey Richter, sharp, original journalists like Jack Hitt and Deanne Stillman, promising underthirty practitioners of literary nonfiction like Sarah L. Courteau, and a *sui generis* author of picaresque futuristic satires named Liz Jensen. And there are more....

These are the lineal descendants of an earlier generation of men and women who realized that the artist's role is to stand outside society, not pander to it like a servile waiter. Twenty years ago, Edward Abbey, Thomas McGuane, Peter Matthiessen, Richard

Ford, and others drew a new map of America. Abbey may not have been the most literary of the three, but he had a way of making words rise from the page as if they were tangible. I was at a tender age then, and romantic enough to hit the road simply because of a book or two. After reading *Desert Solitaire* and *The Monkey Wrench Gang*, I packed my college-girl Honda Civic and headed west, in the rather questionable tradition of Abbey, Lewis and Clark, John James Audubon, and a small army of drifters, grifters, and at least a few serial killers. It wasn't long before I, too, found it hard to live without the pure, frightening blue of a desert sky. I discovered a measure of solitude could set me right, preferably in a landscape of charred volcanic mountains. And I developed a righteous hatred for anyone who would trample those things.

I was hardly the only reader to be so seduced. "A man wrote a book and lives were changed. That doesn't happen often," David Quammen wrote in an obituary for Ed Abbey in *Outside* magazine. But Abbey was only one of a generation of writers whose passion for the natural world was too intense for sentimentality and mercifully inhospitable to self-righteousness. Abbey's correspondence, some of which is published for the first time in this anthology, includes letters from literary figures like McGuane, Jim Harrison, Wendell Berry, and Cormac McCarthy. But the most revealing notes are from writers who never managed to stop working for a living, like John Mitchell, a National Geographic editor who supplied his friend with rowdy gossip-laden reports from the urban field. Abbey also corresponded with Mitch's best friend, Tom Watkins, a working-class California boy, historian, biographer, and magazine editor who had been Wallace Stegner's protégé. When Watkins died, Bruce Weber wrote in *The New York Times* that he had earned the reputation, "like Stegner and Edward Abbey, of one who accepted the might and spiritual tug of nature as factual rather than dreamy and who consequently sought to convey those qualities with literary force but without sentimentality." I knew Tom, if only slightly, and I couldn't describe him better myself, or his peers.

Sadly, by the time Weber wrote these words, this school of writing was in decline. "Too angry," some said. "Irresponsible," said others. And definitely not politically correct. The next crop possessed ambitions grander in scope, perhaps, but their efforts lacked a reprobate's charm. Who can mark the exact moment when the zeitgeist changes? I date it to a Jan. 2, 1988 letter from Barry Lopez to Edward Abbey. Two years before, Lopez had won the National Book Award for *Arctic Dreams: Imagination and Desire in a Northern Landscape.* Despite the book's title, passion held little sway in Lopez's world; rather he aimed for, in the words of one reviewer, "a kind of learned understanding of wild places, in this case the vast, scarcely knowable northern landscape." The book was an impressive achievement. But does anyone fall crazy in love with a painting because they understand the brushwork?

Abbey often berated himself for not doing more for the places he loved. He did the same to writers he admired, including Lopez. Lopez responded: "I chide myself for not standing up publically (sic) more often. But in the end I think I am better off trying to understand our relationship to polar bears and writing clearly about it, about preserving it, the urgency of this, than I am storming those bleak, adamantine caves on the Potomac."

Certainly preachiness is antithetical to good art. But artists have an obligation to renounce cant and caution in the service of truth. This is especially true for writers. I would argue that the difference between these two schools of environmental writing is not between those who feel politically committed and those who don't, but a divide between people who take themselves rather too seriously and those who are passionate, funny, and unpretentious—in other words, people who not only acknowledge their inconsistencies but revel in them. Without their voices, environmentalism became impossibly moral. No wonder the American public turned away.

The cost has been terrible. As Lopez and less talented imitators of his magisterial tone ("those bleak, adamantine caves") came to dominate environmental writing, the politics of the environment plunged so precipitously it is difficult to find an historical analogue short of revolution—or, in this case, counter-revolution. In an interview on Salon.com, environmental attorney Bobby Kennedy Jr. accused the Bush administration of rolling back more than two hundred environmental regulations. "If even a fraction of those are actually implemented, we will effectively have no significant federal environmental law left in our country," Kennedy said. "That's not exaggeration, it's not hyperbole, it is a fact."

Is there a correlation between the abdication of writers and a flaccid, defeated political movement? I believe there is. Only in America is the intimate relationship between culture and politics so vehemently denied, as if art were something not quite respectable, perhaps even illicit. This is a serious mistake. Saving the environment is as much an aesthetic issue as a moral one. Pseudo-utilitarian arguments about preserving rainforests because they might contain a wonder drug merely demean our cause. It simply isn't permissible to destroy beauty. Neither is it morally defensible to drive another species into extinction. In the 1960s, advertising wunderkind Gerry Mander fought construction of a dam in the Grand Canyon by asking: "Would you flood the Sistine Chapel to get closer to the painting?" It worked, and there is a lesson in that.

If you look back, to a time when the whole damned enterprise was still fun, the remedy becomes clear. It's not money; the bad guys will always have more. It's not politics *per se*; at least not right now, when environmental activism veers madly between corrupt pandering and self-indulgent vandalism. It's not the media, lost to the empty pornographic thrill of celebrity journalism.

No, it's beauty that will save us. Beauty and passion, along with honesty, irreverence and an occasional jolt of creativity, were the only advantages that we ever had. We were fools to give them up. We slipped into defeated silence, as if we had resigned ourselves to losing the things that really mattered to us. Or we decamped for "those bleak, adamantine caves"—believing that politics alone could solve everything, or anything.

Edward Abbey swore that he derived more pleasure from nature than from all the works of man (except perhaps the works of Mahler). Yet he wrote books that possessed more humanity than nearly anything written under the environmental banner since his death. Abbey's characters worshiped the desert, but they also threw beer cans out their truck windows. Their flaws engaged and sometimes shocked us. (They drank beer in *cans?*) Abbey freighted his books—some say too heavily—with plot, narrative drive, and humor.

I'm not sure what Abbey would say about the state of world if he were alive today. I imagine his view wouldn't be particularly sunny. But I don't believe, as Paul Theroux once wrote, that it's all over, that we live on a violated planet. Or, I should say, I only half-believe it. The world is a lover lying on rumpled sheets; older, scarred by hard living. But still beautiful. A world that can be loved despite everything.

That's the kind of love we need now—love that isn't blind to experience—and it's the kind of writing that will bring us back to ourselves.

NAKED

From *The Songlines*

BRUCE CHATWIN

IT WAS AFTER FIVE. The evening light was raking down the street and through the window we could see a party of black boys, in chequered shirts and cowboy hats, walking jerkily under the poincianas in the direction of the pub.

The waitress was clearing up the leftovers. Arkady asked for more coffee but already she had turned the machine off. He looked at his empty cup, and frowned.

Then he looked up and asked, abruptly, "What's your interest in all this? What do you want here?"

"I came here to test an idea," I said.

"A big idea?"

"Probably a very obvious idea. But one I have to get out of my system."

"And?"

His sudden shift of mood made me nervous. I began to explain how I had once tried, unsuccessfully, to write a book about nomads.

"Pastoral nomads?"

"No," I said. "Nomads. 'Nomos' is Greek for 'pasture.' A nomad moves from pasture to pasture. A pastoral nomad is a pleonasm."

"Point taken," said Arkady. "Go on. Why nomads?"

When I was in my twenties, I said, I had a job as an "expert" on modern painting with a well-known firm of art auctioneers. We had sale-rooms in London and New York. I was one of the bright boys. People said I had a great career, if only I would play my cards right. One morning, I woke up blind.

During the course of the day, the sight returned to the left eye, but the right one stayed sluggish and clouded. The eye specialist who examined me said there was nothing wrong organically, and diagnosed the nature of the trouble.

"You've been looking too closely at pictures," he said. "Why don't you swap them for some long horizons?"

"Why not?" I said.

"Where would you like to go?"

"Africa."

The chairman of the company said he was sure there was something the matter with my eyes, yet couldn't think why I had to go to Africa.

I went to Africa, to the Sudan. My eyes had recovered by the time I reached the airport.

I sailed down the Dongola Reach in a trading felucca. I went to the "Ethiopians," which was a euphemism for brothel. I had a narrow escape from a rabid dog. At an understaffed clinic, I acted the role of anaesthetist for a Caesarean birth. I next joined up with a geologist who was surveying for minerals in the Red Sea Hills.

This was nomad country—the nomads being the Beja: Kipling's "fuzzy-wuzzies," who didn't give a damn: for the Pharaohs of Egypt or the British cavalry at Omdurman.

The men were tall and lean, and wore sand-coloured cottons folded in an X across the chest. With shields of elephant hide and "Crusader" swords dangling from their belts, they would come into the villages to trade their meat for grain. They looked down on the villagers as though they were some other animal.

In the early light of dawn, as the vultures flexed their wings along the rooftops, the geologist and I would watch the men at their daily grooming.

They anointed each other's hair with scented goat's grease and then teased it out in corkscrew curls, making a buttery parasol which, instead of a turban, prevented their brains from going soft. By evening, when the grease had melted, the curls bounced back to form a solid pillow.

Our camel-man was a joker called Mahmoud, whose mop of hair was even wider than the others. He began by stealing the geo-

logical hammer. Then he left his knife for us to steal. Then, with
hoots of laughter, we swapped them back and, in this way, we
became great friends.

When the geologist went back to Khartoum, Mahmoud took
me off into the desert to look for rock-paintings.

The country to the east of Derudeb was bleached and sere, and
there were long grey cliffs and dom palms growing in the wadis. The
plains were spotted with flat-topped acacias, leafless at this season,
with long white thorns like icicles and a dusting of yellow flowers.
At night, lying awake under the stars, the cities of the West seemed
sad and alien—and the pretensions of the "art world" idiotic. Yet
here I had a sense of homecoming.

Mahmoud instructed me in the art of reading footprints in the
sand: gazelles, jackals, foxes, women. We tracked and sighted a herd
of wild asses. One night, we heard the cough of a leopard close by.
One morning, he lopped off the head of a puff-adder which had
curled up under my sleeping-bag and presented me with its body on
the tip of his sword blade. I never felt safer with anyone or, at the
same time, more inadequate.

We had three camels, two for riding and one for waterskins, yet
usually we preferred to walk. He went barefoot; I was in boots. I
never saw anything like the lightness of his step and, as he walked,
he sang: a song, usually, about a girl from the Wadi Hammamat who
was lovely as a green parakeet. The camels were his only property.
He had no flocks and wanted none. He was immune to everything
we would call "progress."

We found our rock-paintings: red ochre pin men scrawled on
the overhang of a rock. Nearby there was a long flat boulder with a
cleft up one end and its surface pocked with cup-marks. This, said
Mahmoud, was the Dragon with its head cut off by Ali.

He asked me, with a wicked grin, whether I was a Believer. In
two weeks I never saw him pray.

Later, when I went back to England, I found a photo of a
"fuzzy-wuzzy" carved in relief on an Egyptian tomb of the Twelfth
Dynasty at Beni Hassan: a pitiful, emaciated figure, like the pictures

of victims in the Sahel drought, and recognisably the same as Mahmoud.

The Pharaohs had vanished: Mahmoud and his people had lasted. I felt I had to know the secret of their timeless and irreverent vitality.

I quit my job in the "art world" and went back to the dry places: alone, traveling light. The names of the tribes I traveled among are unimportant: Rguibat, Quashgai, Taimanni, Turkomen, Bororo, Tuareg—people whose journeys, unlike my own, had neither beginning nor end.

I slept in black tents, blue tents, skin tents, yurts of felt and windbreaks of thorns. One night, caught in a sandstorm in the Western Sahara, I understood Muhammed's dictum, "A journey is a fragment of Hell."

The more I read, the more convinced I became that nomads had been the crankhandle of history, if for no other reason than that the great monotheisms had, all of them, surfaced from the pastoral milieu . . .

Arkady was looking out of the window.

From *Don't Let's Go to the Dogs Tonight*

ALEXANDRA FULLER

Loo Paper and Coke

DAD TAKES VANESSA AND ME with him while he's out looking for stray wild cattle and fencing the vast, unfenced ranch. We drive for two days to reach this particular herd. Dad is in the front, smoking, alone with his thoughts. Vanessa and I are in the back of the Land Rover with the dogs and the African laborers, bumping with our skinny bottoms on the spare tire and singing against the loud scream of the diesel engine cutting through roadless land, "If you think Ah'm sexy and you want my body . . ." The Africans are crouched, quiet, gently rocking with the sway of the Land Rover. We travel for two days like this, blowing out tires on camel thorns, climbing over fallen trees, churning through dried-out flash-flood riverbeds.

"Come on," Dad shouts, "everyone *getoutandpush!*"

And we leap over the edge of the back, all of us tumbling, scrambling for earth under numb muscles, hurrying before the Land Rover loses what little momentum it has. And we shout in Shona, "*Potsi, piri, tatu, ini!*" One, two, three, four!

And "Push!"

"Ah, ah, ah!"

The men start to sing. "*Potsi, piri, tatu, ini!*"

The Land Rover bites. The dogs are out, too, herding, barking at the back tires. "Yip-yip."

The Land Rover finds edible ground and surges forward; we

cling to the tailgate, jostling for a place. Dad won't stop in case he gets stuck again. We climb aboard while the Land Rover spins ahead.

Dad stops on level, solid ground and we all get out to pee. The men congregate at the front of the Land Rover; Vanessa and I crouch behind the back wheels.

She says, "Keep boogies for me. Make sure they aren't spying."

So I keep boogies. And when she has finished I say, "Keep boogies for me," and she nonchalantly climbs back into the Land Rover. "Hey, that's not fair. I kept boogies for you."

"So?"

"Then keep boogies for me."

"You're just a kid, you don't count."

I pee quickly, crouching, looking over my shoulder. The sweet smell of pee steams up to me from the burning sand, sand hot enough to evaporate pee on contact.

Dad has a compass. He looks at the sun, lights a cigarette. He gets down on his haunches and looks through the trees for a straight passage, wide enough for the Land Rover to fit between the trunks of the thickly-growing mopane.

The men, who have been saving their own cigarettes, stick by stick from one payday to the next, relight old stompies and take two or three drags, holding the smoke deep in their lungs before exhaling, and then carefully pinching the end off their cigarettes, saving them for later.

Cephas has found impala tracks while we are waiting for everyone to pee and to stretch the kinks out of their bones. He shows Dad, without talking, his shoulders shrugging casually in the direction of the thick bush.

"Fresh?" asks Dad.

Cephas reads the ground the way we read a map or a signpost. "They passed this way within one hour."

"Can we catch them?"

"They are moving slowly." Cephas points to newly pinched shrubs. "Eating."

So Dad says, "You girls want to come or stay here?"

The sun is starting to fall into its own fiery pool of color behind the mopane trees and the air is releasing night smells. Vanessa and I know that in less than an hour, we are going to be bunched-up, shivering cold.

"Stay here, thank you, Dad."

"Keep the dogs, hey?"

"Ja."

We hold the dogs by the scruff of the neck until Dad is out of sight. Dad shoulders his .303. He lights a cigarette. Cephas starts to run ahead, darting, ducking, zigzagging. It's as if he's sniffing the ground. Dad follows, his quick strides swallowing ground.

Vanessa and I hunker down next to the Land Rover with the dogs. We have both brought books, but the books need to last us for weeks while we are in camp. We have been in charge of our own packing. Dad said, "You girls are old enough now to pack for yourselves."

We have packed teabags, powdered milk, sugar, and bran flakes for breakfast. Zimbabwean bran flakes taste like barely crushed tree bark. We have tins of baked beans and fish in tomato sauce for lunch. We have brought two shirts, two pairs of shorts, two pairs of brookies, and a jersey each. We already realize that we have forgotten to pack loo paper.

Dad has packed cigarettes, brandy, bullets, and his gun.

Vanessa pulls out the packet of cards. "Want to play war?"

"Okay."

She deals. We play in the failing evening light, which is going in fast stages from mellowing yellow-red into dusky gray, filtered through the trees. The sun sets below the horizon and it is suddenly dark-black. The moon has not yet risen. We put the cards away. The temperature drops from strangling heat to goose-pimple cold in a matter of minutes. The men climb out of the back of the Land Rover and build a fire, to the west of the vehicle, using the body of the car as a windbreak. They slump on their haunches and stretch out their hands to the fire, resting elbows on knees. They relight their stumps of cigarettes and start to talk, their voices rising and falling like wind coming from a distance.

Vanessa and I hunch beside the men, arms outstretched to the warmth of the fire. The men shuffle aside to make room for us, offer us a pull off their carefully smoked cigarettes, and laugh when we shake our heads.

We wait for Dad.

When the men get hungry they boil water and add a fistful of cornmeal into a pot for sadza. Into another pot they throw beans, oil, salt, and sliced dry meat for the relish. One man gets up and fills a small bowl with water from the drums in the back of the Land Rover. The water bowl is passed around and we all wash our hands. Now we eat, squashing balls of hot sadza with the fingers of our right hands and scooping up a little of the gravy onto the ball of meal. The men eat communally from dishes that sit in the middle of us, everyone eating slowly, eyeing their neighbors, careful not to take too much. Each man finishes when he is full, washes his hands from the small bowl. The men relight their cigarettes.

By the time Dad and Cephas return, the moon has risen in the east and is hanging low over the trees, sending a silver light over the faces around the fire. Cephas comes first. He is walking effortlessly with an eighty-pound impala ram slung over his shoulders, the little black-socked feet caught in his fists. Dad follows with the gun. The impala has been field-dressed; the stomach and guts have been left in the bush for hyenas, jackals, and the morning-circling vultures.

Dad has killed the impala with one shot to the heart. I insert my forefinger into the passage where the bullet has gone. It is still warm and wet with quickly robbed life. There is a tinny smell of blood and there are animal smells that waft up from the carcass— the smells this ram carried with it in life: dust, rutting, shit, sun, rain. Live ticks still suck from the dead animal, clustered where the skin is most soft, near the animal's ears and genitals and on its stomach. Its eyes bulge hugely under eyelashes as long as my finger.

Cephas hangs the impala from a tree and slits its throat, and blood gushes out onto the ground where the dogs are waiting, tongues hanging.

We pull out sleeping bags and set up to sleep around the fire. Dad heats up some baked beans for supper, which he washes down with brandy and warm, silty-tasting water. We can hear the hyenas starting their evening scour: *"Waaaaoooop!" "Waaaa-oooop!"* The dogs, blood-spattered and bellies distended, growl and press themselves against our sleeping bags.

"*Waaaa-ooooop!*"

THE NEXT MORNING we are up before dawn. It is too cold to sleep. The men stoke the fire and boil water for tea. Dad smokes. We curl stiff-cold hands around our tin cups and suck on the milky sweet tea until the sun startles up over the horizon, flooding pink light through the trees to our camp. It is almost immediately warm. In an hour it will be so hot that sweat will run in stinging rivulets into our eyes and dust will stick onto fresh sweat. For now, it is cool enough. Food and tea, wood-smoke flavored, are sweet comfort. The mourning doves begin their sad call, "*Wumu-woo. Wumu-woo*" The Cape turtledove is crying, "*Kuk-KOORR-ru! Work hard-er. Work hard-er.*"

The men wash up from breakfast and Vanessa packs the breakfast food and tea back into Dad's old ammunition box. We scramble up into the back of the Land Rover and sit in a circle, perched around the impala. The men begin to sing, picking up songs and tunes from one another. They are songs of work and love and war. They are the songs of men who live too long at a stretch without women.

When we reach the permanent camp on the banks of the Turgwe River, Dad skins the impala and hangs it from the bush pole that holds up the tarpaulin under which we keep food, dishes, and the drums of water for washing. Dad points to the drums. "Don't ever drink this water," he tells Vanessa and me. It comes from the shrinking, slime-frothed pools of water, warm and green with stagnant life, that are all that remains of the Turgwe River's last flood.

During the day, Dad and the men drive to the fence lines and continue to set stakes in the ground, stretching wire into which they will one day herd the wild Brahmans. Some days, Dad drives all day with maps to find the old, decaying dips and kraals. He leaves a span of men at these old cattle camps to fix the holes in the concrete walls and reinforce the old races. He leaves them with food, cigarettes, matches. "I'll be back in two days," he tells them, "you fix this place by then?"

"Yes, boss."

"Then *faga moto!*"

Dad wants to dip the wild cattle before the rains come in October-November.

Vanessa and I stay in camp and read, or climb the boulder that overlooks the Turgwe River and sing into microphone-baobab pods, "If you think Ah'm sexy and you want my body, come on baby let it show."

"Those aren't the words."

"Okay, then." I stick out thin hips and rock back and forth: "There's a brown girl in the rain, tra-la-la-la-la! There's a brown girl in the rain, tra-la-la-la-la-la. Brown girl in the rain. Tra-la-la-la-la. She looks like sugar in your bum. Tra-la-la!"

"I'm telling Dad."

"What?"

"You said 'bum.'"

I climb higher on the boulder until I am balanced precariously on the thin-shouldered top. "Bum!" I shout into the stunned mid-day heat. "Bum! Bum!"

Vanessa says, "You're so *immature*." She goes back into camp and I am left with my bad word echoing around in the dusty quiet bush. *Bum.*

That is a day Dad has gone with old maps to find a kraal and he is late coming back into camp. We have been in camp for two weeks and the drinking water is running low. We must use the drinking water carefully, only for brushing teeth and drinking. When the plastic containers of drinking water have run out we will have to turn to the tanks of river water pulled from the Turgwe. We are already making tea from boiled river water—boiled for ten minutes and strained to get rid of the lumps of dirt, hippo shit, the worst of the silt.

Vanessa is reading under the tree. She has set Shea up as a pillow and is lying on Shea's belly.

I say, "I'll make a cake."

Vanessa doesn't answer.

"Do you want to make a cake with me?"

"No."

I make a cake out of dirt, leaves, bark, and water. I decorate it with stones and sticks, sprinkle it with shiny white sand. I put it on a rock to bake in the dying light of the sun. Then I am bored. I lie on my stomach in the flat dirt, poking pieces of grass into ant lion traps. I catch ants and drop them into the tiny funnel-shaped traps and watch the ant lions scurry up, minute claws waving, to catch the scrambling ants. I lie on my back and squint up at the sky, watching blue through the fronds of the ivory palm tree.

I roll back onto my knees. "Should we have tea?" I ask Vanessa.

Vanessa has fallen asleep over her book. Shea is sleeping, too. I watch their stomachs rise and fall in soft, warm slumber.

The fire has gone out. I soak a teabag in the tepid water from the drum which sits under a fresh impala carcass. This is river water for tea and washing. Powdered milk dropped into my cup floats on top of the water in lumpy obstinance. I take a few sips before the taste of it swells in my throat and I grimace. "Yuck."

By the time Dad comes into camp, Vanessa is holding me up over a fallen log, rear end hanging over one side of it, head hanging over the other. I am naked; all my clothes are in a bag in the tent, soiled with frothy yellow shit. Vanessa has a grip on my shoulders; there is shit streaming from my bum, vomit dribbling into a pool between Vanessa's feet.

"She drank the wrong water," says Vanessa when Dad comes. "She made tea without boiling the water first."

Then there is nothing left inside me, I gag dryly, my bowels clutch and spasm but all that comes out of me is thin yellow liquid. Vanessa wipes my mouth and bum with a fistful of leaves and grass. She bathes me, running water over my burning skin from a bucket, and then wraps me in a towel. She carries me to the tent, which is rank with the smell of my soiled clothes. Dad throws them into a pit fire at the back of the camp where we burn garbage—old baked-bean tins, cigarette packets, empty cereal boxes, and used teabags. Vanessa props me up and tries to feed me some hot tea. I am so thirsty my throat seems stuck together, my tongue feels swollen and cracked. As soon as the liquid hits my belly, I vomit again.

My bum and mouth are raw and both begin to bleed.

Dad says, "We should have packed some Cokes."

"And loo paper," says Vanessa. She licks her finger and wipes the edges of my mouth with her moist fingertip. I loll back against her arm. She says, "Hold on, Chookies." She strokes sweat-wet hair off my forehead and rocks me. "Hold on," she tells me.

WE HAVE A RADIO IN THE LAND ROVER. Dad drives up to the top of a small rise overlooking the river and calls headquarters. The radio hisses and crackles.

"Devuli HQ, Devuli HQ, this is Devuli mobile. Do you read? Over."

The radio squeaks, swoops, "*Wee-arrr-ooo.*"

Dad calls again, but there is no answer.

Dad comes back to camp. "We'll have to try again at seven, when they're waiting for us." We have been checking in every evening at seven to see if Mum has had the baby.

He says, "I'll mix up some rehydration salts." He stirs two level teaspoons of sugar and half a teaspoon of salt into a liter of boiled water. Vanessa holds up my head, and Dad feeds teaspoons of the liquid into my mouth. I start to retch; bile dribbles, bitter and stinging, down my chin.

At seven, Dad drives the Land Rover back up to the rise and radios again. "Bobo's sick; vomiting and diarrhea. She's too sick to move. If we try and move her . . . she won't make it back. Any advice? Over."

The ranch manager's wife comes onto the radio. "Have her sip some salt, sugar, and water. You know the amounts? Over."

"Affirmative. We've tried that. No go. Over."

The manager's wife is quiet. At last she replies, "Don't know what to say, Tim."

Dad slumps over the radio.

THE NEXT DAY DAD STAYS IN CAMP with me instead of going out to herd wild cattle. I am feeling light-headed, losing the feeling of my body. When Dad pinches the skin on my arm, it stays puckered up in a tiny tent of skin. My feet are starting to swell. He tells Vanessa to keep on trying to feed me the rehydration salts. I keep vomiting. By late the next afternoon, I am too tired to keep my eyes open. Vanessa goes into the old ammunition box and finds a wrinkled orange, the last saved piece of fresh food in our store. She slices it open and comes back into the tent. "Here"—she presses a quarter of orange between my teeth—"suck on this."

Dad says, "I don't think she should eat fruit."

Vanessa looks at him.

Dad hunches miserably. He lights a cigarette. "You're right," he says. "Might as well, hey. Try it."

The orange juice trickles down my throat; and falls into my empty, air-blown belly. It stays.

That night Dad feeds me a bowl of soft, watery sadza. He says, "Eat this. If this doesn't plug you up, I don't know what will."

The mealie porridge sticks against my teeth and slides into my belly.

"One more bite."

I swallow and take one more bite, then I say "Enough" and lie back on my cot and shut my eyes.

I can hear the men around the campfire singing softly, taking it in turns to pick up a tune, the rhythm as strong as blood in a body. The firelight flickers off the blue and orange tent in pale, dancing shapes and there is the sweet smell of the African bush, wood smoke, dust, sweat. My bones are so sharp and thin against the sleeping bag that they hurt me and I must cover my hip bones with my hands.

I make a vow never to leave Africa.

Dogology

T. CORAGHESSAN BOYLE

Rumors

IT WAS THE SEASON OF MUD, drainpipes drooling, the gutters clogged with debris, a battered and penitential robin fixed like a statue on every lawn. Julian was up early, a Saturday morning, beating eggs with a whisk and gazing idly out the kitchen window and into the colorless hide of the day, expecting nothing, when all at once the scrim of rain parted to reveal a dark, crouching presence in the far corner of the yard. At first glance, he took it to be a dog—a town ordinance that he particularly detested disallowed fences higher than three feet, and so the contiguous lawns and flower beds of the neighborhood had become a sort of open savanna for roaming packs of dogs—but before the wind shifted and the needling rain closed in again he saw that he was wrong. This figure, partially obscured by the resurgent forsythia bush, seemed out of proportion, all limbs, as if a dog had been mated with a monkey. What was it, then? Raccoons had been at the trash lately, and he'd seen an opossum wavering down the street like a pale ghost one night after a dreary, overwrought movie Cara had insisted upon, but this was no opossum. Or raccoon, either. It was dark in color, whatever it was— a bear, maybe, a yearling strayed down from the high ridges along the river, and hadn't Ben Ober told him somebody on F Street had found a bear in their swimming pool? He put down the whisk and went to fetch his glasses.

A sudden eruption of thunder set the dishes rattling on the drainboard, followed by an uncertain flicker of light that illuminated the dark room as if the bulb in the overhead fixture had gone loose in the socket. He wondered how Cara could sleep through all this, but the wonder was short-lived, because he really didn't give a damn one way or the other if she slept all day, all night, all week. Better she should sleep and give him some peace. He was in the living room now, the gloom ladled over everything, shadows leeching into black holes behind the leather couch and matching armchairs, and the rubber plant a dark ladder in the corner. The thunder rolled again, the lightning flashed. His glasses were atop the TV, where he'd left them the night before while watching a sorry documentary about the children purportedly raised by wolves in India back in the nineteen-twenties, two stringy girls in sepia photographs that revealed little and could have been faked, in any case. He put his glasses on and padded back into the kitchen in his stocking feet, already having forgotten why he'd gone to get the glasses in the first place. Then he saw the whisk in a puddle of beaten egg on the counter, remembered, and peered out the window again.

The sight of the three dogs there—a pair of clownish chows and what looked to be a shepherd mix—did nothing but irritate him. He recognized this trio; they were the advance guard of the army of dogs that dropped their excrement all over the lawn, dug up his flower beds, and, when he tried to shoo them, looked right through him as if he didn't exist. It wasn't that he had anything against dogs, per se—it was their destructiveness he objected to, their arrogance, as if they owned the whole world and it was their privilege to do as they liked with it. He was about to step to the back door and chase them off, when the figure he'd first seen—the shadow beneath the forsythia bush—emerged. It was no animal, he realized with a shock, but a woman, a young woman dressed all in black with her black hair hanging wet in her face and the clothes stuck to her like a second skin, down on all fours like a dog herself, sniffing. He was dumbfounded. As stunned and amazed as if someone had just stepped into the kitchen and slapped him till his head rolled back on his shoulders.

He'd been aware of the rumors—there was a new couple in the neighborhood, over on F Street, and the woman was a little strange, dashing through people's yards at any hour of the day or night, bay-ing at the moon, and showing her teeth to anyone who got in her way—but he'd dismissed them as some sort of suburban legend. Now here she was, in his yard, violating his privacy, in the company of a pack of dogs he'd like to see shot—and their owners, too. He didn't know what to do. He was frozen in his own kitchen, the omelette pan sending up a metallic stink of incineration. And then the three dogs lifted their heads as if they'd heard something in the distance, the thunder boomed overhead, and suddenly they leaped the fence in tandem and were gone. The woman rose up out of the mud at this point—she was wearing a sodden turtleneck, jeans, a watch cap—locked eyes with him across the expanse of the rain-screened yard for just an instant, or maybe he was imagining this part of it, and then she turned and took the fence in a single bound, vanishing into the rain.

Cynomorph

WHATEVER IT WAS THEY'D HEARD, it wasn't available to her, though she'd been trying to train her hearing away from the cease-less clatter of the mechanical and tune it to the finer things, the wind stirring in the grass, the alarm call of a fallen nestling, the faintest sliver of a whimper from the dog three houses over, begging to be let out. And her nose. She'd made a point of sticking it in any-thing the dogs did, breathing deeply, rebooting the olfactory recep-tors of a brain that had been deadened by perfume and underarm deodorant and all the other stifling odors of civilization. Every smell was a discovery, and every dog discovered more of the world in ten minutes running loose than a human being would discover in ten years of sitting behind the wheel of a car or standing at the lunch counter in a deli or even hiking the Alps. What she was doing, or attempting to do, was nothing short of reordering her senses so that she could think like a dog and interpret the whole world—not just the human world—as dogs did.

Why? Because no one had ever done it before. Whole hordes wanted to be primatologists or climb into speedboats and study whales and dolphins or cruise the veldt in a Land Rover to watch the lions suckle their young beneath the baobabs, but none of them gave a second thought to dogs. Dogs were beneath them. Dogs were common, pedestrian, no more exotic than the housefly or the Norway rat. Well, she was going to change all that. Or at least that was what she'd told herself after the graduate committee rejected her thesis, but that was a long time ago now, two years and more—and the door was rapidly closing.

But here she was, moving again, and movement was good, it was her essence: up over the fence and into the next yard, dodging a clothesline, a cooking grill, a plastic trike, a sandbox, reminding herself always to keep her head down and go quadrupedal whenever possible, because how else was she going to hear, smell, and see as the dogs did? Another fence, and there, at the far end of the yard, a shed, and the dense rust-colored tails of the chows wagging. The rain spat in her face, relentless. It had been coming down steadily most of the night, and now it seemed even heavier, as if it meant to drive her back indoors where she belonged. She was shivering—had been shivering for the past hour, shivering so hard she thought her teeth were coming loose—and as she ran, doubled over in a crouch, she pumped her knees and flapped her arms in an attempt to generate some heat.

What were the dogs onto now? She saw the one she called Barely disappear behind the shed and snake back out again, her tail rigid, sniffing now, barking, and suddenly they were all barking—the two chows and the semi-shepherd she'd named Factitious because he was such a sham, pretending he was a rover when he never strayed more than five blocks from his house, on E Street. There was a smell of freshly turned earth, of compost and wood ash, of the half-drowned worms that Snout the Afghan loved to gobble up off the pavement. She glanced toward the locked gray vault of the house, concerned that the noise would alert whoever lived there, but it was early yet, no lights on, no sign of activity. The dogs' bodies moiled. The barking went up a notch. She ran, hunched at the waist, hurrying.

And then, out of the corner of her eye, she caught a glimpse of A1, the big-shouldered husky who'd earned his name by consuming half a bottle of steak sauce beside an overturned trash can one bright January morning. He was running—but where had he come from? She hadn't seen him all night and assumed he'd been wandering out at the limits of his range, over in Bethel or Georgetown. She watched him streak across the yard, ears pinned back, head low, his path converging with hers until he disappeared behind the shed. Angling round the back of the thing—it was aluminum, one of those prefab articles they sell in the big warehouse stores—she found the compost pile her nose had alerted her to (good, good: she was improving) and a tower of old wicker chairs stacked up six feet high. AI never hesitated. He surged in at the base of the tower, his jaws snapping, and the second chow, the one she called Decidedly, was right behind him—and then she saw: there was something there, a face with incendiary eyes, and it was growling for its life in a thin continuous whine that might have been the drone of a model airplane buzzing overhead.

What was it? She crouched low, came in close. A straggler appeared suddenly, a fluid sifting from the blind side of the back fence to the yard—it was Snout, gangly, goofy, the fastest dog in the neighborhood and the widest ranger, AI's wife and the mother of his dispersed pups. And then all five dogs went in for the kill.

The thunder rolled again, concentrating the moment, and she got her first clear look: cream-colored fur, naked pink toes, a flash of teeth and burdened gums. It was an opossum, unlucky, doomed, caught out while creeping back to its nest on soft marsupial feet after a night of foraging among the trash cans. There was a roil of dogs, no barking now, just the persistent unravelling growls that were like curses, and the first splintering crunch of bone. The tower of wicker came down with a clatter, chairs upended and scattered, and the dogs hardly noticed. She glanced around her in alarm, but there was nobody to be seen, nothing moving but the million silver drill bits of the rain boring into the ground. Just as the next flash of lightning lit the sky, AI backed out from under the tumble of chairs with the carcass clenched in his jaws, furiously shaking it to snap a neck that was already two or three times broken, and she was startled to see how big the thing was—twenty pounds of meat, gristle, bone, and hair, twenty pounds at least. He shook it again, then dropped it at his wife's feet as an offering. It lay still, the other dogs extending their snouts to sniff at it dispassionately, scientists themselves, studying and measuring, remembering. And, when the hairless pink young emerged from the pouch, she tried not to feel anything as the dogs snapped them up one by one.

Cara

"YOU MEAN YOU DIDN'T CONFRONT HER?" Cara was in her royal-purple robe—her "wrapper," as she insisted on calling it, as if they were at a country manor in the Cotswolds entertaining Lord and Lady Muckbright instead of in a tract house in suburban Connecticut—and she'd paused with a forkful of mushroom omelette halfway to her mouth. She was on her third cup of coffee and wearing her combative look.

"Confront her? I barely had time to recognize she was human." He was at the sink, scrubbing the omelette pan, and he paused to look bitterly out into the gray vacancy of the yard. "What did you expect me to do, chase her down? Make a citizen's arrest? What?"

The sound of Cara buttering her toast—she might have been flaying the flesh from a bone—set his teeth on edge. "I don't know," she said, "but we can't just have strangers lurking around anytime they feel like it, can we? I mean, there are *laws*—"

"The way you talk you'd think I invited her. You think I like mental cases peeping in the window so I can't even have a moment's peace in my own house?"

"So do something."

"What. You tell me."

"Call the police, why don't you? That should be obvious, shouldn't it? And that's another thing—"

That was when the telephone rang. It was Ben Ober, his voice scraping through the wires like a set of hard chitinous claws scrabbling against the side of the house. "Julian?" he shouted. "Julian?"

Julian reassured him. "Yeah," he said, "it's me. I'm here."

"Can you hear me?"

"I can hear you."

"Listen, she's out in my yard right now, out behind the shed with a, I don't know, some kind of wolf, it looks like, and that Afghan nobody seems to know who's the owner of—"

"Who?" he said, but even as he said it he knew. "Who're you talking about?"

"The dog woman." There was a pause, and Julian could hear him breathing into the mouthpiece as if he were deep underwater. "She seems to be—I think she's killing something out there."

The Wolf Children of Mayurbhanj

IT WAS HIGH SUMMER, just before the rains set in, and the bush had shrivelled back under the sun till you could see up the skirts of the sal trees, and all that had been hidden was revealed. People began to talk of a disturbing presence in the jungle outside the tiny village of Godamuri in Mayurbhanj district, of a *bhut*, or spirit, sent to punish them for their refusal to honor the authority of the maharaja. This thing had twice been seen in the company of a wolf, a vague pale slash of movement in the incrassating twilight, but it was no wolf itself, of that the eye witnesses were certain. Then came the rumor that there were two of them, quick, nasty, bloodless things of the night, and that their eyes flamed with an infernal heat that incinerated anyone who looked into them, and panic gripped the countryside. Mothers kept their children close, fires burned in the night. Then, finally, came the news that these things were concrete and actual and no mere figments of the imagination: their den had been found in an abandoned termitarium in the dense jungle seven miles southeast of the village.

The rumors reached the Reverend J. A. L. Singh, of the Anglican mission and orphanage at Midnapore, and in September, after the monsoon clouds had peeled back from the skies and the rivers had receded, he made the long journey to Godamuri by bullock cart. One of his converts, a Kora tribesman by the name of Chunarem, who was prominent in the area, led him to the site. There, the Reverend, an astute and observant man and an amateur hunter acquainted with the habits of beasts, saw evidence of canine occupation of the termite mound—droppings, bones, tunnels of ingress and egress—and instructed that a machan be built in an overspreading tree. Armed with his dependable 20-bore Westley Richards rifle, the Reverend sat breathlessly in the machan and concentrated his field glasses on the main entrance to the den. The Reverend Singh was not one to believe in ghosts, other than the Holy Spirit, perhaps, and he expected nothing more remarkable than an albino wolf or perhaps a sloth bear gone white with age or dietary deficiency.

Dusk filtered up from the forest floor. Shadows pooled in the undergrowth, and then an early moon rose up pregnant from the horizon to soften them. Langurs whooped in the near distance, cicadas buzzed, a hundred species of beetles, moths, and biting insects flapped round the Reverend's ears, but he held rigid and silent, his binoculars fixed on the entrance to the mound. And then suddenly a shape emerged, the triangular head of a wolf, then a smaller canine head, and then something else altogether, with a neatly rounded cranium and foreshortened face. The wolf—the dam—stretched herself and slunk off into the undergrowth, followed by a pair of wolf cubs and two other creatures, which were too long-legged and rangy to be canids; that was clear at a glance. Monkeys, the Reverend thought at first, or apes of some sort. But then, even though they were moving swiftly on all fours, the Reverend could see, to his amazement, that these weren't monkeys at all, or wolves or ghosts, either.

Denning

SHE NO LONGER BOTHERED with a notepad or the pocket tape recorder she'd once used to document the telling yip or strident howl. These were the accoutrements of civilization, and civilization got in the way of the kind of freedom she required if she was ever going to break loose of the constraints that had shackled field biologists from the beginning. Even her clothes seemed to get in the way, but she was sensible enough of the laws of the community to understand that they were necessary, at least for now. Still, she made a point of wearing the same things continuously for weeks on end—sans underwear or socks—in the expectation that her scent would invest them, and the scent of the pack, too. How could she hope to gain their confidence if she smelled like the prize inside a box of detergent?

One afternoon toward the end of March, as she lay stretched out beneath a weak pale disk of a sun, trying to ignore the cold breeze and concentrate on the doings of the pack—they were excavating a den in the vacant quadrangle of former dairy pasture that was soon to become the J and K blocks of the ever-expanding development—she heard a car slow on the street a hundred yards distant and lifted her head lazily, as the dogs did, to investigate. It had been a quiet morning and a quieter afternoon, with AI and Snout, as the alpha couple, looking on placidly as Decidedly, Barely, and Factitious alternated the digging and a bulldog from B Street she hadn't yet named lay drooling in the dark wet earth that flew from the lip of the burrow. Snout had been chasing cars off and on all morning—to the dogs, automobiles were animate and ungovernable, big unruly ungulates that needed to be curtailed—and she guessed that the fortyish man climbing out of the sedan and working his tentative way across the lot had come to complain, because that was all her neighbors ever did: complain.

And that was a shame. She really didn't feel like getting into all that right now—explaining herself, defending the dogs, justifying, forever justifying—because for once she'd got into the rhythm of dogdom, found her way to that sacred place where to lie flat in the sun and breathe in the scents of fresh earth dung, sprouting grass was enough of an accomplishment for a day. Children were in school, adults at work. Peace reigned over the neighborhood. For the dogs—and for her, too—this was bliss. Hominids had to keep busy, make a buck, put two sticks together, order and structure and *complain*, but canids could know contentment, and so could she, if she could only penetrate deep enough.

Two shoes had arrived now. Loafers, buffed to brilliance and decorated with matching tassels of stripped hide. They'd come to rest on a trampled mound of fresh earth no more than twenty-four inches from her nose. She tried to ignore them, but there was a bright smear of mud or excrement gleaming on the toe of the left one; it *was* excrement, dog—the merest sniff told her that, and she was intrigued despite herself, though she refused to lift her eyes. And then a man's voice was speaking from somewhere high above the shoes, so high up and resonant with authority it might have been the voice of the alpha dog of all alpha dogs—God himself.

The tone of the voice, but not the sense of it, appealed to the dogs, and the bulldog, who was present and accounted for because Snout was in heat, hence the den, ambled over to gaze up at the trousered legs in lovesick awe. "You know," the voice was saying, "you've really got the neighborhood in an uproar, and I'm sure you have your reasons, and I know these dogs aren't yours—" The voice faltered. "But Ben Ober— you know Ben Ober? Over on C Street? Well, he's claiming you're killing rabbits or something. Or you were. Last Saturday. Out on his lawn?" Another pause. "Remember, it was raining?"

A month back, two weeks ago, even, she would have felt obliged to explain herself, would have soothed and mollified and dredged up a battery of behavioral terms—proximate causation, copulation solicitation, naturalistic fallacy—to cow him, but today, under the pale sun, in the company of the pack, she just couldn't seem to muster the energy. She might have grunted—or maybe that was only the sound of her stomach rumbling. She couldn't remember when she'd eaten last.

The cuffs of the man's trousers were stiffly pressed into jutting cotton prows, perfectly aligned. The bulldog began to lick at first one, then the other. There was the faintest creak of tendon and patella, and two knees presented themselves, and then a fist, pressed to the earth for balance. She saw a crisp white strip of shirt cuff, the gold flash of watch and wedding band.

"Listen," he said, "I don't mean to stick my nose in where it's not wanted, and I'm sure you have your reasons for, for"—the knuckles retrenched to balance the movement of his upper body, a swing of the arm, perhaps, or a jerk of the head—"all this. I'd just say live and let live, but I can't. And you know why not?"

She didn't answer, though she was on the verge—there was something about his voice that was magnetic, as if it could adhere to her and pull her to her feet again—but the bulldog distracted her. He'd gone up on his hind legs with a look of unfocussed joy and begun humping the man's leg, and her flash of epiphany deafened her to what he was saying. The bulldog had revealed his name to her: from now on she would know him as Humper.

"Because you upset my wife. You were out in our yard and I, she—Oh, Christ," he said, "I'm going about this all wrong. Look, let me introduce myself—I'm Julian Fox. We live on B Street, 2236? We never got to meet your husband and you when you moved in. I mean, the development's got so big—and impersonal, I guess—we never had the chance. But if you ever want to stop by, maybe for tea, a drink—the two of you, I mean—that would be, well, that would be great."

A Drink on B Street

SHE WAS UPRIGHT AND SMILING, though her posture was terrible and she carried her own smell with her into the sterile sanctum of the house. He caught it immediately, unmistakably, and so did Cara, judging from the look on her face as she took the girl's hand. It was as if a breeze had wafted up from the bog they were draining over on G Street to make way for the tennis courts; the door stood open, and here was a raw infusion of the wild. Or the kennel. That was Cara's take on it, delivered in a stage whisper on the far side of the swinging doors to the kitchen as she fussed with the hors d'oeuvres and he poured vodka for the husband and tap water for the girl: *She smells like she's been sleeping in a kennel.* When he handed her the glass, he saw that there was dirt under her nails. Her hair shone with grease and there were bits of fluff or lint or something flecking the coils of it where it lay massed on her shoulders. Cara tried to draw her into small talk, but she wouldn't draw—she just kept nodding and smiling till the smile had nothing of greeting or joy left in it.

Cara had got their number from Bea Chiavone, who knew more about the business of her neighbors than a confessor, and one night last week she'd got through to the husband, who said his wife was out—which came as no surprise—but Cara had kept him on the line for a good ten minutes, digging for all she was worth, until he finally accepted the invitation to their "little cocktail party." Julian was doubtful, but before he'd had a chance to comb his hair or get his jacket on, the bell was ringing and there they were, the two of them, arm in arm on the doormat, half an hour early.

The husband, Don, was acceptable enough. Early thirties, bit of a paunch, his hair gone in a tonsure. He was a computer engineer. Worked for I.B.M. "Really?" Julian said. "Well, you must know Charlie Hsiu, then—he's at the Yorktown office?"

Don gave him a blank look.

"He lives just up the street. I mean, I could give him a call, if, if—" He never finished the thought. Cara had gone to the door to greet Ben and Julie Ober, and the girl, left alone, had migrated to the corner by the rubber plant, where she seemed to be bent over now, sniffing at the potting soil. He tried not to stare—tried to hold the husband's eye and absorb what he was saying about interoffice politics and his own role on the research end of things ("I guess I'm what you'd call the ultimate computer geek, never really get away from the monitor long enough to put a name to a face")—but he couldn't help stealing a glance under cover of the Obers' entrance. Ben was glad-handing, his voice booming, Cara was cooing something to Julie, and the girl (the husband had introduced her as Cynthia, but she'd murmured, "Call me C.f., capital 'C,' lowercase 'f,'") had gone down on her knees beside the plant. He saw her wet a finger, dip it into the soil, and bring it to her mouth.

While the La Portes—Cara's friends, dull as woodchips—came smirking through the door, expecting a freak show, Julian tipped back his glass and crossed the room to the girl. She was intent on the plant, rotating the terra-cotta pot to examine the saucer beneath it, on all fours now, her face close to the carpet. He cleared his throat, but she didn't respond. He watched the back of her head a moment, struck by the way her hair curtained her face and spilled down the rigid struts of her arms. She was dressed all in black, in a ribbed turtleneck, grass-stained jeans, and a pair of canvas sneakers that were worn through at the heels. She wasn't wearing socks, or, as far as he could see, a brassiere, either. But she'd clean up nicely, that was what he was thinking—she had a shape to her, anybody could see that, and eyes that could burn holes right through you. "So," he heard himself say, even as Ben's voice rose to a crescendo at the other end of the room, "you, uh, like houseplants?"

She made no effort to hide what she was doing, whatever it may have been—studying the weave of the carpet, looking at the alignment of the baseboard, inspecting for termites, who could say?—but instead turned to gaze up at him for the first time. "I hope you don't mind my asking," she said in her hush of a voice, "but did you ever have a dog here?"

He stood looking down at her, gripping his drink, feeling awkward and foolish in his own house. He was thinking of Seymour (or "See More," because as a pup he was always running off after things in the distance), picturing him now for the first time in how many years? Something passed through him then, a pang of regret carried in his blood, in his neurons: Seymour. He'd almost succeeded in forgetting him. "Yes," he said. "How did you know?"

She smiled. She was leaning back against the wall now, cradling her knees in the net of her interwoven fingers. "I've been training myself. My senses, I mean." She paused, still smiling up at him. "Did you know that when the Ninemile wolves came down into Montana from Alberta they were following scent trails laid down years before? Think about it. All that weather, the seasons, trees falling and decaying. Can you imagine that?"

"Cara's allergic," he said. "I mean, that's why we had to get rid of him. Seymour. His name was Seymour."

There was a long braying burst of laughter from Ben Ober, who had an arm round Don's shoulder and was painting something in the air with a stiffened forefinger. Cara stood just beyond him, with the La Portes, her face glowing as if it had been basted. Celia La Porte looked from him to the girl and back again, then arched her eyebrows wittily and raised her long-stemmed glass of Viognier, as if toasting him. All three of them burst into laughter. Julian turned his back.

"You didn't take him to the pound—did you?" The girl's eyes went flat. "Because that's a death sentence, I hope you realize that."

"Cara found a home for him."

They both looked to Cara then, her shining face, her anchorwoman's hair. "I'm sure," the girl said.

"No, really. She did."

The girl shrugged, looked away from him. "It doesn't matter," she said with a flare of anger. "Dogs are just slaves, anyway."

Kamala and Amala

THE REVEREND SINGH had wanted to return to the site the following afternoon and excavate the den, convinced that these furtive night creatures were in fact human children, children abducted from their cradles and living under the dominion of beasts—unbaptized and unsaved, their eternal souls at risk—but urgent business called him away to the south. When he returned, late in the evening, ten days later, he sat over a dinner of cooked vegetables, rice, and dal, and listened as Chunarem told him of the wolf bitch that had haunted the village two years back, after her pups had been removed from a den in the forest and sold for a few annas apiece at the Khuar market. She could be seen as dusk fell, her dugs swollen and glistening with extruded milk, her eyes shining with an unearthly blue light against the backdrop of the forest. People threw stones, but she never flinched. And she howled all night from the fringes of the village, howled so that it seemed she was inside the walls of every hut simultaneously, crooning her sorrow into the ears of each sleeping villager. The village dogs kept hard by, and those that didn't were found in the morning, their throats torn out. "It was she," the Reverend exclaimed, setting down his plate as the candles guttered and moths beat at the netting. "She was the abductress—it's as plain as morning."

A few days later, he got up a party that included several railway men and returned to the termite mound, bent on rescue. In place of the rifle, he carried a stout cudgel cut from a mahua branch. He brought along a weighted net as well. The sun hung overhead. All was still. And then the hired beaters started in, the noise of them racketing through the trees, coming closer and closer until they converged on the site, driving hares and bandicoot rats and the occasional gaur before them. The railway men tensed in the machan, their rifles trained on the entrance to the burrow, while Reverend Singh stood by with a party of diggers to effect the rescue when the time came. It was unlikely that the wolves would have been abroad in daylight, and so it was no surprise to the Reverend that no large animal was seen to run before the beaters and seek the shelter of the den. "Very well," he said, giving the signal, "I am satisfied. Commence the digging."

As soon as the blades of the first shovels struck the mound, a protracted snarling could be heard emanating from the depths of the burrow. After a few minutes of the tribesmen's digging, the she-wolf sprang out at them, ears flattened to her head, teeth flashing. One of the diggers went for her with his spear just as the railway men opened fire from the machan and turned her, snapping, on her own wounds; a moment later, she lay stretched out dead in the dust of the laterite clay. In a trice the burrow was uncovered, and there they were, the spirits made flesh, huddled in a defensive posture with the two wolf cubs, snarling and panicked, scrabbling at the clay with their broken nails to dig themselves deeper. The tribesmen dropped their shovels and ran, panicked themselves, even as the Reverend Singh eased himself down into the hole and tried to separate child from wolf.

The larger of the children, her hair a feral cap that masked her features, came at him biting and scratching, and finally he had no recourse but to throw his net over the pullulating bodies and restrain each of the creatures separately in one of the long, winding *gelaps* the local tribesmen use for winter wear. On inspection, it was determined that the children were females, aged approximately three and six, of native stock, and apparently, judging from the dissimilarity of their features, unrelated. The she-wolf, it seemed, had abducted the children on separate occasions, perhaps even from separate locales, and over the course of some time. Was this the bereaved bitch that Chunarem had reported? the Reverend wondered. Was she acting out of a desire for revenge? Or merely trying, in her own unknowable way, to replace what had been taken from her and ease the burden of her heart?

In any case, he had the children confined to a pen so that he could observe them, before caging them in the back of the bullock cart for the trip to Midnapore and the orphanage, where he planned to baptize and civilize them. He spent three full days studying them and taking notes. He saw that they persisted in going on all fours, as if they didn't know any other way, and that they fled from sunlight as if it were an instrument of torture. They thrust forward to lap water like the beasts of the forest and took nothing in their mouths but bits of twig and stone. At night they came to life and stalked the enclosure with shining eyes like the *bhuts* that half the villagers still believed them to be. They did not know any of the languages of the human species, but communicated with each other—and with their sibling wolves—in a series of grunts, snarls, and whimpers. When the moon rose, they sat on their haunches and howled.

It was Mrs. Singh who named them, some weeks later. They were pitiful, filthy, soiled with their own urine and excrement, undernourished, and undersized. They had to be caged to keep them from harming the other children, and Mrs. Singh, though it broke her heart to do it, ordered them put in restraints, so that the filth and the animal smell could be washed from them, even as their heads were shaved to defeat the ticks and fleas they'd inherited from the only mother they'd ever known. "They need delicate names," Mrs. Singh told her husband, "names to reflect the beauty and propriety they will grow into." She named the younger sister Amala, after a bright-yellow flower native to Bengal, and the elder Kamala, after the lotus that blossoms deep in the jungle pools.

Running with the Pack

THE SUN STROKED HER LIKE A HAND, penetrated and massaged the dark yellowing contusion that had sprouted on the left side of her rib cage. Her bones felt as if they were about to crack open and deliver their marrow and her heart was still pounding, but at least she was here, among the dogs, at rest. It was June, the season of pollen, the air supercharged with the scents of flowering, seeding, fruiting, and there were rabbits and squirrels everywhere. She lay prone at the lip of the den and watched the pups—long-muzzled like their mother and brindled Afghan peach and husky silver—as they worried a flap of skin and fur that Snout had peeled off the hot black glistening surface of the road and dropped at their feet. She was trying to focus on the dogs—on AI, curled up nose to tail in the trampled weed after regurgitating a mash of kibble for the pups, on Decidedly, his eyes half closed as currents of air brought him messages from afar, on Humper and Factitious—but she couldn't let go of the pain in her ribs and what that pain foreshadowed from the human side of things.

Don had kicked her. Don had climbed out of the car, crossed the field, and stood over her in his suède computer engineer's ankle boots with the waffle bottoms and reinforced toes and lectured her while the dogs slunk low and rumbled deep in their throats. And, as his voice had grown louder, so, too, had the dogs' voices, until they were a chorus commenting on the ebb and flow of the action. When was she going to get her ass up out of the dirt and act like a normal human being? That was what he wanted to know. When was she going to cook a meal, run the vacuum, do the wash—his underwear, for Christ's sake? He was wearing dirty underwear, did she know that?

She had been lying stretched out flat on the mound, just as she was now. She glanced up at him as the dogs did, taking in a piece of him at a time, no direct stares, no challenges. "All I want," she said, over the chorus of growls and low, warning barks, "is to be left alone."

"Left alone?" His voice tightened in a little yelp. "Left alone? You need help, that's what you need. You need a shrink, you know that?"

She didn't reply. She let the pack speak for her. The rumble of their response, the flattened ears and stiffened tails, the sharp, savage gleam of their eyes should have been enough, but Don wasn't attuned. The sun seeped into her. A grasshopper she'd been idly watching as it bent a dandelion under its weight suddenly took flight, right past her face, and it seemed the most natural thing in the world to snap at it and break it between her teeth.

Don let out some sort of exclamation—"My God, what are you doing? Get up out of that, get up out of that now!"—and it didn't help matters. The dogs closed in. They were fierce now, barking in savage recusancy, their emotions twisted in a single cord. But this was Don, she kept telling herself, Don from grad school, bright and buoyant Don, her mate, her husband, and what harm was there in that? He wanted her back home, back in the den, and that was his right. The only thing was, she wasn't going.

"This isn't research. This is bullshit. Look at you!"

"No," she said, giving him a lazy, sidelong look, though her heart was racing, "it's dog shit. It's on your shoes, Don. It's in your face. In your precious computer—"

That was when he'd kicked her. Twice, three times, maybe. Kicked her in the ribs as if he were driving a ball over an imaginary set of uprights in the distance, kicked and kicked again—before the dogs went for him. Ai came in first, tearing at a spot just above his right knee, and then Humper, the bulldog who, she now knew, belonged to the feathery old lady up the block, got hold of his pant leg while Barely went for the crotch. Don screamed and thrashed, all right—he was a big animal, two hundred and ten pounds, heavier by far than any of the dogs—and he threatened in his big animal voice and fought back with all the violence of his big animal limbs, but he backed off quickly enough, threatening still, as he made his way across the field and into the car. She heard the door slam, heard the motor scream, and then there was the last thing she heard: Snout barking at the wheels as they revolved and took Don down the street and out of her life.

Survival of the Fittest

"YOU KNOW HE'S LOCKED HER OUT DON'T YOU?"

"Who?" Though he knew perfectly well.

"Don. I'm talking about Don and the dog lady?"

There was the table, made of walnut varnished a century before, the crystal vase full of flowers, the speckless china, the meat, the vegetables, the pasta. Softly, so softly he could barely hear it, there was Bach, too, piano pieces—partitas—and the smell of the fresh-cut flowers.

"Nobody knows where she's staying, unless it's out in the trash or the weeds or wherever. She's like a bag lady or something. Bea said Jerrilyn Hunter said she saw her going through the trash one morning. Do you hear me? Are you even listening?"

"I don't know. Yeah. Yeah, I am." He'd been reading lately. About dogs. Half a shelf of books from the library in their plastic covers—behavior, breeds, courting, mating, whelping. He excised a piece of steak and lifted it to his lips. "Did you hear the Leibowitzes' Afghan had puppies?"

"Puppies? What in God's name are you talking about?" Her face was like a burr under the waistband, an irritant, something that needed to be removed and crushed.

"Only the alpha couple gets to breed. You know that, right? And so that would be the husky and the Leibowitzes' Afghan, and I don't know who the husky belongs to—but they're cute, real cute."

"You haven't been—? Don't tell me. Julian, use your sense: she's out of her mind. You want to know what else Bea said?"

"The alpha bitch," he said, and he didn't know why he was telling her this, "she'll actually hunt down and kill the pups of any other female in the pack who might have got pregnant, a survival-of-the-fittest kind of thing—"

"She's crazy, bonkers, out of her *fucking* mind, Julian. They're going to have her committed, you know that? If this keeps up. And it will keep up, won't it, Julian? Won't it?"

The Common Room at Midnapore

AT FIRST THEY WOULD TAKE NOTHING BUT RAW MILK. The wolf pups, from which they'd been separated for reasons both of sanitation and acculturation, eagerly fed on milk-and-rice pap in their kennel in one of the outbuildings, but neither of the girls would touch the pan warmed milk or rice or the stewed vegetables that Mrs. Singh provided, even at night, when they were most active and their eyes spoke a language of desire all their own. Each morning and each evening before retiring, she would place a bowl on the floor in front of them, trying to tempt them with biscuits, confections, even a bit of boiled meat, though the Singhs were vegetarians themselves and repudiated the slaughter of animals for any purpose. The girls drew back into the recesses of the pen the Reverend had constructed in the orphanage's common room, showing their teeth. Days passed. They grew weaker. He tried to force-feed them balls of rice, but they scratched and tore at him with their nails and their teeth, setting up such a furious caterwauling of hisses, barks, and snarls as to give rise to rumors among the servants that he was torturing them. Finally, in resignation, and though it was a risk to the security of the entire orphanage, he left the door to the pen open in the hope that the girls, on seeing the other small children at play and at dinner, would soften.

In the meantime, though the girls grew increasingly lethargic—or perhaps because of this—the Reverend was able to make a close and telling examination of their physiology and habits. Their means of locomotion had transformed their bodies in a peculiar way. For one thing, they had developed thick pads of callus at their elbows and knees, and toes of abnormal strength and inflexibility—indeed, when their feet were placed flat on the ground, all five toes stood up at a sharp angle. Their waists were narrow and extraordinarily supple, like a dog's, and their necks dense with the muscle that had accrued there as a result of leading with their heads. And they were fast, preternaturally fast, and stronger by far than any other children of their respective ages that the Reverend and his wife had ever seen. In his diary, for the sake of posterity, the Reverend noted it all down.

Still, all the notes in the world wouldn't matter a whit if the wolf children didn't end their hunger strike, if that was what this was, and the Reverend and his wife had begun to lose hope for them, when the larger one—the one who would become known as Kamala—finally asserted herself. It was early in the evening, the day after the Reverend had ordered the door to the pen left open, and the children were eating their evening meal while Mrs. Singh and one of the servants looked on and the Reverend settled in with his pipe on the veranda. The weather was typical for Bengal in that season, the evening heavy and close, every living thing locked in the grip of the heat, and all the mission's doors and windows standing open to receive even the faintest breath of a breeze. Suddenly, without warning, Kamala bolted out of the pen, through the door, and across the courtyard to where the orphanage dogs were being fed scraps of uncooked meat, gristle, and bone left over from the preparation of the servants' meal, and before anyone could stop her she was down among them, slashing with her teeth, fighting off even the biggest and most aggressive of them until she'd bolted the red meat and carried off the long, hoofed shinbone of a gaur to gnaw in the farthest corner of her pen.

And so the Singhs, though it revolted them, fed the girls on raw meat until the crisis had passed, and then they gave them broth, which the girls lapped from their bowls, and finally meat that had been at least partially cooked. As for clothing—clothing for decency's sake—the girls rejected it as unnatural and confining, tearing any garment from their backs and limbs with their teeth, until Mrs. Singh hit on the idea of fashioning each of them a single tight-fitting strip of cloth they wore knotted round the waist and drawn up over their privates, a kind of diaper or loincloth they were forever soiling with their waste. It wasn't an ideal solution, but the Singhs were patient—the girls had suffered a kind of deprivation no other humans had ever suffered—and they understood that the ascent to civilization and light would be steep and long.

When Amala died, shortly after the wolf pups had succumbed to what the Reverend presumed was distemper communicated through the orphanage dogs, her sister wouldn't let anyone approach the body. Looking back on it, the Reverend would see this as Kamala's most human moment—she was grieving, grieving because she had a soul, because she'd been baptized before the Lord and was no wolfling or jungle *bhut* but a human child after all, and here was the proof of it. But poor Amala. Her, they hadn't been able to save. Both girls had been dosed with sulfur powder, which caused them to expel a knot of roundworms up to six inches in length and as thick as the Reverend's little finger, but the treatment was perhaps too harsh for the three-year-old, who was suffering from fever and dysentery at the same time. She'd seemed all right, feverish but calm, and Mrs. Singh had tended her through the afternoon and evening. But when the Reverend's wife came into the pen in the morning Kamala flew at her, raking her arms and legs and driving her back from the straw in which her sister's cold body lay stretched out like a figure carved of wood. They restrained the girl and removed the corpse. Then Mrs. Singh retired to bandage her wounds and the Reverend locked the door of the pen to prevent any further violence. All that day, Kamala lay immobile in the shadows at the back of the pen, wrapped in her own limbs. When night fell, she sat back on her haunches behind the rigid geometry of the bars and began to howl, softly at first, and then with increasing force and plangency until it was the very sound of desolation itself, rising up out of the compound to chase through the streets of the village and into the jungle beyond.

Going to the Dogs

THE SKY WAS CLEAR all the way to the top of everything, the sun so thick in the trees that he thought it would catch there and congeal among the motionless leaves. He didn't know what prompted him to do it, exactly, but as he came across the field he balanced first on one leg and then the other, to remove his shoes and socks. The grass—the weeds, wildflowers, puffs of mushroom, clover, swaths of moss—felt clean and cool against the lazy progress of his bare feet. Things rose up to greet him, things and smells he'd forgotten all about, and he took his time among them, moving forward only to be distracted again and again. He found her, finally, in the tall nodding weeds that concealed the entrance of the den, playing with the puppies. He didn't say hello, didn't say anything—just settled in on the mound beside her and let the pups surge into his arms. The pack barely raised its collective head.

Her eyes came to him and went away again. She was smiling, a loose, private smile that curled the corners of her mouth and lifted up into the smooth soft terrain of the silken skin under her eyes. Her clothes barely covered her anymore, the turtleneck torn at the throat and sagging across one clavicle, the black jeans hacked off crudely— or maybe chewed off—at the peaks of her thighs. The sneakers were gone altogether, and he saw that the pale-yellow soles of her feet were hard with callus, and her hair—her hair was struck with sun and shining with the natural oil of her scalp.

He'd come with the vague idea—or, no, the very specific idea—of asking her for one of the pups, but now he didn't know if that would do, exactly. She would tell him that the pups weren't hers to give, that they belonged to the pack, and though each of the pack's members had a bed and a bowl of kibble awaiting it in one of the equitable houses of the alphabetical grid of the development springing up around them, they were free here, and the pups, at least, were slaves to no one. He felt the thrusting wet snouts of the creatures in his lap, the surge of their animacy, the softness of the stroked ears, and the prick of the milk teeth, and he smelled them, too, an authentic smell compounded of dirt, urine, saliva, and something else also: the unalloyed sweetness of life. After a while, he removed his shirt, and so what if the pups carried it off like a prize? The sun blessed him. He loosened his belt, gave himself some breathing room. He looked at her, stretched out beside him, at the lean, tanned, running length of her, and he heard himself say, finally, "Nice day, isn't it?"

"Don't talk," she said. "You'll spoil it."

"Right," he said. "Right. You're right."

And then she rolled over, bare flesh from the worried waistband of her cutoffs to the dimple of her breastbone and her breasts caught somewhere in between, under the yielding fabric. She was warm, warm as a fresh-drawn bath, the touch of her communicating everything to him, and the smell of her, too—he let his hand go up under the flap of material and roam over her breasts, and then he bent closer, sniffing.

Her eyes were fixed on his. She didn't say anything, but a low throaty rumble escaped her throat.

Waiting for the Rains

THE REVEREND SINGH sat there on the veranda, waiting for the rains. He'd set his notebook aside, and now he leaned back in the wicker chair and pulled meditatively at his pipe. The children were at play in the courtyard, an array of flashing limbs and animated faces, attended by their high, bright catcalls and shouts. The heat had loosened its grip ever so perceptibly, and they were, all of them, better for it. Except Kamala. She was indifferent. The chill of winter, the damp of the rains, the full merciless sway of the sun—it was all the same to her. His eyes came to rest on her where she lay across the courtyard in a stripe of sunlight, curled in the dirt with her knees drawn up beneath her and her chin resting atop the cradle of her crossed wrists. He watched her for a long while as she lay motionless there, no more aware of what she was than a dog or an ass, and he felt defeated, defeated and depressed. But then one of the children called out in a voice fluid with joy, a moment of triumph in a game among them, and the Reverend couldn't help but shift his eyes and look.

(*Some details here are from Charles MacLeans "The Wolf Children: Fact or Fantasy?" and "Wolf-Children and Feral Man," by the Reverend A. L. Singh and Robert M. Zingg.*)

From *The Snakebite Survivors' Club*

JEREMY SEAL

PROLOGUE

I STOOD IN THE DOORWAY, deferring the moment with a fretful cigarette. One of the gorillas across the way returned my gaze through the bars of its cage, and we eyed each other for some time. The ape had sad, fathomless eyes. The human, I guessed, must have anxious, haunted ones.

The gorilla scratched itself, yawned and toppled back into the straw. I turned towards the building behind me. It was square and neo-classical in style. A decorative frieze ran round the portals in which were carved iguanas, snails, salamanders, frogs, alligators, pythons and, in place of prominence on the keystone, three hooded cobras wearing berets of black bitumen that had dripped from the roof in the heat of a former London summer. A group of school children approached. "Oh no, Priscilla!" yelled a young boy. The contents of the building had dawned upon him. "This is the scary one!"

Years before, as a child, I had stood in this same doorway. I remember how I had imagined within a bottomless pit overflowing with snakes, plaits of snakes spilling on to the shiny floor to untangle themselves and slither numberless down long corridors, and the images had stopped me in my tracks. My palms had prickled with sweat and tears had welled up in my eyes, and thirty years later little had changed.

I was not, of course, alone in my fear of snakes. Ever since the world's first "serpentarium" or "reptilium" opened at London Zoo in June 1849, in the Swiss chalet-style building which had formerly

38

housed the zoo's carnivores, children have screamed between the portals and adults have turned away, pale-faced. Beatrice Thompson, who enjoyed frequent visits to the zoo at the end of the last century, remarked how she had "known many women of the educated classes firmly refuse to enter the Reptile House at all."

True, the image of the overflowing snake-pit had since left me, but a more particular, more threatening vision had taken its place: a single snake seething at my feet, a wave of chevrons and diamonds breaking yellow and brown, then the instant of sharpness and blood nudging scarlet from the puncture marks as the disappearing snake flicked its tail at the grass. The snakebite sequence began as a recurring dream. I then started imagining it, imagined it so often that I began to anticipate it and it became in time a fact of my future, as if I was living in a world littered with live ordnance which I was one day destined to tread upon. I began to believe that I was going to die of snakebite.

So what was I doing here, so close to my fear? The answer perhaps lay in an 1805 penny tract called *Wonderful Account of the Rattlesnake and other Serpents of America* that I recently came across in a library, where I found the suggestive description of snakes possessing their prey—birds, rabbits and other rodents—"with infatuation," so that they "flutter or move slowly, but reluctantly, towards the yawning jaws of their devourers, and creep into their mouths. . ." I knew that feeling. So too, I suspect, had everyone who had ever stood at the entrance of reptile houses and snake parks, daring themselves to cross the threshold despite their abhorrence of what they would find inside. I was drawn to snakes even as they disgusted me. The fascination was as strong as the fear; a kind of transfixing awe, an infatuation, was the result. The presence of snakes seemed to cast a strange light across the landscape, a light that might attend the end of the world; spare, stark and alive with a crackly energy. A charge pulsed through such moments, and made them among the most compelling of my life.

Just as I could not keep myself from snakes, so I was drawn to survivors of snakebite, that singular clique, that club whose members had been touched by something dark, exotic and preternatural.

They were like those who had experienced shipwreck, lightning strike or even alien abduction; they wore a badge of otherness that the rest of us could only shiver at even as we asked, our mouths slack with fascination: *being bitten; what did it feel like?* That was the point; we wanted to know. If we examined our curiosity deep enough, I suspected we might even acknowledge that these people, these survivors, had experienced something far stranger than we would ever know, and what we truly felt, despite our shivers, was something akin to a kind of dangerous envy, even a yearning for the experience they had survived.

Which perhaps explained why I should be standing outside the reptile house at London Zoo on a spring afternoon in 1996, gathering myself to step inside.

AMERICA I

Defense Counsel: How many of you are afraid of snakes?
(*Many jurors raise hands.*)
Defense Counsel: How many of you are not afraid of snakes?
(*No response.*)

—Trial transcript extract, *The State* versus *Summerford*,
February 1992, Jackson County Courthouse,
Scottsboro, Alabama

April 1996

ON A FRIDAY EVENING in the fall of 1991, as people all over Alabama sat down to TV dinners, or mowed the twilit lawn for the last time till spring, Darlene Summerford Collins took a bite from a diamondback rattlesnake. She saw only a blur of motion, a pink flash of gaping jaws as it lashed up at her descending hand. Its fangs found flesh high on the thumb, close to the wrist joint of her left hand.

Darlene had been bitten before. The Lord knows, she'd handled enough snakes over the years. Used even to carry photos of snakes in her purse to show to friends; favourite ones—copperheads, moccasins, that greenish timber rattler she so liked. And her husband Glenn had been handling them for the best part of ten years, lately in the little church with the teetering steeple on Woods Cove Road outside of town, letting them get into his hair or using them to wipe the sweat from his face, handling Satan just like any true believer.

Only now, her husband was standing over her with a gun, the pistol she'd bought at Scottsboro Pawn just six months earlier, his hand twisting cruel, thick plaits in her red hair as she looked down at her thumb and the bead of blood that stood proud a brief moment before running across her palm, seeking out the lifelines.

"The lid," hissed Glenn. "Put the lid back on the box." As she did so, the snake rattled its tail in anger. She had heard its tindery buzz many times, but never before had the sound made her nauseous. In the musty shed, she could smell the snake and the fetid scent of its anger, the drink on her husband's breath and the coal-dust smell of gunmetal. Now Glenn was dragging her to another box. She could plainly see the contents: two large rattlesnakes whose diamond patterned backs were faintly echoed in the mesh tracery of the chicken-wire lid.

"You praying now?" he whispered. He smiled. "I bet you praying now."

Foreboding coiled tight in her belly. Around her thumb, there was already a vicious clamping pain where the venom was going to work. But what was making her sick was something else: it felt as if her senses had gone. She was sure she could hear the river—and when had she ever done that?—and smell doughnuts from somewhere, and every consonant Glenn had uttered was now careening around her head, just in no particular order and a couple of octaves lower. There were times she had thought every moment in her life was leading her downwards, but not to this, not to murder from multiple rattlesnake bite. Not by her husband.

That was over four years ago. By the time I reached the house, Glenn and Darlene were long gone, but something of that distant fall evening still clung to the place, a baleful, poisoning mood that had spited time and made me shiver. The house lay beyond Scottsboro's outskirts, where the neat lines of weatherboard homes fronted by mailboxes gave way to the scruffy smallholdings on Barbee Lane, a long nibbled ribbon of blacktop that cut into the countryside. Chained dogs lay among the gutted auto parts—the engine blocks, radiators and rusted exhausts—of pick-ups spray-painted in bright pinks and purples. Workshop radios interspersed music and commercial messages. Save a light breeze mussing its mane, a single horse stood motionless in a field.

The house stood at Barbee Lane's far extent, among the stands of pine, hickory and beech that led down to the Tennessee River. The river threw a big southerly lassoo loop through Alabama. It entered the state in the north-east from Tennessee and, mindful of its name, left it for Tennessee to the north-west. For much of its length, however, it was a shapeless thing. A series of bloated blackwater sloughs had backed up behind dams all the way to the Mississippi, depriving the river of its sinuous, serpentine coils. As if in compensation for the loss of its grace, the flabby river had at least acquired an excellent reputation for catfish, lurking monsters that weighed up to a hundred pounds. Fishermen never knew what might fetch up along the Scottsboro stretch of the Tennessee.

The Barbee Lane house lay in permanent shadow. It had a tin roof, ripped tar-paper walls and a highly visible sign warning against trespass. A cardboard-coloured dog, a large one, barked fiercely and baulked my uncertain approach. For a while, we just looked at each other. The dog's look was more direct. Guessing he might not be a patch on the house's current tenant, I returned to the car.

I drove past the imposing brick courthouse in Scottsboro's main square, and the flourishing attorney's offices that fed off it. Beyond their brief affluence, however, were autopart stockists emphasizing the essential—"Need a new engine? We can help"—and pawn shops that had long since quit claiming any measure of discernment—"Car title pawn. And guns, jewellery, anything"—and the unclaimed luggage dealers that airports from New Orleans to Atlanta supplied with job lots of umbrellas, coats, suitcases, boots, hats, paperbacks, bottles of aspirin, walkmans, laptops, pens, even forgotten photos of loved ones caught in distant, suburban sunshine, posing beside car ports in Ohio, or on the balconies of Florida condos with just-about views of the ocean.

Woods Cove Road wound out of town on the west-side, passed the Jackson County hospital, crossed the railroad tracks and headed through cornfields before being sucked into the wake of the interstate to die premature, serving just a few loose farmsteads—and the old church—on the way. The church looked old enough. Less like a church though. Concrete plinths where the fuel pumps once stood still fronted the former country store and gas station, set to catch unwary shins. The building was flat-roofed, whitewashed and jerry-built. Spare squares of sorry chipboard patched the front. A poor, hand-painted sign said "Paster Frank. Everyone welcome. Friday night. Sunday night 7.00 P.M." Pastor Frank, I figured, must have followed in Glenn's footsteps for a while. The first rime of rust on the padlock suggested, at best, an irregular ministry.

I rubbed at the window. A spider's web slung across the pane gave even the indistinct gloom within a fractured appearance. There was the suggestion of old lino switchbacking across the floor. A chair lay on its back, like a man with his knees tucked up to his chest as if to protect himself from an unholy kicking. Around the back of the church, a stack of decrepit pews were turning into mould among the sycamore trees, their ply sheets yawning open like the pages of well-thumbed Bibles.

More effort had gone into painting the church's name, The Church of the Lord Jesus Christ, in a blue arc around a cross. In Glenn's time, I mused, this had been the Church of Jesus With Signs Following. At that time the words "Mark 16, vs 15–18" were painted with a shaky reverence on an inside wall; "And these signs shall follow them that believe," read the verses referred to. "In my name shall they cast out devils; they shall speak with new tongues; They shall take up serpents; and if they drink any deadly thing, it shall not hurt them; they shall lay hands on the sick, and they shall recover." In Glenn's church, like others scattered throughout the Southern Appalachian mountains, a place unto itself among a jumble of intersecting southern state lines, they had taken the Bible at its every word.

Glenn Summerford did the lot. Spoke in tongues, drank deadly strychnine and drain cleaner, and even took electric shocks in God's name. But it was the snake-handling he really took to. Did it with an abandon that frankly scared his packed congregation as much as it inspired them. Glenn had come to the Lord the hard way, leaving in his turbulent wake a trail of criminal charges from illegal racoon-hunting and grand larceny to the attempted murder of his mother-in-law—with a vase.

Darlene could tell you all about his violent temper, drinking bouts and infidelities. She was one of thirteen children who had grown up on handouts near Dutton township on Sand Mountain, the looming plateau on the eastside of the Tennessee River that stands between Scottsboro and the sunrise. She and Glenn had met when they were young. By the mid-1970s, she was falling for his considerable, if diabolical charisma. He had fire and life. What he'd noticed were her enormous blue eyes and that hair you couldn't ignore, ginger-red as agricultural twine. Within months of their marriage, however, he was kicking her around, accusing her of cheating on him with young boys, even with her own brother, and drinking with a ferocity that drove him still deeper into sloughs of jealousy and murderous rage.

Then, one day in 1982 Glenn wove out of a bar and, promising himself a new start, fell into a friend's pick-up bound for a church service across the state line in Kingston, Georgia. Propped in a pew, he watched men remove rattlesnakes from wooden boxes stacked by the altar, and pass them among themselves during the singing with a strength and confidence that he had only ever got out of bottles. He could not hear the snakes' angry rattles above the cacophonous wailing, the Hallelujahs and the music—thumping drums, twanging guitars, crashing cymbals and the roar of miked-up male voices—but he could see them tense in the initial grip of their handlers and then, miraculously, go rope-limp. Even as the men draped them round their shoulders or held them by the midriff, letting them hang by their sides, the snakes made no attempt to strike. One man tucked a young rattler in his shirt pocket; its tail protruded like a limp, gorgeously patterned dandy's kerchief. Later, when things got a little crazy—women were keeling over, shuddering like cardiac cases or were slumped, sobbing against the altar—the men even threw the rattlesnakes into the air, sending lightbulbs swinging, hustling the shadows away, and caught them on their descent.

It might, granted, have been on the road to Cartersville, the nondescript strip of fast-food joints and budget motels huddled along Georgia Highway 41 some forty miles north of Atlanta, rather than to Damascus, but Glenn nevertheless sensed redemption in that small, clapboard church on a hill. This was simple instruction. The Word of the Book guaranteed salvation through the act of lifting the hinged wire lid of a wooden box, reaching in and taking from it writhing rosaries of evil incarnate. Belief would do the rest. Faith would disarm the devil. Perfect victory, they called it. By the end of the service, Glenn was converted. He was set on becoming a preacher, and handling snakes.

Soon, he had seventeen snakes in the shed at the bottom of Barbee Lane. Supportive preachers provided him with some. Others told him to go out into the woods, to sit down and pray and let the Lord send the snakes to him. Some he bought for a few dollars from local boys who caught them in the brushwood. He even found a couple of his own, sunning themselves among the pine trees in the spring and learned how to box them without harming himself. He took them to his first church services in Scottsboro, itinerant, short-notice arrangements that convened in borrowed rooms and old buildings all over town. His congregation even did a spell above a chicken restaurant. Locals accused them of being "freaks," "Holy Rollers" and "Jesus Onlys," even broke what panes remained in their windows. So they came at last to the old gas station on Woods Cove Road.

They were content to hold their services outside of town. They were used to the margins; heaven, they and their kind had spent their lives on them, living out of trailers on disability or scraping occasional work in the cornfields or for local concerns like the Church Pew Factory out at Rainsville.

As for the trouble, well, it just seemed to come with snake-handling. And anybody who regularly handled diamond-patterned

Death in the Lord's name could take any number of the eggs and insults that were hurled during the services. In their grandparents' time, stirred-up bees had been released by disbelievers in the churches. Sometimes, churches had been torched. Brief infernos would light up the night sky, ashy smuts dancing on the breeze to put down gently on distant fields or shingle roofs.

Three nights a week, and for hours at a time, Glenn's growing congregation just sang over the car horns sounding down Woods Cove Road, or ignored the sneering faces glimpsed at the windows, joyous to be worshipping the Lord in a place they could finally call their own. As for Glenn, he had a purpose and a congregation, a congregation that gave him status—and regular funds. For a while, those closest to the preacher dared even believe the violence and the drinking was behind him for good and all.

Their forebears, mostly from the Scottish Borders and from Northern Ireland, had first come to the Southern Appalachians, the frontier uplands of West Virginia and the Carolinas, Southern Kentucky and Eastern Tennessee, the hills of Northern Georgia and Alabama, as pioneering settlers in the 1700s. They had brought with them little more than the clothes they stood in, some livestock, a few tools and the King James Bible. Their isolated lives were parcelled out in work: clearing the land, building homesteads and churches with tramped earth floors, raising their stock for milk and food, hides and lard, and growing potatoes and corn. The rest was sleep and prayer. They kept to themselves, and called themselves Holiness people after their strict beliefs. They kept Christian houses, read from the Scriptures, abjured alcohol and tobacco, lies and "backbiting."

They dressed with a sober modesty. In the same spirit, later generations favoured shirts buttoned to the neck or workman's bib overalls. Citing Corinthians, the women mistrusted jewellery and wore their hair long and unstyled except perhaps fastened in a modest bun. In the 1950s, they wore thrifty dresses made up from the cheap floral patterns printed on the sacks of canny feed manufacturers.

The twentieth century, however, increasingly set the Holiness people at odds with the American way. Unversed in commerce and contract, they had too often sold their upland plots, and their holy self-reliance into the bargain, to timber and farming interests for a pittance. The only work was elsewhere, in the cities of Chattanooga, Huntsville, Knoxville, Atlanta and Nashville, or in towns like Scottsboro and Fort Payne in Alabama, Cleveland in Tennessee and Rome in Georgia. They worked in the lumber mills and coal mines, in construction and on the railroad, in the stores, factories and restaurants. They drove trucks. And they felt defiled.

The modern world had touched, even tempted them, with its abominations. Society was fallen, awash with the filth of homosexuality and the provocative attires of Jezebel: strumpet make-up, earrings and bangles; beer, whiskey and cigarettes; the unpardonable utterances of the movie houses, of radio and television; chewing gum, soda pop and coffee; and, latterly, rock music, drugs and even homosexual marriages. For the Holiness people, the twentieth century was one long crisis. Seeing their kind being swept away on the foul currents of modern American life spurred them to return with renewed spiritual vigour to their rickety churches, where living right became once more a simple thing enshrined in the unchanging Scriptures. It was here, in the first decade of the century, that men among them first found instruction in the final utterances of Mark to take up serpents. Snakes were evil; they embodied the century's very mood. Handling them meant perfect victory over Satan. Handling them was to rise above the wickedness of modern America.

But Glenn Summerford's redemption was to prove short-lived. By October 1991, the bad old ways that he had disavowed at Kingston nine years before had reclaimed Glenn with a vengeance. In the aftermath of some bad bites earlier that summer—notably from an exotic, a Mojave Desert rattlesnake out of Arizona that somebody had got off of a dealer—the preacher had been going under, leaving vodka bottles, crumpled Winston cigarette packets, trashy rented videos with dues to pay, serial infidelities and too many public brawls bubbling in his wake. For a few days, a bite from an eastern diamondback had turned his vision yellow. Too much booze and strychnine, too much suspicion, and too much plain rattlesnake venom in his blood had finally pushed him over the edge, pushed him to park the car out of sight one Friday evening so nobody might guess them in, to lock the front door and drag his wife to the shed where the snakes were kept, a gun to her head.

I took a motel room just off the interstate outside of town. The room smelt of stale cigarettes and lingering pizza. I dug out the phone book and found, between Chiropractors and Cigar, Cigarette and Tobacco Dealers, entries for fifty-one local churches of a bewildering range of denominations. There was African Methodist Episcopal, the Assemblies of God, Baptist, Catholic, Church of Christ, Church of God, Church of Jesus Christ of Latter Day Saints, Episcopal, Interdenominational, Jehovah's Witnesses, Lutheran, Methodist, United Methodist, Nazarene, Pentecostal, Presbyterian and Seventh-day Adventist, but there was nothing under Holiness. Pastor Frank, Glenn Summerford and their like evidently inhabited a world outside the phone book.

The phone rang.

"What's happening?" a voice asked me. Male.

"Who do you want?" I asked, assuming a wrong number.

"You," he replied. I laughed. "After a good rubdown tonight?" he asked, cutting to the chase. I dropped the phone and went out in search of somewhere to eat.

Geno's Pizzeria, down by the lights on the edge of town, seemed safe enough from unsolicited rubdowns. Not that it was the kind of place to invite conversation. Peaky blondes served large men who stared at television screens from under baseball hats advertising agricultural machinery. Occasionally, they wiped beer froth from their moustaches with the back of their hands. I turned to Scottsboro's *Daily Sentinel*. "Dear Abby," a correspondent wrote on the letters page. "My husband and I have a difference of opinion about what the date on a carton of milk represents. He says it is the 'sell by' date, and I say it indicates that the milk is good until that date. Would you please consult your experts and let us know the answer."

The man who walked through the door just at that moment—big boots, black beard, bandanna, khaki flak jacket—seemed less the sort to respect sell-by dates on cartons of milk than to grievously molest the dairy herds from which they came. Until he walked in, the other newspaper item that had caught my eye—Major Public Auction! Complete Liquidation of a Rocket Fuel Manufacturing Facility—had seemed most improbable. Now, the market was all too apparent. When he placed a bag on the counter, I expected him to growl *Fill it from the till, bitch. And don't try my itchy trigger finger*. I did not expect him to tell the waitress, perfectly respectfully, that she had given him Thousand Island dressing.

"And I actually asked for Italian, miss," he added. "Mind if I ask you to change it?"

So, I mused, driving back to my motel, Scottsboro folk were a bit fastidious about milk and burger dressings. I just couldn't square that with people who regularly got bitten handling snakes of their own free will and then refused hospital treatment to die in agony— an estimated one hundred of them since the first decade of the century when snake-handling had begun to be practised, without apparent precedent but with a fervent enthusiasm, initially among the country churches around Chattanooga, Tennessee, about fifty miles to the north of here. As the spring gnats danced in the head-lights, I imagined the most recently dead, Melissa Brown in Middlesboro, Southern Kentucky, just seven months earlier in August 1995, being welcomed by earlier generations of Appalachia's snakebite dead into an afterlife that they all believed in with the kind of untroubled, everyday conviction normally reserved for concepts such as a roundish earth.

Melissa Brown had been bitten just below the elbow at the little church out the back of Middlesboro by a four-foot long timber rattler, one of some fifty snakes being handled during the morning service that Sunday. Fifteen minutes after the bite, she had lost the use of her legs. She had laid up at her preacher Jamie Coots's apartment in Bella Gardens until Tuesday morning, almost forty-eight hours later, when her husband, Punkin, unsuccessfully urged her to think of their five children, ranging between sixteen months and nine years, and allow herself to be taken to hospital. "She suffered hard the whole time," said Jamie Coots, suffered until she lost consciousness on the same afternoon, when an ambulance was finally called at 3.38 P.M. By that time, however, Melissa Brown was in full

arrest and was pronounced dead on arrival at Middlesboro
Appalachian Regional Hospital.

Wherever Melissa went that Tuesday afternoon, she had no
doubt what she'd find there: joy unspeakable in the arms of the
Lord, and all the snakebite dead whose example she'd followed. People she knew from the church revivals and homecomings that
attracted Holiness communities from all over the Southern Appalachians, days of prayer, song and hog roasts in churches and sum-
mertime brush arbors, simple shelters raised in fields and on hill-
tops. There was Bruce Hale who had died just six months before her
after taking two bites from a rattlesnake at the New River Free
Holiness Church outside of Lenox, South Georgia. There was
Jimmy Ray Williams who died in Tennessee in 1991, and his father,
Jimmy Ray senior, who had died in the same county as his son eighteen years earlier, but after drinking strychnine. There was the
handsome preacher Charles Prince who'd grown up with rattlesnakes under his bed (Tennessee, 1985), Mack Wolford (West
Virginia, 1983) and John Holbrook (West Virginia, 1982). There
was Claude Amos (Kentucky, 1980) and the three who died in 1978.

Further back, there were those whom Melissa knew only by
repute or through familiarity with their sons and daughters; happy
Lee Valentine (Alabama, 1955) and, three weeks before him, snake-
handling's founding father, George Went Hensley. Hensley, whose
name sounded more like a direction, was said to gather up serpents
in his arms "like a boy would gather stovewood" and claimed to be
able to cure the dying and to walk the Tennessee River. He finally
succumbed to an eastern diamondback near Altha, Northern
Florida after surviving some four hundred previous bites that had
left him "speckled all over like a guinea hen." There were the four
who died in just six weeks of 1946 within just a few miles of each
other near Cleveland, Tennessee—Joe Jackson on 13 July, Henry
Skelton on 17 August, Walter Henry on 25 August and Hobart Wil-
son on 2 September. There were the three who had died in September 1945—Anna Kirk in Virginia, Lewis Ford in Tennessee and
George Coker in Kentucky—and Johnny Hensley, Maudie Lank-
ford and Jesse Coker in 1944. From August 1940, there were

Martha Napier and Jim Cochran, who both died in Kentucky. Melissa was in the company of the faithful. She had come home.

"LIFT THE LID," said Glenn as they stood over the second box. "I said lift it." Darlene's left hand was now throbbing so bad from the bite that she did so, gingerly, with her right hand. A charge ran through the box's contents; the snakes drew themselves tight.

"Tell you what," said Glenn, kneading the barrel of the pistol in the nape of her neck. "You handle that snake right there," he pointed to the larger one, "without it biting you, the Lord says I'll let you live." But the Lord, Darlene knew, had nothing to do with this. If the Lord was anywhere, he was certainly not here. She tasted bile. She was in danger of joining Appalachia's posthumous rattlesnake bite club.

Only thing was, she was not willing.

From *The Shadow of the Sun*

RYSZARD KAPUŚCIŃSKI

NOW THAT I HAD a powerful, four-wheel-drive vehicle, I could set off. And there was reason to: in early October, a neighbor of Tanganyika's, Uganda, was gaining its independence. The wave of liberation was sweeping the entire continent: in one year alone, 1960, seventeen African countries ceased being colonies. And this process was continuing, though at a diminished pace.

From Dar es Salaam to Uganda's capital, Kampala, where the ceremony was to take place, is three days' solid driving, going from dawn to dusk at maximum speed. Half the route is asphalt, the other half consists of reddish laterite roads, called African graters because they have a crenellated surface over which you can only drive fast, so as to skim over the tops of the crenellations.

A Greek went along with me, Leo—a part-time broker, part-time correspondent for various Athenian newspapers. We took four spare tires, two barrels of gasoline, a barrel of water, food. We set out at dawn, heading north, to the right of us the Indian Ocean, invisible from the road, to the left first the massif of Nguro, and then, for the rest of the way, the plain of the Masai. Both sides of the road are dense with greenery. Tall grasses, thick, fleecy shrubs, spreading umbrella trees. It's this way all the way to Kilimanjaro and the two little towns nearby, Moshi and Arusha. In Arusha we turned west, toward Lake Victoria. Two hundred kilometers on, the problems started. We drove onto the enormous plain of the Serengeti, the largest concentration of wild animals on earth. Everywhere you look, huge herds of zebras, antelopes, buffalo, giraffes. And all of them are grazing, frisking, frolicking, galloping. Right by the side of the road, motionless lions; a bit farther, a group of elephants; and farther still, on the horizon, a leopard running in huge bounds. It's all improbable, incredible. As if one were witnessing the birth of the world, that precise moment when the earth and sky already exist, as do water, plants, and wild animals, but not yet Adam and Eve. It is this world barely born, the world without mankind and hence also without sin, that one can imagine one is seeing here.

The Cobra's Heart

This mood of elation quickly dissipated in the fact of the realities and riddles of the journey. The first, most important question was, which way should we go? For when we emerged onto the great plain, what was heretofore a single broad trail suddenly forked into several identical-looking dirt paths, all leading in entirely different directions. And no guidepost, sign, or arrow in sight. The plain smooth as a tabletop, overgrown with tall grasses, no mountains or rivers, no natural orientation points of any kind, only this unending, increasingly unreadable, tangled net of trails.

There weren't even any intersections, but every few kilometers, sometimes every few hundred meters, more and more radiating tentacles, coils, and knots, from which secondary offshoots of the same kind branched out chaotically this way and that.

I asked Leo what he thought we should do, but he just looked about uncertainly and answered my question with an identical one. We drove on randomly, choosing roads that seemed to head west (and therefore toward Lake Victoria), but whichever the road, suddenly, after several kilometers and for no apparent reason, it would begin to turn in some unknown direction. Utterly confused, I would stop the car, wondering, now where? It was an especially urgent question, since we had neither a detailed map nor even a compass.

Soon, a new difficulty developed, for noontime arrived, and with it the hours of the greatest heat, when the world sinks into insensibility and silence. Animals seek shelter in the shade of trees. But the herds of buffalo have nowhere to hide. They are too large, too numerous. Each might be a thousand strong. Such a herd, in the hour of the greatest heat, simply grows motionless, dead still. It so happens that one has frozen this way precisely on the road along which we want to drive. We approach. Before us stand a thousand dark, granitelike statues, firmly set on the ground, as if petrified.

A mighty force slumbers in the herd, mighty and—should it explode anywhere near us—deadly. It is the force of a mountain avalanche, only inflamed, frenzied, driven by foaming blood. The zoologist Bernhard Grzimek tells of flying a small plane over the Serengeti and observing for months on end the behavior of buffalo. A lone buffalo didn't react at all to the whir of the descending plane: it calmly continued grazing. When Grzimek flew over a large herd, however, it was different. It sufficed for there to be among them a single overly sensitive one, a hysteric, a hothouse flower, who at the sound of the engine would start to thrash around waiting to flee. The entire herd would immediately panic and, in terror, begin to move.

And here is just such a herd. What should we do? Stop and stand? For how long? Turn around? It's too late for that; I am afraid to turn around, for they might rush us. They are fantastically swift, stubborn, and persistent animals. I make a sign of the cross and slowly, slowly, in first gear, the clutch only half engaged, drive into the herd. It is enormous, stretching almost to the horizon. I observe the bulls, who are at the head. Those who are standing in the path of the car begin drowsily, sluggishly to step aside so that the car can pass. They do not move even a centimeter farther than is absolutely necessary, and still the Land Rover is constantly scraping against their sides. I am drenched in sweat as we drive through this minefield. Out of the corner of my eye I look at Leo. His eyes are shut. One meter after another, meter by meter. The herd is silent. Immobile. Hundreds of pairs of dark, bulging eyes in massive heads, filmy, dull, expressionless. The passage lasts a long time, a crossing seemingly without end, but at last we emerge on the other shore— the herd is now behind us, its deep, dark stain against the green surface of the Serengeti growing smaller and smaller.

THE MORE TIME PASSED, the farther we drove, circling and straying, the more anxious I became. We had not encountered any people since morning. We had also not come upon either a larger road or any kind of signpost. The heat was terrifying, and it intensified with every minute, as if the road we were on, and all the others as well, led directly toward the sun, and as we drove we were inexorably approaching the moment we would be consumed by fire, like offerings laid at its altar. The burning air started to quiver and undulate. Everything was becoming fluid, each view blurred and washed out as in a film left running out-of-focus. The horizon receded and smudged, as if subject to the oceanic law of ebb and flow. The dusty gray parasols of the acacias swayed rhythmically and moved about-as if some confused madmen were tossing them here and there, at a loss for anything better to do.

But the worst by far was that the tangled net of roads that had held us in its treacherous and suffocating grip for several hours now itself twitched and began to move. I could see that the web, the entire intricate geometry, which admittedly I had not been able to decipher but which nonetheless was a kind of constant, a fixed element upon the surface of the savannah, was now thrashing about and drifting. Where was it drifting to? Where was it pulling us, entwined in its coils? We were all being swept somewhere, Leo, the car and I, the roads, the savannah, the buffalo, and the sun, toward some unknown, shining, white-hot space.

Suddenly, the engine stopped and the car came to an abrupt halt. Leo, seeing that something was wrong with me, had turned off the ignition. "Give it to me," he said. "I'll drive." We continued this way until the heat diminished, and it was then that we spotted two African huts in the far distance. We drove up. They were empty, with no doors or windows. There were some wooden bunks inside. The houses clearly did not belong to anyone, and were simply intended for travelers who happened by.

I don't know how I found myself on one of the bunks. I was half-dead. My head was pounding from the sun. To overcome drowsiness, I lit a cigarette. It didn't taste good. I wanted to put it out, and when I looked at my hand, which was reaching instinctively for the ground, I saw that I was about to extinguish the cigarette on the head of a snake lying under the bed.

I froze. Froze to such a degree that instead of quickly pulling back my hand, I left it suspended, cigarette burning, over the snake's head. Slowly, the reality of my position dawned on me: I was the prisoner of this deadly reptile. I knew one thing for certain: I could not move a muscle, because then the snake would attack. It was an Egyptian cobra, yellowish gray neatly coiled on the floor. Its venom brings death quickly, and in our situation-with no medicines, and the nearest hospital probably a day's driving away-death would be inevitable. It was possible that at that very moment the cobra was in a state of light catalepsy (a condition of numbness and lethargy apparently typical of these reptiles), because it did not stir. My God, what should I do? I thought feverishly, by now completely wide awake.

"Leo," I whispered loudly. "Leo, a snake!"

Leo had been in the car, getting our luggage out. We stared at each other silently, not knowing how to proceed. Yet time was running out: Were the cobra to awaken, it would probably attack instantly. Because we had no weapons of any kind, not even a machete, we decided that Leo would get a metal canister from the car and with it we would try to crush the cobra. It was a risky plan, but it was all we could come up with. We had to do something. Our inaction was giving the snake an advantage.

The canisters, from old British army supplies, were large, with sharp, protruding edges. Leo, who was a powerful man, grabbed one and started to creep toward the hut. The cobra was still just lying there, motionless. Leo, grasping the canister by its handles, lifted it up and waited. He was calculating, positioning himself, aiming. I lay still as stone on the bunk, tense, ready. And then suddenly, in a split second, Leo, holding the canister before him, threw his entire weight upon the snake. At which moment I too fell with my whole body on top of him. In these seconds, our lives hung in the balance-we knew this. Actually, we only thought of it later, for the instant the canister, Leo, and I came down on top of the snake, the interior of the hut exploded.

I never suspected there could be so much power within a single creature. Such terrifying, monstrous, cosmic power. I had assumed that the canister's edge would easily cut through the snake—nothing of the kind! I now saw we had beneath us not a snake, but a throbbing, vibrating steel spring, impossible to either break or crush. The cobra was thrashing and pounding the ground with such demented fury that the hut's interior grew dark from the dust. Under the powerful blows of its tail, the clay floor was crumbling and scattering, blinding us with clouds of debris. At one point it suddenly occurred to me with horror that we wouldn't manage, that the reptile would slip out from under us and, in pain, wounded, enraged, would start to bite us. I pressed down even harder on my friend. He was groaning, his chest crushed against the canister, unable to breathe.

Finally, but this took a long time, an eternity, the cobra's blows started to lose their impetus, vigor, frequency. "Look," Leo said. "Blood." Indeed, into a crevice along the floor, which now resembled a shattered clay dish, a narrow trickle of blood was slowly seeping. The cobra was weakening, and the vibrations of the canister, which we felt the whole time and by means of which the snake signaled us about her pain and her hatred, vibrations that terrified and panicked us, were also diminishing. But now, when it was all over, when Leo and I rose and the dust began to settle and thin out and I gazed down again at the narrow ribbon of blood being quickly absorbed, instead of satisfaction and joy I felt an emptiness inside, and something else as well: I felt sad that that heart, which inhabited the very pit of hell we had all shared through a bizarre coincidence only a moment ago, that that heart had stopped beating.

From *On Bullfighting*

A. L. KENNEDY

An Introduction to Death

I'M THINKING I MIGHT ACTUALLY ENJOY THIS, if I had more time.

It's Sunday, the first day of the week: the one that's for resting and possibly talking to God, but I am doing neither. I am sitting across my window ledge and thinking that Sundays are always much the same: vaguely peaceful and emptied and smug: and I am looking out over my gutter and four storeys down to my street. It's late in a mild afternoon and there are flickers of spring in the trees. The smell of young grass drifts up to me from the park and the air is also coloured very slightly with waking earth and sunny masonry. Cars beetle past, roofs gleaming, but there's no one out walking. Although I'd expect there might be on such a pleasant day, there is no one about.

Which means I should do this. I should jump now, while I can.

Because I don't want anyone looking, or there to be hurt by me when I fall. It's only me I want to kill. And I don't wish to be gawped at while I'm killing. I believe I've had enough embarrassment for one life.

But I can do this now, it's all clear, no observers—I can jump.

Not that I feel despairing—I don't—not any more. I'm not even remotely upset: I am only very heavy, only that. I have turned into something new, unworkably substantial, too solid to last. I'm already straining my grip on the window frame, finding it hard to keep myself above the street.

So I should go.

I wanted to do this naked. There aren't many things I like to do undressed, but I did want to leave life as I met it, because that seemed neat and I can be neat if I choose to, on this day of all days. And because, with no clothes to disguise me, there would be no more pretence that I'm anything more than function, mechanics, butcher's shop window stuff. I would like to think otherwise, but currently, I don't.

Still, the thought of myself on the pavement with my skin against the stone—the idea of that little discomfort, which I wouldn't even feel—made me squeamish. It made climbing up to the window too difficult. So I've kept on my clothes and made the climb. But I have taken off my shoes.

The only proper eccentricity I've managed to cultivate in all this time: I take off my shoes to do anything important, it helps me concentrate. I always, for example, used to get shoeless before I wrote. And this is pretty unimpressive, I do know, as a trick of personality, I had hoped for something more: like keeping a parrot that screamed obscenities, or randomly screaming obscenities myself, or perhaps just affecting an eye-catching limp. When I was a kid I would secretly practise all kinds of limp.

But it's rather too late for that kind of nonsense now.

I look at the sky and it's all a broad, dumb blue. I bought this flat because I could finally afford one and it felt happy and had a study where I could write—my first ever study—and because it had high windows that showed nothing but the sky.

I should really go.

And now I have been in this flat and unhappy for far longer than I'd have wished. Which is of no particular consequence to anyone much beyond myself. I do know that. The inadequacy of my misery hasn't escaped me, the fact that I'm literally boring myself to death. This all started with such utterly commonplace stuff, things other people can manage and that I should have managed, too: a man that I loved has died and another has hurt me, I am not in good health and don't sleep, I have a rather averagely broken heart and no more need for the flat someone else would be glad of, or for its study, because I don't write. I'm a writer who doesn't write and that makes me no one at all. I don't look very different, but I have nothing of value inside.

So why stay here, when I have no further use.

Although this proves that I am a coward, I close my eyes before making what I hope will be my last voluntary move.

And then the music starts.

By this I don't mean that the music of my past life is dashing down to flutter by my ears, or that I experience some kind of filmic interlude, or the hymns of choirs angelic, demonic, or revelatory. I mean that I hear a man's voice droning from a distance, cheaply amplified and criminally flat and singing what has always been my least favourite folk song in all of the world—*Mhairi's Wedding*.

For those of you lucky enough to have never encountered this piece of pseudo-Celtic pap I will say that it's first words are *Step we gaily, on we go, heel for heel and toe for toe,* and that it then deteriorates. It mentions—I can hear it fucking mentioning herring and oatmeal and peat and several other rustic elements vital to the noble, rural, ceilidhing Gaelic life.

I had to sing *Mhairi's Wedding* in school music lessons for, if recollection serves me, thirty or forty years. I need hardly say that its tune, what there is of it, is precisely annoying enough to be utterly unforgettable without having a single moment of genuine muscle, emotion or charm. I have never truly liked anybody called Mhairi, quite simply because of this song.

But here it is, coming from nowhere that I can see, from nowhere that makes any sense, from some unlikely outdoor concert, some especially elaborate practical joke. Verse and chorus, it spindrifts in towards me from the suburbs and the carriageway to the west and it breaks the day. I can't do this any more. I can't wait here and listen to *Mhairi's Wedding* and still prepare myself to die with even a rag of credibility. Equally, I can't face jumping while the bloody thing is still being sung. Murdering myself to this accompaniment is more than I can bear. So now I can't even die. It seems that, having been fucked over by every other part of my existence, I am now being splendidly, finally fucked by either divine intervention or simple chance.

I get back down into my living room and I put on my shoes and I stand for a while, having nowhere else to go, and I cry, because the life I had hoped I would not have to meet with again is still here and still waiting and still mine. Divine intervention wasn't something I happened to want.

Oh, and do feel free to imagine my unparalleled delight whenever I remember that *Mhairi's Wedding* is, at least in part, why I'm alive and typing this today.

And, just in case you've wondered, I only mention these things by way of a preamble because this book will be, at least in part, about people who risk death for a living. Whatever you or I think of how and why they do this, they are making that commitment every working day—a commitment which I'm pointing out I know that I can't equal. But my little confession of a contemplated sin is intended to indicate that I will give you as much as I can. I do promise that.

I will tell you about bulls, the *toros bravos* of Spain, bred to be killed in the rink as the culmination of the three acts which form the *corrida de toros*.* There are, in the world, many other bull spectacles— US rodeo confrontations, Portuguese and French displays of arena athleticism, Spanish *charlotadas,* or "comic" plaza circuses, and *rejoneos* where mounted *rejoneadors* use lances to kill bulls, there are bulls set to fight or race other bulls in the Far East—but the traditional, Spanish corrida will be the subject of this book. I will focus on the meetings between bulls and matadors, unmounted men.

And I will point out now that the corrida is not, accurately speaking, a bullfight, although this is the standard English term for it. No man, as has often been noted, can actually *fight* half a ton or so of bull. What happens in the ring is more complicated, repellent, fascinating, grotesque, sacramental, ugly, ritualistic, haphazard, sacred and blasphemous than any fight.

*Literally, a running of the bulls, harking back to more disorganised, rural fiestas with elements in common with the current annual running of the bulls towards a ring in Pamplona. It is now the name attached to a traditional Spanish "bullfight."

I will use a glossary and footnotes,[+] which attempt to translate or at least to explain the vocabulary of the corrida; the particular, peculiar, partly gypsy, fastidiously detailed and occasionally mystical language in which the corrida has come to be defined. And I will write about the *toreros*,[*] the men (and the handful of women) whose job it is to kill the bulls and who may, themselves, be killed by bulls. Such deaths are infrequent, particularly in these days of effective antibiotics, but they are still by no means impossible. Toreros must also accustom themselves to a career which will inevitably involve injury by goring: sometimes serious, if not, grotesque, goring. No matter what your personal opinion of the corrida may happen to be, these facts are inescapable: in the corrida, bulls and men meet fear and pain and both may die.

The proximity of so much dying tends to demand a certain honesty from observers. So, in the spirit of my earlier promise, I will be honest with you. As a former author and former suicide, honesty's about all I have left. Which means that I can tell you this book does not come from any prior interest or enthusiasm on my part. I have no love for the hairy, manly Hemingway approach to the corrida, no anxious need to lurk at the bedsides of wounded toreros, fiddling with the dressings on tight, young thighs. I am not a woman who finds the facts of death erotic (although we will discuss such matters in due course) and the sight of boys in spangled satin and slippers stiff-legging it through their required paces does nothing for me, per se.

I was simply asked if I would write this and I simply agreed. When I began the necessary research, I could have heard that the corrida had been banned throughout the world for ever and ever amen and I would have remained unconcerned. I came to this with entirely selfish motives. I wanted to see if I was still capable of writing anything at all. I wanted to keep my mind occupied, because—

[+]Something I hate. Sadly, some subjects demand them. Sorry.

[*]*Torero*, sometimes used interchangeably with *matador*, properly applies to any of the three classes of human participants in the corrida—the *matador* who kills the bull, the *picador* who is mounted and tests the bull with spear-thrusts, and the *peones* who assist the matador and must draw bulls away from fallen or terror-stuck men.

left to its own devices—it might very well manage to kill, or at least torment me. And I wanted to discover if the elements which seemed so much a part of the corrida—death, transcendence, immortality, joy, pain, isolation and fear—would come back to me. Because they were part of the process of writing and, good and bad, I miss them.

I will try to make this book as accurate as I can, although there are others that any would-be *aficionado** might do better to consult: they're listed in the bibliography. For those who are already implacably repulsed by the corrida, I don't wish to change your mind, but I may be informative and it's certainly always my policy to know my enemy—it may also be yours. For those of you who are already gripped by *afición*;* I can't even promise to inform, in fact, I will probably irritate. You may well be enraged by my attempt to anatomise your passion and, like experts the world over, may well be keen to enjoy correcting an interloper's mistakes. Whoever you are, you and I both know that you're the reader—this book is, therefore, yours to do with as you'd like. It is a record of both the progress and the conclusions of a relatively brief study of the corrida. It is a personal view. If you feel this will not suit you, you can, of course, leave now.

But before we begin in earnest with the bulls I will add a postscript to my window-sill interlude.

A few months after I studied the pavement and then didn't meet it, I was talking to a friend of mine who is an undertaker and also a writer: or a writer and also an undertaker, depending on your frame of mind. When I told him how much I still wanted to die, to finish up the job, he said—and I do remember this exactly, "Don't do that, Alison. You would look so silly." He had guessed, quite correctly, that the last thing I'd want my death to be is silly.

This is, naturally, why the strains of *Mhairi's Wedding* stopped me jumping—dying in time to that tune would have been entirely ridicu-

*Literally, someone who has a liking for anything, or who is a fan of anything. Quite often used specifically of those who have a knowledge of and enthusiasm for the corrida.

*The quality of liking, having one's fancy taken by something. Again it can be used specifically to denote an informed, even opinionated, passionate interest in the corrida. To have it, is to be an initiate in taurine circles, to be a believer.

lous and I wanted to keep my dignity. Or, to be more precise, I still
had my pride. Undoubtedly, I could see no point in going on—still
can't. And I was thoroughly sick of several types of pain—still am—
but there was one last hook of interest in life for my ego and me: I
very much wanted to make one last, grand gesture and to make it
properly. If there was nothing else for me to say and no one to listen, in
any case, then at least I could find a way to make my death speak.

Then my kind friend made it beautifully plain that I could
make myself dead very easily, but not dead and in control, not dead
and also eloquent.

Although recent research seems to show that a torero's body
chemistry predisposes him, or occasionally her, to crave risk, the
average *matador** is not exactly suicidal. He goes into the ring to face
both destruction and survival. The matador is at the heart of a
strange balance between the demands of safety and of fame,
between the instinct for self preservation and the appetite for the
ultimate (and therefore ultimately dangerous) execution of the corrida's three traditional acts. He is both threatened and exalted by a
process intended to make death eloquent. The torero, the *cuadrilla**
(the men who support him in the ring), the *ganadero* (the rancher
who breeds the bulls) and the whole regiment of other interested
parties are intended to be held by rules which attempt to make the
bull's death more than slaughter, something beyond ten or fifteen
minutes of torment and clumsy flight.

Human injury or death also has its place within the fabric of the
corrida, and its effects can be ambivalent. While a wound received
in the ring may assure one matador's reputation and drive forward
his skills, it may destroy the courage of another. The death that

---

*A killer of bulls, as opposed to a butcher, or a murderer of bulls. (Obviously some
would think this distinction overly fine.) The matador is the only one permitted to
make full passes with the *capote de brega* and then the *muleta* and to wear gold decora-
tion on both the jacket and trousers of his suit. Becoming a torero can be called "taking the gold." All toreros, apart from the picador, wear the *coleta*—a pigtail—as did
Roman gladiators.

*The team which supports the matador in the ring. This comprises two *picadors*, three
banderilleros (also known as *peones*) and the *mozo de espada*, or sword boy, and his assistant.

stalks all toreros can give their life meaning, offer moments of delirious intensity, even while it drives them into drug abuse, compulsive sexuality and suicide.

And if it does so happen that a human being finds death in the corrida's rarefied afternoon, if a torero, or perhaps one of his cuadrilla, is fatally wounded, then the corrida is intended to redefine the moment of death, to act as our translator. Even the almost always inevitable death of the bull, is meant to be controlled within the corrida's physical language, the structure and the sad necessities of its world. The corrida can be seen as an extraordinary effort to elevate the familiar, mysterious slapstick, the irrevocable, indecipherable logic of damage and death, into something almost accessible. The corrida can be seen as both a ritualised escape from destruction and a bloody search for meaning in the end of a life, both an exorcism and an act of faith.

I am not unaware that faith makes living supportable, can make sense out of death, can make any communication both possible and worthwhile. In writing this book, I am looking for faith. I am not unaware that I need it. I begin with a slender point of connection: that, in attempting to control death, the toreros and I may have a little in common. We have attempted the impossible, something which stands in the face of nature.

And, like many people who feel themselves opposed by forces greater than themselves, I am inclined to be superstitious. Matadors are superstitious, too. Most people have some familiarity with higher and lower types of faith and, when religion seems inadequate or impossibly exalted, we can all resort to courting luck. Every bull ring of any size at all offers some variety of space set aside for toreros who wish to pray and, beyond prayer, toreros and the members of their cuadrillas have patterns and layers of habits and charms to coax in and secure good luck.

Contrary to theatrical tradition, it is not considered unlucky to wish a matador good luck—which is to say, "*Suerte*."* Not uncoinci-

---

*Variously defined as (good) luck, fortune, chance, destiny, lot. *Una suerte de capa* is a cape pass. *Cagar la sierte*—a highly charged phrase, almost impossible to define, even

dentally, the same word describes each of the three stages of the corrida. Even the most talented matador, the most talented "killer of bulls," would acknowledge that each gesture with the bull, successfully completed, is a concrete proof of not only skill, but also good fortune. A matador of any standing draws his confidence from both and then puts himself at risk, while in a condition of acute readiness. Throughout the corrida, he must be as alert and prepared as his training and disposition can make him, because he cannot know the absolute fact of the bull until he meets it, cannot guarantee his safety until he has struck the killing blow. Even then, he should be wary.

On 30th August 1985 José Cubero Sánchez "El Yiyo" turned his back on a bull he had mortally wounded and, while he acknowledged the crowd's applause, was knocked to the ground by the dying animal. All attempts to distract the bull were unsuccessful and, as its strength failed, it gored its killer where he lay. The bull's right horn entered the matador's heart and its last efforts to toss up his body succeeded only in lifting the man to his feet. For an instant, the dead man and the dead bull both stood on the sand. Then "El Yiyo" walked a few paces and fell. A friend of mine who saw this happen has, quite understandably, never forgotten it.

In his death, "El Yiyo" confirmed an old corrida tradition—that a man who kills a bull which has already killed a man, will himself be killed by a bull. "El Yiyo" had stepped in to finish the bull which killed "Paquirri" exactly a year previously in Pozoblanco. The corrida provides a setting intended to display its own blend of chaos and coincidence, chance and death.

But, of course, the torero seeks order, a way to live through the afternoon, or leave it with the required dignity. His aim is to control a bull of which he has no real prior knowledge, to dominate it with style and to conjure up its death correctly. If needs be, he must also present his own injury as perfectly as he can. In this respect, mata-

---

literally. Means something like "to carry/load/hear a pass." Very loosely it would mean the flowing performance of passes in absolute good faith, according to whichever style the observer thinks best. It has also been elegantly translated as "pushing your luck."

dors are like the rest of us, naked in the grip of reality—they have to rely on what chance gives them. In the execution of their accepted duties, they make this exposure plain.

And chance will make itself plain, from time to time, without any human assistance. For example, I am filling this page on a Sunday, in the cottage I've borrowed from my friend who writes and undertakes, or undertakes and writes, because it may be a place where I can get well. It is a cottage containing both oatmeal and peat and is not far from a spot on the coast where those so inclined can fish for herring. *Mhairi's Wedding* has crept up and caught me at last, but this reality is far more pleasant than the song's unmelodious fiction.

In the byre next to the cottage there are cows in calf and I will mention now that it so happens cows carry their offspring for nine months, in the way that human beings do. And this morning, while I did what passes for my work, a cow in the byre went under the knife. It turned out that her calf was deformed and dead in the womb: she couldn't give birth and would die without a Caesarean section being performed to remove the corpse.

So the thin song of starlings came out with the sun and I sat here and tried to put one word after another and, now and then, provided hot water for the vet who stood and waited in my doorway. He was wearing a surgical gown and gloves, just as he would if he were operating on a person. His arms were up to the shoulder in blood which might as well have been the blood of a person for all that I could tell. I rinsed the bucket for him and filled it when required and then washed away the blood from round the sink—blood which thickened and darkened and dried in just the way that human blood would—most blood being much the same in these respects.

When the procedure was over, I walked into the byre with the farmer to see the dead calf where it lay, milk-white, something of the spider about it: long legs curled impossibly from its perfect hooves to its oddly small body. It was born without a ribcage, and an uncontained sprawl of purple, glossy organs was spread behind it, forced out through its skin by the pressure of the womb. The calf looked very far from human and barely animal, only incapable of holding life.

Back beside the wall was the cow, entirely alive and standing and chewing impassively, as no human mother could at such a time. Her belly hair was clotted with mud and her own blood, a shaved and sewn scar glinted in her side, made strange by a silvery preparation, painted on to prevent infection.

Both the vet and the farmer had wondered if I should look at these things, in case I was squeamish and because the calf seemed so disturbing, a thing against nature. But of course I looked, because my training and disposition made me look. They always do. So today I saw death and survival among animals and men in a way that might almost have been intended, because my life can be quite eloquent without any special maneuvering from me: I need only be in it.

Life's definite *sense*, of course, remains nothing if not opaque. For example, the farmer and I sat together after the Caesarean and drank tea and agreed that we didn't know why such things happened: why a cow should survive after being cut wide open, why matter should grow strange inside the womb. The farmer wondered, half-serious, if he hadn't had to lose the calf because he'd been working on too many Sundays—not giving the day an adequate respect. I nodded, half-serious myself, saw him out and then went back to work.

From *Tierra Incognita*

SUSAN ZAKIN

I MET A LAWYER who lives in the unforgiving southern California desert where Charles Manson chewed gum and dreamed of dismemberment. With his milky freckled skin and red hair, this man seemed an unlikely candidate to live in a place where the sun never lets you go for very long. "Why do certain people love the desert?" I asked him. "For example, why are *you* here?"

"Claustrophobia," the lawyer answered, without missing a beat. I laughed; it seemed so obvious now that he had said it. Deserts are Meccas for intellectuals with high heat tolerance and higher anxiety. The lawyer had grown up in Los Angeles and like other shell-shocked urban refugees, he found in the desert correlative and antidote, a place that surprises yet calms. That explanation had never occurred to me, even though I, too, come from a family of urban-bred claustrophobes. My mother hugged the shoreline of Manhattan island as if it were her last vestige of sanity. She liked to look at the river, she said. I think she needed to believe she could escape, if it really came down to that.

Phobias can seem self-referential because they appear as non sequiturs. Why should one person be afraid of snakes, another of attending the theater? But experts say all phobias stem from the same causes. There are explanations for people like us, and, quite frankly, they aren't flattering. "Bravery, rebellion, ambitiousness, desertion from the army, playing truant from school, criminality and polygamy may be defenses against claustrophobic anxieties," wrote Melitta Schmideberg in "A Note on Claustrophobia," a brief but devastating paper published in a 1948 edition of the *Psychoana-*

lytic Review. "Claustrophobia may be transferred onto the inability to fit into existing conditions, to submit to authority, to accept limitations, a steady job, or marriage, in fact, any sort of emotional independence." (sic) A typographical error, no doubt. These personalities avoid emotional *dependence*, not independence.

Recent research indicates that claustrophobia and agoraphobia are essentially the same thing. William James arrived at a theory that sounds oddly relevant to twenty-first-century ears tuned to sociobiology and neuropsychology. James believed these phobias are not diseases but instincts from the days of sabretooth cats and dire wolves. Agoraphobia: our ancestors were vulnerable on the open savanna. Claustrophobia: the darkness of caves hid predators. In *The Songlines*, Bruce Chatwin writes of a researcher in South Africa who hypothesized that *Dinofelis*, a cat with jaws more powerful than a sabretooth, was a specialist killer of primates. He based his theory on the preponderance of human bones found at the mouths of caves inhabited by these cats. The lawyer, my mother, and I may be throwbacks to days of darkness.

Certainly no one would argue with the idea that claustrophobia and other anxieties stem from the fear of death. At its worst, the paradoxical effect of this misplaced survival instinct is that one forgets to live.

I was stunned to discover that a present-day remedy for phobias is called "flooding." "This involves practically overloading the person with whatever it is the person is afraid of," one brochure reported chirpily. The method sounds positively Victorian, like locking a child in a dark closet to punish bad behavior. But apparently it is still in use.

I may have used it on myself. Late that winter someone taught me to meditate. This was the politically acceptable way to deal with grief in San Francisco in 1989. The weather was getting warm, but most days I stayed wrapped in a heavy blue bathrobe. Despite being slovenly and disoriented, each morning at exactly ten o'clock I religiously parked myself on a rattan chaise lounge. Very deliberately, I closed my eyes. I imagined sitting on a hill in Vermont. I looked in the four directions for five minutes each, visualizing what I had seen during my childhood summers. My last stop was a grove of trees. They were short and dark and whorled, like the trees in *The Wizard of Oz*, the ones that threw their apples at Dorothy. The trees seemed to be closing in on me. The more I concentrated, the more sinister they looked. I checked my watch, twice, three times, cracking open my eyes just enough to see. I clenched and unclenched my jaw. I tried to breathe deeply. I made it through the requisite five minutes, but barely.

God, I hated meditating. But I was willing to try anything. Fortunately it wasn't long before I had to get on the road. There's nothing like travel for abandoning good intentions.

WE'RE GOING TO MEXICO. Yee-hah! But it's midnight already and we haven't made it past Gila Bend.

"I think we should stop now, don't you?" asked Art.

"I guess that makes sense," I said.

I wanted to drive all night, but, hey, Gila Bend had its merits. In Arizona, a state losing an acre an hour to sprawl, Gila Bend was an oasis of old-time sanity. The only millennial spillover came in the form of a Dairy Queen, a Subway sandwich shop, and a few chain motels encrusting the highway on-ramp. On the main drag, the Space Age Motel, a masterpiece of circa-1964, NASA-inspired kitsch, was still the most heavily booked place in town.

Art and I met when we worked at the same daily newspaper in Connecticut. He adopted me as mentor, not that I knew much more than he did. I took him for granted, bossed him around, and occasionally worried about him. Art appeared to be a regular modern person but in reality he is a first-generation immigrant from a vanished America. Art's family had lived for generations in a small Connecticut town. His mother is—still, I think—known as the Muskrat Baby because his grandfather had trapped a dozen muskrats to pay the doctor who attended her birth. Art was the youngest of three boys, and at five feet, ten inches, the smallest. His two brothers were enormous, grease-stained, pot-smoking, and probably methamphetamine-producing Harley riders. As a scrawny kid, Art never had to worry about getting beaten up: everyone was too afraid of his brothers. But he worried about everything else. Ten years ago he was agonizing over a screwed-up relationship with a Puerto Rican girlfriend and a meaningless job on Wall Street. Fortunately, underneath his brand-new suits custom-made by an Italian tailor (their wide lapels and padded shoulders gave him a look best described as "Poindexter-turned-bookie") Art was an experienced outdoorsman. So he threw off his anxieties and jumped at the chance to go to the place the author Edward Abbey had called "the final test of desert rathood." This was, of course, the Pinacate Desert. Abbey claimed that the Pinacate was the postdoc for degreed desert rats, a place of not-quite-extinct volcanoes and light that played tricks with your mind. This wasn't all hype. Back in those days, the Pinacate truly was a no man's land. The roads were faint tracks in the dirt; the only signs sun-blasted wooden posts marked by faded lettering. The highest of the Pinacate cinder cones, Pinacate and Carnegie peaks, were incongruous slices of night sky. At four thousand and three thousand seven hundred feet respectively, they were barely tall enough to be called mountains yet they were visible from great distances. I always had the feeling they were watching me. At their bases, the sandy playa ran into a seductive nothingness.

I know that Art was looking for a way out then. In retrospect, I may have been running away, too. Everything seemed circumstantial at the time, a case of putting one foot in front of the other.

In spite of our worries, or perhaps because of them, the trip took on a certain demented jollity. One could hardly be serious at the Space Age Motel. The Space Age was indeed a door to another world, but it was a world cadged from a low-budget 1960s TV show; *Lost in Space*, I think. We ate breakfast under floor-to-ceiling murals of Apollo missions. The pancakes tasted like a failed experiment in astronaut food. Outside the dining room's picture window, a flying saucer straddled a patch of dried, curling Bermuda grass.

After leaving behind this ratty tribute to the space program—if not the ultimate escape fantasy, certainly the nerdiest—Art and I headed south. In this direction, only the spooky underwater landscape of the Sonoran Desert crossed our windshield. The saguaro cactus is the postcard icon of this desert, a tall, columnar cactus whose arms strike out in unpredictable directions. Like many of the plants and animals that evolved here, saguaros lead a double life. In the rainy season, water pulses through them as invisibly as the secret life of a bigamist. In a drought, the saguaro's rib cage becomes fragile as straw, hollow as a reed. You discover this only after one has died and the broken pieces are lying on the ground. The delicacy of this enormous, treelike cactus is shocking, just as you are shocked by the death of a lithe young basketball player whose heart unaccountably stops in the middle of a game. One writer suggested that saguaros resemble stage props: papier-maché boulders or a false-front Western town. This is not true. For years now I have touched their green skin. I know they are alive.

Ten years ago, I had touched nothing. But I had read books. The poet Richard Shelton compared this desert, all deserts, to a lover. This is what the desert means to all men, he wrote.

What does it mean to a woman? If the desert is a lover, can it take the place of a husband, of children, of family? Of normal human contact? Love? "I am convinced now that the desert has no heart," Edward Abbey once complained.

Squinting into the sun as I drove, I imagined a featureless man dressed in sun-faded clothes. A desert rat. His skin, his clothes, and his hair are coated with golden dust. He is a loner, a smaller, wiry version of Gary Cooper, capable of superhuman feats. This man must be a creature of the 1940s, I think, a time when life was clean and simple, the moral code clear. His face is blurred, hidden by a hat. Always hidden.

ART AND I WERE HEADED to Organ Pipe Cactus National Monument to meet a park ranger named Peter Travis. Organ Pipe Cactus National Monument is more than three hundred and thirty thousand acres of mountainous desert on the US-Mexico border; a valley, essentially, bounded by two mountain ranges: the Ajo Mountains and the Bates Mountains. Today Organ Pipe is called the most dangerous national park in the United States. The park earned this distinction because of a single incident. A law enforcement ranger gave chase to a Mexican drug dealer who had crossed the border after killing four men. The park ranger followed the drug dealer into an arroyo, where he was shot for his efforts. This was tragic, but the ranger hadn't followed police procedure: cowboy cops who fail to wait for backup only live to tell the tale in the movies. But the tragedy, if it is that, is not without meaning. The scenario could be viewed as one of those thinly veiled puppet shows scoring arch political points just before the French Revolution. The real story here is US government hypocrisy. The border has always been corrupt. The recent explosion of the border drug trade is not unrelated to the increasing intimacy of the two countries. US corporations open manufacturing plants in Mexico to take advantage of cheap labor and lax regulation, but their lackeys in government keep the border closed—or as closed as they can manage—to prevent Mexicans from taking advantage of America's affluence. The edge is ragged, and violent.

Before the last decade's intrusion of various police agencies to the border region, the drug dealer would have crossed the desert quietly and disappeared, like a contrail dissolving in the sky, or a lizard burrowing in sand. When Art and I first traveled there, Organ Pipe was merely obscure; the Pinacate Desert, less than thirty miles south, even more so. The desert was a place of quiet so pervasive it filled the air. A phone booth at a crossroads gas station had the gravity of an Edward Hopper painting.

Peter Travis was the guide to this uncharted place. "He knows that desert and he loves it," a colleague had said of Peter. I hesitated before dialing Peter's telephone number. I was in San Francisco, engaging in my pathetic attempts to meditate and, in general, trying to recover from the events of the past weeks. It was hard to talk to anyone at all, but harder still to talk to someone I didn't know.

Finally, I called. As I held the receiver to my ear, the lines gave off a faint, rattling ring. They sounded antiquated and very far away. But Peter and were instantly close, or so it seemed. Peter had the kind of deep voice that makes you believe vocal chords are the *homo sapiens* equivalent of a male bird's plumage. He even seemed to have something to say. He had lived in Berkeley. He knew restaurants and culture and music. He said he would take us to the Pinacates. "Are you sure you don't mind?" I asked. "It's not an imposition?"

"I'm the resident tour guide around here," he said, with a self-deprecating laugh; nearly a cough, really. "It's a great excuse to get out, showing people around."

"Do you get bored?" I asked him. "Living there?"

"Bored? It's the least boring place in the world. The desert never ceases to amaze." Peter said this mockingly, as if reciting a park service motto; he sounded, I thought, embarrassed by his own passion. *Just doin' my job, ma'am.*

We were set for the trip. Peter told me he had a Baja Bug, a VW retrofitted for the desert with big wheels and a fancy suspension. There was only one problem, according to Peter. "It's going to be hard to fit three people in the Bug—and the beer," he said in a tone of phony concern.

"Are you saying we should ditch Art?" I said.

"Well, it would be easier. Who is this guy, anyway?"

"A friend," I said. "Just a friend. Look, I can't ask him not to come. I already invited him." *This guy's got some nerve,* I thought. But I remember looking up from the phone and smiling as I watched the fog blotting out the sun, the way it did every afternoon in San Francisco.

WHEN ART AND I REACHED ORGAN PIPE, Peter was nowhere to be found. *Out in the field,* said his boss, a stocky youngish man with a fleshy, sunburned face. We left a six-pack of beer on the doorstep of Peter's house with a note promising we'd be back.

Art and I decided to hike up to Bull Pasture, a rugged saddle high up in the Ajo Mountains. This is one of only two real trails in the park. In the book *Cactus Country*, Edward Abbey told the story of a woman who disappeared here in 1971 while hiking alone. Before setting off she left a note in the trail register, mentioning that she was wearing a yellow windbreaker, a garment that would be easy to spot at a distance. Just in case.

The woman simply vanished. She evaporated like a drop of rain lofted across the sky, a whisper from a lone summer cloud to a sun-baked rock, disappearing at the point of contact. Rangers searched for twelve days. This was about a week longer than anyone could have survived.

Art and I stopped to talk at the base of the Ajo Mountains, probably within a few feet of where the woman started her walk to the saddle. There were two trails: one led straight up, the other meandered through the canyon.

"Which way do you want to go? I want to take the steep one," Art announced. He sounded as if he were spoiling for a fight. Both of us were tired, driven out.

"Listen," I said, "why don't you take that one, and I'll meet you at the top. Okay?"

"Are you sure?"

"Yeah. Just wait for me at the top if you get there first."

Art didn't move.

"Go," I ordered.

I may have bossed Art around like an older sister, but I was still young enough to experience certain things for the first time. On that day I discovered the comforting feeling of insignificance familiar to anyone who has spent time in large landscapes. I remember looking up at canyon walls, realizing I might not be able to reach the place where they met the sky, not that day, possibly not ever. I navigated the heat, inseparable from the sound of birds. I walked alone, following their drifts of complicated code in the air.

I learned about rain that summer, when planes couldn't land, when the airport was cut off and the world held at bay, if only for a day or two. I learned about the all-encompassing heat of the desert. I breathed heat in like a narcotic, or perhaps a balm, erasing everything that had come before. The heat affected me like an illness. I felt I could not go on. Yet, as time passed, I found it pleasant to submit to something larger than myself; something that, like H. Ryder Haggard's campy goddess She, could not be denied.

That day, as I walked silently through arroyos filled with fleeting, unknowable scents, I thought of that bright yellow streak tumbling down the canyon wall. If a foreign body wrapped in a cheery piece of plastic clothing falls through geologic time, charted only in an inexact fashion by crumbling rhyolite, hurtles in a soundless void of a canyon and disappears; well, who can know what happened? Was she pushed? Did she fall? Or did she choose something? Not to die, perhaps, but to *be* in that canyon in another way. . . . On that afternoon I glimpsed the barest edge of something but felt mercifully released from any need or desire to name it.

Art and I met at the top, friends again. We ran down the steep side of the canyon back to the car. The sun crashed behind us.

I FELT A RUSH OF DISAPPOINTMENT when I saw Peter. He was waiting for us, the last one left in the office. Peter wore cheap chrome glasses and his bulbous features seemed out of place on a narrow face. But the minute he opened his mouth, I softened. He still had that edge of humor in his voice. I noticed that his sun-streaked hair looked startling, incongruous over his tanned, dark skin.

Peter invited us to his house for dinner. He lived in a place where signs warned you off if you were a mere member of the public. We followed a curving road under twin saquaro-studded hills. The rangers lived in low-slung, 1970s suburban tract-style houses. Every part of Peter's government-issue house was beige, as if the sand of the desert had seeped in beneath the doors and windows.

Peter not only lived in a government-issue house, he also shared it with a government-issue roommate; a woman. "I want to show you something," he said, leading me down a darkened hallway. He opened a door and switched on a light. I had never seen so many orange ruffles in my life. Everything in the bathroom was orange, and, if scientifically possible, also ruffled, from the shower curtain to the toilet paper cover. The bathroom glowed as if it were a bubble from outer space. "It's a theme park," I gasped.

"The only one around here, fortunately," he laughed. Obviously he had never been to the Space Age Motel. "We're assigned roommates. It's kind of random," he said. He said random with an emphasis I had never heard before. I found out later that Peter had been something of a math prodigy. He had entered the California Institute of Technology at sixteen. Random, as in "random number," as in unsorted, unchosen, undesirable, had been a popular word. "She's a Christian," added Peter.

"Well, *that* explains it," I said. "She's definitely handy with a sewing machine."

"I thought you'd appreciate it."

"I do. But do you think I could use it for its original purpose? I mean, I might have to close my eyes. It's a little distracting." I waited for him to leave. "So, uh..."

"Oh, right. Sorry." He backed away, but he didn't seem particularly embarrassed.

"Thanks for the tour," I said, shutting the door.

AFTER DINNER, Peter showed us the topographic map on the wall. The map gave us the basic information about Organ Pipe Cactus National Monument. "The Organ Pipe cactus can only be found in Mexico and in this part of Arizona. Protecting this huge cactus, whose bunched columns can reach twenty-five feet into the air, was the reason for creating the national monument in the 1930s," I read aloud from the legend.

"Do you want to know the real reason?" Peter asked.

"Of course," Art said. "Don't reporters always want to know things like that?" He looked over at me. I shook my head and laughed.

"The bootleggers wanted a faster road up from Rocky Point," said Peter. "So they called their friends in the federal government."

"Cool," said Art.

"Is it true?" I asked.

"Who knows?" Peter said. He walked over to a battered desk. "Maps are very valuable, you know. They're like icons. Religious objects. Especially in Mexico, it's hard to find accurate ones." He plucked out what looked like an ordinary piece of eight-by-eleven paper.

He sat on the ugly old plaid couch. Art and I huddled on either side of him like children so we could see the hand-drawn map he was holding. *The Pinacate Desert*, read the curlicued lettering. The style was that of a pirate's map torn from an old edition of *Treasure Island*. "A friend of mine who works here did this. She got all the people who knew the place to work on it," Peter said.

"Who are they?" I asked.

"Oh, geologists, botanists. Various weirdoes of the right sort."

"As opposed to the wrong sort," I said.

"Exactly," Peter said, smiling. His teeth looked very white against his tan, which seemed baked in, not the intentional kind people get on vacation.

"So we drive in here?" Art said. He spoke in a very male-bonding, 1950s sort of way, a tone of voice he never used with me.

Peter nodded. He pointed to a spot on the map. "I thought we'd camp here," he said. "It's like a beach, but the sand is black. It's very soft, so it's comfortable to sleep on. They call it Paradise. Or maybe I made up that name. I can't remember anymore." He laughed, that short, coughing sound again. Then he looked over at me, a bit too meaningfully. "How does that sound?"

"What do you think?" I asked Art. I felt responsible for him. And slightly guilty.

"I'm just along for the ride," Art said.

I looked at Peter. "Who could turn down Paradise?" I said.

ART AND I HAD ARRIVED TOO LATE that day to get into the primitive campground, so we were stuck with the RVers in the "developed" campground with its picnic tables and bathrooms. We both were drunk enough for the task of pitching a tent to seem dauntingly complex so we threw our sleeping bags on two of the picnic tables. The hard redwood slats made me think of a John O'Hara story I had read as a teenager. A couple making love on top of a picnic table. Or were they leaning against it? I tried to think about something else.

"What's your take on Peter?" I asked from inside my sleeping bag.

"He's great," Art said. "Maybe a little Peter Pan. I mean, the guy's a park ranger, for Chrissake." He paused. "He's got a wife stashed somewhere in town."

"He does?"

"Yeah, he told me." Another pause. "You're not interested in him, are you?"

"Nah," I said. "I just figure we're trusting our lives to the guy."

I don't remember what we talked about after that, only that we chatted companionably under the dense scatter of stars. I tried to remember the last time I had slept next to a man who was not my lover; simply shared a room without touching. The only time I could remember was twenty years before. It was the year after my parents' divorce. Money was tight. My brother and I shared a room in the small apartment my mother had rented. This was fine with me. In our previous home, when nightmares woke me in the middle of the night, I had generally opted to sleep with my brother instead of going to my parents' room. Our new arrangement eliminated the archetypal childhood terror of walking down the dark hallway.

Each night, my brother and I talked for hours. We could not see each other; a bookshelf separated our beds in deference to our genders. This freed us. We made up characters: a brother and sister who lived on a farm. I can't remember their names, but I know they had red hair and freckles, a bit like Howdy Doody. We seemed to have an uncanny ability to imitate hayseed accents. We acted out these stories in character. We had just moved to Manhattan. Perhaps a rural life seemed simpler than our new sophisticated existence. For whatever reason, these stories fascinated us, then lulled us to sleep.

I don't remember what Art and I talked about that night. But I can still feel the aimless pleasure of the conversation. Before dropping off, I gathered the last of my wakefulness to take in the sight of cactus and mountains cast blue-grey by the underlight of the night sky. I reminded myself, not for the first time, that I had never intended to settle in San Francisco. Six months. That was the original plan. Somehow I had gotten stuck, along with all the other pathetic pilgrims.

WE MET AT PETER'S HOUSE the next morning. Art had invited a dark-haired woman we had met in the campground. ("You have Peter," he had said. "What am I supposed to do? Talk to myself?") This woman struck me as an enigma. I don't think she said more than a few sentences during the entire trip. I wonder now if she was in mourning for someone, too. A dead child, a lost father. Perhaps, less melodramatically, a lost lover. Maybe she was on the wrong medication. We never get to know her well enough to find out, at least I didn't.

Art and the woman drove in my old Honda Civic while I rode with Peter in the highly touted Baja Bug. The VW was a retrofitted sixties model with too many original parts. Mexican blankets covered the torn upholstery, but stalks of stuffing escaped through the loose weave and poked into my legs. The Bug was just like a car in Africa or Mexico. I recognize this now, but back then I had never been in a car with holes in the floor. It felt jaunty and fun.

We stopped at a town just over the border to buy tortillas, avocados, and cheese. In a dusty little plaza we perched on the edge of a concrete fountain that hadn't seen water in a long time. Peter leafed through his mail. "Looks like I'm divorced," he said, holding up an official-looking envelope bled by the glare.

"What do you mean?" I asked. He handed the letter to me. A judge informed Peter that his wife's motion to divorce had been granted.

"I'm sorry," I said, somewhat disingenuously.

"Oh, it's not a surprise," he said. For the first time, I saw lines in his face. They weren't deep; more like creases in a shirt worn by someone traveling too long. "Ready to go?" he asked rhetorically, getting to his feet. I stood up. Art was paralyzed, no doubt aghast at Peter's disclosure of personal information to relative strangers. "Come on, Art, let's go," I said, tugging his arm. The dark-haired woman was already halfway to the car.

Despite my bravado, I too must have been a bit uncomfortable. I remember launching into a set piece about the first time I had heard of the Sonoran Desert. A few months after Rupert Murdoch bought *The New York Post*, I landed a college kid's summer job on a magazine in New York. Journalism seemed exciting then; central to our lives. The sixties were over, of course. But the engaging if hubristic idea that art or passion or even a single individual could change the world was lingering like the haze from the pot we all grew up smoking. It was not unusual for someone to read two or three newspapers a day. *The Post* came out in the afternoon and people even read that. "There was a newsstand downstairs in the office building where I worked," I told Peter. "When I got out of work that day, the paper had a huge headline. I mean *huge*. ALIENS FOUND IN DESERT! I thought, 'Finally, they're here!'"

Peter laughed. "You must have seen *E.T.*"

"It was *Rupert Murdoch*," I said frostily.

The aliens from outer space were Mexicans, of course. Nine migrants had roasted to death in a van when their *coyote*, their smuggler, abandoned them at Organ Pipe Cactus National Monument. The real news was that while I was innocently away at college studying Oscar Wilde and J. K. Huysmans, our good gray liberal afternoon paper had turned into *The Weekly World News*.

Now I find tabloid journalism amusingly innocent compared to the subtler, stage-managed marketing copy that masquerades as journalism in more respectable places. But, for me, at least, the transformation of *The New York Post* went beyond the bare-knuckled tradition of the Yellow Kid, beyond even the onerous but impressive feat of William Randolph Hearst starting the Spanish-American War. I don't know why the loss of this particular newspaper meant so much. Perhaps I instinctively understood that an epoch was over. When words become a commodity, truth turns into a substance that is not exactly a lie, but something far worse: an ersatz truth. Even then, we were barely hanging on to the old values: truth, ethics, the social compact, art for its own sake, catchphrases that sound so implausible now. I didn't know yet how difficult it is, even for well-intentioned people, to tell the truth. All I knew was that the religion of art, even art supposedly based on truth itself, was turning out to be as fragile as any other faith.

Peter patted my leg, chuckling at my indignation. I laughed, too, mostly at my own credulousness. But I was still angry. "I swore I'd never buy that goddamn paper again," I said.

"I read that, too. I was in California then," Peter said.

"You did?"

He looked at me. "You're not the only naïve schmuck around," he said. "Did I say that right?"

"Not bad," I said. "Incredibly well for a person who pronounces the *h* in *where*." I imitated him, blowing out the *h,* and he laughed. I was only pretending to give him a hard time and we both knew it. We lapsed into silence; this time a comfortable one.

Peter was still new to the Park Service then. He carried extra bottles of water to give to Mexicans crossing the border illegally. He stored dead rattlesnakes in his freezer. He wrapped the dead snakes in plastic bags, saving them for the herpetologist he assisted in the field. Their corpses were thick and coiled, like sausages. Peter was only a year older than me. We had grown up with the same ridiculously unhealthy cultural influences. At thirty-seven, he still had the loose-limbed awkwardness of a teenager. I'm reluctant to say it. I must have felt that we were almost like brother and sister.

In the car that day, though, I wasn't thinking very much, just having an incredibly good time. This surprised me: it felt like cheating. I wasn't just excited about Peter. It was the whole exotic setting. The atmosphere of Peter's beige Australian outback ranger house felt heightened in a sensory way. Even the ruffled bathroom, with its creepy density of captive light, seemed like another world. Yet Peter felt so familiar. Perhaps, I thought, he was more like a high school sweetheart than a brother.

Peter must have arrived at a similar conclusion because his hand migrated back to my thigh, like the boy who pretends to yawn and then puts his arm around you, but in a more definite and adult way. I took if off, giving him a *pro forma* explanation of journalistic ethics. Sleeping with sources is not such a good idea, I explained. Conflict of interest, that sort of thing.

"I'm not a source," he told me. "I'm a person."

There wasn't much I could say because I thought he was right. I stared out the window, as silent as the woman in the other car.

Look at the side of the road, Peter had instructed earlier. *See how many flowers grow there? It's because of the runoff, it shears off from the tarmac.*

AS YOU LEARN ABOUT LANDSCAPE, the information seems so obvious, so *familiar*, you almost feel as if you had known it forever. Thick rows of vegetation divide on either side of the road, bright white, bright yellow, like the boys' line and the girls' line in grammar school. That day I remember thinking the flowers were pretty but not quite right. I preferred the hypnotic grace of the loping bajada, where plants grow at the proper distance from one another, not demanding extra water or nutrients from the soil. Without having experienced it yet, I wanted the clean, alive feeling after a rain, when the scent of creosote bathes the air.

Go back. Start over. "Do you want to stop somewhere, Peter? Call your wife?" I asked. We had crossed the border. Escape routes were disappearing. "Oh, no," he said quickly. "We've been all through that ."

So we reached the subject of D-I-V-O-R-C-E. Peter and his wife had been married for ten years when they came to Tucson from California. Peter's wife wanted to live in town. She was starting a new career as an urban planner. He was ecstatic at the idea of working for practically nothing in the park. They tried to stay married but lived separately.

For the past year Peter had inhabited a world contained by two mountain ranges. Sunsets opened out the edges of this world like a box unfolding. In my ignorance, I imagined that he missed nothing from his former life. This is what I thought: There is one road and it has very few pullouts. He must believe it is better not to stop. Foolishly, I admired him for this.

The silence that followed us then was as concrete as the cattle tanks we passed in the desert. Eventually Peter shifted back into evangelical mode. The line we had just crossed, he told me, shows up on satellite photos. Not because there is a fence on the border between the US and Mexico—although six years later the US government would erect one amid much controversy in the town of Douglas, Arizona—but because cattle on the Mexican side have denuded the vegetation. The landscape shows up as a different color under the satellite's electric eye. Cattle grazing has even changed the weather.

Changes both dramatic and subtle tell us when we cross a border: men with guns at a checkpoint, fewer trees, a bumpier road. Sometimes we don't realize how drastic a change we've made. We cross these borders on a postcollege adventure or perhaps an exotic vacation. Often we find another life entirely, one we could never have foreseen. Sometimes we find no life at all.

All of us: me, Peter, Art, even, I suspect, the silent mourning woman, crossed more than one border that day; lines drawn by our imagination as much as anything else. Ten years ago, no fence marked the Pinacate Desert. The Pinacate was a Mexican national park but there was no money to pay a park ranger or to do much of anything else. Mexico's problems could hardly be stayed by a rusted, barbed wire fence. After the revolution of 1919, the government parceled out the land of the old haciendas to peasants. The least arable land was the last to be distributed. It was not until the 1970s that the government established communal farms, called *ejidos*, near the Pinacates. The farms failed for the obvious reasons of aridity and isolation. *Ejido* members turned to the region's traditional sources of income: smuggling and poaching.

Small airplanes full of drugs landed on the playa at night. Men cut down ironwood and mesquite trees to fill bags of charcoal "briquets" for the US market. Trespass cattle ate the tentative green plants that appeared each spring on sand whipped up from the Colorado River. Miners scooped hollows out of monumental black cinder cones to make blocks for houses.

Pyramids got torn down to make shacks.

Peter touched my shoulder. A sandy road led off the rutted two-lane highway across the playa. We turned and the Baja Bug, despite its fancy suspension, rumbled painfully. "Do you know the two ways to drive on washboard?" Peter asked. I looked at him noncommittally, unwilling to admit my ignorance. He laughed. Then he explained that tire vibrations created a rippled surface on dirt roads. "So there are two ways to drive it. Really slow or..." he smiled and gunned it—if you can truly be said to gun a 1965 VW Bug. "Really fast."

The next time I looked back, my small white car had disappeared.

THAT NIGHT WE FOUND PARADISE. As Peter had promised, the black sand playa was a felicitous location. There are places in the world where angles of hills and gradations of color conspire to create beauty. For a brief time, one desires neither the future nor the past.

Just before dark we climbed one of the smaller cinder cones. The silent woman stayed at camp. I walked with the others but I found myself wanting to be alone. Art tried to keep up with me. I saw Peter bend his head close to Art's. Unless Art had revealed my secret, Peter didn't know what had happened to me. But I suppose he knew enough. He may simply have understood the decorum of such a place.

The fever of walking was upon me. Effortlessly I found my footing on broken pieces of lava. There are times when motion has a life of its own. If you trust it, you are safe. But you must stop caring about safety.

Evan that safety is an illusion.

I reached the top of the cone. Everything around me was a darkening blue. The sky and the desert were the colors of the ocean. The color was not quite like the sea itself, but like an exhalation from the deepest part of the sea, where volcanoes lie in wait.

I thought of the person I had just lost. I warned myself not to confuse him with Peter, who reminded me so powerfully of my past. I did not trust Peter's sudden intimacies.

Peter and Art rose up the hill, soldiers storming a beach. "Hey, how 'ya doin'?" Art asked me. "Okay?"

Peter touched my arm. "You have to see this," he told me softly. A fine-edged cinder cone descended from turquoise to scarlet like the sun falling into water. "That's Cerro Colorado," Peter said. "The colors change all the time. Every night. "

The light clicked down with the inexorability of a stopwatch. I could not keep up with it. The lava, the volcanoes, the lowering sky; everything changed too quickly.

Now I understand more. I believe the Pinacate Desert is a dark piece of the larger landscape surrounding it. Yet it is as discontinuous as the volcanoes that rupture the earth. More than a decade later I can make out the deviation. The Pinacates, in their stillness, paused between breaths, tell a highly colored version of an often forgotten truth. The colors: night blue of mountains, lavender sand verbena, waxy white of Ajo lily. The air has an altered quality; the light, the smell. The cinder cone Cerro Colorado moves by degrees into dusk, never the same shade twice. I grew addicted to this kind of truth.

I knew so little about the desert then, and even less about myself. On that first trip to the Pinacates, though, I did see something. A shadow perhaps. I didn't identify it then; I struggle to do so now. But the feeling of differentness refused to leave me. I had reached what is hidden around the bend in the canyon.

From *Kinski Uncut*

KLAUS KINSKI

H ERZOG, WHO'S PRODUCING THE FILM, also wrote the script—and he wants to direct it, too. I promptly ask him how much money he's got.

When he visits me in my pad, he's so shy that he barely has the nerve to come in. Maybe it's just a ploy. In any case, he lingers at the threshold for such an idiotically long time that I practically have to drag him inside. Once he's here, he starts explaining the movie without even being asked. I tell him that I've read the script and I know the story. But he turns a deaf ear and just keeps talking and talking and talking. I start thinking that he'll never be able to stop talking even if he tries. Not that he talks quickly, "like a waterfall," as people say when someone talks fast and furious, pouring out the words. Quite the contrary: His speech is clumsy, with a toadlike indolence, longwinded, pedantic, choppy. The words tumble from his mouth in sentence fragments, which he holds back as much as possible, as if they were earning interest. It takes forever and a day for him to push out a clump of hardened brain snot. Then he writhes in painful ecstasy, as if he had sugar on his rotten teeth. A very slow blab machine. An obsolete model with a nonworking switch—it can't be turned off unless you cut off the electric power altogether. So I'd have to smash him in the kisser. No, I'd have to knock him unconscious. But even if he were unconscious, he'd keep talking. Even if his vocal cords were sliced through, he'd keep talking like a ventriloquist. Even if his throat were cut and his head were chopped off, speech balloons would still dangle from his mouth like gases emitted by internal decay.

I haven't the foggiest idea what he's talking about, except that he's high as a kite on himself for no visible reason, and he's enthralled by his own daring, which is nothing but dilettantish innocence. When he thinks I finally see what a great guy he is, he blurts out the bad news, explaining in a hardboiled tone about the shitty living and working conditions that lie ahead. He sounds like a judge handing down a well-deserved sentence. And, licking his lips as if he were talking about some culinary delicacy, he crudely and brazenly claims that all the participants are delighted to endure the unimaginable stress and deprivation in order to follow him, Herzog. Why, they would all risk their lives for him without batting an eyelash. He, in any case, will put all his eggs in one basket in order to attain his goal, no matter what it may cost, "do or die," as he puts it in his foolhardy way. And he tolerantly closes his eyes to the spawn of his megalomania, which he mistakes for genius. Granted, he sincerely confesses, he sometimes gets dizzy thinking about his own insane ideas—by which, however, he is simply carried away.

Then suddenly, out of a clear blue sky, he knocks me for a loop: He tries to make me believe that he's got a sense of humor. That is, he almost unintentionally, sort of carelessly hints at it—and, half in jest, he's embarrassed, as if caught with his pants down.

If he initially applied some cheap tricks to get me drunk, he now throws caution to the winds and starts lying through his teeth. He says he enjoys playing pranks; you can go and steal horses with him, and so forth. And since he's already confessed all that, he doesn't want to hide the fact that he can now laugh his head off at his own roguishness. While it's quite obvious that I've never in my life met anybody so dull, humorless, uptight, inhibited, mindless, depressing, boring, and swaggering, he blithely basks in the glory of the most pointless and most uninteresting punch lines of his braggadocio. Eventually he kneels before himself like a worshipper in front of his idol, and he remains in that position until somebody bends down and raises him from his humble self-worship. After dumping these tons of garbage (which stinks so horribly that I felt like puking), he actually pretends to be a naive, innocent, almost rustic hick—a poetic dreamer, or so he emphasizes, as if he were living in his own little world and didn't have the slightest notion of the brutal material side of things. But I can very easily tell that he considers himself ever so cunning, that he's waiting in ambush, dogging my every step and desperately trying to read my mind. He's racking his brain, trying to determine how he can outfox me in every clause of the contract. In short, he has every intention of outwitting me.

Still and all, I agree to do the movie—but only because of Peru. I don't even know where it is. Somewhere in South America, between the Pacific, the desert, and the glaciers, and in the most gigantic jungle on earth.

The script is illiterate and primitive. That's my big chance. The jungle smolders in it like something that infects you when you see it, a virus that invades you through your eyes and enters your bloodstream. I feel as if I knew this land with the magical name in some other lifetime. An imprisoned beast can never forget the reality of freedom. The caged bird cranes its neck through the bars to peer at the clouds racing by.

I tell Herzog that Aguirre has to be crippled because his power must not be contingent on his appearance. I'll havé a hump. My right arm will be longer than my left, as long as an ape's. My left arm will be shortened so that since I'm a southpaw I have to carry my sword on the right side of my chest, and not in the normal way, on my hip. My left leg will be longer than my right, so that I have to drag it along. I'll advance sideways, like a crab. I'll have long hair—down to my shoulders by the time we start shooting. I won't need a phony hump, or a costumer or a makeup man smearing me up. I will *be* crippled because I *want* to be. I'll get my spine used to my crippling. Just as I'm beautiful when I want to be. Ugly. Strong. Feeble. Short or tall. Old or young. When I want to be. The way I hold myself will lift the cartilage from my joints and use up their gelatin. I will be crippled—today, now, on the spot, this very instant. Henceforth everything will be geared to my condition: costumes, cuirasses, scabbards, weapons, helmets, boots, and so on.

I determine the costume: I tear a couple of pages out of books showing Old Master paintings. I explain the changes I want, and I fly to Madrid with Herzog to find armor and weapons. After days of rummaging through mountains of rusty scrap metal, I fish out a sword, a dagger, a helmet, and a cuirass, which has to be trimmed because I'm a cripple.

Traveling all the way to the jungle is the worst kind of agony. Penned up in old-fashioned trains, wrecks of trucks, and cagelike buses, we eat and camp out like pigs. Sometimes in Quonset huts or other torture chambers. We can't even think about getting any sleep. We can barely breathe. No toilets, no way to wash. Many days and nights. I stay dressed day and night; otherwise the mosquitoes would eat me alive. I feel as if I'm standing under a nonstop jet of boiling water. Indoors the heat is lethal. But outdoors it's just as venomously hot. Whole mountains of garbage, inundated by a cesspool of human piss and shit. The populace tosses the ripped-out eyes and innards of slaughtered animals into this sewage from hell. Huge carrion birds the size of great Danes strut and squat on this horror as if it were their private playground.

Wherever I go I see these disgusting Quonset huts. If only I didn't have to lay eyes on these half-finished cement barracks with corrugated-iron roofs. Nothing is completed. Everything is abandoned halfway through, as if it had been surprised by the decay. Iron window shades and fences jeer at you. Why?

Garbage heaps, sewage, eyes, innards, breeding grounds, carrion birds and—TV antennas. Just like in New York, Paris, London, Tokyo, or Hong Kong, but more loathsome.

The road into the wilderness is long and tortuous—but no abomination is too unbearable to escape this hell on earth

And as if Minhoï and I were to be rewarded for our getaway, we feel that our hair is becoming silkier, our skin softer, like the fur of wild beasts that have been set free; our bodies are lither and suppler, our muscles are tensing for a leap, our senses are more alert and receptive. Minhoï has never been more beautiful since the tiger trap in Vietnam.

Swelling up from mosquito bites without having eaten or drunk anything, we reel toward the next leg of our journey.

A little Inca girl stands on the runway for military aircraft. She's got a small monkey on her arm and she wants to sell it. But the terrified monkey clings to the girl, afraid that the buyer might take it away.

Here we clamber into ancient, battered transport planes for paratroopers, and the propellers rage in my temples like pneumatic hammers. A pungent stench, the odor of gasoline, hunger, thirst, headaches, and stomach cramps, and no toilet here either. Pent up and huddling together on the hot steel floor of the windowless plane. Hour after hour. During the flight each passenger in turn can spend one moment climbing from the plane's tomblike rear into the cockpit and peering out through a tiny window. Far below, the green ocean, thousands of miles of jungle, with a yellow tangle of vipers winding through it—the biggest river network in the world.

Next, single-engine amphibians that have to nose-dive to avoid missing that slim chance when the jungle opens—and promptly closes again.

Then more trucks and bus cages. Indian canoes. And finally the rafts, on which we stand, chained to one another, to the cargo, and to the raft, as we shoot over raging rapids. Our fists clutching ropes, as if we were making a laughable effort to halt runaway horses by clasping their reins even though the horses have already plunged off a cliff. The raft is too heavily loaded; the Indians warned us. But blowhard Herzog, arrogant and ignorant as he is, mocked their warnings and called them ridiculous. We're all in costume and fully equipped, because we wanted to shoot while riding the rapids. Herzog misses out on the grandest and most incomprehensible things because he doesn't even notice them. I keep yelling at the stupid cameraman through the thunder of our nose-dive, telling him to at least roll the camera because we're risking our lives. But all he says is that Herzog ordered him not to press the button without his, Herzog's, say-so.

I'm disgusted by this whole movie mob—they act as if you're supposed to shoot a flick in a pigpen.

My heavy leather costume, my long boots, helmet, cuirass, sword, and dagger weigh over thirty pounds. If the raft were to capsize because of Herzog's delusions of grandeur, I'd be doomed. I'd be unable to get out of my cuirass and leather doublet, which are buckled in back. Besides, the rapids are cut through with a chain of jagged reefs, and their razorlike tips lurk under the spume like piranhas, sometimes even looming out of the lashed waters.

And so, like a fired missile, we hurtle downstream while the steep waves attack our raft like hysterical bulls and clap together way over our heads. The air is filled with foam like white drool.

Suddenly, as if the plunging water had furiously spat us out, we glide almost soundlessly along a calm and powerful branch of the river in the middle of the jungle and deeper and deeper into its interior. There it lies: the wilderness. It seizes me. Sucks me in—hot and naked like the sweaty, sticky, naked body of a lovesick woman with all her mysteries and wonders. I gape at the jungle and can't stop marveling and worshipping....

Animals as graceful as in fairy tales... Plants strangling one another in their embraces... Orchids stretched on stumps of rotten trees like young girls on the laps of dirty old men... Radiant metallic-blue butterflies as big as my head... Pearly floods of butterflies alighting on my mouth and my hands—the panther's eye blending into the flowers... Frothy streams of flowers; green, red, and yellow clouds of birds... Silver suns... Violet fogs... The kissing lips of the fish... The golden song of the fish...

We're going to be living exclusively on rafts for the next two months. Drifting downstream toward the Amazon. Minhoï and I have a raft to ourselves. We either float way ahead of the other rafts or lag behind as far as possible. When night falls, we moor our raft to lianas. Then I lie awake, diving into the galaxies and starry archipelagoes, which hang down so low that I can reach out and feel them.

We have a small Indian canoe that we tie to the raft, towing it along. If I don't have to shoot, we sneak away in the canoe, searching for cracks in the jungle wall. Sometimes we penetrate a tight slit that may have never existed before and that will instantly close up again. The water inside the flooded forest is so still that it barely seems affected by our paddles, which we dip cautiously to avoid making any noise.

Perhaps no boat has ever glided across these waters, perhaps no man has set foot here in millions of years. Not even a native. We wait without speaking. For hours on end. I feel the jungle coming nearer, the animals, the plants, which have been watching us for a long while without showing themselves. For the first time in my life I have no past. The present is so powerful that it snuffs out all bygones. I know that I'm free, truly free. I am the bird that has managed to break out of its cage—that spreads its wings and soars into the sky. I take part in the universe.

Although I constantly try to keep out of his way, Herzog sticks to me like a shithouse fly. The mere thought of his existence here in the wilderness turns my stomach. When I see him approaching in the distance, I yell at him to halt. I shout that he stinks. That he disgusts me. That I don't want to listen to his bullshit. That I can't stand him!

I keep hoping he'll attack me. Then I'll shove him into a side branch of the river, where the still waters teem with murderous piranhas, and I'll watch them shred him to bits. But he doesn't do it; he doesn't attack me. He seems unfazed when I treat him like a piece of shit. Besides, he's too chicken. He attacks only when he thinks he'll keep the upper hand. Herzog pounces on a native, an Indian who's taken the job to keep his family from starving and puts up with anything for fear of being kicked out. Or else he assails a stupid, untalented actor or a helpless animal. Today he ties up a llama in a canoe and sends it tearing down the rapids—supposedly because this is required by the plot of the movie, which he wrote himself! I find out about the llama only when it's too late. The animal is already drifting toward the whirlpool, and no one can save it. I spot it rearing in its mortal fear and yanking at its fetters, struggling to escape its gruesome execution. Then it vanishes behind a bend of the river, shattering against the jagged reefs and dying a torturous death by drowning.

Now I hate that killer's guts. I shriek into his face that I want to see him croak like the llama that he executed. He should be thrown alive to the crocodiles! An anaconda should strangle him slowly! A poisonous spider should sting him and paralyze his lungs! The most venomous serpent should bite him and make his brain explode! No panther claws should rip open his throat—that would be much too good for him! No! The huge red ants should piss into his lying eyes and gobble up his balls and his guts! He should catch the plague! Syphilis! Malaria! Yellow fever! Leprosy! It's no use; the more I wish him the most gruesome deaths, the more he haunts me.

We drift down the river all day long, shooting endlessly. Night falls. Nevertheless we all gather ashore, where a night scene is to be filmed. Herzog and his production morons haven't even supplied illumination—no flashlight, nothing. The night is pitch-black and we keep falling on our faces, one after another. We tumble into swampy holes, stumble over roots and tree trunks, run into the knives of thorny palms, get our feet caught in lianas, and almost drown. The area is teeming with snakes, which kill at night after storing up their reserves of poison throughout the day. We're completely exhausted, and once again it's been an eternity since we ate or drank anything, including water. No one has a clue as to what, where, and why we're supposed to shoot in this garbage dump, which stinks to high heaven.

Suddenly, in full armor, I plunge into a swarm hole. The harder I try to get my body out of the mud, the deeper I sink. Finally, in a blind fury, I yell, "I'm splitting! Even if I have to paddle all the way to the Atlantic!"

"If you split, I'll ruin you!" says that wimp Herzog, looking scared of the chance he's taking.

"Ruin me how, you bigmouth?" I ask him, hoping he'll attack me so I can kill him in self-defense.

"I'll shoot you," he babbles, like a paralytic whose brain has softened. "Eight bullets are for you, and the ninth is for me!"

Whoever heard of a pistol or a rifle with nine bullets? There's no such thing! Besides, he has no firearm; I know it for a fact. He's got no rifle or pistol, not even a machete. Not even a penknife. Not even a bottle opener. I'm the only one with a rifle: a Winchester. I have a special permit from the Peruvian government. To buy bullets I had to spend days on end running my legs off from one police station to the next for signatures, stamps, all that shit.

"I'm waiting, you vermin," I say, truly glad that things have reached this pass. "I'm going back to my raft now and I'll be waiting for you. If you come, I'll shoot you down."

Then I stride back to our raft, where Minhoï has fallen asleep in her hammock; I load my Winchester and I wait.

At around four A.M. Herzog comes paddling up to our raft and apologizes.

Herzog is a miserable, hateful, malevolent, avaricious, money hungry, nasty, sadistic, treacherous, cowardly creep. His so-called "talent" consists of nothing but tormenting helpless creatures and, if necessary, torturing them to death or simply murdering them. He doesn't care about anyone or anything except his wretched career as a so-called filmmaker. Driven by a pathological addiction to sensationalism, he creates the most senseless difficulties and dangers, risking other people's safety and even their lives—just so he can eventually say that he, Herzog, has beaten seemingly unbeatable odds. For his movies he hires retards and amateurs whom he can push around (and allegedly hypnotize!), and he pays them starvation wages or zilch. He also uses freaks and cripples of every conceivable size and shape, merely to look interesting. He doesn't have the foggiest inkling of how to make movies. He doesn't even try to direct the actors anymore. Long ago, when I ordered him to keep his trap shut, he gave up asking me whether I'm willing to carry out his stupid and boring ideas.

If he wants to shoot another take because he, like most directors, is insecure, I tell him to go fuck himself. Usually the first take is okay, and I won't repeat anything—certainly not on his say-so. Every scene, every angle, every shot is determined by me, and I refuse to do anything unless I consider it right. So I can at least partly save the movie from being wrecked by Herzog's lack of talent.

After eight weeks most of the crew are still living like pigs. Penned together on rafts like cattle going to slaughter, they eat garbage fried in lard, and, most dangerous of all, they guzzle the river water, which can give them all kinds of diseases, even leprosy. None of them is vaccinated against any of these deadly scourges.

Minhoï and I cook alone on our raft. We dump soil on the wooden floor and start a fire. If either of us dives into the river to swim or wash, the other watches out for piranhas. Normally we have nothing to cook, and we feed on fantastic jungle fruits, which contain enough liquid. But these heavenly fruits are hard to get since we float downstream almost nonstop, and often there are long stretches when we can't go ashore to look for produce.

Eventually we start feeling our malnutrition. We grow weaker; my belly swells up, and I'm all skin and bones. The others are even worse off.

The wilderness isn't interested in arrogant bigmouth movie makers. It has no pity for those who flout its laws.

At three in the morning we're violently awakened on our rafts. We're told there's no time for breakfast, even coffee. We'll only be traveling for twenty minutes, up to the next Indian village on the river. There we'll get everything. The alleged twenty minutes turn into eighteen hours. Herzog has exaggerated again.

With our heads in heavy steel helmets that get so hot from the pounding sun that they burn us, we're exposed to the ruthless heat for days on end, without shelter, without the slightest shade, without food or drink. People drop like flies. First the girls, then the men, one after another. Almost everyone's legs are festering from mosquito bites and distorted by swelling.

Toward evening, we finally reach an Indian village, but it's blazing away. Herzog set it on fire, and even though we're starving and dying of thirst, reeling, exhausted after eighteen hours of infernal heat, we have to attack the village—just as it says in the mindless script.

We spend the night in the village, camping in the miserable barracks that haven't burned down. Giant rats insolently frolic about, circling closer and closer, drawing nearer and nearer to our bodies. They probably sense how feeble we are, and they're waiting for the right time to pounce on us. More and more of them appear.

Someone tells Herzog that his people can't continue if we don't get better food and especially water. Herzog answers that they can drink from the river. Besides, he goes on, they ought to collapse from exhaustion and starvation: That's what's called for in the script. Herzog and his head producer have their own secret cache of fresh vegetables, fruit, French camembert, olive oil, and beverages.

As we drift along, one of the Americans falls dangerously ill; he's got yellow fever and a high temperature, and he's writhing on the raft. Herzog claims that the American is malingering; he refuses to let him be brought ashore at Iquitos, which is getting closer and closer.

When we're near Iquitos and our rafts drift into the Amazon, we ignore Herzog and carry our patient ashore, to a hospital. We take the day off in order to buy the most necessary food, mineral water, bandages, medicines, and salves for mosquito bites.

Ten weeks later the final scene of the movie is shot: Aguirre, the sole survivor, his mind gone, is on his raft with several hundred monkeys, floating downstream toward the Atlantic. Most of the monkeys on the raft jump into the water and swim back to the jungle. A gang of trappers plans to sell them to American laboratories for experiments. Herzog has borrowed them. When only some hundred monkeys are left, waiting to dive into the waves and regain their freedom, I order Herzog to film right away. I know that this opportunity won't knock twice. When the take is done, the last monkeys spring into the river and swim toward the jungle, which receives them.

Minhoï and I have to spend three days in the Iquitos hospital getting vitamin transfusions.

When the jet plane, amid the murderous booming of its turbines, rises steeply, leaving the green sea of the jungle far below me, I launch into a crying jag. My soul is so deeply shaken and my body so violently convulsed that I think my heart is about to rip open. I hide my face from the other passengers, pressing it against the window and trying to stifle my sobs. Imagine someone weeping because he has to leave the wilderness, and because he's not happy and grateful to be back in the civilization ghettos, which are haunted by madness! If it's a human being, he'll be locked up in a nuthouse, and if it's an animal, it'll be put to sleep.

On the way back. Minhoï and I fly around the globe again. When we finally reach Vietnam, Minhoï is happy. In Saigon a Vietnamese teenager spits at me in the ricksha because he thinks I'm an American.

Once again, someone spitting at me! First it was the Belgians because I wasn't American. Then American strafers shoot my mother down. And now here in Vietnam, where Minhoï was orphaned by the dirtiest of all wars, someone spits at me because he thinks I'm American! Maybe the boy thinks that I'm one of those men who at Christmas sent home color Polaroids showing the corpses of massacred women and children. Minhoï, next to me, cries. I jump out of the ricksha to chase after the teenager, who scurries away—but then a Vietnamese soldier sticks a pistol into my chest, releasing the safety catch. I have to pull myself together, choke back tears of rage, at this glaring injustice. Nevertheless I love this nation more than any other in the world.

The streets are filled with barricades of sandbags. A little boy, at most seven or eight years old, stands there with gaping mouth and eyes, performing a pantomime. I don't understand what he means! Minhoï's caught on. His body language says that he's seen me in a movie in which I play an American soldier who, with gaping mouth and eyes, croaks in the hatch of a tank.

So we're back in the human hell, the hell of adults.

From *Blue Desert*

CHARLES BOWDEN

Blue

THEY PLAY A GAME HERE but nobody watches from a box seat. The players are called wets by those who hunt them. They cross a hot desert, a dry desert, one of North America's benchmarks for thirst and they cross with one or two gallons of water. They walk thirty, forty, fifty, sixty miles in order to score. The goal line here means not six points but a job.

Here are the rules. Get caught and you go back to Mexico. Make it across and you get a job in the fields or backrooms. Don't make it and you die.

Each month during the summer about two hundred and fifty people try the game in this particular section of western Arizona, a 3,600-square-mile stretch that runs from Yuma on the Colorado about a hundred miles eastward. Many get caught, mainly because the heat and thirst and miles grind them down. A bunch go down and wait to die.

Some die.

Nobody pays much attention to this summer sport. The players are nameless and constantly changing and so there is little identification with them or with their skills and their defeats. And the players are brown and this earns them a certain contempt and makes the attraction difficult to sell to spectators. The arena, a section of desert 100 miles long and 30 to 60 miles wide, is too unwieldy for easy viewing—no zoom shots here, no instant replay—and very uncomfortable with its heat, dryness, serpents, and thorns. A massive folk movement is pounding its way out of Mexico and Central America and this sector of the line and these deaths are but a small noise amid the clamor of the American border.

Those who play this desert game do pay attention. And they learn many things.

My education in these matters began months before. I was sitting at my desk in September when a news story caught my eye: seven Mexicans had died of thirst east of Yuma and several more had been snake bitten. It seemed like a high price for a job I would not take if offered. I began to train, walking around the city with my backpack stuffed with five or six gallons of water. The weight and feel of the load seemed impossible and then, before I fully appreciated this fact, my knee went out. A month later I was in the hospital looking up at two eyes staring over a surgical mask. The operation kept me a bit gimpy for two months and then it was too late to pursue my idea.

By then the desert had gone cold and there was little to learn in walking forty or fifty miles on the winter ground. I waited until June, until the solstice of June, thinking the longest day of the year surely would provide the heat and thirst required. The whole notion captivated me. I had separated from my wife and taken a studio apartment in a huge complex full of others in temporary flight from maimed marriages. On the wall I taped large topographic maps of the area where I would cross the line and march north. I sat there for hours sipping a drink and studying the vast expanses of sand and mountain, the delicate lines tracing the Cabeza Prieta National Wildlife Refuge, the warning announcements for the huge Air Force Gunnery range. I would move slowly northward, leave the truckstop in Sonora where wets gather, slip through the legendary fence between the two nations, slide across the burning ground until finally, finally, I would come out at Interstate 8, the big road linking Phoenix and Tucson with San Diego, come out and be safe on this artery of commerce that followed the Gila River westward.

In the evenings I ran. In the mornings, I lifted weights. Always, I thought about the crossing and made the journey day after day in my mind. I told people I was angered by the news coverage of such events, by the way the deaths were ignored or entombed in tiny clippings. I would piously ask, "What do you think would happen if seven people from Minnesota died out there? Why, it would be on the network evening news!" as if such a result would make everything right again in the world. I half believed this rhetoric but it had little to do with my desire for the crossing.

I get up at 4 A.M. and make coffee and sit in the small apartment and stare at the maps. The women I am seeing tell me, "Don't die out there. Don't get hurt." I smile and shrug. It is all false, all melodrama. I do not consider getting hurt; I do not consider not making it. That is not the threat or the attraction. I smell the aroma of the coffee and savor the bitterness on my tongue.

I have no interest in Central America and believe it a fact of life that the United States will meddle in the affairs of nearby countries that are small and weak. I feel little concern about Mexicans coming north. I don't care if they take jobs and I don't care if they are blocked by a wall of steel and weapons and forced to live with the nation they created, Mexico.

When I drift in my thoughts of the desert, then in those good moments, the desert is always blue. I am going to blue desert. Of course, this will not suffice for a newspaper so I focus on the Border Patrol, the tactics and problems of Mexicans coming north, the harshness of the land. But at 4 A.M. over that first cup of coffee, I warm myself in blue desert. I have no idea why the color attracts me. As a boy, I had a succession of hand-me-down blue suits and I hated them and have hated the color in clothing ever since. But I keep seeing this image and everything is blue and a great calm settles over me.

It is late at night and we are drinking wine in a club. The woman says, "Don't you die out there on me. You come back."

I smile and shrug and hardly hear.

Everything is blue, luminously blue.

But of course there is a difference between my imaginings over morning coffee and the desert on a June night. The snake rattles by my boot at 2 A.M. and then moves off a foot into a brittle bush. The green-and-tan-banded body is only about twelve inches long. We throw down our packs. Bill Broyles, my companion on this hike, slowly assembles the flash unit on his camera and then pokes the rattler to force a better display.

This is the moment I have been dreading and the key reason I could not face the walk alone. I have this nightmare of being bitten. It is very dark and I am alone and thirty or forty miles from roads, doctors, and salvation. I go slowly berserk or perhaps I quickly die. The snake in my dream has an awful grin, a scaly Satan with fangs buried deep in the muscle of my calf. I can feel my flesh pulse as the reptile injects the poison into my blood.

So I have not come alone. In my backpack, I have a rope. Somewhere in the back of my head, I have this idea that if one of us is bitten, the other can tie up the victim to prevent him from wandering off into the desert in delirium, and then the lucky one will walk out for help. That is how deep run my fears and fantasies of snakebite.

Now the moment has arrived, just an instant ago I felt the snake quiver under my boot and then the rattle and then nothing at all. The small reptile simply slithered off a foot, as shocked at our meeting as I was. And I hardly moved.

As Bill works his camera I lie down on the ground four or five feet away from the snake and take a ten-minute nap. I am not afraid and I am not brave. I am absolutely indifferent.

We are twenty-odd miles into the passage. Around us are all the places I studied on the wall maps back at the apartment. If you have enough water, the names have a picturesque ring. If you do not have enough water, they sound like the lid opening on a crypt. The Lechuguilla Desert is at our backs, the Tule Desert sprawls to the south, and the dunes of the Mohawk Valley yawn before us with the sands glowing under a full moon. We are stopped on the east flank of the Copper Mountains, just north of the Cabeza Prietas. Behind us, Big Pass opens with jaws seven miles wide. Fifteen miles to the southeast, the Tinajas Altas look near enough to touch. All these places are creosote, bare ground, dry washes, stunted trees. This earth is too dry for the deer, too dry for the javelina. This is the furnace room of the Sonoran Desert.

I cannot get the map out of my head with its names, tidy brown contour lines, blue strands hinting at drainages and babble of Spanish words and prospector lingo, all struggling to nail down the land. On my faithful map, this country appears as tidy and organized as a city park.

The photo session winds down, the thirty-pound packs are shouldered and we move on. We do not talk much about the snake or about our reactions. We do not talk about thirst, hunger, or fatigue. There is no need. I sense we are starting to lose it and I do not even consider talking about this at all.

Of course, I suppose there are good tactical reasons for not launching a discussion on the fact that we have just treated a rat-tlesnake as an amusing toy and a media event. But I don't think like a line commander and my silence has nothing to do with careful judgment. We do not talk because there is no need or appetite for words. We have come at least twenty miles tonight and we have more than twenty to go before the sun takes the land back.

We are two specks on an ill-defined strand of migrant trails, faint footpaths that start at truckstops just over the line in Mexico and then lance north thirty to sixty miles, depending on the angle chosen, to Interstate 8. Yuma is more than forty miles to the west and Ajo eighty to the east and in between there is not much at all. There are no springs or streams and no one lives here, no one. A few rock holes hold puddles for desert bighorns for weeks or months at a time and the rains average three inches a year and sometimes for-get to come for years at a time. In the summer, say from Memorial Day to mid-September, daytime temperatures scamper right past 100 and some times touch 120, 125 degrees or more.

This is the basic desert of folklore, one uncluttered with annoy-ing twentieth-century rest areas, water fountains, trail signs, and shortcuts. For me, this is clearly part of the draw. I don't have to think much here because everything is stated very plainly. I have found a place that skips the big words.

We do not know how many are out here with us this night. Before we left El Saguaro truckstop in Mexico hours ago, we watched men glide off in twos and threes and head north. But there are other spots for departure and many more are walking this desert. We are all heading for towns and points along the Interstate, places like Wellton, Tacna, or a roadside rest area at Mohawk Pass. Little dots of flesh inching north and probably by now all hurting.

We go up against seven border patrolmen who work days, the random war games of the gunnery range and full-time companions like hunger and thirst and heat.

Score-keeping is a bit haphazard. The Border Patrol body count runs anywhere from two to twelve dead a summer but no one pretends to find all the bodies or have any real sense of how many rot undiscovered. There is a range here littered with bones and the desire to recover them is slight since a pauper burial costs the county $400. Over the past decade, I calculate at least 200 people have died on this stretch.

Jim Clarida, a Border Patrol agent at the Tacna station, tried to explain the power of the heat to me one day in late May. The afternoon before the thermometer had slapped 125 in the Tacna shade. Clarida patiently sipped his coffee, lit a smoke, and said, "Let me tell you about my son's pet rabbit."

The kid, he sighed, had raised this buck for a 4-H project and then you know how it goes. The rabbit became part of the family and stayed on. The animal lived in a cool hutch under thick vines.

Well, yesterday, he continued, the rabbit got out and ran about fifty yards before the boy caught him and put him back in the hutch. Twenty minutes later, Clarida went out and checked on him and the buck was thrashing around and heaving. Then he just died.

Clarida paused in his tale and snapped his fingers, pop! He died just like that, he smiled.

Of course Mexicans are not rabbits. Once, they found a dead man and the desert all around him was ripped up like he had gone berserk. They could see the marks on the ground where he had crawled on his belly swimming across the sand, acting as if the hot ground were a cooling sea.

Then there are those found with their shoes and clothes piled neatly beside them. Such men reach a point and decide the game is over and try to lie down and peacefully die. This is not an easy thing to do. When the cold takes a man, it is said to be like drifting off to sleep and not unpleasant. I have a friend who was drunk and womanless and depressed in a small pub in the Canadian bush. He walked out in the January night and hobbled off a mile into the snow. And then he lay down and began to fall into dreams. Calm and content, he waited for death. He eventually changed his mind and struggled out but he told me the brief taste of the grave was not bad, not bad at all.

With heat and thirst, death shows a different hand. The body temperature soars and the brain seems to cook. The flesh feels electric with pain as each cell screams out its complaint. People in such circumstances tear off their clothes in the hope of being cooled. They bury their heads in the sand in the hope of comforting their sizzling craniums. Sometimes the Border Patrol finds corpses with the mouths stuffed with sand.

Strange thoughts and desires can be unleashed. A few years ago south of Ajo, a group of Salvadoran men and women crumpled under the heat and began to die. One man, staring at a death that seemed minutes away, tried to fuck a corpse only to find that he was too far gone for even this last pleasure. Dying in the snow and cold is better. On this everyone agrees.

But still they keep coming, day after day, night after night. Some will move only during daylight because they fear the snakes. Some refuse to wear hats. Almost all carry no more than a gallon of water. The desert south of Tacna and Wellton is probably the hardest sector of the American border to cross and survive. But they keep coming and I cannot help but wonder what kind of experiences produce people willing to take on such ground.

Almost always this particular chunk of the Republic is ignored. The 125-mile drive along Interstate 8 from Gila Bend to Yuma is universally decried as a vast boredom of sand, creosote flats, vicious-looking rock piles of mountains, frightening heat, and no decent restaurants to tease the traveler. Because the land south of the highway is locked up by the military and the U. S. Fish and Wildlife Service, it is little known. There are no paved roads there, no picnic benches, no suggested scenic overlooks.

The statistics kept by the game rangers contend that 3,000 Americans a year peek into this country but the numbers are a bureaucratic fraud based mainly on those who drive a short loop road right next to Ajo. In a typical summer, maybe two or three Americans legally take out a permit and go into the hot country. And perhaps a thousand Latins who have other concerns than permits.

I was once having dinner with a woman who proceeded to tell me what a hideous drive it was to go to Yuma, to stare hour after hour at this God-forsaken wasteland. I lost my temper and told her she was a fool and she looked at me with disbelief. But I knew what she said rang with truth, that for almost everyone this country is a flat, dry tedium, something flaming past the window as the air conditioner purrs, the stereo sings, the cold beer sweats in the hand. It is not an idea or felt thing. No one sings its praises or spins legends from its emptiness. It is nowhere.

Now Bill and I are deep into this nowhere and by 2 A.M. we are facing our hurts. Our shoulders ache, our backs ache, our legs ache, and our feet ache. We drink constantly and nibble candy bars and yet our thirst never seems to end and our energy continues to decline. And we are maybe halfway.

The hunger is a fine thing. A month earlier I made a sixteen-mile night march out of this same desert with a half gallon of water and no food. The black sky flashed and sparkled with aircraft playing war and the air hung like a sweet drug full of carnal sensations. When I finally staggered into Tacna, the town's cafes were closed and I banged loudly on the kitchen door of one until a woman appeared and heard my plea. She sold me a small bag of M&Ms.

I tore the packet open and the little candies spilled out onto the gravel, I dove down to my knees and grabbed greedily at them in the dirt. She stood there towering over me and said nothing and I did not give her a moment's thought.

That kind of totally absorbing hunger is the basic menu here. It insists on your attention and yet is strangely sensuous like the feel of your hand caressing a woman's breast. It is not to be ignored.

Besides the aches and the thirst and the hunger, Bill and I sense something else, something we refuse to discuss. Our behavior with the snake had a certain flair but does not seem terribly sensible. Why did he hunker down a foot or so from the snake and keep poking at it with a stick while he fiddled with his camera? Why did I sprawl out next to the snake and nap like I was sharing a bed with a domestic cat back home?

Something is happening at a deep level in our bodies, a revolt in the cells, a shift in the chemical juices, in the intricate synapses that fire information through our flesh and that organize our muscle into motion and purpose. Our will is dissolving as our tissue loses tiny trace elements, things with names I do not even know.

We skip the snake business, brush it off as a detail, and consider the containers of water straining our shoulders. Do we really need that much water? Maybe we should pour some of it out, cut the load?

Then we stop talking about the water and march on. We do not trust our minds any longer. They seem fine and even more interesting than is usually the case but there is something different now about the way thoughts come and go. And we do not want to speak of this feeling of unreliability. How can we even trust our perceptions of warning?

I drift back to our start yesterday afternoon. In that beginning there is warmth, confidence, and good spirits. We sprawl in the shade at El Saguaro truckstop, a dot along the Mexican highway between Sonoyta, eighty miles to the east, and San Luis forty miles to the west. A man, a woman, and a baby rest on pads under a flatbed truck and wait out the afternoon heat. The man is about thirty and he stretches out and smokes. His woman nuzzles against him. The baby gurgles and plays with the man's finger.

It is 105 degrees in the shade and rising.

The truck bears Sinaloa plates, a Mexican state 600 miles south and I imagine them homeward bound. El Saguaro has no electricity no cooling, no well. A few miles to the east is La Joya truckstop another place of dreams. There electric lights hang from the ceiling, a television is mounted in a corner, and at La Joya also there is no electricity, no cooling, no well. Once I was there and I saw a dog eating a dead dog. The food in the café is simple but filling.

These two spots are the principal launching pads for the walks of *los mojados* northward. Water is sold to these travelers at about a buck and a half a gallon. At times Mexico can seem a little weak on compassion. A friend once asked an old patrón of San Luis what people did there for a livelihood.

"They eat each other's bones," he smiled.

All my many Mexicos appear at El Saguaro. There are the tall Sonorans, fairer skinned than many of their countrymen and larger because they possess less Indian blood. *Ricos*, the richer members of the Mexican economy, pull in from time to time in new cars, windows rolled up to announce they have air conditioning. They buy a bottle of pop and a bag of chips, gaze at the slumbering throng with disgust, and then depart. The truckers and poorer folk from farther down are darker and shorter and look out on the desert heat with caution written across their eyes. Forty years ago this stretch of road was sand and many died when their machines bogged down and no help came. For years some residents of San Luis and Sonoyta made a tidy little income salvaging the abandoned cars and trucks. Once a man found the skeleton of an infant on a back seat.

The Mexican poverty that always catches my eye when I am deep into the country is here launching a war of liberation. The truckstops hold small groups of men, each man carrying a clear plastic, gallon milk container full of water and a bag or knapsack with a few cans of chiles for the hike north. I once hitched a ride on this road with a Mexican in an old wreck—we had to stop twice to pour in transmission fluid—and suddenly he pointed north to men going through the fence and laughed, "*Mojados!*" Then he asked, "How good really are wages in the states?"

I lie on a cement slab and stuff down potato chips and Cokes. My body is full of apprehension. Semi drivers carefully string hammocks under their parked rigs and then climb in and sleep. Others sit in a small patio eating and drinking beer.

The baby starts crying and the man gets up, walks into the restaurant, and returns with a canteen of water. He sprinkles drops over the child's body and is very gentle. The crying stops. The woman sleeps on.

The landscape around the truckstop is almost empty of vegetation—some creosote, a few ironwoods huddling in a dry wash, but mainly rock and pale earth and glare. Behind us a road leads to a hilltop micro-wave station. We sit without electricity while high tech sings above our heads.

The Mexicans who travel this road fear the desert and fear the heat. I have walked out of this terrain and had them offer me free meals as if I were some wonder boy of the sands. Once Bill hitched a ride with a trucker on this stretch. When he asked the trucker to stop so he could hike off into the desert, the man refused.

He said, "If I let you go, you will die."

El Saguaro attracts people willing to give it a shot. Around 12:30 two men start north. They wear caps and each carries his gal-lon of water. Three hours later, some men get off a flatbed truck that has stopped. They carefully fold up the tarp for the driver as pay-ment for the ride. Each of these men also has a one-gallon milk con-tainer and heads north. They wear no hats; their shirts do not cover their arms and are dark colors. For shoes, they favor sneakers.

Bill and I watch them depart into the heat. The Border Patrol has found that the men who die are usually in their twenties and quite strong. They do not fear the desert or the sun. They walk right through the heat of the day. And they die. We are both on the edge of forty. We wait.

I content myself with watching the people who must live with heat. They are drinking beer, sleeping in hammocks under trucks, sprinkling water on squawling babies.

Our preparations do not seem to be much as the hot hours roll past. We have run, lifted those weights, studied our safe little maps. Bill is basically a piece of iron. the survivor of thirteen marathons and a man who has run Pike's Peak four times. One room of his house is nothing but weights, the walls plastered with little admoni-tions to lift harder.

Our packs tip the scales at a little over thirty pounds and hold three gallons of water, some raisins, nuts and candy bars, extra socks, medicine, swatches of material for plastering blisters, flashlights trousers and long-sleeved shirts, a sheet to stretch out for shade. Also, we have buried water along the route just in case we need it or run into someone else who does.

We wear hats, running shorts, t-shirts, and light boots.

Of course, there are some black spots in the training record. I sat up half the night before, drinking and drinking and could hardly sleep at all what with the phantoms stalking my dreams.

The Mexicans train differently. They arrive after long truck rides and hitchhikes and carry their one gallon of water and little or no food. They wear shabby shoes or sandals, skip hats as often as not and sometimes are decked out in black from head to foot. According to the Border Patrol, about sixty percent have made the passage before and presumably know what they are getting into. The other forty percent are virgins.

The first-timers are often dropped here by coyotes, the border's smugglers of humans, and are told that the border is a few miles away and they will meet them on the other side. The other forty or fifty miles of the route is apparently considered a detail by these smugglers. The people ignorant of the area tend to come from the interior, from jungles full of parrots or Sierras full of pines. They amble off into the hard desert and discover a different kind of world.

I watch them disappear one by one into the beginning of their education. The walls of the café are red and yellow, and a battery powered radio blares, "Hotel California."

Men are busy working on the truckstop trying to install an air cooler. They fire up a tiny Honda generator to test it. The boss paddles over, a stout man in his fifties. He is dressed very nicely and makes conversation with us.

He explains that his lease on the place expires in fifteen days and he is making improvements in the hope that the landlord will renew it. He points to big holes in the roof and sighs. Out back are two privies, and he dismisses them with a sweep of the hand. He confides that he refuses to use them.

The cooler is really his grand gesture. Surely, he feels, this will win his landlord to his side.

I am charmed by this Mexican Mr. Fix-it, but a little alarm rings in the back of my head. He moves with the unmistakable air of a Mexican official, a kind of predator seldom seen in the states outside the turf of the Chicago police force.

Suddenly, he demands, "Who are you and what are you doing here?"

He produces a badge and says he is an immigration official at San Luis.

He continues his questions with "Where is your car?"

Bill tells him that we are on foot, that we love this beautiful desert and wish to hike it.

The man brushes past such nonsense and asks, "Why are you taking pictures?"

"Oh," Bill smiles, "I take them for memories, Señor."

The official gazes with interest at our bulging backpacks and visions of loot, scams, busts, and bribes dance across his features. It would be difficult to exaggerate the roguery of a Mexican official. I know a man with a federal job in one border community who regularly drives up to Arizona and buys big appliances that are barred by Mexican law from importation into the country. Once, he was heading back with a load of micro-wave ovens when a friend asked him how he proposed to get them past the Mexican customs officials. Ah, he exclaimed, but they are for the wives of the customs officials.

The man with the badge continues to wait for our reply. Bill has brought an ice axe to use as a camera tripod and the agent's eyes light up when he notices it.

"Oh," he muses, "you are prospectors, no?"

He begins to babble of lost gold mines said to be in the area and the thought of ore brings pleasure to his face. Is that not why we have come?

We smile and laugh and shrug. He will not be dissuaded. He has seen the axe.

He punctures this moment of good cheer by noting, "I could ask for your papers right now, you know. I have the right."

This is kind of a sore point for me. The night before I could not find my birth certificate or voter registration card and in any event, I resent the paperwork demanded by governments that claim to own the desert. So I have entered the Republic of Mexico illegally and I start calculating just how much money this technical error will cost me.

We smile at the man.

Then someone calls him from inside the café, something about the new air cooler being installed. He nods and excuses himself from us for a moment.

We grab our packs and melt into the desert to the north knowing he will never follow us into such a country.

It is 5:30 P.M. when we step off and there will be some light for three hours. The border waits five or six miles ahead and many trails streak northward to the line. We follow tracks of tennis shoes, running shoes, soccer shoes, *huaraches*, and boots. The way is lined with empty cans of fish, nectarine juice, and chiles. Black ash marks where fires fought back the night.

The trails braid and wander and cross each other, a kind of stuttered beginning to a long walk. We move along the stone walls of the Tinajas Altas mountains, walking fast, eager to leave the Mexican immigration official behind and powered like all travelers on this path by the pull of the El Dorado to the north.

Then a white masonry obelisk spikes upward a couple of hundred yards to the east. A bunch of stones on the ground at our feet spell out MEXICO/USA, and nearby a huge wooden sign stands there with its surface weathered and perfectly blank. Another and smaller sign warns that motor vehicles are forbidden.

This is the fabled border. There is no fence, just this boast of an imaginary line and footprints, everywhere footprints, and all heading one direction.

We move through the low hills, a gentle roll of land, and after a half hour, the view opens up and we can see across the Lechuguilla to Big Pass. Beyond Big Pass, puffs of smoke rise from fields being burned off near Tacna. Everything looks close enough to touch. It seems impossible that the hike will take more than two, maybe even three hours. The light weakens from white to gold, the valley shines with perfectly spaced creosote and is lanced down the center by ironwood and palo verde lining Coyote Wash. We hardly speak now. The rhythm of our footsteps constitutes our language and to a degree, we are struck dumb by the order and hugeness of the landscape. The big valley could serve as the garden of a Zen monastery.

Two and a half hours out of El Saguaro truckstop, we reach a fork in the trail that leads off to Tinajas Altas, a series of nine rock tanks. All human footprints arc away from the water. All coyote tracks race left toward the water. The small pools lie hidden from view on the steep rock side of the mountain. The rains fill them and historically they have been the only sure water between Agua Dulce spring sixty miles to the east, and Yuma, forty miles to the west. Once hundreds of graves were visible around the tanks and the path was lined on both sides with the mummified carcasses of upright horses and mules. The federal boundary survey of the 1890s found a prospector dead just below the first tank. His fingers were worn raw from trying to climb the rock. He had been too weak to make it to water and died a few yards from his salvation.

At this place, a key medical paper on thirst was created in 1905. W. J. McGee, a nationally known scientist and renowned desert rat, was camped here in August while cancer ate at his body. Pablo Valencia dropped in.

Valencia had been lost for six-and-a-half days and for five days he had lived by drinking his urine. His bowels had completely shut down during this experience and for two days his kidneys failed. He had undergone a change in what we moderns might call his values. He threw all his money away; he hallucinated a desert saturated with wet sand. He had dreams of dying and he had days of staying on the march. He made it to Tinajas Altas and was saved. McGee had heard this bellowing, this deep roaring, a sound he likened to a bull, and wandered out and found the man.

When Bill almost died because coyotes dug up his water supply, he was retracing Valencia's wanderings.

We pass Tinajas Altas without stopping and strike out across the desert for Big Pass, following the footprints of Mexicans. A little after 8 P.M. we stop and eat and drink. We have been drinking steadily, making no effort to conserve water. The problem is not running out of water but pouring it into our bodies fast enough. We sweat like beasts but we can only drink like human beings.

Bill checks his feet for blisters, the sun sinks, and the light goes from gold to rose to gone. We sit beside an ancient trail etched on a field of stone. Broken pottery fragments lie about. I smile and think of an Indian tripping, and I imagine strange curses in the air as the clay vessel smashes on the ground. The Lechuguilla wears the marks of many journeys. Aboriginal trails cross car tracks, tank tracks, game tracks, Mexican tracks, our tracks. Pieces of spent military hardware litter the ground. I can see traces in the sand of lizards, rats, and sidewinders.

Big Pass is so near, so very near. We joke that this walk may be too easy, that Big Pass will be ours in an hour or so. But from Tinajas Altas to the Big Pass is 13.5 miles as the raven flies. We are not ravens. We dodge clumps of creosote, fall into rat holes, stumble down into washes, detour ironwoods, watch for cactus, and zigzag across the terrain.

The moon slams the ground with white light. At our backs, Cipriano Pass knifes between the Tinajas Altas and Gila Mountains, a cut the Border Patrol calls Smuggler's Pass. It is part of a shortcut to the Interstate and the town of Wellton, a nine-hour route. The various trails whipping across the Lechuguilla all have one goal: avoid capture. The Mexicans say that they come across this pan of sand and heat because they think their chances of evading the Border Patrol are enhanced. The Border Patrol denies this and claims such hikes are foolish risks. But then, their federal commitment to the game is not as complete as the Mexicans'—the referee never has the same feel for the sport as the lineman.

We stumble across the valley. The heat ceases to matter, not because it goes away, but because we go into it and join with it and can imagine no life separate from it. The night is soft with warmth, the moon is up, and I feel my sweat as the air brushes against my flesh with a light touch, I have no desire to be cool and no desire to be elsewhere, I do not think of the Border Patrol or of snakes or of thirst, fatigue, thorns, blisters, hunger, and pain.

I think of my wife. I look at the moon and think she is looking up at that moon and we are together. This lunar unity strikes me suddenly as a great insight. The soil crunches under my feet and my legs bleed from the small tears of thorns. I look at that moon.

The collapse of my marriage has not been tidy. I left; then there were no words. Then there were talks. She has seen a counselor and this, she tells me, has helped.

I am sitting in the living room, an exhibition hall of her taste and the sofa is soft and comfortable. My body is rigid, the muscles hard with tension. She speaks and the words pour out for more than an hour—angry jabs, blunt charges, an inventory of my sins. I do not disagree. I listen and I am mute. This is all necessary. The words must be said. She weeps.

We make love on the floor.

Then it falls apart again. The pattern repeats. We begin the process of divorce. Then we have dinner and laugh. I bury myself in work; I go through the motions of preparing for the long walk; I drink.

She has large breasts hanging from a thin body. She finds a lump. There are many tests and the results give different answers. I can see a blue vein just below the surface on one breast, a faint pulsing river of blood. There are more tests. After weeks, they decide cancer. The breast must be cut off.

She tries to be brave but after a while this ceases to be enough. She asks me if I can imagine what this means, if I can conceive of mutilating my sexual identity. Of course, I cannot.

The water sloshes in my pack, my feet pound along like a metronome on a grand piano, and I look up at that moon. In three days, she will be wheeled into surgery. I have had her schedule the operation so that it will not interfere with my walk, with this story. I am inflexible on this point and cannot be budged. My work has become my religion and I use it to keep at bay all demands and duties. She looks into my eyes and sees a sullen stranger there.

They will cut off the breast and they will search her tissue to see—to see if more must be hacked off her body. She stares at a fear much larger than Big Pass. She wants to make love all the time. The shambles of our marriage does not matter. She is like a gladiator about to go into the arena and she wants it all while there is still time.

She has never been more alive and her senses grow keen with this fact of cancer. "Can you imagine what this means to me?" she says. I hear her voice cutting across the Lechuguilla. She collects toys and stuffed animals; she collects images of pigs; she worships cats. As children we both happened to read the same edition of Hans Christian Andersen, one with intricate and magical plates by Nathaniel Wyeth. The illustrations promised a world far beyond my reach.

"Can you imagine?" she asks.

I enter a serenity of walking, dodging cactus, and always those thorns on the small shrubs and large trees slice my arms and legs. I walk into the limbs, these I do not detour and I take pleasure in crashing ahead, in the sound of thorns raking across my nylon pack.

The moon—I draw power from the moon. I think—no, I do not think, I know with certainty—that I will make it and she will make it and that we are both looking at the moon and I will pull her through the dark cave of anesthesia and the knife and the pain and the huge bandage wrapped across where her breast once spread as a generous mound. My will becomes like iron and I know. I am a tiny dab of flesh dragging across a huge valley in the moonlight but I am larger than the mountains, stronger than hard metals, because I know. I know. I feel no guilt now.

Everywhere the earth is beauty. The mountains lift sharply off the valley floor, rockpiles almost naked of plants. Beauty. The moon flashes off the stone walls. Beauty. The creosote, the much derided greasewood, stands spaced like a formal garden. Beauty. Stars crowd the sky and I can hear them buzzing with the fires of their explosive gases. I tear the wrapper from a Granola bar and crunch the grains between my teeth. I tip the plastic jug up to my lips and swallow. I lock on the moon. Beauty.

The desert tonight is an enormous theater full of tracks made by men and women and sometimes children inching north. The air is empty of sound. We all struggle toward Big Pass alone and this is necessary. We are always alone, everywhere alone, but here this fact cannot be denied. It is a condition of this place and other people cannot, this time, alter or obscure that insight.

A flare bursts over our heads. The military sharpens itself for war. We enter a cleared strip of ground, a target area. Something finned like a bomb fragment squats on the sand. And then everything turns blue. The mountains rise azure, the ocotillo waves blue wands, the creosote whispers by my feet, and everything is awash with a rich, bright blue. At first the color is ahead and then I enter it like water and the blue is everywhere. It does not coat the surface but seems to come from the center of things. I look at my hand and the skin glows with blue pigment.

I do not hesitate or wonder. I do not speculate that the sugar flow to my brain has declined, that the pangs of dehydration have addled my mind, that some vast chemical change in my body is altering my perceptions. I have entered this blue world and I accept it totally. It means peace. I long to see a coyote cutting across the flats on a night hunt, to see a blue coyote and hear a blue yell under a blue moon. My senses quicken and yet dull. The peace works deep into my muscle and my body works harder and harder and yet feels ease. I begin to glide. Ahead Big Pass waits with dark blue jaws.

I glance at Bill ten yards off to my side and lurching as I must be over the uneven surface mined with holes, plants, and bad footing. But I glide. I know I glide.

Blue.

Other travelers have probably tasted a different, less serene Lechuguilla. In 1976, the Border Patrol found men harnessed to a cart equipped with auto tires for wheels. They were hauling it across this very desert where Bill and I now stumble. They were on no road or trail. The cart was full of marijuana.

Once Bill was walking a few miles to the south and discovered tracks made by wheels. He carefully measured the marks and realized they were made by wagons in the nineteenth century. I have a friend who served in this area during World War II. He says there is a wagon train lying in ruins in the sands, a relict of a party massacred by bandits a century ago. Men training for the war sighted the wreck. No one has seen it since.

There is a mass grave near a big tree according to old accounts, a burying place for a man, a woman, and their children. The horse died, the wagon stopped, the family perished within ten miles of the waters of Tinajas Altas. People report visiting the site from time to time. Bill and I have tried to find it. There are so few large trees in the Lechuguilla, the task should be simple. We always fail.

To the north and west a ways, the military prepares to test a silo for the MX missile system. Giant doors will endure huge blasts to determine if this clever shell game with the Soviets will really work. Someday, future wanderers can search for this site.

Thoughts trip across my mind without obvious logic. They are soft, soggy clumps of feeling. They produce no argument or insight but seem like the pulps of fruit lying together in a bowl. I solve nothing and do not desire solutions. We are on a treadmill toward Big Pass. The rock walls glow under the fat moon.

Steps. Step after step after step. We tire, we stop. We time the break with our digital watches. Five minutes and no more. We must move, move, move. Move dammit, MOVE.

We must make Big Pass.

We do not ask why.

We do not speak at all.

About 12:30 A.M., Big Pass finally swallows us. We have drunk less than one gallon of water apiece. We are thirsty, constantly thirsty but we cannot seem to pour the fluid into our bodies any faster. My legs are tired, my shoulders sore, and I am beginning to feel the bones in my feet. We move on.

The tracks we lost at Tinajas Altas now reappear and I smile at the reunion. The soccer shoe is back. The running shoe also. We have all converged at the Pass and just beyond the gap, we all take a dirt road hugging against the Copper Mountains. Now the hunt begins in earnest.

The Border Patrol knows tracks. They can read prints on foot, from trucks and from aircraft. Once they pick up a fresh trail below the Interstate, they stay with it until the footprints tell them that the people have gotten out. In part this is because once the tracks make it to the freeway, the person is likely to hitch a ride and slip beyond the federal reach. And in part, this is because if the tracks do not make it to the Interstate, then the person is still in the desert and to the Border Patrol this means the person could be dying. Jim Clarida, the man who watched his son's rabbit die from the heat, once tracked a man for seventy-five miles.

The Mexicans in turn do their very best to avoid the trackers. They walk backwards to confuse their pursuers. They drag brush to obliterate their footprints. They often stay off the roads. When caught, they ask the agents how they bagged them. The agents tell them. The game demands certain courtesies.

After Big Pass, the drag roads begin. The Border Patrol pulls old tires on chains to wipe the dirt clean. Then they know any tracks are fresh. The drag roads are checked often, on the ground and from the air. When a new sign is spotted, the hunt begins.

Tonight, no one seems interested in hiding their tracks. The road shows clear sign. It is now 1 A.M. and the Border Patrol shift will not begin until 6 A.M. Perhaps, everyone counts on being past the Interstate by then. Or perhaps everyone is too weary to care.

The game is played seriously but without anger. If a Mexican cannot make it, his companions often go to the Border Patrol and turn themselves in so that help can be sent to the person left behind. The Border Patrol responds. If someone is trapped in the desert, they say he is down. And that is serious business.

The agents seldom face resistance. Some of the Mexicans have been caught many times in this sector. It is a game. Once Clarida cornered a man in the brush. Suddenly the man walked out and gave himself up. Clarida recognized him as someone he had once rescued. "Anyone else I would have run from," he said, "but I owe you this one."

By 2 A.M. I feel ruin in my limbs. It is not a question of being strong or fit. Such things no longer matter. Something is happening to my body and I cannot alter this decline. The rattlesnake briefly buzzes beneath my foot, the photo is taken, the incident filed but not discussed. We can now see the Interstate more than twenty miles ahead, a thin strand of lights beckoning.

A couple of years back, a nineteen-year-old came out and said his uncle and father were down. They had no water; the father had been snakebitten. The Border Patrol found them a few days later working on a ranch along the Gila River. The father and uncle had walked through their thirst and had drunk their urine. They had poulticed the snakebite with the flesh of a cactus.

The father was sixty years old. He was very angry that his son had gone to the Border Patrol.

We gaze ahead at Tacna, at the big road, at Mohawk Pass, at the twinkling lights of other people and the promise of shade, water food, rest. We have twenty miles more.

We have entered the killing ground.

The people who come this way do not die in the heart of the desert; they go down near their goals. They go down because there is nothing left in them, not even a tiny spark to propel them one more mile.

We begin to consider dumping our water at a point up ahead. When we reach the mouth of a certain canyon. We will be only twelve miles from Tacna. Then, the water must go. Surely nothing can stop us from covering only twelve miles and to be free of the weight of the water would be an utter joy. Why, to keep carrying all this water is madness. We are sure of this fact. Dammit, we will get rid of the stuff. We are not fools. We will pour it out.

The calves in my legs tighten, the bones in my feet hurt, the hips grind and grow sore with each stride. My pack cuts into my shoulders and food no longer seems to work. I eat and walk a ways and the energy disappears. I drink but need more water. I envision drilling straight into my belly, auguring a big hole and just pouring the water in. I will use a funnel and not spill a drop.

The night is still a blue dream. The desert can never be better than what greets my eyes. The forms cannot be questioned. The night world brings no fears. Bats fly just over our heads and they are friends. I am certain of this. An owl lifts off a saguaro and I stop and stare with worship. Nighthawks sweep just off the ground.

Across the blue valley, the Mohawks glow. Once a woman lost all hope on the flanks of the Mohawks. She was just a few short miles from the Interstate and the roadside rest there with its ramadas of shade, its bathrooms, its tap water. She ripped her clothes off, article by article and walked up a canyon and then scaled the rock slope. From up there she could see everything and it must have looked so lovely to her, seeing the green fields, the towns, and snug houses, the traffic, the big highway, the lazy course of the river. Behind she left her dress, her shoes, her panties, her bra littered along her trail.

They never found her body.

The night, the delicious night, denies such stories. The night insists on beauty.

But we hurt. Our bodies whisper: Yes, the stories are here.

At 4 A.M., we strike another drag road, wide and clean and hungry for our footprints. The moon is down and our pace is two miles an hour. We drift closer to the Coppers where we have cached water, all part of our grand strategy. Six gallons lie buried under the sand. We do not touch them and are amused by their uselessness. The water mocks our thirst. We possess this treasure but we cannot get it into our bodies.

We fall down on the road and eat and drink and watch a red glow grow in the east. We empty our packs of canteens and keep only a gallon. The rest we set out for whoever needs it, whoever comes after us. The brotherhood.

Originally, we thought we might stop at dawn in this area, wait out the murderous heat of the day and finish the following evening. We reject this idea now. We want out; that is part of it. But also we want to beat the Border Patrol. We want to win, to gain the big road before they can catch us. We have been playing the game too hard to be indifferent to the final score.

I walk off a ways into the desert, squat down, and take a shit. The sun comes on stronger. The literature of hiking is almost devoid of the simple pleasure of pissing and shitting at will. It is replete with tips on how to dispose of wastes, how to protect babbling brooks from pollution, how to leave a clean camp. But nothing on this pleasure, this return to infancy when there is no distance between the desire and the act.

I feel like I can walk no farther. I feel like I can walk forever. My body, my tired, sore body, is simply something I drag along and I cannot imagine the trip ever ending.

The traffic on the Interstate can now be seen clearly, trucks storming toward Los Angeles markets, cars cruising with the air conditioning blowing hard. I hear the rumble of the engines and delight in the sound of machines.

Bill and I get up and trudge on. We must go twelve miles. We must. We cannot beat the dawn, but we will fight the sun; we will war against the rays. We refuse to stop. Every hour, we pause briefly, drink, snack, and lie down. Then we stagger up, our legs stiff as boards. Tacna seems just ahead but hour by hour comes no nearer. We dream of Tacna, a hamlet of 100 people. Bill sees iced tea, and ice cream; he makes out a waitress holding up a cone and beckoning. We shuffle more than walk, our feet scraping across the soil.

The sun comes up with unbelievable force. I shudder under the rays like a vampire caught far from my coffin. All around us are the unmarked spots where the last dramas of the dying take place. One man went down a mile south of the Interstate. He set fire to a tree in hopes that the smoke would bring help. They found his body.

The dying can be very quick. A few weeks before a man left El Saguaro truckstop at 4 P.M. on a Saturday. By 9 P.M. Sunday he was in a body bag in Tacna. He was twenty-eight. Sometimes the Border Patrol finds people too far gone to risk the ride to the hospital in Yuma. They take them to a grocery in Tacna and put them in the beer cooler in hopes of lowering their body temperatures.

None of these tales stops the flow of people. There was an old man who crossed this desert with his son and nephew. The two boys died ten miles south of the Interstate. The old man was caught and shipped back to Mexico. A week later, he was caught again crossing the same desert with a girl of eighteen. So far the Border Patrol in the Tacna sector has nabbed that old man fifteen times.

We walk on. We must have walked on. But there is no memory of this. We walk on.

We reach Tacna at 9:48 A.M. we have made the crossing in sixteen hours, seventeen minutes, drunk a gallon and a half of water each, and have nothing to say. We have probably walked forty-five miles, but this figure, like our careful recording of the time elapsed, means very little. The weather has been very cool for this country, surely no more than 110.

I will write a story, the newspaper will print it, and there will be awards, the trinkets of the business. But this will happen later.

Now there are other tasks at hand. I must call Tucson and let them know we are out. I fumble at the push buttons of the pay phone and keep getting the operator of an overseas line. I persist and after forty minutes make the simple connection. I begin to grasp what has happened to me. My mind does not work in this world.

We enter a café and eat a breakfast and drink iced tea after iced tea. The food is flat. The cool drinks lack pleasure. We consume coffee, pop, ice cream, eggs, sausage, hash browns, beef, lamb, soup, beer. The gorging continues for hours.

I walk into a bar and order a Budweiser longneck. I cannot sit. My limbs ache too much. I recline on the floor. The bartender says nothing. The Mexicans are still out there. They were there yesterday, they are there today, and they will be there tomorrow and tomorrow and tomorrow. And they cannot walk in here. They are huddling by an irrigation ditch and drinking deeply and then walking ten more miles, fifty more miles, one hundred more miles, whatever it takes to find work. I feel the rush of energy that must be pushing such people. I hear this force pounding like a mighty heart somewhere to the south.

But mainly as I lie there, I feel it all slip away and my senses deaden under the blandishments and delights of my civilization. When I get home in a day I will write the newspaper story in four hours, a torrent of words, statistics, and suggestions on this illegal immigration problem. But I will not mention my wife. There will be nothing about the cancer, the scalpel incising the soft white flesh topped by the faint pink nipple. I will not find room for the insistent feeling that she will triumph, the conviction that everything can be overcome. I will skip my notion that we both looked up at the same moon. And I will write nothing of blue desert. Nor will I speak of that place to anyone.

I have exited the only ground where I truly trust my senses. Most of the Southwest is beyond my belief and strikes me as an outpost of American civilization with the exiled desert merely a faint, scenic mural stretching behind the powerlines and skyscrapers. But the Lechuguilla, the Tule, the Mohawk dunes, these places have a weight with me that makes the cities of my people seem light and insubstantial. There is no point in reasoning with me on this matter. When I touch the steel towers of the Sunbelt, they feel like cobwebs soon to be dispersed by an angry wind. When I touch the earth I feel the rock hard face of eternity.

But as I lie on the saloon floor I can hardly believe in the country I have just left. I feel the bubbles of the beer against my tongue and savor the sour taste. I am busy killing experience with categories and words and leads, striking at it like it were a serpent to be slain and made into a safe skin, perhaps a belt or hatband.

And then I fall back again and see only one word. Blue. Always blue.

They play a game here. We play a game here.

The Luckiest Horse in Reno

DEANNE STILLMAN

WHEN THE MEN APPROACHED, the black foal might have been nursing. Or she might have been on her side, giving her wobbly legs a rest, leaning into her mother under the starry desert sky. The band of wild horses had only recently returned to this patch of scrub; the land had been stripped bare of forage by hordes of roaming cattle, and it was only in the past year that some edible plants—their seeds dropped here by migratory birds who knows when—began to green up the hills and provide nourishment for the critters that brought us all westward ho. At the sound of the vehicle, the band—all thirty-five horses—prepared to move and did move at once, for horses are animals of prey and so their withers twitched, their ears stiffened, their perfect, unshod hooves dug into the scrub for traction and then they began to run. The black foal might have taken a second or two longer than the others to rise. Perhaps the mare, already upright, bolted instantly, turning her head to see if the foal had followed. The headlights of the vehicle appeared over a rise. The men were shouting and then there was another bright light—it trained from atop the vehicle across the sunken bajada and it swept the sands, illuminating the wild and running four-legged spirits as their legs stretched in full perfect extension, flashing across their hides which were dun and paint and bay, making a living mural in 3-D in which the American story—all of it— was frozen here forever, in the desert as it always is, as bullets hissed from the vehicle through the patches of juniper and into the wild horses of the old frontier. It was Christmas. Two thousand years earlier, Christ had been born in a stable.

Statement of Marine Lance Corporal Scott William Brendle, January 14, 1999.

> *I was home in Reno, Nevada on Christmas leave. On the 27th of December, 1998, approximately between 1900 and 2100 hours, I drove Darien Brock and Anthony Merlino to Wal-Mart. We went inside and purchased one box, I believe, of 20 rounds of .270 caliber Winchester rifle ammunition, and two boxes of 12 gauge shotgun shells, brand unknown. The boxes of shotgun shells were green and yellow in color. The color of the shotgun shell itself is read [sic] plastic with brass bottoms. Also, we purchased a hand-held spotlight to spot rabbits in the dark so we could shoot them. We had approximately two to three six packs of beer with us. I drove up the construction road behind Rattlesnake Mountain. My pick up truck is a four-wheel drive, Ford Ranger, green 1992, with an open bed and toolbox in the back. When we left the road Anthony and Darien got into the bed of the truck so driving would be easier. The spotlight was plugged into the cigarette lighter and passed out the sliding rear window so they could shine it around the area of the truck as I drove. As I was driving, both of them pounded on the top of the truck to let me know to stop. I stopped the truck and got out to see what they were looking at. They said, "Hey, look, there is a horse."*

Two months later on a cold and sunny afternoon, a man was hiking in the mountains outside of Reno. She saw a dark foal lying down in the sagebrush, not able to get up. A bachelor stallion had been watching from a distance and now came over and nibbled at the foal's neck. She tried to get up but couldn't, and the stallion rejoined his little band. The hiker called for help. A vet arrived and could find no injuries. As it grew dark, a trailer was pulled across the washes and gulleys until it approached the filly, about a hundred yards away and downhill. The stars were particularly bright that night and helped the rescue party, equipped only with flashlights, lumber across the sands and up the rocky rise where the filly was down. Four men lifted her onto a platform and carried her down the hill and into the trailer. "She was a carcass with a winter coat," said a rescuer. She was covered with ticks and parasites, weak and anemic. She was six months old. Two days later, at a sanctuary near Carson City called Wild Horse Spirit, two women helped her stand. But she kept falling. Over the weeks, they nourished her and she grew strong and regained muscle and she began to walk without falling down. But she was nervous, not skittish like a lot of horses are, especially wild ones, but distracted, preoccupied, perhaps even haunted. Because of her location when rescued, near Rattlesnake Mountain, and because she was starving, her rescuers reasoned that she had been a nursing foal who had recently lost her mother. Without mother's milk, a foal can last for a while in the wilderness, sometimes as long as a couple of months. And because a band of bachelor stallions had been nearby when she was found, her rescuers figured they had taken her in, looking after her until they could do it no longer, standing guard as she lay down in the brush to die. "Something made me stop," the hiker who found the filly would later say. As it turned out, the filly was the lone survivor of the Christmas massacre, and they called her Bugz. Like all survivors, she had a story to tell.

A visitor to the site of the massacre can know part of the story, just as a visitor to Gettysburg or Little Big Horn can bear witness but not fully. But here there are no texts to guide us; no oral histories passed down across time; just skulls and the cages of ribs and shins and intact hooves and manes and tails right where the wild horses were felled, forever preserved in the dry air of the Great Basin that birthed Nevada—mosh pit of America—godforsaken treasure chest of a state that lures big and small spenders alike with five-cent slots and high-roller events and hollow spectacles and all-night pawn and—yes!—"wild horses, just like in the Old West!" says the travel literature—"See them roam free just like they oughtta be!" But Bugz knows better and that's why Bugz is permanently spooked, not unlike another twitchy Nevada character, Bugsy Siegel, said to have been demon-possessed and therefore buggy. No doubt he was, having witnessed—and been the progenitor of—great rivers of desert carnage. But Bugz the horse is our real American hero, mute witness to the history of the West, important remnant of the dwindling wild horse population, help to man in the taming of the frontier, maker of trails, intrepid deliverer of urgent messages (yes, the Pony Express trail is now Nevada Highway 95), fighter of battles, devoted member of the US cavalry, thrill-providing rodeo ride, license plate symbol, name of cool and desirable muscle car, fleet and wild heart of the American wanderer, tameable by no one yet a willing good friend who will carry you into hell if you ask.

"When we got the call, they said one horse was shot and wounded. Two others were dead," Betty Lee Kelly remembered, walking with me across the killing field. Betty and her partner Bobbi Royce are the founders of Wild Horse Spirit, a home for rescued, injured, abandoned, and abused wild horses. They gave their lives over to the horses fifteen years ago. When a wild horse is found shot or injured, which often happens in Nevada, they are usually the first contacted by animal control officers. Betty and Bobbi immediately drove from their home outside Carson City to the Virginia Range east of Reno, parking in a wash at Rattlesnake Mountain and meeting up with the Washoe County Sheriff and the man who had first happened upon the shootings and phoned law enforcement. The man led them to the injured horse whom they had been called to help. Betty guides me to the exact location. Four years after the massacre, a pair of equine leg bones lie crossed, as if running in repose, the cartilage of the hooves still intact. The bones are as white as white can get, radiating almost, a reverse silhouette of wildness frozen in movement and time. "She had probably been here for a day or two," Betty said. "She was lying in the sand. She had dug a small hole with her front legs, intermittently trying to get up. But she was shot in the spinal cord and her hind legs were paralyzed. An animal control officer put her to sleep." Betty and Bobbi would later name this filly Hope; police investigators would identify her as #7 in the final report. As the band of people explored the site, it quickly became clear that the incident was far more horrific—and way less routine—than the shooting of a few horses. Other murdered horses found that day included a nursing mare (#9) and her five- to six-month-old filly (#10) and two stallions (#8 and #11). And then there was the young colt, soon to be known in the Nevada court system as #4. Bobbi and Betty would call him Alvin. He was shot in the chest and then sprayed in the eyes, mouth, rectum, and genitals with a fire extinguisher, although at the time of the discovery, no one really knew what all the foamy white stuff was. Now, Alvin's carcass—the barrel of his chest—lies where he died, picked and blown clean by time, wind, and critters. The spine is flush against the sand, and the ribs curve toward the sky. "There was a stallion watching us that day," Betty said. "Just standing at the perimeter as we found each dead horse. When the sun went down and we got in our cars, he trotted on down the road. His family had been wiped out but we still didn't know how bad it was."

When investigators returned the following morning to complete their report, they fanned out across the area. By the end of the second day, the death toll had climbed to thirty-four. Some horses had been shot—several times—in the head. Others—shot in the stomach—probably died more slowly. Somehow, Bugz had escaped, perhaps even returning to her mother's side to nurse as the mare lay dying on the desert sand. At the base of an old pinon pine lies a large cross of rocks and stones with the bullet-riddled skull of a wild horse at the top. Betty built the cross two years after the massacre, the day the killers went on trial in Virginia City, a blood-soaked frontier town that feeds on its own mythology, charging two bucks to tour a brothel museum wherein, legend has it, a prostitute's hand is entombed in a jar, sliced off when its owner tried to steal from the till. Shortly after the massacre, a state senator rose to make a speech on the Nevada house floor. "If a wild horse comes to your property," he said to much applause, "shoot him." Eventually the killers would plead guilty to a misdemeanor, despite evidence such as a photograph of one of them standing proudly with his foot atop the colt who came to be known as Alvin. But Bugz knows what happened on Rattlesnake Mountain that awful Christmas day. Bugz saw the stallions, mares, fillies, and colts that were her band make their last stand in the West that they made ours and where they still—occasionally—roam.

From *Ill Nature*

JOY WILLIAMS

Save the Whales, Screw the Shrimp

I DON'T WANT TO TALK about *me*, of course, but it seems as though far too much attention has been lavished on *you* lately—that your greed and vanities and quest for self-fulfillment have been catered to far too much. You just want and want and want. You believe in yourself excessively. You don't believe in Nature anymore. It's too isolated from you. You've abstracted it. It's so messy and damaged and sad. Your eyes glaze as you travel life's highway past all the crushed animals and the Big Gulp cups. You don't even take pleasure in looking at nature photographs these days. Oh, they can be just as pretty as always, but don't they make you feel increasingly... anxious? Filled with more trepidation than peace? So what's the point? You see the picture of the baby condor or the panda, munching on a bamboo shoot, and your heart just sinks, doesn't it? A picture of a poor old sea turtle with barnacles on her back, all ancient and exhausted, depositing her five gallons of doomed eggs in the sand hardly fills you with joy, because you realize, quite rightly, that just outside the frame falls the shadow of the condo. What's cropped from the shot of ocean waves crashing on a pristine shore is the plastics plant, and just beyond the dunes lies a parking lot. Hidden from immediate view in the butterfly-bright meadow, in the dusky thicket, in the oak and holly wood, are the surveyors' stakes, for someone wants to build a mall exactly there—some gas stations and supermarkets, some pizza and video shops, a health club, maybe a bulimia treatment center. Those lovely pictures of leopards and herons and wild rivers—well, you just know they're going to be accompanied by a text that will serve only to bring you down. You don't want to think about it! It's all so uncool. And you don't want to feel guilty either. Guilt is uncool. Regret maybe you'll consider. *Maybe*. Regret is a possibility, but don't push me, you say. Nature photographs have become something of a problem, along with almost everything else. Even though they leave the bad stuff out— maybe because you *know* they're leaving all the bad stuff out—such pictures are making you increasingly aware that you're a little too late for Nature. Do you feel that? Twenty years too late? Maybe only ten? Not *way* too late, just a little too late? Well, it appears that you are. And since you are, you've decided you're just not going to attend this particular party.

PASCAL said that it is easier to endure death without thinking about it than to endure the thought of death without dying. This is how you manage to dance the strange dance with that grim partner, nuclear annihilation. When the U.S. Army notified Winston Churchill that the first A-bomb had been detonated in New Mexico, it chose the code phrase BABIES SATISFACTORILY BORN. So you entered the age of irony, and the strange double life you've been leading with the world ever since. Joyce Carol Oates suggests that the reason writers—*real* writers, one assumes—don't write about Nature is that it lacks a sense of humor and registers no irony. It just doesn't seem to be of the times—these slick, sleek, knowing, objective, indulgent times. And the word *environment*. Such a bloodless word. A flat-footed word with a shrunken heart. A word increasingly disengaged from its association with the natural world. Urban planners, industrialists, economists, developers use it. It's a lost word, really. A cold word, mechanistic, suited strangely to the coldness generally felt toward Nature. It's their word now. You don't mind giving it up. As for *environmentalist*, that's one that can really bring on the yawns, for you've tamed and tidied it, neutered it quite nicely. An environmentalist must be calm, rational, reasonable, and willing to compromise; otherwise, you won't listen to him. Still, his beliefs are *opinions* only, for this is the age of radical subjectivism. Some people might prefer a Just for Feet store to open space, and they shouldn't be castigated for it. All beliefs and desires and needs are pretty much equally valid. The speculator has just as much right to that open space as the swallow, and the consumer has the most rights of all. Experts and computer models, to say nothing of lawsuits, can hold up environmental checks and reform for decades. The Environmental Protection Agency protects us by finding "acceptable levels of harm" from pollutants and then issuing rules allowing industry to pollute to those levels. Any other approach would place limits on economic growth. Limits on economic growth! What a witchy notion! The EPA can't keep abreast of progress and its unintended consequences. They're drowning in science. Whenever they do lumber into action and ban a weed killer, say (and you do love your weed killers—you particularly hate to see the more popular ones singled out), they have to pay all disposal costs and compensate the manufacturers for the market value of the chemicals they still have in stock.

That seems. . . that seems only fair, you say. Financial loss is a serious matter. And think of the farmers when a particular effective herbicide or pesticide is banned. They could be driven right out of business.

Farmers grow way too much stuff anyway. Federal farm policy, which subsidizes overproduction, encourages bigger and bigger farms and fewer and fewer farmers. The largest farms don't produce food at all, they grow feed. One third of the wheat, three quarters of the corn, and almost all of the soybeans are used for feed. You get cheap hamburgers; the agribusiness moguls get immense profits. Subsidized crops are grown with subsidized water created by turning rivers great and small into a plumbing system of dams and irrigation ditches. Rivers have become conduits. Wetlands are increasingly being referred to as *filtering systems*—things deigned *useful* because of their ability to absorb urban runoff, oil from roads, et cetera.

We know that. We've known that for years about farmers. We know a lot these days. We're very well informed. If farmers aren't allowed to make a profit by growing surplus crops, they'll have to sell their land to developers, who'll turn all that arable land into office parks. Arable land isn't Nature anyway, and besides, we like those office parks and shopping plazas, with their monster supermarkets open twenty-four hours a day and aisle after aisle after aisle of products. It's fun. Products are fun.

FARMERS LIKE THEIR POISONS, but ranchers like them even more. There are well-funded federal programs like the Agriculture Department's "Animal Damage Control Unit," which, responding to public discomfort about its agenda, decided recently to change its name to the euphemistic Wildlife Services. Wildlife Services poisons, shoots, and traps thousands of animals each year. Servicing diligently, it kills bobcats, foxes, black bears, mountain lions, rabbits, badgers, countless birds—all to make this great land safe for the string bean and the corn, the sheep and the cow, even though you're not consuming as much cow these days. A burger now and then, but burgers are hardly cows at all, you feel. They're not all *our* cows, in any case, for some burger matter is imported. There's a bit of Central American burger matter in your bun. Which is contributing to the conversion of tropical rain forest into cow pasture. Even so, you're getting away from meat these days. You're eschewing cow. It's seafood you love, shrimp most of all. And when you love something, it had better watch out, because you have a tendency to love it to death. Shrimp, shrimp, shrimp. It's more common on menus than chicken. In the wilds of Ohio, far, far from watery shores, four out of the six entrees on a menu will be shrimp something-or-other, available, for a modest sum. Everywhere, it's all the shrimp you can eat or all you *care* to eat, for sometimes you just don't feel like eating all you *can.* You are intensively *harvesting* shrimp. Soon there won't be any left, and then you can stop. Shrimpers put out these big nets, and in these nets, for each pound of shrimp, they catch more than ten times that amount of fish, turtles, and dolphins. These, quite the worse for wear, are dumped back in. There is an object called TED (Turtle Excluder Device) that would save thousands of turtles and some dolphins from dying in the net, but shrimpers are loath to use TEDs, as they argue it would cut the size of their shrimp catch.

We've heard about TED, you say.

At Kiawah Island, off the coast of South Carolina, visitors go out on Jeep "safaris" through the part of the island that hasn't been developed yet. ("Wherever you see trees," the guide says, "it's actually a lot.") The visitors (i.e., potential buyers) drive their own Jeeps, and the guide talks to them by radio. Kiawah has nice beaches, and the guide talks about turtles. When he mentions the shrimpers' role in the decline of the turtle, the shrimpers, who share the same frequency, scream at him. Shrimpers and most commercial fishermen (many of them working with drift and gill nets anywhere from six to thirty miles long) think of themselves as an *endangered species*. A recent newspaper headline said, "SHRIMPERS SPARED ANTI-TURTLE DEVICES." Even so, with the continuing wanton depletion of shrimp beds, they will undoubtedly have to find some other means of employment soon. They might, for instance, become part of that vast throng laboring in the *tourist industry*.

TOURISM HAS BECOME AN INDUSTRY as destructive as any other. You are no longer benign in traveling somewhere to look at the scenery. You never thought there was much gain in just looking anyway; you've always preferred to *use* the scenery in some manner. In your desire to get away from what you've got, you've caused there to be no place to get away *to*. You're just all bumpered up out there. Sewage and dumps have become prime indicators of America's lifestyle. In resort towns in New England and the Adirondacks, measuring the flow into the sewage plants serves as a business barometer. Tourism is a growth industry. You believe in growth. *Controlled growth*, of course. Controlled exponential growth is what you'd really like to see. You certainly don't want to put a moratorium or a cap on anything. That's illegal, isn't it? Retro you're not. You don't want to go back or anything. Forward. Maybe ask directions later. Growth is *desirable* as well as being *inevitable*. Growth is the one thing you seem to be powerless before, so you try to be realistic about it. Growth—it's weird—it's like cancer or something.

As a tourist you have long ago discovered your national parks and are quickly *overburdening* them. All that spare land, and it belongs to you! It's exotic land too, not looking like all the stuff around it that looks like everything else. You want to take advantage of this land, of course, and use it in every way you can. Thus the managers—or *stewards,* as they like to be called—have developed *wise* and *multiple-use* plans, keeping in mind exploiters' interests (for they have their needs, too), as well as the desires of the backpackers. Thus mining, timbering, and ranching activities take place in the national forest, where the Forest Service maintains a system of logging roads eight times greater than the interstate highway system. Snowmobilers demand that their trails be *groomed.* The national parks are more of a public playground and are becoming increasingly Europeanized in their look and management. Lots of concessions and motels. Paths paved to accommodate strollers. You deserve a clean bed and a hot meal when you go into the wilderness. At least, your stewards think that you do. You keep your stewards busy. Not only must they cater to your multiple and conflicting desires, they have to manage your wildlife *resources.* They have managed wildfowl to such an extent that, the reasoning has become, if it weren't for hunters, ducks would disappear. Duck stamps and licensing fees support the whole rickety duck management system. Yes! If it weren't for the people who kill them, wild ducks wouldn't exist! Many a manager believes that better wildlife *protection* is provided when wildlife is allowed to be shot. Conservation commissions can only oversee hunting when hunting is allowed. But wild creatures are managed in other ways as well. Managers track and tape and tag and band. They relocate, restock, and reintroduce. They cull and control. It's hard to keep it straight. Protect or poison? Extirpate or just mostly eliminate? Sometimes even the stewards get mixed up.

THIS IS THE TIME OF MACHINES and models, hands-on management and master plans. Don't you ever wonder as you pass that billboard advertising another MASTER PLANNED COMMUNITY just what master they are actually talking about? Not the Big Master, certainly. Something brought to you by one of the tiny masters, of which there are many. But you like these tiny masters and have even come to expect and require them. In Florida they're well into building a ten-thousand-acre city in the Everglades. It's a *megaproject,* one of the largest ever in the state. Yes, they must have thought you wanted it. No, what you thought of as the Everglades, the park, is only a little bitty part of the Everglades. Developers have been gnawing at this irreplaceable, strange land for years. It's like they just hate this ancient sea of grass. Maybe you could ask them about this sometime. Every tree and bush and inch of sidewalk in the project has been planned, of course. Nevertheless, because the whole thing will take twenty-five years to complete, the plan is going to be constantly changed. You can understand this. The important thing is that there be a blueprint. You trust a blueprint. The tiny masters know what you like. You like a *secure landscape* and *access to services.* You like grass—that is, lawns. The ultimate lawn is the golf course, which you've been told has "some ecological value." You believe this! Not that it really matters—you just like to play golf. These golf courses require a lot of watering. So much that the more inspired of the masters have taken to watering them with effluent, *treated* effluent, but yours, from all the condos and villas built around the stocked artificial lakes you fancy.

I really don't want to think about sewage, you say, but it sounds like progress.

It is true that the masters are struggling with the problems of your incessant flushing. Cuisine is also one of their concerns. Great advances have been made in sorbets—sorbet intermezzos—in their clubs and fine restaurants. They know what you want. You want A HAVEN FROM THE ORDINARY WORLD. If you're a NATURE LOVER in the West, you want to live in a WILD ANIMAL HABITAT. If you're eastern and consider yourself more hip, you want to live in a new town—a brand-new reconstructed-from-scratch town—in a house of NINETEENTH-CENTURY DESIGN. But in these new towns the masters are building, getting around can be confusing. There is an abundance of curves and an infrequency of through streets. It's the new wilderness without any trees. You can get lost, even with all the "mental bread crumbs" the masters scatter about as visual landmarks—the windmill, the water views, the various group-ings of landscape "material." You *are* lost, you know. But you trust a

Realtor will show you the way. There are many more Realtors than tiny masters, and many of them have to make do with less than a loaf—that is, trying to sell stuff that's already been built in an environment already "enhanced" rather than something being planned—but they're everywhere, willing to show you the path. If Dante returned to Hell today, he'd probably be escorted down by a Realtor talking all the while about how it was just another level of Paradise.

WHEN HAVE YOU LAST WATCHED A SUNSET? *Do you remember where you were? With whom? At Loews Ventana Canyon Resort, the Grand Foyer will provide you with that opportunity through lighting that is computerized to diminish with the approaching sunset!*

THE TINY MASTERS are willing to arrange Nature for you. They will compose it into a picture that you can look at at your leisure, when you're not doing work or something like that. Nature becomes scenery, a prop. At some golf courses in the Southwest, the saguaro cactuses are reported to be repaired with green paste when balls blast into their skin. The saguaro can attempt to heal themselves by growing over the balls, but this takes time, and the effect can be somewhat...baroque. It's better to get out the pastepot. Nature has become simply a visual form of entertainment, and it had better look snappy.

Listen, you say, we've been at Ventana Canyon. It's in the desert, right? It's very, very nice, a world-class resort. A totally self-contained environment with everything that a person could possibly want, on more than a thousand acres in the middle of zip. It sprawls but nestles, like. And they've maintained the integrity of as much of the desert ecosystem as possible. Give them credit for that. Great restaurant, too. We had baby bay scallops there. Coming into the lobby there are these two big hand-carved coyotes, mutely howling And that's the way we like them, mute. God, why do those things howl like that?

Wildlife is a personal matter, you think. The attitude is up to you. You can prefer to see it dead or not dead. You might want to let it mosey about its business or blow it away. Wild things exist only if you have the graciousness to allow them to. Just outside Tucson, Arizona, there is a structure modeled after a French foreign legion outpost. It's the *International Wildlife Museum*, and it's full of dead animals. Three hundred species are there, at least a third of them—the rarest ones—killed and collected by one C. J. McElroy, who enjoyed doing it and now shares what's left with you. The museum claims to be educational because you can watch a taxidermist at work or touch a lion's tooth. You can get real close to these dead animals, closer than you can in a zoo. Some of you prefer zoos, however, which are becoming bigger, better, and bioclimatic. New-age zoo designers want the animals to *flow right out into your space*. In Dallas there's a Wilds of Africa exhibit; in San Diego there's a simulated rain forest, where you can thread your way "down the side of a lush canyon, the air filled with a fine mist from 300 high-pressure nozzles . . ."; in New Orleans you've constructed a swamp, the real swamp not far away being on the verge of disappearing. Animals in these places are abstractions—wandering relics of their true selves, but that doesn't matter. Animal behavior in a zoo is nothing like natural behavior, but that doesn't matter, either. Zoos are pretty, contained, and accessible. These new habitats can contain one hundred different species—not more than one or two of each thing, of course—on seven acres, three, one. You don't want to see *too much* of anything, certainly. An *example* will suffice. Sort of like a biological Crabtree & Evelyn basket selected with *you* in mind. You like things reduced, simplified. It's easier to take it all in, park it in your mind. You like things inside better than outside anyway. You are increasingly looking at and living in proxy environments created by substitution and simulation. Resource economists are a wee branch in the tree of tiny masters, and one, Martin Krieger, wrote, "Artificial prairies and wildernesses have been created, and there is no reason to believe that these artificial environments need be unsatisfactory for those who experience them. . . We will have to realize that the way in which we experience nature is conditioned by our society—which more and more is seen to be receptive to responsible intervention."

FIDDLE, FIDDLE, FIDDLE. You support fiddling, as well as meddling. This is how you learn. Though it's quite apparent that the environment has been grossly polluted and the natural world abused and defiled, you seem to prefer to continue pondering effects rather than preventing causes. You want proof, you insist on proof. A Dr. Lave from Carnegie-Mellon—and he's an expert, an economist and an environmental *expert*—says that scientists will have to prove to you that you will suffer if you don't become less of a "throw-away society." *If you really want me to give up my car or my air conditioner, you'd better prove to me first that the earth would otherwise be uninhabitable*, Dr. Lave says. *Me is you,* I presume, whereas *you* refers to them. You as in me—that is, *me, me, me*—certainly strike a hard bargain. Uninhabitable the world has to get before you reign in your requirements. You're a consumer after all, *the* consumer upon whom so much attention is lavished, the ultimate user of a commodity that has become, these days, everything. To try to appease your appetite for proof, for example, scientists have been leasing for experimentation forty-six pristine lakes in Canada.

They don't want to *keep* them, they just want to *borrow* them.

They've been intentionally contaminating many of the lakes with a variety of pollutants dribbled into the propeller wash of research boats. It's *one of the boldest experiments in lake ecology ever conducted*. They've turned these remote lakes into huge *real-world test tubes*. They've been doing this since 1976! And what; they've found so far in these *preliminary* studies is that pollutants are really destructive. The lakes get gross. Life in them ceases. It took about eight years to make this happen in one of them, everything carefully measured and controlled all the while. Now the scientists are slowly reversing the process. But it will take hundreds of years for the lakes to recover. They think.

REMEMBER WHEN YOU USED TO LIKE RAIN, the sound of it, the feel of it, the way it made the plants and trees all glisten? We needed that rain, you would say. It looked pretty too, you thought, particularly in the movies. Now it rains and you go, Oh-oh. A nice walloping rain these days means *overtaxing our sewage treatment plants*. It means *untreated waste discharged directly into our waterways*. It means . . .

Okay. Okay.

Acid rain! And we all know what this is. Or most of us do. People of power in government and industry still don't seem to know what it is. Whatever it is, they say, they don't want to curb it, but they're willing to study it some more. Economists call air and water pollution "externalities" anyway. Oh, acid rain. You do get so sick of hearing about it. The words have already become a white-noise kind of thing. But you think in terms of *mitigating* it maybe. As for the *greenhouse effect*, you think in terms of *countering* that. One way that's been discussed is the planting of new forests, not for the sake of the forests alone, oh my heavens, no. Not for the sake of majesty and mystery or of Thumper and Bambi, are you kidding me, but because, as every schoolchild knows, trees absorb carbon dioxide. They just soak it up and store it. They just love it. So this is the plan: you can plant millions of acres of trees, and you go on doing pretty much whatever you're doing—driving around, using staggering amounts of energy, keeping those power plants fired to the max. Isn't Nature remarkable? So willing to serve? You wouldn't think it had anything more to offer, but it seems it does. Of course, these "forests" wouldn't exactly be forests. They would be more like trees. *Managed* trees. The Forest Service, which now manages our forests by cutting them down, might be called upon to evolve in its thinking and allow these trees to grow. They would probably be patented trees after a time. Fast-growing, uniform, genetically created toxin-eating *machines*. They would be *new-age* trees, because the problem with planting the old-fashioned variety to *combat* the greenhouse effect, which is caused by pollution, is that they're already dying from it. All along the crest of the Appalachians from Maine to Georgia, forests struggle to survive in a toxic soup of poisons. They can't *help* us if we've killed them, now can they?

ALL RIGHT, you say, *wow, lighten up, will you? Relax. Tell about yourself.*

Well, I say, I live in Florida . . .

Oh my god, you say. Florida! Florida is a joke! How do you expect us to take you seriously if you still live there! Florida is crazy, it's pink concrete. It's paved, it's over. And a little girl just got eaten by an alligator down there. It came out of some swamp next to a subdivision and carried her off. That set your Endangered Species Act back fifty years, you can bet.

I . . .

Listen, we don't want to hear any more about Florida. We don't want to hear about Phoenix or California's Central Valley. If our wetlands—our vanishing wetlands—are mentioned one more time, we'll scream. And the talk about condors and grizzlies and wolves is becoming too de trop. *We had just managed to get whales out of our minds. Now there are butterflies, frogs even that you want us to worry about. And those manatees. Don't they know what a boat propeller can do to them by now? They're not too smart. And those last condors are pathetic. Can't we just get this over with?*

Aristotle said that all living beings are ensouled and strive to participate in eternity.

Oh, I just bet he said that, you say. That doesn't sound like Aristotle. He was a humanist. We're all humanists here. This is the age of humanism. Militant humanism. And it has been for a long time.

YOU ARE DRIVING WITH A STRANGER in the car, and it is the stranger who is behind the wheel. In the backseat are your pals for many years now—DO WHAT YOU LIKE and his swilling sidekick, WHY NOT. A deer, or some emblematic animal—something from that myriad natural world you've come from that you now treat with such indifference and scorn—steps from the dimming woods and tentatively upon the highway. The stranger does not decelerate or brake, not yet, maybe not at all. The feeling is that whatever it is *will get out of the way.* Oh, it's a fine car you've got, a fine machine, and oddly you don't mind the stranger driving it, because in a way, everything has gotten too complicated, way, way out of your control. You've given the wheel to the masters, the managers, the comptrollers. Something is wrong, *maybe,* you feel, a little sick, *actu-*

ally, but the car is luxurious and fast and you're *moving*, which is the most important thing by far.

Why make a fuss when you're so comfortable? Don't make a fuss, make a baby. Go out and get something to eat, build something. Make *another* baby. Babies are cute. Babies show you have faith in the future. Although faith is perhaps too strong a word. They're everywhere these days; in all the crowds and traffic jams, there are the babies too. You don't seem to associate them with the problems of population increase. They're just babies! And you've come to believe in them again. They're a lot more tangible than the afterlife, which, of course, you haven't believed in in ages. At least not for yourself. The afterlife now belongs to plastics and poisons. Yes, plastics and poisons will have a far more extensive afterlife than you, that's known. A disposable diaper, for example, which is all plastic anal wood pulp, will take around four centuries to degrade. But you like disposables—so easy to use and toss—and now that marketing is urging you not to rush the potty training by making diapers for four-year-olds available and socially acceptable, there will be more and more dumped diapers around, each taking, like most plastics, centuries and centuries to deteriorate. In the sea, many marine animals die from ingesting or being entangled in discarded plastic. In the dumps, plastic squats on more than 25 percent of dump space. But your heart is disposed toward plastic. Someone, no doubt the plastics industry, told you it was convenient. This same industry avidly promotes recycling in an attempt to get the critics of their nefarious, multifarious products off their backs. That should make you feel better, because *recycling* has become an honorable word, no longer merely the hobby of Volvo owners. The fact is that people in plastics are born obscurants. Recycling won't solve the plastic glut, only reduction of production will, and the plastics industry isn't looking into that, you can be sure. Waste is not just the stuff you throw away, of course, it's also the stuff you use to excess. With the exception of *hazardous waste*, which you do worry about from time to time, it's even thought that you have a declining sense of emergency about the problem. Builders are building bigger houses because you want bigger. You're trading up. Utility companies are beginning to worry about your constantly rising consumption. Utility companies! You haven't entered a new age at all but one of upscale nihilism, deluxe nihilism.

With each election there is the possibility that the environment will become a political issue. But it never does. You don't want it to be, preferring instead to continue in your politics of subsidizing and advancing avarice. The issues are the same as always—jobs, defense, the economy the economy the economy, maintaining the standard of living in this greedy, selfish, expansionistic, industrialized society.

You're getting a little shrill here, you say.

You're pretty well off. And you expect to become even better off. You do. What does this mean? More software, more scampi, more square footage, more communication towers to keep you in touch and amused and informed? You want to count birds? Go to the bases of communication towers being built all across the country. Three million migratory songbirds perish each year by slamming into towers and their attendant guy wires. The building of thousands of new digital television towers one thousand feet and taller is being expedited by the FCC, which proposes to preempt all local and state environmental laws. You have created an ecological crisis. The earth is infinitely variable and alive, and you are moderating it, simplifying it, killing it. It seems safer this way. But you are not safe. You want to find wholeness and happiness in a land increasingly damaged and betrayed, and you never will. More than material matters. You must change your ways.

What is this? Sinners in the Hands of an Angry God?

The ecological crisis cannot be resolved by politics. It cannot be resolved by science or technology. It is a crisis caused by culture and character, and a deep change in personal consciousness is needed. Your fundamental attitudes toward the earth have become twisted. You have made only brutal contact with Nature; you cannot comprehend its grace. You must change. Have few desires and simple pleasures. Honor nonhuman life. Control yourself, become more authentic. Live lightly upon the earth and treat it with respect. Redefine the word *progress* and dismiss the managers and masters. Grow inwardly and with knowledge become truly wiser. Think differently, behave differently. For this is essentially a moral issue we face, and moral decisions must be made.

A moral issue! *Okay, this discussion is now over. A moral issue . . . And who's this we now? Who are you, is what I'd like to know. You're not me, anyway. I admit someone's to blame and something should be done. But I've got to go. It's getting late. Take care of yourself.*

Die, Baby Harp Seal!

LYDIA MILLET

I'M GAZING WISTFULLY at a towering red rock butte bathed in gentle sunset light, shades of brown to violet framed against a meek background of sky. It's massive but tame, brooding but well mannered, broad shouldered but shy. Its silence is nothing short of submissive. ·

In short, it's the January pinup in the Nature Conservancy's calendar. Environmental organizations and independent entrepreneurs yearly churn out glossy wall charts and engagement books for the consumption of nature-loving citizens like myself—grizzly cubs from TNC are on the menu, for instance; spotted dolphins and two albatrosses with their beaks interlocked from the Sierra Club; and from Audubon a polar bear perched with all four paws together like a performing bear in a circus, as well as a mother and baby baboon and mother and baby koala, perfectly groomed, hugging each other cutely and looking straight at the camera with big, dark, inviting pools of eyes.

As I flip through these adorable menageries I'm reminded of nothing so much as my twenty-something days working for slaves' wages as a copy editor at *Hustler* magazine. I'm reminded of models named Tammi and Lynda, buck naked and intertwined, long tresses artfully arranged to frame obscenely augmented breasts, who also hugged each other—though not so cutely—and looked straight at the camera with big, dark, inviting pools of eyes.

Sometimes, as copy editor, I had to pen what are called girl tags: lines of loopy, babyish script, ostensibly the models' own, scrawled over their Coppertone-silicone bodies in a vacuous and beckoning voice. In a leopardskin-clad jungle-themed photoset, *Prrr... yours to maul. Luv xxx Tammi.*

At first glance a girl-girl spread in *Hustler* has little in common with a twin-albatross picture in an Audubon engagement calendar. For one thing, the latter doesn't sell on newsstands in a brown wrapper. But both are clearly porn. They offer to the viewer the illusions of control, ownership, and subjugation; they tell us to take comfort: they will always be there, ideal, unblemished, available. They offer gratification without social cost, satiate by providing objects for fantasy without making uncomfortable demands on the subject.

The landscape photographs featured in the calendars may not play quite as facilely on the heartstrings of the average American wildlife consumer as baby animals, but they too are blatantly pornographic. We see the Grand Canyon, cliffs lit orange, with snow in the foreground; we see a fuchsia fog unrolling endlessly over Ross Lake in the northern Cascades under a golden sky; we see an emerald green pool surrounded by red rock in Havasu Canyon. In a daybook called *Heaven on Earth*, we see lush trees, river scenes, and rolling green landscapes with pithy pastoral proverbs accompanying each image.

This is picture-book nature, scenic and sublime, praiseworthy but not battleworthy: Tarted up into perfectly circumscribed simulations of the wild, these props of mainstream environmentalism serve as surrogates for real engagement with wilderness the way porn models serve as surrogates for real women. They are a voyeur's vice, a Utopian habit, placebos substituting for triage.

To add insult to injury, they don't even get us off. At least *Hustler* is reliable: it offers an aesthetic that changes (albeit marginally) with the times, faithfully fulfilling its monthly function as a stroke rag for, among others, tens of thousands of irritable prison inmates.

But nature calendars rely on a hackneyed canon of evocations that no longer serves a purpose. Their girlish good looks have aged poorly. At best they elicit a regretful nostalgia for a never-known past of unspoiled landscapes; at worst they reassure us disingenuously that the last great places are safe and sound.

They go largely unnoticed as they drop through the mail slot; even hanging on the wall in office carrels or beside foyer telephones they're nothing more than cheap wallpaper. And yet they reveal a broad truth about the environmental movement: it has failed to generate a compelling language for itself. Its propaganda falls flat, its style is outdated, its rhetoric is stale. It needs to be reborn.

A straight line can be drawn between the complacent prettiness of the conservation aesthetic and the vaguely Dutch, vaguely golf-course universe lived in by the BBC's *Teletubbies*, complete with fake flowers and fuzzy bunnies hopping to and fro, which is apparently serving as a fair approximation of nature for a new generation of infants. What the natural world actually looks like these days is neither airbrush nor pastorale. It's more like *120 Days of Sodom*.

To a generation that feeds on novelty and violence, whose cinema and videogames and TV are a hopped-up, full-frontal assault of jump cuts and dizzying Handicam movement, whose music is amphetamine driven and whose news is always already bad, the environmental movement pathetically and stubbornly offers up static postcards of hillsides and lakes. It whines on about moral virtue like a sad minister in a derelict Episcopalian church, preaching resignedly to a congregation of Sunday drivers and aging hippies.

So what's next? Next is all or nothing—either a critical facelift for environmentalism or a long slow slide into obsolescence. Medium-as-message is the message: a soft aesthetic produces soft results. So-called "radical" environmentalists and little-read deep ecologists hark to our "duty" to preserve and caretake nature, poignantly calling for a profound paradigm shift that will allow the human race to see beyond its own wants, needs, and foibles to a Higher Love—quite a tall order for people who can't decide whether to use paper or plastic.

If we acknowledge the unlikelihood of such a shift coming about just because we asked for it, we're left with two options. We can throw up our hands in despair or we can jump into the fray. We can do, in fact, what the far right has done so well since the advent of Reagan: find base and selfish selling points for our product. Make people afraid not to buy.

Wilderness and biodiversity conservation in the twenty-first century will mean national security, food security, atmospheric security, in short survival; environmentalists have a powerful product and the onus is on them to use powerful tools for the sale.

But of course, doomsaying is not the ticket. At least, not the brand of doomsaying we've seen in the past, which reminds the unconvinced of nothing so much as a nagging and petulant wife or a disgruntled fringe. Rather, environmental advertising has to define a new style for itself—a style with unapologetic momentum, a hardball-playing, fast-moving engagement with the realities of anthropogenic devastation that doesn't shrink from the rude, the vicious, or the unsightly. Think of Richard Misrach's stunning photography book *Violent Legacies*, which features desecrated toxic landscapes rendered lovely by tragedy and good composition. Consider the gentler and colder work of Lee Friedlander in *The Desert Seen*, which sacrifices touristic prettiness for a near clinical complexity, or the photography of Lynn Davis in *Wonders of the African World*, the companion book to the Henry Louis Gates PBS series, which shows us that an arid landscape and pre-industrial architecture, the natural and the contrived, may be similarly formal expressions of a dignity elicited by the desert's rigors.

In pop culture, where music is loud, movies have turned into souped-up rollercoaster rides with only the vaguest of nods toward antiquated props like character and meaning, and video games hurtle players through extreme landscapes at breakneck speeds, perpetrating violence as they go, there's no time for stately, quiet glimpses of scenic far-off fjords. David O. Russell's *Three Kings*, for instance, is a testosterone-driven party with a visual style gleaned from color Xerox, night-vision goggles, and MTV that climaxes with a deliberately sympathetic Iraqi torturer cramming crude oil down Marky Mark's all-American throat—a gritty, glamorous assault that successfully wreaks destruction on the propaganda myth of Desert Storm.

Our legacy is not the landscapes nature gave us, the voluptuous tropics or the lofty peaks of the Himalayas; these were the gifts we found waiting when we got up on Christmas morning. Our legacy is the wrapping paper we left crumpled and scattered around the house, the old, bare trees we abandoned later on the sidewalk. These are the aesthetic forms we have made all by ourselves—the forms that speak to us of what we have done and what we stand to do. What environmentalism needs is not a well-meaning posse of smiling grannies handing out Hallmark cards in the mall, but the guts to assault us with the impacts of our own desires.

Letters

EDWARD ABBEY

Edward Abbey was born in Home, Pennsylvania, in 1927. As a young man, he discovered the American Southwest on a memorable if ill-conceived hitchhiking trip around the country. After a stint in the US Army—he saw a bit of the world—and earning a master's degree in philosophy at the University of New Mexico, Abbey built a career as a novelist. In his twenties and thirties, Abbey bankrolled his writing with stints as a fire lookout and park ranger. In later years, he refused to allow his first novel, Jonathan Troy, *to be republished. *Troy *is a clumsy Bildingsroman about a lust-dazed young man who is chronically angry at his deer-poaching card sharp Appalachian father. Abbey became one of America's foremost novelists dealing with ideas of freedom, nature, and the frontier.* The Brave Cowboy, *Abbey's postmodern Western, was made into a film starring Kirk Douglas; Douglas has said that* The Brave Cowboy *is his favorite of the many films he's starred in.* The Monkey Wrench Gang *was the most successful, artistically and commercially, of several books about ecosabotage written in the 1970s, including novels by revered authors Jim Harrison and William Eastlake. Perhaps because of its controversial endorsement of what Abbey called nachtwerk,* The Monkey Wrench Gang *has yet to be filmed. Abbey's book,* Desert Solitaire, *continues to have iconic status. Abbey's many novels and essay collections remain in print.*

Abbey was married five times, fathered four children, and died in March of 1989.

He made peace with many of his demons, but never sold out.

This is apparently a form letter Abbey kept on file to send to recipients he deemed appropriate, including novelist Tom McGuane.

THE REVEREND EDWIN P. ABBOTT, JR.
Christ-of-the-Rocks Rescue Mission
Box 628
Oracle, Arizona 85623

Perhaps you have heard of me and my nationwide campaign in the cause of temperance. Each year, for the past fourteen years, I have made a tour of Arizona, Colorado, Utah, Nevada and Texas and have delivered a series of lectures on the evils of drinking.

'On this tour I have been accompanied by my young friend and assistant, Clyde Lindstone. Clyde, a young man of good family and excellent background, was a pathetic example of a life ruined by excessive indulgence in whisky and women.

Clyde would appear with me at the lectures and sit on the platform, wheezing and staring at the audience through bleary, bloodshot eyes, sweating profusely, picking his nose, passing gas, and making obscene gestures to the ladies present, while I would point him out as a perfect example of what over-indulgence can do to a good man.

Last fall, unfortunately, Clyde died.

A mutual acquaintance, Dr. Stan Silverman, has given me your name and suggested that you may be seeking employment in the near future. I wonder if you would be available to take Clyde's place in my forthcoming lecture tour?

Yours in faith,

Rev. Edwin P. Abbott
EPA/wn

It is unclear how many responses Abbey received as a result of his recruitment effort, but McGuane was one who responded enthusiastically. However, Abbey and McGuane's letters seem to have crossed in the mail.

Jan 82

Dear Tom,
I see by the papers that you have definitely decided that Montana will be your new home. I'm glad to hear that. Welcome to the West.

Maybe now you'll help us try to save what's left of it. And I dont mean just write about it, that's already been done, many times over, but actually get down off the fence and join in the fight. We need the help.

Dont worry so much about getting depressed. Once you get involved in a real fight, something serious and important and therefore <u>interesting</u>, your existential angsts will drop away like old wives and girl friends. You wont need your hobbies anymore. The only depressing thing I see are those people with time and money and talent who tell us how much they love the West but won't lend a hand to help defend it.

What's more, if you join us, you'll meet the best people. Like me. Like Doug Peacock and Bruce Hamilton and Ed Dobson and Howie Wolke and Dave Foreman, and many others; once you get to know them, real outdoorsmen, you'll realize how dreary and mean and trivial those Hollywood coke-sniffers and rodeo cowboys are—them <u>Marlboro</u> types. (Their main passion is really real estate.)

You know I admire your novels very much. All four of them. I think you are one of the half dozen or so best fiction writers now working in these U.S. I like your style and wit. But your heroes are too short. I mean, self-obsessed. What they need, it finally occurs to me, is something to <u>do</u>. They are dying of too much money, education, leisure and boredom. They need some work—man's work.

Indolence leads to melancholy, as Sam Johnson pointed out. And Burton and Shakespeare and Ecclesiastes et al.

Of course your main job is writing novels. I sympathize with that. But in your spare time, you know, between typewriters, you might—lend a hand. Grab a-hold. We need all the help we can get. I know you'll enjoy this kindly advice from your older brother.

Ed

18 Feb 1982

Dear Ed,

A warm and hearty no-thanks to your invitation to join your no-frills moral paradise, the West. It's still too operatic for me.

As to you "those who love the West but", you got the wrong Joe.

I don't love it. And like the man said, I got a wife, ten kids and a monkey on my back.

I hope you get a nice tan.

Tom

Tom McGuane
Rte. 38
Livingston, MT. 59047

PS: You write good, Eddy. Don't throw your talent away on virtue.

March 5, 82

Dear Tom,

Can't blame you for getting mad: nobody likes to be smoked out of his hole in the middle of February. But when did I ever accuse you of "loving" the West? I was merely suggesting, in my discreet and subtle way, that if youre gonna make a home out here you might be interested in helping to protect your own home (for chrissake!) from all those eastern and midwestern relatives of yours who want to flood you out or stripmine you or radiate you or smother you w/smog etc.

Passive non-resistance will get you nothing. "Westerners" like that are no better, in my eyes, than common tourists. Or worse: like ticks on a dog, ornamental but dysfunctional. Or as my neighbor Joe McKearny says (he's a mining engineer), "useless as tits on a motor."

Oh, well. Nobody's perfect. Look at me: though born and raised on a submarginal Appalachian farm, and though I've spent most of my life in the rural West, I have never yet—not once!— fallen in love with a horse.

Either end.

And if you really don't "care about the country" (I don't believe you), than where to next? Oahu? Take up surfing? O'Neil space capsule? Zero-gravity masturbation? Etc?

Yours fraternally,

Ed Abbey

Oracle, Arizona

8 March 1982

Dear Rev,

Thank you for the invite. Clyde is right down my alley. I knew if I waited long enough, you would think of something for which I had some talent.

I tell you, boy, it's sure nice here, even to an old snake oiler like me. Hot spring sun on white snow. Evergreens giving up their balsamic ghosts.... Even enlightened people like you and Clyde couldn't ruin a day like mine. I ate a whole bowl of iron crosses and stared at my checkbook. Springtime in the North Rockies, a Cordilleran idyll.

Stay in touch now. We're letting the tourists empty their saddle tanks in the garden this summer. Beats settling ponds, grows big tomatoes and shows real hope of making The Whole Earth Catalog.

Ed: just got your post-Clyde letter, somewhat in response to mine. Of course you're right about the place, and I feel the same. Don't know exactly what to do about it. As to my relatives coming out here, they all drank themselves to death. Besides they were genial slum Irish, in all respects preferable to the tonguetied simian local here in the West. As you may guess, I think the joint is wasted on white people anyway, rather like when they gave Spotted Tail's people over to the Episcopalians of Nebraska. I'd love to think of something though, so long as it didn't put me with Kounterkulture types or, in fact, the illuminati of the eco movement; in my opinion, they let the air out of things without moving the ball down the field.

All best,

Tom

Tom McGuane

Today Desert Solitaire *is one of the most loved books in America. But in the late 1960s, Abbey had to hustle to get it published in paperback. This letter documents the beginning of Abbey's long association with book editor Jack Macrae. He also seems to have taken an interest in publicity, especially when the publicist assigned to his book was female.*

June 23, 1969

Mr John Macrae III
E.P. Dutton & Co Inc
201 Park Avenue South
New York, NY 10003

Dear Mr Macrae:
Thank you for your letter of June 17th.

I am naturally pleased and honored that you should ask me to write another book on the subject of wilderness preservation, industrial tourism, and the general triumph of the yahoos. However, I feel that I have said most of what I want to say on these matters in the book DESERT SOLITAIRE. I am not a professional in any field of social or natural science and anything that I might propose could only be more or less a rehash of what I have already stated in the role of concerned amateur and onlooker. I lack expert knowledge; in fact I am an ignorant man.

What I should like to propose to you is a paperback edition of DESERT SOLITAIRE. The response to that book, although it hasn't sold very well, has been highly gratifying. Most of those who have read it seem to like it very much; and a few—even more satisfying to me—have detested it heartily. But it seems to me that the book has reached only a part of the audience it was meant for— mainly older people already interested in conservation questions. I had hoped to reach a different group, the college-age militants with whose aims and activities I am in deep sympathy, in an effort to close the gap that now exists between conservationists on the one hand and political activists on the other. It seems to me that the two groups should be allies, since our basic goals and our basic enemies are the same, e.g., the people now busily engaged in poisoning the forests and farmlands of Vietnam are the same or closely connected with the people whose business it is to complete the pollution of our environment here in the States. Anyway, I think that a paperback edition of DESERT SOLITAIRE, perhaps with some revisions and additions, available in college bookstores, might help establish contacts between the wilderness preservers and the war-resisters.

Thanks again for writing to me.

Yours truly,

Edward Abbey
North Rim
Arizona 86022

Oct. 3, 1975

Dear Dianita:

Idea: next time you write up an ad for MONKEY WRENCH (or any other book for that matter) it seems to me that it might be useful, make the ad more interesting, if you juxtapose the con with the pro. Rather than attempt to overwhelm the reader with a sea of encomia carefully culled from selected reviews, tease his/her mind (if any) with paired-off praise and censure. E.g., though I no longer have the reviews on hand, I think I remember one writer comparing the end of MWG to "a cheap Hollywood trick"; another calls the attempts at humor "flat and arch"; another speaks of the style as "swollen with verbiose verbiage"; and one says of my mild sex scenes that they are "the least arousing since Lord Wimsey's honeymoon". Etc etc. This is great stuff, and if counterposed to opposite opinions might well titivate the biblio-freak's skeptical curiosity.

Incidentally, though I know his intentions were good and I am grateful for his interest, I cannot forgive our friend John Baker of PW for making me talk like an Englishman in that so-called interview. No matter how drunk or incoherent I may actually have been, I know that I do not—never could—talk like an Englishman.

Do all his interviewees talk like Englishmen? Perhaps—and no doubt I should regard it as an intended compliment.

Well, what the phukk, gotta get back to work now. Am typing up a piece on "life in a Lookout Tower" for Audubon while postponing as long as possible the dread moment in which I must somehow resume work on the novel which, for seven years now (and they have been <u>very</u> kind and forbearing), I have owed to your colleagues McGraw and Hill.

Good luck with <u>our</u> book.

Yrs,

Edward Abbey

Box 66
Moab, Utah

Abbey corresponded with Edward Hoagland, author of Walking the Dead Diamond River *and other nature books. But eventually their friendship turned fractious, at least on Abbey's side. Hoagland, who teaches at Bennington College, was just a bit too . . . Eastern.*

Box 66
Moab Utah

April 16, 76

Dear Ted,

Thanks for your letter. I presume you've just returned from Africa and that we'll read all about it in the next book. I hope so. Me, I'm on my way to Australia in two weeks: will spend a month or so there exploring the desert interior (for the Geographic), then on to Calcutta, Bombay, Tehran, Athens etc etc for a rather hasty return to the States. Got to be back in Utah in time for the fall watermelon festival, rodeos, roundups and alfalfa harvest. Will stop off in NYC in August and look for you.

I am grateful for your attempts to find out what happened to my Monkey Wrench book in New York. Actually, I'd gotten over my bitterness about it and pretty well forgotten the whole mysterious business—until your letter. Now all my exasperations have revived and I am outraged all over again.

The Monkey Wrench book, nation-wide, did very well compared to anything else I've ever had published. It's sold more copies in six months than the Desert Solitaire book (my only other "popular" production) has sold in eight years, got five times more reviews (mostly favorable), and resulted in more letters decent and indecent, friendly and hateful than I care to try to answer anymore.

But in New York itself (the big puddle?) there were no reviews at all, unless you count Newsweek as a NYC publication. I don't. Even the Sunday Times failed or declined to have it reviewed and that I find absolutely inexplicable, unjust and unfair. And am still mighty pissed about it, now that youve reminded me. I don't care if they dont like the book, they should have the guts to say so and say <u>why</u> they don't like it, rather than try to bury it alive.

Oh well, what the hell. There's still the inner satisfaction. Of all the books I've composed so far, two give me that sensation Nabokov calls "aesthetic bliss", the feeling that I've finally done something right, and one of those two is The Monkey Wrench Gang and the other is Black Sun. The rest is juvenilia and journalism (though not without art, I hope). So to hell with the New York book reviewing crowd. I can survive without them. Except for your generous plug in the Sunday Times several years ago, none of them ever were any help to me anyhow.

As for frogs and puddles, who can say? That is a matter of perspective. Except for the publishing industry, New York City appears from here as a small and waning force in American culture. I feel that the real battle to determine the character of America's future (if any) will take place west of the Mississippi. I certainly do not feel isolated from your "red hot center"—quite the contrary. The West is now the scene of what may be seen decades from now as epic struggles, of which the Kaiparowits affair is merely one minor skirmish. (Our greatest negative victory so far though—we had an epic celebration in Salt Lake City a couple of nights ago.) If I really wanted peace and quiet in my life I'd go home to Pennsylvania—or back to Hoboken or Brooklyn. I always felt, living in those places, that things were pretty well shaken down and settled; that in fact there was really nothing very interesting going on, that the dominant emotional atmosphere is one of cynical hopelessness, humorous resignation. The <u>European</u> phase in the maturing and decay of America. No doubt it will eventually creep over the West as well.

But not while I'm around.

To belabor this subject a bit further, I wonder if there even really is such a thing as a "red-hot center" in American literary life? When I try to think of the contemporary American writers, poets, novelists I most admire, they seem to be scattered all over the landscape: McGuane in Montana, Harrison in Michigan, Eastlake and Harrington in Arizona, Creeley in California, Pynchon in California (or so I HEAR), Berry in Kentucky, McMurtry in DC, Kesey in Oregon (although he has apparently quit), Kinnell in Spain, old Henry in California, Algren somewhere in New Jersey now, Hoagland in Vermont and all over, Gary Snyder in California, Mumford in—well I dont know—he is my candidate for the Nobel Prize, by the way, Hunter Thompson in Colorado, John Graves in Texas, Exley in Florida, and so on. Well, there must be others but I cant think of them offhand.

And I think this is right and wholesome. I think that writers and artists should be scattered, spread out, living among working people (as most of us do) rather than clustered together in herds, interlocking elbows w/agents & editors.

There's a topic for your next essay: "The Desolation and Barrenness of the New York Literary Scene." . . .

Enough of all this gibberish. Good luck. Write again.

Ed

Abbey wrote this letter for publication in High Country News, *a fledgling pub-lication back in 1976 that aimed to cover stories about the West that were—and still are—neglected by the New York City-centric media.*

May 1, 76

HCN
Lander Wyo

Dear Friends:
Please dont print that dumb interview from the New Mexico Inde-pendent. I mustve been drunk or hungover. That's not me talking. That's me trying to impersonate a responsible conservationist. I am not a responsible conservationist, I am a wild preservative. If I knew how to blow up Glen Canyon Dam I'd be out there working on it tonight. Print this letter instead.
    Yrs truly,

Ed Abbey

    Wolf Hole, Arizona

Abbey had a penchant for criticizing editors. This only occasionally resulted in get-ting assignments. But he seemed to prefer being right to being popular.

    Box 66
    Moab, Utah

Sept. 11, 1976

    Editors
    Esquire Magazine
    New York

Dear Sirs:
I read with interest your two stories in the September issue promoting "Traction"—ORVs or "escape machines," as your writers call them.
    Let me tell you what a lot of us who live out here in the American West think about your goddamned Off-Road Vehicles. We think

they are a goddamned plague. Like the snowmobile in New England, the dune buggy on the seashore, the ORV out here in the desert and mesa country is a public nuisance, a destroyer of plant life and wild life, a gross polluter of fresh air, stillness, peace and solitude.

The fat pink soft slobs who go roaring over the landscape in these over-size over-priced over-advertised mechanical mastodons are people too lazy to walk, too ignorant to saddle a horse, too cheap and clumsy to paddle a canoe. Like cattle or sheep, they travel in herds, scared to death of going anywhere alone, and they leave their sign and sort all over the back country: Coors beercans, styrofoam cups, plastic spoons, balls of Kleenex, wads of toilet paper, spent cartridge shells, crushed gopher snakes, smashed sagebrush, broken trees, dead chipmunks, wounded deer, eroded trails, bullet-riddled petroglyphs, spray-paint signatures, vandalized Indian ruins, fouled-up waterholes, polluted springs, and smoldering campfires piled with incombustible tinfoil, filtertips, broken bottles. Etc.

It is not the bureaucrats back in Washington who are trying to stop this motorized invasion of what little wild country still remains in America; on the contrary, the bureaucrats are doing far too little. What feeble resistance has so far appeared comes from concerned citizens here and there who are trying to prod and encourage the bureaucrats to do their duty: namely, to save the public lands for their primary purpose, which is wildlife habitat, livestock forage, watershed protections and non-motorized human recreation.

Thank God for the coming and inevitable day of gasoline rationing, which will retire all these goddamned ORVs and "escape machines" to the junkyards where they belong.

Ed Abbey

Wolf Hole, Arizona

Box 702
Oracle, Arizona

January 22, 1977

Editors
Bookletter
New York

Dear Editors:

I was shocked by Seymour Krim's review of <u>Mauve Gloves</u> etc. Tom Wolfe a "major American writer"!? That's an insult to the living memory of the <u>real</u> Tom Wolfe—Thomas Wolfe the <u>novelist</u>. This current Tom Wolfe is merely a journalist, and one of the most sycophantic of that generally spineless species. He has all the instincts of the intellectual courtier, defending the rich, the sleek, the powerful from their critics by attacking safe and easy targets like professors, schmierkunst painters, NY intellectuals, of which he is one, and penthouse liberals. Where was Wolfe when the Pentagon was waging its cowardly war against the rice farmers of Vietnam? Why he was dancing on the sidelines, cheerleading for the Grim and Roaring Majority, idolizing the bomber-colonels eating steak in air-conditioned wardrooms while the victims were trying to remove steel flechettes from the bodies of children, women, and teenage soldiers. <u>Tom Wolfe is the leading pom-pom girl of American journalism</u>. If he worked in Prague he'd be doing the same thing he does here, denouncing dissidents. As for his much admired style, it looks to me like laboriously-contrived, imitation-teenybopper, hippie-type hype, a barely controlled hysteria verging continually on the edge of a screaming breakdown. On the other hand—let's be fair—he is sometimes very funny. I wouldn't miss a word.

Ed Abbey, Novelist

June 17, 1977

Mr. Kenneth Atchity
Ms. Marsha Kinder
The Dream Journal
Los Angeles

Dear Sir and Madam:

Thank you for the invitation to contribute a dream to your Journal. I am honored and flattered by your interest, and went to bed last night resolving to dream a good dream for you. However, nothing much occurred; if I dreamt anything at all it evaporated with the dawn.

I believe I've had the usual assortment of weird, satirical, comical, paranoid and nonsensical dreams that everyone else apparently has. I've never found any of my own dreams very interesting or, so far as I could tell, of much significance. The nearest thing to a significant dream that I remember is one which I retold in a novel called BLACK SUN—the dream of the incompleted house on a seashore. If you want to, you're welcome to reprint that passage. The book was published by Simon and Schuster in 1971, reprinted in paperback by Pocketbooks in 1972. Havent got a copy on hand.

I find other people's dreams even less interesting than my own; nothing is more boring, really, than free fantasy unattached to the real—especially in literature. Most dreams, I think, are simply the horseplay of the brain; an unwinding and running down after the tensions and efforts of the day. NO dream I've ever read or heard of gives me one-tenth of the pleasure I get from awakening in the morning, watching the sun come up over the mountains, hearing the curved-bill thrasher whistle as I stroll down the path to the old shithouse and sit there for a while, smoking a cigar, and thinking about—nothing much at all.

Yours sincerely,

Edward Abbey

Oracle, Arizona

DeWitt's indentity is lost to history—at least this history. But Abbey's words on Steg-
ner are worth saving.

25 Feb 1989

Dear DeWitt:
Thanks for the Stegner tape.

Stegner hardly needs praise from me, but if you wish you may
quote me as follows re that old gent:

There are only two living American authors fully deserving of
the Nobel Prize. One is Lewis Mumford. The other is Wallace
Stegner, whose novels and essays provide us a comprehensive
portrait of industrial society in all its glittering corruption and
radiant evil.

By the way, thinking of good old Wally, I'd sure appreciate it if
you'd delete his quote about me from future editions of your
catalogue. I've always resented that crap about a "gadfly with a
stinger" etc. It typifies the most narrow kind of view of my work
and I'm certain Stegner himself would retract it now. After all, he
wrote it more than twenty years ago, when I was just getting started
as a writer.

If you want a blurb for my tape, my favorite is this from
Wendell Berry, as quoted on the jacket of the The Fool's Progress:

"We are living... among punishments and ruins. For those who
know this, Edward Abbey's books remain an indispensable solace.
His essays, and his novels, too, are antidotes to despair."

Good luck and best regards,

E.A.
Edward Abbey

One of Abbey's last letters, or perhaps his very last, was a kind note to John Nichols,
author of The Milagro Beanfield War. *Edward Abbey died ten days after*
writing this letter.

27 Feb 89

Dear John,
My friend Jack tells me you've suffered another heart attack

recently. Sorry to hear that. You take care of yourself; we're all expecting at least six more fat novels and a dozen screenplays out of you. DON'T CHOP WOOD; GET YOUR NEW WIFE A NEW AXE. Etc.

Me, I'm living under a sword too, as Jack may have told you. An old wino's disease, which could lay me in the grave most anytime. Not that I mind; too much; I've done everything I ever wanted to do. But. . . . as you know, one would like to continue doing the good things over and over again, so long as there's pleasure in it.

We saw your movie Milagro. A charming, delightful film: that Reuben Blades is a lovable guy. And the old folks in the show, they upstaged everyone else.

Whatre you doing now? Another book? Another film? Sure wish I could get back in that Screenwriters' Guild again: I need the medical insurance. Any ideas?

Me, I finished HAYDUKE LIVES! a couple of weeks ago, should be out a year from now. Only a potboiler but easy and fun to write. A sequel to MONKEY WRENCH, of course. What next? Maybe an expose of the public lands ranching swindles . . . or a book on Mexico before Mexico erupts: call it . . . On the Edge of the Volcano. Or a book on Australia, my favorite land and favorite people (next to Sweden and Norway and Ireland and Italy); call that one . . . The Last Good Country. Or a book on music; I've always wanted to write a book on music from the layman-listener's point of view; music has played a bigger part in my life than anything else except love, nature, sex, poetry and philosophy.

Give my regards to old Malcolm Brown next time you see him—a friend of mine from long long ago—and the only person I know, aside from yourself, still living in bleak grim cold picturesque Taos. He thinks that Norton Bildad, in my Fool novel, is a parody of him. Not so of course; as I told him, reality and real people are too subtle and complicated for anybody's typewriter, even Tolstoy's, even yours, even mine.

Enuf of this maundering. You be careful. Best regards,

EA

Even by 1975, Ed Abbey had come a long way from the awkward but talented young man who wrote Jonathan Troy. *A letter to his ailing father, John Paul Abbey, contained a presagement of Abbey's own death. In the spring of 1989, Abbey's wife and friends took him out of the hospital so he could die at home, in the desert that he loved. After his death, the same friends hauled his body to a landscape of sand and volcanoes on the border of the US and Mexico, where the remains of Edward Abbey, who loved many women but whose greatest intimacy may have been with the desert, lie beneath a pile of jagged rocks in a location known only to a few.*

March 14, 1975

Dear Dad,

Got your long letter and feel very bad. I am terribly sorry if I hurt your feelings. I did not mean to; I was responding to a letter from Mother in which she said you seemed to be wasting away, in effect, by staying in bed all the time. At least that was my impression of what she said, though I'm not sure where I put her letter now.

You know damn well you have always been my hero, and I know damn well you have worked very hard most of your life, and maybe you did, as you say, overstrain your heart at some time. Nor did I know that you have seen two more doctors in addition to Bee. Of course, if all three doctors agree that you should take it easy then I agree with them: you should. I guess it is unrealistic of me to think that you could continue to do the extraordinary things you used to do right up to the end of your days.

Painful subject—but surely we can be open with each other. I know that you are going to have to die sometime, probably before I do, and I hope very much that it doesn't happen to you in a goddamned hospital bed. Having witnessed that kind of end for someone I love already, I don't want to see it happen that way to you. On the other hand I do want you to hang around as long as possible, just as I plan to do myself.

I suppose each of us has his own fantasy of how he wants to die. I would like to go out in a blaze of glory, myself, or maybe simply disappear someday, far out in the heart of the wilderness I love all by myself, alone with the Universe and whatever God may happen to be looking on. Disappear—and never return. That's my fantasy. And I suppose, unconsciously, I have imagined that kind of death for you. But why should <u>you</u> want to fulfill <u>my</u> fantasy?

And furthermore, by the time I'm your age (if I live that long), I'll probably see things in a different, not quite so romantic, light. Anyway, I apologize, and do look forward to seeing you here in Moab this spring. Then we'll go out on Grand View Point and talk the whole matter out, to the very end. I love you, old man, never mind all the stupid things I may have said.

Ed

From *Beyond the Last Village*

ALAN RABINOWITZ

It is only with the heart that one can see rightly; what is essential is invisible to the eye.
—Antoine de Saint-Exupery

Pygmies of the Adung Wang Valley

ALTHOUGH IT WOULD HAVE SEEMED IMPOSSIBLE to me a few days earlier, I returned to Tazundam more tired than when I had left. The members of the team who had stayed behind were well rested and eager to be off again, but we needed to rest an extra day. Not only were both knees bothering me continuously now, but my left knee was also swollen with fluid. Zawgan had fashioned a new walking stick for me, and I used it constantly. Hobbling along, sporting a monthlong gray beard on my face, I felt very old.

I tried to maintain the illusion that if I just ignored the pain, it would go away. It had worked when I was younger. In my more lucid moments, however, I realized that my age and the abuse I had inflicted upon my body over the years were catching up with me. Injury, illness, and even the possibility of an untimely death were realities that I'd learned to deal with during my years in the field. But aging, manifested by the irreversible breakdown of my body parts, was something I couldn't yet accept.

The next village on the trail from Tazundam, Tazhutu, was only six miles or a three-hour hike away, but we ended up spending the night there. The monk had been through several days earlier, looking weak and feverish, but we heard that he was back safely at his

169

monastery now. Zawgan, who had been teasing me about walking like an old man, sprained his ankle. It gave me some satisfaction that we'd both be limping to our final destination. That evening, the team had an infusion of animal protein, feasting on a freshly killed Assamese macaque brought in by a hunter. I ate some of the meat but passed on the offer of a special dish of cooked brain.

We were nearly four weeks into the expedition. Despite the fluid in my knee, I still walked faster than anyone else on our team. Fortunately, the soldiers no longer felt the need to keep someone assigned to me, so my solitary walks were more pleasant. I was alone when I rounded a bend in the trail and saw the large swinging bridge spanning the Adung Wang River. On the far side, I could hear children's voices and dogs barking among the nearly thirty huts that dotted the narrow piece of land between the river and the mountains. The sights and sounds were like those of all the other Rawang villages we had visited so far, but my heart beat faster as I approached the bridge. This was not just any village. I had been anticipating this moment since the morning I had burst into Khaing's room over the railroad station in Myitkyina. Soon a mystery would be solved. This was the home of the Taron.

In 1954, the Myanmar military officer Colonel Saw Myint, while leading a reconnaissance expedition to the northern borders of the country, came upon a group of fifty-eight people (twenty-six males, thirty-two females) living in three settlements in the Adung Wang Valley; most were in the village of Arundam, which I was looking at now. In his report to the government, Colonel Saw Myint called them Taron, describing them as a separate pygmoid racial group originating in the upper reaches of the Tarong River in China, with distinctive behavior, language, and cultural beliefs. The Taron first migrated into Burma in the 1800s, the elders told him, when they were trying to escape tribal warfare with the Tibetans who dominated the Tarong River basin at that time.

Earlier explorers who had also met these people described them as "a pygmy forest tribe of unknown origin" and "queer, stunted simian beings...with scarcely any clothes, an unsavory smell, and great mops of curly black hair." But they had mistakenly grouped them together with another Rawang tribe, the Daru, which also lived in the area. Eight years after Colonel Saw Myint's expedition, a team from the Burma Medical Research Society journeyed to collect physical and physiological data on the Taron. Their report, published in the book I had shown Khaing and in the international journal *Nature*, stated that the sixty-nine pygmies they examined were of Mongoloid racial stock. Due to inbreeding, the Taron had a disturbingly high rate of infant mortality, insanity, cretinism, and mental retardation. Such defects, combined with the natural hardships and dangers of living in this rugged region, took a heavy toll, as illustrated by the family tree Colonel Saw Myint recorded of a 70-year-old Taron male who had taken two wives:

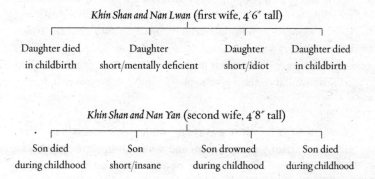

Khin Shan and Nan Lwan (first wife, 4´6˝ tall)

| Daughter died in childbirth | Daughter short/mentally deficient | Daughter short/idiot | Daughter died in childbirth |

Khin Shan and Nan Yan (second wife, 4´8˝ tall)

| Son died during childhood | Son short/insane | Son drowned during childhood | Son died during childhood |

In the decades that followed, the outside world had lost touch with the Taron, and I didn't know what I would find. We were about to learn the status of perhaps the only pygmies of Asian ancestry in the world.

To most people, the capitalized term *Pygmies* refers to the several hundred thousand racially distinct people of equatorial Africa who have been around for at least 4,000 years. Of these, the Mbuti Pygmies of the Ituri Forest in Congo (formerly Zaire) are the smallest, with the men averaging less than five feet tall and 106 pounds, and the women averaging less than four and a half feet tall and 92 pounds. But the lowercase term *pygmy* can refer to any short person with a stunted or dwarfish condition. It is a diminutive of a

Greek word meaning "fist," originally used to refer to a measure of length from the elbow to the fist. The earliest use of the word is most often ascribed to Homer, who used it when describing a battle between Greek and Trojan forces in the *Iliad*.

The Myanmar Medical Society Expedition of 1962 found the average height of the Taron to be four and a half feet for both men and women, with the men averaging 91 pounds and the women 84 pounds. Professor Mya-Tu, who led the expedition, noted the similarities in stature between the Taron and both the African pygmies and the Oceanic Negrito pygmies, but the Taron had typical Mongoloid, not Negrito, features, he commented, and differed in other ways as well. One of the generally accepted theories among nineteenth-century anthropologists was that all people of small stature, typically those living in humid tropical areas of Asia, Oceania, and Africa, belonged to the same racial group. It was not until the 1960s that this theory was disproved, when studies using blood groups as genetic markers showed that pygmies of various geographic regions are more similar to their non-pygmy neighbors than to each other.

AS I CROSSED THE BRIDGE and entered the village, now renamed Karaung, all movement and sound around me ceased. The houses here were rougher, more poorly built than those in other Rawang villages. My first impression was that the village, rather than being filled with short-statured Taron, was populated by people who were merely less attractive, aberrant forms of the Rawang. I stopped to take a picture of a woman who looked terrified of me and had frozen in place as I approached her. Focusing the camera, I felt, and then saw out of the corner of my eye, a child brushing up against my leg. Turning with the camera still to my face, I was surprised to watch the viewfinder fill not with the body of a child but with the misshapen, dwarfish form of an old man with sad, rheumy eyes. Before I could snap the picture, the viewfinder was empty. I looked up in time to see him hobbling off before disappearing into a nearby house. I had just seen my first Taron.

That night we bought a chicken and some eggs from the village headman and asked him to join us for dinner. During the meal I learned why the people of this village, apart from the Taron, looked different from other Rawang. Of the twenty-eight families comprising 170 people in the village, most were Htalu, with nearly a third of them claiming Taron blood from mixed marriages. I suspected that the proportion of mixed-blood families might in fact be even higher, because few of these people had the characteristic taller stature and sharply delineated facial features that we had seen among the Htalu in Tazundam.

Over tea, I asked the headman why I saw so few of the Taron, and how the Htalu had come to live with them in the first place. He seemed reluctant to answer and changed the subject. A little later I instructed Khaing to give the headman a bag of medicine that we had planned to leave for the village. He was grateful for such an important gift, as I knew he would be. Then I asked my questions again.

"The Taron have a hard life," the headman finally answered. "Many people have hurt them. We help them build houses and cut their taungyas now. But soon there will be only Htalu. That is better."

I asked what he meant by that last statement, but he wouldn't explain. Would he help me talk with the remaining Taron in the village? He looked toward his elder daughter, who had been standing unnoticed in the shadows. She nodded. Then she moved into the firelight as her father stood and left the room.

I spent that evening and the next day visiting the few huts where the Taron lived. In contrast to the friendliness and hospitality of other tribal groups, the Taron seemed fearful, listless, and sad. Colonel Saw Myint had reported that the Taron were extremely shy in the presence of outsiders, harboring feelings of inferiority built up through a history of persecution and enslavement by neighboring Tibetans and Chinese. At one point, he said, the Taron had built their huts in trees in order to escape continual slave raids. Even during Colonel Saw Myint's trip, Tibetans in the village of Tahundan still owned Taron slaves.

Using the headman's daughter as a translator, I was shocked to learn that while there were sixty-eight people from sixteen families who claimed mixed Rawang-Taron heritage, there were only twelve pure-blood Taron left, down from more than a hundred just forty years earlier. I thought again of Colonel Saw Myint's report, which stated that after the Taron crossed the mountains into Myanmar, they lost contact with their original tribal settlements in China when earthquake closed the passes and isolated their settlements. No longer able to obtain matrimonial partners from other Taron groups, the Taron here started condoning marriage between brothers and sisters in an effort to maintain ethnic purity. The result was a high rate of infant mortality and a sizable proportion of mentally defective children. Yet that still didn't seem to fully explain how quickly and dramatically the Taron's situation had deteriorated.

Questioning the Taron was a laborious and sometimes frustrating process. I would pose a question to Khaing, and he would translate from English to Burmese for our local Rawang forester, U Myat Soe. U Myat Soe talked to the headman's daughter, translating from Burmese to Rawang. The headman's daughter questioned the Taron in the local Htalu dialect, which the Taron could speak and understand even though it wasn't their first language.

The Taron were reluctant to talk about their past, and it turned out that much of their oral history was forgotten. I was also uncertain as to the accuracy of the translations I was getting. Answers to questions about animals and hunting were much easier to confirm than responses to personal questions. Sometimes I asked the same question three or four different ways to make sure I understood the answer. But there was always some doubt in my mind as to the original wording of the answer from the mouths of the Taron.

The Taron houses were more decrepit than those of other Rawang groups, as were the Taron themselves. Although they had a lighter facial complexion than the Rawang, my first impression was that the few Taron left looked much like the typical portrayals of Stone Age people. They were disheveled and dirty, their simple cotton clothing almost in tatters, as if they cared nothing about their appearance. Even in Colonel Saw Myint's time, the simple coarse cloth dress of the Taron, barely covering much of their bodies, was described as "inferior" and as little better than what one would expect from "jungle-dwelling savages."

The remaining Taron were mostly elderly. Two individuals I interviewed were retarded, and a third had advanced goiter. Colonel Saw Myint described watching Taron male children wrestling and playing with crossbows while Taron girls wove cloth alongside their mothers. There was none of that now. Instead, I was struck by the look of resignation on the villagers' faces. It was a look I had seen only once before in my life, in an AIDS ward in a New York City hospital.

The results of the Taron-Htalu marriages in the village didn't seem advantageous to the Htalu, whose children were shorter and far less physically attractive than the Htalu we'd seen in Tazundam. The diet of the village was mostly wheat, corn, beans, millet, and taro from local village plantations. The Taron, unlike the Htalu and other Rawang, had no livestock and rarely included meat or fish in their diet anymore, although they were considered skillful hunters in the past, with the ability to bring in any species they desired. Colonel Saw Myint speculated that the appearance of the Taron was due to dietary deficiencies in nutrients such as iodine, but the medical team that came later found the Taron to be no more nutritionally deficient than any other human group in the area.

The Taron men became excited for the first time when I showed them pictures of animals, as memories of their past suddenly surfaced. Before their conversion to Christianity, I was told, a special ceremony overseen by a shaman was held after the birth of a Taron male child, involving small models of animals that they valued, such as serow, bear, and musk deer. These models were placed around a foot-high sculpted mountain made of corn flour, and the corn mountain was burned to invoke the protection of the Spirit of the Mountain. Afterward the animal figures were taken into the forest to ensure the hunting success of the child when he reached adulthood.

One old Taron started jabbing his gnarled hand at one of the pictures in my book. I had seen this behavior often by now, usually when the hunter was familiar with the species. This time the picture was of a yellow-throated marten, a four- to five-pound weasel-like animal that was common over a wide area in forests between 600 and 9,000 feet in elevation.

The Taron reached behind him and pulled a small rolled-up skin from under a bundle of clothes, then handed it to me. I didn't really want to see the skin of another yellow-throated marten, but I felt I had to examine it to be polite. As I unrolled the skin, I was already framing the false words of admiration I'd use. But the words died in my throat.

"Ask him where exactly he killed this animal, and if there are many others like it around here," I said to the headman's daughter through Khaing.

"He says there are some, but not many," Khaing eventually replied. "He is giving you the skin as a present."

It was a present I wanted. The skin I held was not from a yellow-throated marten but from a stone marten, a related species that was known mostly from central China and the Himalayas above 4,500 feet in elevation. Although it was not uncommon at higher elevations, its fur was valued by traders and it had never before been documented in Myanmar. This was the fourth new mammal species I had identified in the country.

Khaing was unusually quiet that first night when we returned to our hut. I thought he was exhausted after hours of helping me with tedious translation. As we prepared our bedrolls, we agreed to give the Taron all the extra salt and clothing we had left. They seemed the neediest of all the groups we'd met so far. I asked Khaing what he thought about the Taron.

"They are a pitiful people," he said. "When I was translating for you, I felt bad for the Taron, and I had to be careful that I didn't put my own feelings into what they said. Sometimes the meaning of what I was told they said was difficult to understand."

"You did the best you could," I said. "We learned a lot." I crawled into my sleeping bag.

"I told you they don't like themselves," he said, suddenly stopping what he was doing and looking up at me through the light of the candle on the floor between us. "I think that was right, although it might have been said with different words. But I didn't tell you something I should have. U Myat Soe said that the Taron said of themselves that they are ugly. *I* thought they were ugly too. So I wasn't sure if we were just putting our own feelings into words that were supposed to have come from them. How could they know what 'ugly' is? I felt bad about what I was thinking, so I didn't tell you this."

I sat up, leaning on one elbow and facing Khaing. He had my full attention now.

"If we're to understand anything about these people, I need to know exactly what they say, or at least what you think they say. You know that, Khaing." He nodded sheepishly. "Besides, I was thinking and feeling the same things you were as we talked with them. I didn't even want to sit close to them."

"But maybe they're not ugly to each other," Khaing said. "Maybe we're putting words in their mouth."

"That's possible. In such a short time, it's hard to really know what's going on here," I replied. "But I think you were right about what they said. I think they see in each other some of what we see from the outside, though maybe they wouldn't describe it as we do."

I wrote in my field notes what Khaing had just revealed to me and then lay back in my sleeping bag, letting the candle burn itself out. In the darkness, I again faced toward where Khaing was lying.

"You still awake?" I asked, hearing snoring from another part of the hut.

"Yes," he said, in a way that suggested he was still thinking about our conversation.

I tried to explain to Khaing why I had said what I did. The beliefs that "beauty is in the eye of the beholder" and that physical attraction is completely culturally determined were not borne out by scientific studies, I said. While the criteria for beauty were often influenced by our cultural backgrounds, there actually seemed to be a universal perception of attractiveness, one that was governed by natural selection and was programmed in the circuitry of the human brain. In other words, features that were considered universally beautiful in women might be external cues to men indicating that a woman is herself healthy and fertile and thus capable of bearing healthy children. Features considered attractive in men were often those indicating strength and dominance in a group. That's why it would be no surprise to me, I said, if some of the Taron and even the mixed Taron-Htalu appeared unattractive not only to us but also to themselves.

AS SOON AS I ENTERED THE HUT, the man sitting by the fire turned away from me. He had known I was coming. Two Taron women, his older and younger sisters, stood beside him. As Khaing worked with the translator to ask the women questions, I sat down beside the man, sipping tea and looking into the fire. Out of the corner of my eye, I saw him cast furtive glances toward me. I waited.

I reached for the teapot sitting in the fire, forgetting that my hands were not as work-hardened as those of the villagers whom I'd watched do this many times.

"Yow!" I hollered, dropping the pot, spilling the tea, and spraying myself with hot ashes. "Damn," I said, pounding out the smoking embers that were burning holes in my clothes. Suddenly, I heard the strangest sound and turned. The Taron man was now facing me, rocking back and forth, cackling with high-pitched laughter. Unwittingly, I had broken the ice between us.

His name was Dawi and, at 39, this stocky, impish-looking man was the youngest of the surviving Taron in Myanmar. He and his two sisters were the only pure Taron family left. The other eight Taron were part of Htalu families. As he poured the tea for me, I took out my last remaining PowerBar, which I'd been saving for an emergency, and gave it to him.

He sat facing me now. He was wearing a coarse, dirty blanket thrown over his shoulder, light cloth pants tied at the knees, and cloth leggings that ended at black, hardened feet that had never seen shoes. He was one of the few who still wore remnants of the Taron traditional dress. I asked him several questions that went unanswered. He nibbled around the edges of the PowerBar, smiling and speaking to his sisters in the Taron dialect; suddenly, the whole bar was gone in a gulp.

After many cups of tea and a long hard look at me, Dawi began to speak, straining to put into words thoughts he'd perhaps never voiced before. He'd remembered everything I had asked him, and the intensity of his gaze hinted at an intelligence that had probably been long suppressed.

"For many years the Taron only marry each other," Dawi started, almost in a whisper. "But when we have babies, the babies have small brains and small bodies. It was no good." He turned his eyes away for a moment and then looked back at me.

"We don't want Taron babies anymore," Dawi continued. "Long ago, the Taron decided not to have babies with each other. Only with Htalu. Some Htalu marry Taron, many do not want to. If Htalu won't marry Taron, then we die alone."

His voice became almost defiant. "There are few Taron left. Many die alone."

Dawi shifted his body away from me again and faced the fire. It must have taken a lot for him to tell me what he did, to face images of a past that was gone and a future that would never be. Kingdon Ward called the Taron "one of nature's unsuccessful experiments." I think Dawi might have agreed. I didn't need to ask him what he thought of his own future. He was among the last. And he was dying alone.

From Audubon's Watch

JOHN GREGORY BROWN

Audubon's Inquiry

D EAR LUCY, DEAR ROSE: The wild thrashing of wings in
my ears has become a roar, indescribable in its intensity and
the ruin it would cause me. No, my daughters. No. I once encountered such an unholy din in my youthful wanderings. Outside of
Louisville, I discovered inside a sycamore of sixty or seventy feet, in
the stump of a broken, hollowed branch some forty feet from the
ground, the roost of no less than a thousand swallows. I rose early
the next morning, long before daylight, and found the tree so I
might learn more of the swallows' habits. I leaned my head against
the tree, which was utterly silent, and remained in that posture until
light began to penetrate the woods, when suddenly I sensed that the
tree had begun to fall and would surely crush me.

I leapt away and looked up, astonished to see that the tree still
stood. Instead, the swallows poured from the stump in a black
stream, the noise of their wings like that of a mill's giant wheel
revolving within the rushing torrent of a rain-swollen river. For half
an hour they rose like smoke swirling from a chimney, darkening the
sky until finally they passed from view, and I fell to the ground then
in simple and complete depletion, as though I had come face to face
with the devil's dark minions and fought them off with my bare
hands and arms.

That, my beloved daughters, is the noise I hear now. That is the
exhaustion I feel. I wake to it in the morning, pass my days in its company, seek sleep that I might forget the deafening roar. Your mother

attends me still, though she has given up her pretense of happy bustle and sits by my side for an hour each evening, clasping my hand.

I cannot hear the voices about me, nor my own, except in the rare moments, no longer than a few minutes in length, when the roar suddenly quiets. I call to your mother then, though my words are mere wisps of air, a snake's hiss or the dull swish of leaves on a branch, too faint to rise above even the spit of the fire that does nothing to warm me.

Then the cacophony continues. To preserve my reason, I attempt to extract from the din the call of my birds, of Townsend's finch and the black-necked still, of the eider duck and the Florida cormorant, the arctic jaeger and the red-necked grebe, the solitary vireo and the welcome partridge, the great marbled godwit and the black-backed gull, the little night owl and the sora rail.

My study is of birds, I insisted.

No, not of birds. Of truth, Emile Gautreaux said.

He would have me get at the truth of his wife's death, my daughters. He would have me turn from the ornithological to the human. But hadn't I already gotten at the truth, known it the moment I saw that she had drunk herself into an everlasting sleep?

I will answer your every question with candor and completeness, no matter how deeply you probe.

So I made a show of my inquiry. I learned the man's full history, and Myra Richardson's as well. I learned the nature of her melancholy, her spells of confusion and despair, how she would retreat to the very house to which I had been invited to draw her figure, at which I had been stirred to such desire, urged by her toward its fulfillment but then cast out as though I would challenge her virtue and propel her toward ruin.

"Did she," I asked Emile Gautreaux, "ever speak of these spells when they had ceased, when she had returned to her true character?"

"She did," he answered, pacing about the room, "though she spoke as though her memory were dim."

"As though her very character had been altered?" I inquired.

"Not altered. No," Gautreaux replied. "Diminished."

"And did she seem so to you?"

"Diminished?" Gautreaux laughed. "How would she be diminished, Mr. Audubon, if she possessed more of my devotion with each passing hour?"

I recognized, my daughters, the calamitous truth of the man's words, for I too wished to forget all other intimacies, the countless hours of devout and spirited coupling that steered your mother and me through our wedded evenings, and remember instead my hands on Myra Gautreaux's breasts, my lips on her lips, how I clung to her, stirred passion in her, my lips on her breasts, my hands and mouth descending to explore and taste the warm folds of her sex. Though illicit and profane, never again would I know, I believed, so fierce an ache and longing, a dalliance that possessed the grace and recklessness, the sublime wonder, the immeasurable distances of flight.

Would I get at the truth now, my daughters? Would I confess that thirty years later, I cannot provide a contrary answer?

The flight of the swallow-tailed hawk, of the golden eagle. The downy feathers of the white-tailed ptarmigan. The acrobatics of the violet-green swallow. The night-hawk's wings spread out against the burnished sky, the prairie wood-warbler's joyous trill and song. Would I exchange these as well?

Emile Gautreaux spoke to me that evening in quiet reverence of Myra Gautreaux's carnal appetite and how she would call to him and bid him to speak of his desire. *I did not speak*, he said. *I did not speak. I would speak now, that she might hear.*

Again the man wept, at this admission, and stood before his wife's body and clasped her hands in his own.

And I too did not speak.

Then, outside, we heard the Negroes shouting. Gautreaux joined me at the window. The Negroes had stopped their work and stood with their knives lowered at their sides or raised above their heads as though they would defend themselves. The oxen snorted and kicked, their brutish faces shining in the firelight. Something had struck terror among the Negroes, and the oxen sensed this change, as though the air about them had become unsettled, had taken on a new and unfamiliar scent. They strained against their yokes.

I leaned closer to the window, to discover what had stopped the

Negroes' work. In the distance, as though he were an apparition invented out of the black night, a man on horseback emerged. The Negroes cowered at his approach. It was the devil himself, they seemed to believe, the devil come to set the fields on fire, to set them all aflame or lead them on a final march to the fiery regions and shadowy air of hell. Many of them fell to their knees. The wind whipped at their torn and mud-streaked clothes.

Is that not the region I now occupy, my daughters? It is as though at any moment I will find as company not you or the gentle creatures of the air but the foul odor of the condemned, the monstrous roar of the three-headed beast Cerberus, every scarred soul and forsaken spirit a poet might conjure to convey the torment of the damned.

Would my birds shed their feathers on my behalf, so that I might shape for myself a pair of wings for an airy descent into that dark realm?

I'll see this story done, my daughters.

The horse and rider drew closer. My breath clouded the window, and I raised my hand to wipe it clear. Then I saw that the Negroes had determined with relief, as had I, that here was no ghostly apparition nor the devil himself nor even James Pirrie, who would provoke in them a kindred fear. It was a young man, the physician Ira Smith, come to confirm and certify Myra Gautreaux's death, to assert his authority by inventing the story whereby this woman would remain in the eyes of the church wholly blameless, her soul unsullied.

It was to me that Gautreaux had assigned the task of affixing blame.

Peace to her soul, for my own had turned as black as the evening, as ash.

The golden eagle, my good and fair and loving daughters, clutches a white rabbit's carcass, talons embedded in the head, piercing the rabbit's eye. The white-headed sea eagle stands on the shore over a gutted catfish. The beak of a peregrine falcon drips with a mallard's blood, the mallard's feathers strewn about him, the mallard's chest gaping. A lifeless vole dangles in the clutches of a sharp-shinned hawk.

Not of birds, Emile Gautreaux declared. *Not of birds. Of truth.*

If he makes this journey, if he is at this very moment on his way, I will hold the demons at bay, withstand the roaring in my ears, turn death a while from my door—so that I might speak, might tell him.

Not of birds. Of truth.

Habits and Habitat
of the Southwestern Bad Boy

STACEY RICHTER

N ONE OF THIS WOULD HAVE HAPPENED, none of this mess with the phone calls and the bad boy and the sandwich and the cow, if I'd been able to find a time that would have me. For a brief period, I seriously considered the 1980s. It's my luck in life to have big hair naturally, and I've always felt jaunty wearing those floppy boots that turned into socks at the top. But I decided only rocker chicks with ratted hair and white bustiers yellowed by cigarette smoke were fully able to pull that off, and I was too uptight for that look. Then, for a while, I believed my time to be the 1920s. I wore sleeveless shifts and adorable shoes and made an effort to express myself spontaneously through flowing movements, like Isadora Duncan. A shitload of gin and one whole day spent spontaneously vomiting into the commode suggested that the twenties were not going to embrace me either.

I finally gave up. If a time wasn't going to have me, I wasn't going to waste my time pursuing one. Of course, whenever one gives up a fond hope, a hole springs open in the empty space. My life, a motheaten sweater, was laced with such holes. And so when my dear friend Walter turned to me and said, "Holy Toledo. Check it out. Bad boy at two o'clock," I turned, I looked, and I saw. I saw the bad boy.

The grim lesson I'd learned, in renouncing my search for a time that would have me, is that the only time is now, and it is impossible to inhabit now. For me, now is debased and vaguely embarrassing. Now is a limerick where everything rhymes with *pants*. The bad boy was bizarrely beautiful and young, with a pink bloom in his cheeks. You could almost see the desperation rising from him like the puff of dirt that enveloped Pig Pen in Peanuts cartoons. He was clearly a creature of the present. In his clothing, his fluid movements, the thick curtain of hair—for him, now was a sonnet. He could probably name three or four presidents, tops. Walter and I pivoted our heads and stared. The bad boy took a long drag from his cigarette, broodingly, his mouth pursed in a rock star pout, a pubescent Mick Jagger and Jimi Hendrix and Evan Dando rolled into one. O, I thought O, that I might be a carcinogen within that deep-sucked breath!

Sun streamed through the windows of the café. The boy got up and lurched across the room. He was flooded by sun, then doused in shadow—bad boy, bright and dark. Walter and I watched him openly; we watched him the way we might track the antics of a squirrel in a park. He found a stack of ashtrays and detached one from the top before going back to his seat.

"Three sheets," Walter noted, and cocked a brow.

We tittered. How naughty. Weeks earlier, to kill some time, we'd filled out sex surveys for a semirisqué magazine, and in the space after: "What is your favorite sexual fantasy?" Walter knew I had written: "Drunken teenage boys."

The boy ignored his cup of coffee and poked at a shiny set of keys on the table in front of him with distressed concentration, like an obsessed crow. On the basis of this, I guessed that he must be sixteen, with a new license and his mom's gleaming, innocent Saturn in the lot, waiting to be wrecked. I was probably only a few years younger than his mother, as was Walter, my friend and social escort, though we were not of parental ilk. We were easily distracted and underemployed—I sold low-fat scones to espresso joints and Walter worked in a bookstore. When we weren't doing those things, we wrote poetry and smoked cigarettes and painted the insides of our apartments "interesting" colors like "soil" and "yams." Walter had found *his* time: the 1940s. He wore smoking jackets and sported a

pencil-thin mustache, like William Powell's. He glided around the
bookstore with the air of a bemused sophisticate. People were afraid
to ask him questions for fear of an acerbic reply.

"Look at him," I said.

Walter was already looking—at the adorable bangs, the long-
lashed eyes, the restless feet. "The little buckaroo," he said.

"No one understands him."

"No," he agreed.

"Do you think he would, you know, *go* somewhere with us?" I
gave him a significant look. He gave me a look in return. It said: "Are
you psycho?" but with a subtext of prurient interest. I felt the stir-
rings of a conspiracy—about what, I wasn't clear. About the boy I
guess, the beautiful, shit-faced bad boy. He couldn't possibly be
allowed to drive himself home.

"Our best chance," he said, with a wry smile, "is if he's
impressed by the fact that we're poets."

We laughed again, with a bit more tension this time. We really
were poets, or at least attempting to be. Walter kept a list of all the
little magazines and journals that had published his work over his
desk. His list was up to twenty. I kept a list of all the journals that
had published my poetry over my desk, if you can call two names "a
list." That the boy would be impressed by this or anything at all
appeared unlikely. Words in particular were a long shot considering
his T-shirt. It seemed to be from a foreign country where English
was admired rather than understood, and said: "Do To Others As
Others Have To You Be."

The bad boy noticed our interest and began to stare back. I
tried a smile.

"What?" he blurted.

Walter and I traded amazed glances. It was like a bunny rabbit
had spoken.

"We were admiring your nail polish," Walter tried, in a suave,
lying tone.

"Oh, yeah," said the boy, looking at his hand, "it's 'Savagery.'" He
clawed the air with mock ferociousness. "It's new."

"Of course it is," Walter said, with an indulgent grin. It occurred to me that he might like the boy too.

And by like, I mean *like* like.

"QUESTION!" screamed the boy. The three of us were sitting in the capacious front seat of my 1957 Chevy Bel Aire, which I acquired during a brief, meaningless flirtation with the fifties. Below our feet zipped the ribbon of I-19 that stretched from Tucson to the Mexican border, past road signs that, in some incomprehensible burst of optimism, were calculated in metric.

"Answer!" yelled Walter. He and the boy gripped 40s. With the extra alcohol and the rush of air through the windows, our bad boy seemed to have boomeranged out of his brood and into an edgy mania. It was like he'd just been released from a room where they administered horrible tests. His thigh fell heavily against mine, and when the breeze hit right I could smell the bad boy aroma of lemons and dirt.

"No, wait—no. Question!"

I gave him a sideways glance. His cheekbones were drop dead but his eyes were glazed. He was, I had to admit, utterly blotto.

He yelled, "What do you get if you cross Lassie with a pit bull?"

"Cross them how?" I teased. "Do you mean *crossbreed* them?"

"Or cross Lassie, make-Lassie-mad-cross her?" Walter was babbling. He had regressed, the way he did around boys he liked, mixing babiness with his innate sophistication until he became like a very suave ten year old. He sat there and giggled at nothing. I wondered if he might think he was on a date with the bad boy, with me as a chaperone. Whereas I thought of it more as kidnapping.

"Grrr," said the boy, showing Walter a set of white, even teeth.

"Grrr indeed," he replied, and took a little nip out of the bad boy's T-shirt. They tossed their heads and laughed and gazed at each other.

"No, come on," he protested, "you know what I'm saying! Just, like, *cross* them. Together."

"Oh," I said. "Okay. I see." Then I reached over and tousled his hair. What the hell. "What do you get?"

"Some type of bitch," Walter mumbled to the side mirror.

Since I'm a chump who is nice to Walter no matter what, I ignored this. The bad boy didn't answer either. He'd faded out of the debate and was pawing at the radio knobs, trying, I suppose, to find some of the music of today. He popped us away from Peggy Lee on my oldies station. *Is that all there is?* She was wondering. It was hot in the car. One of the many problems of devoting oneself to the Eisenhower era is that air conditioning was seen as an impossible luxury. As if in agreement, the boy bent an elbow over the top of his head and, with that inimitable bad boy flair, pulled his T-shirt clean off.

Walter and I looked at each other. That look, I believe, was a combination of shock, lust, and mutual panic, garnished with a sprig of deadly competition. There we were, speeding toward the border with a half-naked, underage boy pressed between us. It made me think of Audubon's painting of pintail ducks, wherein a pair of waterfowl lunge across a vacant, primordial landscape, beaks hanging open, both of them straining with every quill toward a single, yellow fly, hanging like a dollop of custard at the top of the frame.

We drove on, flanked by low mountains and dust and parched desert plants. The boy had given up on the radio and the Chevy filled with the sound of wind. In the café we had offered the bad boy an adventure and he hadn't thought twice, brushing his bangs back and squinting up at us. "Yeah," he said, "let's rally." We had simply volunteered to take him on an expedition to see a giant cow skull.

After a while, the bad boy blurted: "A dog that rips off your hand, then goes and runs for help."

EVERYTHING WONDERFUL HAD ALREADY DIED OFF. That was my feeling about it. Secretly, without telling Walter, I believed I might have located my time—the first half of the nineteenth century. That was when John James Audubon roamed the hills and wetlands of the American continent, killing anything feathered. He killed then drew virtually every bird there was, and they had them all then. Audubon witnessed flocks of now-extinct passenger pigeons so vast they blackened the sky for hours at a time.

He drew them on a lichen-covered branch, a pair of slender birds with blue-tipped feathers. The girl bird is thrusting her beak into the boy bird's mouth in a moment of languorous instinct. Back then Indians picked berries on the ground where my apartment is and the Santa Cruz River flowed through Tucson year round, fed by a giant prehistoric lake percolating up through the desert floor. Now the river is a gravel trough, drained by golf courses and copper mines and neat little flower beds. Nothing is wild anymore.

The giant cow skull had once been a snack bar. It was about twenty feet high, including the horns. Hungry visitors had entered through the nasal cavity, but the interior had long since been boarded up and the glory of the skull could now only be viewed from the outside. We parked and climbed out onto the packed dirt. We were right off the highway, in the middle of a lonely stretch of desert, at the start of a little road that led to a microscopic town called Sin Vacas, which translates to *without cows* in Spanish.

"Heavens me," intoned Walter. "There seems to be a freakishly large cow skull over there."

The boy swayed on his feet and informed us that he had to pee. He stepped to the side of the car and did just that, upon my tire. Walter and I wandered away and stared solemnly into the distance. When he was finished, the boy zipped up and began to walk toward us. His pants were slipping off his hips so that a crescent of boxer shorts showed above his waistband. His stomach was flat and his skin was a warm, tawny brown. The boy's shadow slipped into the gap between Walter's shoulders and mine. He had a last minute chance to reach for me—I held my breath—but no, he stumbled toward Walter, drunker than ever, stretching his arms up over his head. Then he leaned in, and, with the open mouth so indicative of messy teenage kissing, crushed his lips to Walter's.

Reserved, suave Walter just *went* for it. He ground himself into the boy. He abandoned himself. I found myself standing there, mesmerized, staring at their mouths as they made out. It was completely unrestrained. When was I going to get a chance to observe something like this again? I had to remind myself that I was striving to be a nineteenth-century lady, and with this in mind I managed to walk across the lot and climb into the car. The sun was low in the sky and the shadows of cholla and knife-edged agaves stretched over the ground. Slanted light tumbled through the windshield and spilled all over the upholstery of the Chevy. I thought that maybe the fifties weren't so bad after all. Anything was preferable to the depravity of now.

After a while, I heard an electronic wheezing coming from the backseat. I followed the noise to a small phone inside the boy's backpack.

"Hello?"

"Hello?" said a woman's voice.

"Yes?"

After a pause, the woman said, "Where the fuck is Zach?"

"One moment please."

I ferried the phone across the dirt. By the time I arrived, the bad boy was being very bad indeed. He had Walter pressed up beneath the eye socket, mashed against a plate of faux bone. Clothes were falling off. I sort of ignored this, and tapped the boy on the shoulder.

"What?" he hissed.

I waved the phone. "It's your mother."

The boy looked at me with hating eyes. I have to admit I loved him in a sick way at that moment—O youthful rebellion, O reckless spirit! It was a brief, fleeting moment, I knew. I could scrawl poems until my fingers bled but there was no way to capture it. He'd grow up and become a real estate broker or an alcoholic or both. The window of opportunity to live a life of pure rage is very small.

He took the phone. "Yeah?" he said, in a sulky tone. Then, flatly: "I don't know"; and then, with anger: "I *said* I don't know"; and then, with a rising note of distress: "I don't have to tell you everything I'm doing." Finally, just like the classic song, he proclaimed: "You don't own me!"

He jabbed off the phone and glared at it. When I refused to take it back, he placed it on the ground and stepped away. He dug his hands into his hair, seizing it by the roots. His eyes began to roll from side to side. I was witnessing a display of pure, animal agony. It was fascinating; it was charming. Yet I only got to observe it for a moment, because then the boy turned, and with an easy, athletic gait, sprinted off into the desert.

Walter and I looked at each other with disbelief. For a second the ember of our camaraderie flared to life. Then I watched as it doused itself in Walter's eyes.

"Oh my God!" he commented. He patted his hair, smoothed down his pencil-thin mustache, and dashed off into the desert after the boy with an awkward, stiff-armed sprint.

I didn't even know what this was. We smoked, we cracked wise, we drank coffee so strong we could stand spoons in it. In seven years, I'd never seen him *run*.

I lingered by the cow skull, walking in circles. The sun was sinking and everything was turning salmon pink. After a while the phone squeezed out another little chirp from where it rested, antenna up, on a pile of rocks. I could see where things were heading. Pretty soon we wouldn't have real birds anymore. We'd have electronic avian simulators activated by motion detectors placed along a nature path with a corporate sponsor. To enter, you'd slide your card.

I decided to leave the phone to its ringing and walked into the desert in its last, fading hour. I believed that this was what Audubon would have done, though probably not in flip-flops. I could see no trace of Walter or the boy. I had to pick my way carefully, watching for cacti and other thorned plants. It hadn't rained in months and everything was shrunken and yellow. I, personally, wasn't particularly well acquainted with the outdoors, but was willing to learn. I walked over a rise into a shallow arroyo. I rounded a knot of mesquite and found myself staring into the huge, syrupy eyeballs of a small cow. It swung its head around and looked at me.

"Hello," I said.

The cow nibbled a dainty clump of brush.

"There's a snack bar made out of your bones around the corner."

The cow regarded me skeptically. It switched its tail; it allowed a few flies to crawl on the wet membrane around its eye. It seemed unperturbed by its surroundings. Like the bad boy, the cow was now.

I walked over to the cow and threw my arms around its neck. It resisted me for a second or two, then forgot about that and again became preoccupied with the task of chewing. I pressed my cheek against its shoulder. It was warm and dusty and smelled like a dirty horse. I loved the cow. The cow was my consolation prize.

We stayed that way for a while, the cow and I, until I heard a murmur of voices above me. I looked up and was greeted by the silhouette of a little boy, vaguely extraterrestrial in his drop-shaped, plastic bike helmet. He peered at me over his handlebars.

"Dad," he inquired, "why is that lady hugging a cow?"

Dad wheeled his mountain bike closer to the edge of the gully and looked down at me for a silent moment. "C'mon," he said, with a note of uneasiness in his voice, "Let's get out of here. Let's get going."

From far away, I heard the phone chirp faintly.

NIGHT WAS FALLING. In the west, the sky clung to the faintest tinge of pale blue like Isadora Duncan clinging to the last thread of her scarf. I had returned to the car. I sat on the hood, still warm from the sun, and listened to the phone ringing weakly every few minutes. I supposed the batteries must be wearing down. Somewhere north of us, in a sprawling desert city under a darkening sky, some lady was sitting at a kitchen table, with nails like talons, madly dialing the same number over and over again, driven by rage or spite or love. In a sick way I sort of admired her. She stuck with it. She took her connection to the boy seriously. That was more than I could say.

When it was almost dark, I heard Walter and the boy's feet crunching over the rocky ground before they came into view. Walter appeared, his expression reserved and grim. Behind him staggered the boy, head hanging like a sack on his neck. He seemed a whole lot less manic and bad than he had earlier, and a lot more tired and young. I have to admit, I literally couldn't take my eyes off him. In the gathering dark his bone structure was more freakishly perfect, his silhouette more overwhelmingly luscious than I remembered. He truly was a rare specimen, gorgeous and condemned, like the Roseate Spoonbill, a shore feeder once found in plentiful supply on the Florida coast and hunted nearly to extinction. Audubon's portrait shows a lone bird in full postparty dishevelment, with hot pink plumage and bloodshot eyes, wandering in a desolate swamp beneath thick clouds. The poor thing looks like it should be clutching a handbag full of condom wrappers.

"Are you okay?" I asked.

"Oh, probably not," said Walter.

The boy was still drunk or exhausted or both. I was sure Walter had done something to him, I just wasn't sure what. The zipper to the boy's fly, however, was only half way up. It seemed like the action was always taking place somewhere else—all the passion, the anguish, it was always elsewhere—on the phone, in the past. I hated it and it was exactly the way I wanted it. My only comfort was in knowing it was the same for Walter. A zipper half way up is also only half way down.

We drove back to civilization in silence. Walter smoked cigarettes and stared out the side window into the night. He wouldn't look at me. The boy slept behind us in the back seat. After a while the city lights reappeared, and we coasted off the highway and into town. When we stopped at a light, I turned to look at Walter. He angled his body to look back at me.

"You didn't have to leave me there," I said.

"It's not like I made you wait."

"You knew I liked him."

He took a drag off his cigarette. "Yeah. I knew you wouldn't really do anything with him either."

"You don't know that," I said. "You have no idea what I'd do."

Walter squinted off into the mysterious veil of the night. "My God," he exclaimed, "look how they spelled *sandwiches*."

There was a coffee shop on the opposite side of the intersection. The marquee said: "Fresh Sandwhiches Daily."

"I think I like it better that way."

"Me too," said Walter.

The light changed and I drove forward. Walter, meanwhile, dug around in the boy's backpack and pulled out a book that said "math" on the cover—not algebra or geometry—just "math." The boy's address was scrawled in a psychotic hand inside. Walter thought it was in the Sam Hughes neighborhood, so I turned the Chevy around and headed that way. It turned out the boy lived in a nice area, on a block of bungalows built in the 1930s. Looking at those little porches, I could almost picture men from the old days in fedoras, sitting on metal chairs, slowly dying of lung ailments.

We idled to a stop in front of a beige-and-white house. It was brightly lit, with some shrubs and a little rectangle of lawn in front.

"C'mon kiddo." Walter poked the boy in the arm. "End of the line."

The boy looked at us blankly, then rolled over and burrowed his face into the upholstery. "Noooo," he moaned.

We opened the rear doors and went around to prod him better. I tried to lift his head. It flopped back onto the seat as though there were neither muscles nor tendons within. "Noooo," he said, and covered his ears with his hands. Walter finally got a grip on the boy's arms and hauled him headfirst from the Chevy. He balanced him on the curb, half in the car, half out, until I came around from the other side and helped prop him up.

"Where are we?" he said.

"We're home!" I said brightly. This seemed to inspire the boy to begin a low, constant moaning.

We'd walked him halfway to the front door before his knees crumpled and he slithered to the grass, which was wet, from the sprinklers I suppose. He crawled on his belly for a few feet then gave up and sprawled out in a twisted, dissipated heap. He lay there, retching a little.

"Hey," said Walter, bending over the boy and patting him on the face. "Hey little guy. Upsadaisy. Come on. Let's rally!"

The boy's eyes slid open. He stared at Walter for a while, as though he were trying to place him. Then he groaned, "I love you."

Walter looked from the house to the boy to the Chevy, then back again. "Oh my God," he said wearily.

"What do you want to do?"

"I don't know." He seemed baffled. "I mean, we can't stay here, we can't just dump him."

The boy lay on his stomach, damp, panting, and oddly flat to the ground. *Dump him.* It sounded so light, so breezy. O breezy day.

"Yeah," I said, "Let's do that. Let's just go."

"Wait," moaned the boy, "fuck."

I sighed. I suppose he was having a life crisis. I suppose he'd experienced his first blow job or similar sexual episode while he was with Walter, and now he expected us to be as concerned about it as he was. I found it remarkable that anything could affect anyone so much. All that rage, all that confusion, all that love. What a mess. Someone should have warned him not to get in a car with a couple of poets. All we wanted to do was to get home and write about him.

"You want to leave him here all," Walter looked at the boy, "twisted?"

"Yes," I said. "Yes I do."

The edge of a smile appeared at the corners of Walter's mouth. Just like that, I felt our camaraderie flare back to life. For once I felt very of-the-moment, very now. I didn't have to wait for him to agree. We were already jogging away from the house, toward the car. Walter tossed me his lighter and I managed to torch the end of a cigarette just as I sprang open the door to the driver's seat. The night was warm and the lights of the city sparkled around us, better than stars. We hopped into the Chevy and peeled out.

I could make out the figure of the bad boy receding in the rearview mirror as we drove away. Audubon's portrait would have shown him rearing up, his knees digging into the grass while a vomity stain on the front of his shirt glowed a faint, noxious yellow. His mouth is open as though he's about to utter his cry, the cry of the Southwestern Bad Boy—perhaps "fuck it" or "motherfucker"—something ardent and vague. Audubon would have done a fine job capturing his beauty, with all the outlines precise and crisp, all the colors vivid and true, painting him with the remarkable care he took with all his subjects, all of those doomed creatures, so beloved and so used.

From *Ark Baby*

LIZ JENSEN

Darwin's Paradox

I WAS STILL REELING from the sight of the magnificent corseted woman—reality or apparition of my crazed mental state, I knew not which—when the door of 14 Madagascar Street opened abruptly, and I found myself face to face with a thin, grey-bearded, grumpy-looking gent whose mouth appeared to be bristling with pins. In his right hand, he was wielding a hoof.

"Dr. Scrapie?" I stammered.

"Yes?" With a gesture of disgust, he spat out his pins into his hand and settled his eyes on me, where they blazed uncomfortably. The shirt beneath his frock-coat was splattered with what might have been cochineal, or blood. A hole gaped in the sleeve of his jacket. "Well, young man? What is it?"

"May I come in, sir?"

"What for?" he barked. "I'm busy. State the nature of your business, sir, or bugger off."

My heart began to thump crazily under my ribs. I must persevere, I thought. I have come this far. What I have started, I will finish. Betty Botter bought some butter. Peter Piper picked a peck. Axelhaunch. Fib's Wash. Blaggerfield.

"Well?"

"I would like to request you, sir—" I begin, trying to effect an entry. But he blocks my path.

"Yes?"

"—And as a matter of fact require you—" (Courage, Tobias!)

"Yes?" He was scowling at me now.

"—And furthermore demand you, sir—" (Yes!)

"What, dammit?"

"Humbly, sir, to—"

"To what? Get on with it, fellow!" His voice has growling thunder in it.

Three words left. Grasp those thistles, Tobias, and prove you are a man!

"Examine my body. Sir."

Silence. He's looking at me as if I'm mad.

"I'm not a bloody physician," he spits finally. "I am a taxidermist. I stuff and mount animals. Whoever directed you here is an imbecile. Now bugger off."

"Please, sir. Please!" I am wedging my way in now, and reaching in my pocket. "There is something only you can answer."

"I said NO!" he shouted. "Now bugger off! I'm in the middle of stuffing—" He stops.

I'm pointing my revolver at him. My hand is shaking. Dr. Scrapie freezes.

I can hear how thin and desperate my voice sounds. Like a tin whistle.

I say, "You will do it, sir, or I shall blow your head off, and then my own!"

Yes: a man at last!

NONE OF THE PLASTIC REPLICAS of primates or the hologram exhibits resembled my towel-holder in any way. There was an interactive CD ROM, though. I scrolled through, beginning to feel that my visit here was already a waste of time. I'd been through all my old veterinary books, and even rung a friend who specialised in primates. He'd never heard of the Gentleman Monkey, and when I described my towel-holder, he drew a blank. The CD ROM display repeated a lot of the stuff I'd already come across in the virtual library that I'd accessed from Thunder Spit: how the monkey differs from the ape in crucial ways such as DNA structure, teeth, skull size, and skeletally, in

particular with regard to the tail. There are only three living excep-
tions to this rule: Kitchener's Ape, which has a cingulum on its molar
teeth, more in keeping with the monkey family, the Yeoman Baboon,
whose skull is closer to the fossilised humanoid Neanderthal than an
ape as such, and the extinct Ape of Mogador.

Mogador rang a bell. Wasn't Mogador mentioned in Scrapie's
treatise?

"MY GOD," says Dr. Scrapie, a minute later when Tobias Phelps
has bashfully undressed. A brief glimpse of Tobias Phelps' anatomy
would be enough to tell any zoologist that they had something
remarkable on their hands. As Scrapie's expert eyes take in the sight
of the creature before him, he stifles a gasp.

"Extraordinary," he murmurs.

The hand-like feet.

The abundance of orange body hair, peppered with animal fleas.

The mutilated coccyx.

"And then there's that," says Tobias Phelps, pointing to the jar.

Scrapie peers at its contents, and soon his pulse is racing furiously.

"Am I the first to—?" he asks Tobias Phelps in a haunted whisper.

"Apart from Dr. Baldicoot, when I was a baby. And my mother,
but she is dead." Tobias Phelps is silent for a moment, and then confesses, "I rarely have occasion to be entirely naked, sir. Even when
alone." Scrapie raises his eyebrows. "My upbringing, you know,"
Tobias Phelps whispers sadly. "My parents—discouraged nakedness."

Scrapie's heart does a complicated somersault.

"Yes," he says, clearing his throat. "I quite understand. Now lie
down, please," he instructs the young man. The phrase "on a plate,"
keeps running through his head. Meanwhile Tobias Phelps, for his
part, cannot help noticing that the taxidermist's manner has altogether altered, in the direction of sudden, extreme interest.

"Now," announces Scrapie, forcing his mouth into a smile. "My
dear young man. I need to investigate you further."

I KEYED IN "APE OF MOGADOR," and waited for further details. As the computer was running the search, I looked about: the schoolkids were flowing up the stairs like an anti-gravitational pancake mix. Everything echoed. I didn't like this place. It gave me the creeps.

Just then there was a muted beep, and some text came up on the screen: in pink, on a yellow background, with an insistent techno-beat of music behind it. I began to read.

The Ape of Mogador: Also known—erroneously, because of its misleading tail—as the Gentleman Monkey.

Jesus Christ. And there was more.

As I read on, I began to feel sick with excitement.

PETER PIPER PICKED A PECK OF PICKLED PEPPER, I said to myself as Dr. Scrapie took out a small roll of measuring tape and encircled my skull with it. Miss Mosh mashes some mish-mash, I thought, as he shone a little torch into my eye. Minewort, lungwort, I thought, as he peered first into one ear, and then the other. Gudderwort. The arid Gudderwort. I can see his face. I can see his face and the distaste on it as he hands me the jar. And other faces, too: the Mulveys, the Cleggses and the Balls and the Tobashes. Tommy Boggs' wife was a Tobash. Jessie, who had called me Prune-Face. Jessie's belly, rounded with child.

The girl in my rooms, her hand down a student's trousers, fishing about for his—

The woman I had glimpsed in the upper window, beneath whose corset—

The jar that contained my—

"Now breathe in slowly," Scrapie is saying; he has a cold stethoscope to my chest. Can he hear how fast my heart is pounding?

From this angle, with his flowing white hair, grizzled beard, and authoritarian expression, Dr. Scrapie resembles God; the same God whose beard dissolved into the white storm-clouds of the Great Flood in the Noah's Ark picture on my bedroom wall at home. Have I not come to the expert of experts? The man who single-handedly peopled the Queen's ghastly Animal Kingdom Collection with its human-eyed bestiary?

His eyes are all fired up with a strange gleam, and it dawns on me that I will have no more need of my revolver. I have his attention.

"*Sir* Ivanhoe," I hear him murmur.

"I beg your pardon?"

"Nothing," he replies quickly. "I am just trying to think how I can—"

There is a long pause as he appears to search the recesses of his memory for the right word. "Help you," he says finally.

Now he is questioning me intensively, scribbling notes as he does so, and I am suddenly telling him everything. About being a foundling, discovered by the altar of St. Nicholas's Church in Thunder Spit, the day after the Travelling Fair of Danger and Delight left Judlow, with a ghastly mutilation to my lower spine which had nearly killed me. About the way the animals of Thunder Spit growled at me, and how I was rejected by humans, too. About the Contortionist at the Travelling Fair, who had handed my father the jar containing the—

"The object in question," I falter. Scrapie's eyebrows shoot up.

"Aha," he says. "Now we are getting somewhere."

But he does not say where. Instead, he questions me in detail about what he calls my "well-spokenness." This prompts me to impress him further with a few tongue-twisters, and I recount how I used to read long passages from the Bible in church.

"Speech came to me late," I tell him, "prompted by the sight of a cake on my fifth birthday." This seems to stir even more excitement in him.

"And before that? How did you communicate?"

"In squeaks and grunts, as far as I am aware," I told him. "They said it was a miracle."

"A case of nurture overcoming nature, perhaps?" mutters Scrapie, almost to himself. And then, addressing me: "In what manner were you raised?"

"In a Christian manner, sir," I tell him. "Cleanliness, reading, self-improvement and piety were encouraged. Indulgences of the flesh, nakedness and childish play were not. A traditional English upbringing, sir."

He questions me further, and I find myself telling him more: about how I believed the jar to contain an umbilical cord, until it had smashed, and about how Kinnon had put me right. About how, when I had told Kinnon my fears, he had assured me I was mad. About how I had insisted on knowing the truth. About how he had advised me to come to London, and search out an expert.

"You could not have come to a better place, young man," murmurs Scrapie reassuringly, as he begins to carry out a series of quick sketches of me in his notebook. "You can trust me implicitly."

This is a profound relief.

"AND YOU SAY YOUR FOSTER-FATHER WILL NOT SEE YOU?" Scrapie asked when I had finished telling him about Parson Phelps' removal to the Fishforth Sanatorium for the Spiritually Disturbed.

"That is so, sir." I hung my head.

"I am—sorry to hear that," he said thoughtfully. "And nobody has any idea that you are here in this house? With me?"

"No, sir. Why should they?"

"No reason at all. Indeed not. My poor young man. No relatives? No friends? You are here completely—alone?"

It seemed important to him, though I could not see why.

"Completely alone," I confirmed. Although I did not like this lonely thought, Dr. Scrapie seemed to find it particularly appealing; he started rubbing his hands as if I were a warm hearth.

Finally he blurted excitedly, "You looked familiar to me, young man, as soon as I saw you."

I was surprised.

"Are there others like me, then?" I asked, filled with a sudden tremulous hope.

"In a manner of speaking, yes," said Scrapie. "Or at least there were. What I mean is, I have seen a creature that resembles you. Resembles you so closely, and according to my records so accurately, anatomically speaking—"

He went over to his desk and pulled out a notebook full of measurements and sketches. Then he said, "Have you heard of a creature called the Gentleman Monkey? An extinct primate, from Morocco?"

"No." I said. Why was my heart suddenly plummeting downwards like a leaden fishing weight?

"That is the creature you resemble, young man."

I PRESSED THE KEY to call the picture up from the CD ROM, and watched the 3-D image emerge. It was an artist's impression, and was accompanied by an etching of the creature, made in 1843 by a wildlife artist who had visited the last remaining specimen in the Jardin Zoologique in Mogador, Morocco. I gasped when I saw it. It showed the monkey standing with its hands on its hips, in a defiant and disconcertingly human posture, behind the bars of a large cage.

"It's him!" I shouted. "It's bloody-well him!"

"*Lang*uage!" said the man in the mauve tracksuit. The pancake mixture had finished its progress up the stairs, and was now slurping Coke from cans and mock karate-kicking each other with feet clad in blocky trainers. "There's kids about," the teacher went on. "If you can't keep your mouth clean you shouldn't be here in school hours."

"Sorry," I lied, desperate to get rid of him. He was glaring at me now like I was some kind of paedophile. When he finally shuffled off, trailing his charges behind him like a pedagogical jellyfish, I turned my attention to the text that accompanied the etching. The Gentleman Monkey was an unusual specimen, and had baffled naturalists at the time. Strikingly humanoid, with a larger brain than man's, and a fun-loving temperament.

Polygamous by nature.

That word "polygamous" got me thinking. It was then that some phrases from Dr. Ivanhoe Scrapie's eccentric treatise came floating back into my head, and my brain began to whirr.

"SO THIS—GENTLEMAN MONKEY," I croaked finally, gulping at air.
"What is it, exactly?"

"Was," Dr Scrapie corrected me. "It is no more. It was an interest-ing species of monkey; not so much a monkey, in fact as a tailed ape. Anyway, highly intelligent, and strikingly human in appearance. Polygamous by nature, and a fructivore, but in other respects remark-ably similar in many ways to the human. Child-like but courteous by nature; that's why they called him the Gentleman, I suppose. And probably also why he became extinct," he added thoughtfully.

I was having trouble breathing by now. "And what happened to it?"

"The last remaining member of its race is now housed in Buck-ingham Palace," said Scrapie. "I stuffed him and he became a towel-holder for the ladies' powder room in the banqueting suite. That's where he is now."

If only I had heeded Kinnon's advice, accepted his diagnosis of madness, and remained in Hunchburgh! I would be ordained by now! I would be Parson Phelps the Second, preaching my anti-Dar-winian sermon loud and clear from the pulpit!

I pictured the creature's skin being removed from its body, and filled with sawdust, then dressed in human clothes, like the crea-tures I had seen at the Museum.

"And the—carcass?" I mustered finally, following the ghastly thought through to its conclusion.

"You'd rather not know about that, young man," said Scrapie, looking suddenly tired and slightly throttled. "Suffice it to say that it was highly toxic. It contained poison."

"Poison?"

"So it would appear. Not something I discovered till—later," said Scrapie. "When I had cause to investigate the creature's remains."

"You mean the monkey was poisonous by nature, or it had been poisoned?"

"It had been poisoned," he said slowly. "With praxin."

"But why? Where? Who did it?" I felt my sanity slipping away as I spoke.

"Nobody knows," sighed Scrapie. "But I have my suspicions."

THE LAST OF THIS SPECIES OF APE, according to the inter-active CD-ROM display, had been purchased by the entrepreneur Horace Trapp from a Moroccan menagerie for Queen Victoria's collection and shipped over to Britain, but it had died in mysterious circumstances on the voyage back to London, following a mutiny on board Trapp's vessel, the *Ark*. The creature had later been stuffed by the Taxidermist Royal, Dr. Ivanhoe Scrapie, as part of Queen Victoria's Animal Kingdom Collection, most of which was housed in the Museum. But the Queen had so taken a liking to the primates that she decreed they should grace the rooms of Buckingham Palace, which was where the ape was dispatched, once stuffed, sometime in the 1850s. But in 1864, to the dismay of later generations of evolutionary scientists specialising in primates, the stuffed creature was stolen from Buckingham Palace. And never traced.

It was there, as I flicked through the interactive zoology encyclopedia, that I realised. The Gentleman Monkey in my bathroom was the only known specimen in the whole world of this breed of extinct primate. The only remaining evidence that such a creature had ever existed. There was no mention of its having been stolen in Scrapie's treatise. Could he perhaps have written it before the creature had disappeared from the Palace? And if he had not been lying about the rarity and the final extinction of the species—was it (I got all choked up at the thought), was it possible that the rest of his extraordinary document was also true?

That word "polygamous" kept haunting me.

Yes: I'd definitely have to think about this.

"WE FOUND THE GENTLEMAN MONKEY dead on the *Ark*," said Scrapie, after he had finished telling me what he knew about Horace Trapp's career, first as a slave-trader, then as an animal collector for the Queen. "Along with all the other creatures. Over a thousand of them. Most of them half torn to bits. Nature's cruel, you know, young man," he said, eyeing me in a strange way. "But there wasn't a mark on the monkey. It was the praxin that killed him. It must have been injected."

I winced.

"We found Trapp's head, too," Scrapie continued, going slightly pale. He paused for a moment and re-filled his pen with ink. He did it slowly, applying great concentration to the task. "Not a pretty sight," he said finally.

"When was this?" I asked. "When did Trapp's *Ark* arrive in London?"

"1845, the same year Violet was born," said Scrapie. "It was found floating on the Channel, and hauled in."

"Violet?"

"My youngest daughter." I remembered the face of a woman in the window. So this was Violet Scrapie. I felt my heart shift, and desolation sweep through me like a cold wind. "It was a bloody nuisance," Scrapie was saying. "Had to ship an iceberg over to deal with it. Trapp's *Ark* kept me busy for fifteen years."

I gulped.

"1845 was the year of my birth," I told him. "As far as it is known."

Scrapie picked up his notebook again, and began to scribble furiously.

I HAD DISMISSED THE ASSERTIONS in Scrapie's treatise as nonsense; the ravings of a demented man.

But—

Hope gobbled at my innards, and my brain raced. I found myself actually having to grab hold of a fibreglass gibbon to keep my balance. The kids had moved off, but their voices wafted up from the hall below, a faint echo buzzing in my head.

What I was thinking was that, by a quirk of fate—that chance meeting in the pub with Norman Ball? Or was it even earlier, when the threatened litigation over Giselle catapulted me north? Or did it date back to my childhood wish to work with animals? In any case, by some quirk of fate, some kind of extraordinary missing link had fallen into my lap.

The de Savile Theory of Evolution, they would rename it. I

would insist on it. I'd hold the Gentleman Monkey hostage, if necessary, until it was official. You try stopping me.

I'd be given a Euro Award.

Then I started thinking about the other stuff in the document, and my stomach heaved. There were implications. Phelps, the man was called. Tobias Phelps. I didn't recognise the name from the twins' family tree. But they hadn't finished it.

I was hallucinating now, surely. I had never seen their feet. They didn't have tails, that was for sure. But it was still possible— was it not? That—

No. I was going mad. It was impossible.

"IMPOSSIBLE!" I said.

Scrapie said, "So you know, since you have become aware of Mr. Darwin's theories, that we are all descended from the humble primate?" He spoke slowly, as if I were suddenly a child, or a creature not too quick on the uptake. Perhaps he was right. "*All* of us," he said. "Even Her Majesty Queen Victoria."

No, I thought. It wasn't like that. *The earth was without form and void, and darkness was upon the face of the deep.*

"Human beings stand at the top of Darwin's ladder of nature, you know, Mr. Phelps. Of all the species of primate, we are the most evolved."

Blasphemy!

"Have you ever seen a fossil, Mr. Phelps?"

"I have. My father used to say that they were God's jokes," I told him. My voice sounded weak and thin.

"Jokes?"

"God moves in a mysterious way," I said, scraping about in my memory for the comfort of my fledgling sermon on God and the fossils. "Fossils are clearly the Lord's doing, and evidence of His grand design."

But my heart wouldn't stop pounding; I felt that I might explode and scatter, like a distraught firework.

"Well, according to Darwin and others," said Scrapie, "they are evidence of a distant past, of which we are the biological inheritors. Have you heard of natural selection, young man?"

"Yes," I said. "It is Darwin's theory. I have studied his book, and his profane ideas."

"Natural selection," said Scrapie, brushing my remarks aside, "is Nature's way of making advancements. From simple to complex, from complex to even more complex, until you reach man. Darwin says that we must not, however, forget the principle of correlation, by which many strange deviations of structure are tied together, so that a change in one part often leads to other changes of a *quite unexpected nature*."

Scrapie stopped in his tracks and steered me towards a *chaise-longue*.

"Sit down here," he said. Obeying him, I found myself face to face with the male object and related accoutrements of a stuffed horse.

"A fine specimen, your horse," I mustered politely. Miss Mosh mashes some mish-mash. The creature looked nothing like the horses back in Thunder Spit.

"Well, it would be an odd specimen, if it were a horse," says Scrapie. "Actually, it's a mule. An ass. A hybrid."

"A hybrid? A sort of cross?"

Mildred doesn't like this idea one little bit, and wrenches violently at my long-suffering sphincter.

"Exactly. Father a stallion, mother a donkey. Or occasionally vice versa. They are always sterile," continued Dr. Scrapie slowly, keeping his eyes levelled on my face. "They are sterile," he said, "because Nature doesn't like breeding across species. Yet—*paradoxically*—it has always happened. In the case of the mule, it has been virtually an institution. Most examples occur in the world of botany, but there are plenty of zoological examples as well. More than you'd think. Wallabies and kangaroos. Crocodiles and alligators. Lions and tigers, even. And then there are historical cases, or should I say mythological ones, though where mythology ends and history begins we can only guess at."

"Cases such as, sir?" I falter faintly.

"Such as the Minotaur, the Centaur, the mermaid; Pegasus, the winged horse. Medusa, the snake-headed woman. The Devil is half goat, is he not? And then of course there's the Angel."

Blasphemy and more blasphemy!

"I cannot agree with that, sir," I retort, my cheeks burning. "The Angel is a creature of Heaven." But then I feel my face slacken, and I reach for my whelk. For I know, suddenly, and, with a force that sets Mildred attacking my innards, that if a creature of Heaven is possible, then so is a beast from Hell.

"So how—? What—?" I stammered.

"Darwin," said Scrapie, "asked the following question: *'If the cross offspring of any two races of birds or animals be interbred, will the progeny keep as constant, as that of any established, breed; or will it tend to return in appearance to either parent?'* I'll say this much for Darwin: he's asked some sensible questions. But he doesn't have all the answers. Not by a long chalk."

I am perched stiffly now on the edge of the *chaise-longue*.

"And—do you have answers, sir?"

"I think your existence upon this earth is beginning to provide me with some," he replied. He sat still for a while, lost in thought. "A form of natural selection," he finally murmured to himself. "An evolutionary tangent. A new branch of the family. Or an old one." Then he jumped up and began to pace the room. I could see his mind was tumbling in all directions. "Yes; very possibly an old one. Humans are evolved from other primates. Apes. Monkeys, too, but further back. But what if—?" He paused then began to drum his fingers on a table.

"Hypothesis," he said, his eyes dancing with excitement. "Hypothesis. A human mates with another species of primate. On board Trapp's *Ark*, let's say. Mates, let us speculate, for the purposes of argument, with the Gentleman Monkey. And creates a new breed of human-like primate. You, Mr. Phelps!"

I was winded by the very absurdity of the suggestion, but there was no stopping Scrapie by now. He was leaping up and down.

"Yes, you!" he yelled, slapping me hard on the back. "Raising the intriguing scientific question: Can the unaccountable leaps and bounds of our evolutionary path be explained by the occasional injection of the blood of other species into the veins of some creatures? Could the mouse have emerged from the elephant, or vice versa, by an incredible act of sexual union? Which occasionally bore fruit?"

I gulped.

Scrapie said that a man called Mendel had bred peas that told such a story. The botanical examples were all about us. I thought of the gourd plant on my mother's grave. Had it been trying to tell me something, after all?

"Yes!" Scrapie was almost shouting. "There's not enough time, you see, for everything to have happened! To get from a fish to an amphibian to a man takes longer than it should. It doesn't work on paper. So there have to be sudden changes, not just gradual ones. And you are the answer!"

My head was thudding, and the air about me seemed suddenly strangely dappled, as though my vision were disintegrating. "I still don't understand."

"Two different species, breeding, Mr. Phelps! Imagine such a thing! Not possible now, to create a new species, out of two. But *was once*, maybe. Why on earth not? So imagine this, as the answer to Darwin's time-paradox: that man didn't evolve slowly from a gorilla or a chimpanzee. He appeared suddenly, like Adam and Eve in the Bible. Just one. A freak cross-breed. From two completely different—and perhaps incompatible—species. Two species that would perhaps otherwise not have *survived*! That would have *died out*! Two wrongs, therefore, Mr. Phelps, making a right! You are living proof that it's possible."

One of the briefest, but also the most potentially historic conversations on the theory of evolutionary science, had just taken place.

"I'M ALL SHOOK UP!" I sang. "*Oooh!*"
  Pedal to the metal. Go, cats, go.
  This was the biz.
  And I was the King.

SO, I THOUGHT MISERABLY, Genesis *was* a lie. And evolution *was* a fact. But its mechanics—its mechanics were not quite as Mr. Darwin thought. It had progressed at times in great magical leaps. And I was proof of it. A mutant, an aberration, a misbegot. One year a green and stippled gourd. The next a yellow, blotchy one. The following year an orange fruit, with warts. The year after that, a mauve one with stripes. The year after that, a green one again, but with warts, or stripes, or mottled patches. A bit of this, a bit of that. Fling it in the primordial soup pot and await God knows what! The world looked different, all of a sudden. It had transformed itself, before my eyes, from an ordered place, a hierarchy created by God, into a floating Darwinian whorehouse. There reigned a new, chaotic higgledy-piggledyness that defied belief and astonished the heavens. And I, Tobias Phelps, was part of this crazy hotchpotch of nature called evolution, a dangerous and wild and virtually unexplored new territory of understanding. But was I a victim or a pioneer?

Was I one of God's jokes, or the butt of it?

I hung my head in an unfathomable mixture of pride and shame.

Scrapie was fingering a syringe now, and giving me a strange look.

"Have you ever had laudanum?" he asked.

"Yes. Kinnon gave me some before I left Hunchburgh. To calm my nerves."

"He did well. I would now like to give you some more. I shall administer it by injection; it'll act faster and more effectively that way. Now roll up your sleeve for me."

Betty Botter bought some butter, I murmured to myself as the needle entered my vein and he squeezed. But, she said, this butter's bitter. Scrapie had been right; I began to feel both relaxed and dizzy immediately.

"How tall are you, Mr. Phelps?" he is asking.

"Five feet two," I reply, sinking back on to the *chaise-longue*.

"That's right. Make yourself comfortable. And your waist measures—approximately?"

"I have no idea, sir," I murmured, feeling drowsy.

"Will you permit me then," he asked, "to measure you again?"

"With a view to what, Dr. Scrapie?" I moaned.

But before I could hear his answer, I had succumbed to blackness.

Gunnison Beach

RITA WELTY BOURKE

THEY CALL US PARK SERVICE BITCHES: Geneva Hart-
land, Sallie Bailey, and me, Kylie Wheeler from Birmingham,
Alabama. This past May I walked off the stage at the University of
Colorado with a ribbon around my neck, a medallion hanging
between my breasts, and a leather-bound diploma swinging from
my fingertips. That's how I snagged this job with the National Park
Service. The federal government is impressed with stuff like that.

We girls walk, and sometimes ride, the beaches at Sandy Hook,
New Jersey, wearing Department of Interior outfits: olive green
shorts and matching blouses with insignias on the shoulders, Vasque
boots, and wide-brim hats. We put on sunglasses, sun block, and
insect repellent before we venture out of our housing units. Sallie
and I live in an old army barrack dating from pre-Civil War days.

A biological science technician, GS 5 level, I was hired to protect
endangered species on the island. Specifically, I am to document
sightings of black skimmers, least terns, and piping plovers. I am to
follow them through their mating and nesting cycles and protect
them from harm. I carry government issue, high-powered binoculars. Sometimes, in the pursuit of my duties, I have to become a Park
Service Police Officer. Hence the name Park Service Bitch.

Sallie is an intern, unpaid except for free housing and uni-
forms. She dreams of getting a job with Greenpeace one day.
Geneva is our boss.

The swimmers and sunbathers who come over from the mainland don't like it when we close their beaches, which we do from
time to time. And the nudies up on Gunnison don't like women

who are clothed coming into their private world. Mostly gay and largely male, they especially dislike women in authority.

Right off the bat, one of them got smart with me about roping off an area of the beach where he wanted to set up a badminton court.

"Every year you're taking more of the beach away from us," he whined. "I'm a taxpayer, like everyone else. I have rights."

Yeah, right. Get a life, Mister. "Sir, we're here to protect the piping plovers. We have no control over where they decide to nest. Our job is to find the nests, build an exclosure, and rope off the surrounding area. If you have a problem with that, write your congressman. He voted for the Endangered Species Act." Get out of my way; I have a job to do.

Geneva trained us to be tough. Uncompromising. Anyone who won't listen, throw them off the island, she said. Ban them from coming onto the Hook for the rest of the season. And don't hesitate to call security if you need extra muscle.

She handed me a radio, which I hooked onto my belt. It became part of my uniform.

Geneva takes nothin' off nobody. She's been here seven years, and she just got tossed out of her house because she has a live-in boyfriend. The government frowns on what they call "fraternization." Since her eviction, Geneva's been in a constant state of mad.

Yet she can be soft in ways that catch you unexpectedly. Like last week, when she got after some New York City trash who decided to picnic inside one of our nesting areas. She grabbed one of our signs off the truck and waved it in their faces. "Can't you read English? Do you understand what this says? A-r-e-a C-l-o-s-e-d?" She was so mad she sprayed spit when she spelled out the letters.

It was a family of foreign-looking people who probably did not speak English. They never said a word, just looked scared and backed away from her. The father ushered his wife and carbon copy kids under the wire and they scrambled off as fast as hermit crabs.

The nest had been trampled. The two plovers scampered around on the sand, one of them doing the broken wing act, trying to draw us away from the nest.

"She thinks her babies are still alive," Geneva said, and she walked over to the smoothed-out hollow in the sand.

All four eggs were squashed, the nest wet with mucous. You could see the imprint of a kid's shoe; he'd run right through it.

Geneva hunkered down and picked up a piece of broken egg, and I thought she would cry. She held it in the palm of her hand, just looking at it for the longest time. "It was no more than a day or two from hatching," she said.

With Sallie and me looking on, it felt as if we were attending a funeral there on the beach.

Inside the curve of the shell was a wet cotton ball. Geneva touched its beak, its orange stick legs, its tiny feet. Baby plovers look like little puffs of cotton stuck on orange toothpicks. This one would never run on the beach, never do the broken wing trick, never have a nest of his own.

Damn stupid people.

I ARRIVED ON THE ISLAND during a thunderstorm that cut the electricity, doubled trees over, and nearly toppled the lighthouse up on the north shore. I spent the night huddled in an empty dorm room wondering why I ever left Boulder, wishing I'd brought a flashlight, praying the ocean didn't rear up and sweep right over the island.

The next morning I had to clean up the road that runs down the spine of the island. In the afternoon I set fox traps. And I saw my first nude, an old gay man jogging on the road well beyond the area where he should have been.

I let him go. He was wearing a shirt, so he wasn't totally nude. And with my new uniform still stiff from the sizing, I could afford to wait another day or two.

That first week I caught a feral cat, but I let her go, too. She was a nursing mother, and she'd eaten every bit of the raw chicken I'd tied to the trip wire inside the cage. Her belly was pouched out from the chicken and her breasts swollen with milk.

Geneva was ready to send me packing for that. "Don't you realize she'll eat the birds as soon as they hatch?" Sand birds who run on the beach, preferring to walk rather than fly, are no match for a hungry mother cat with kittens hidden away. "Find her kittens and take them over to the shelter in Red Bank," she ordered.

But I never did. The mother cat avoided the trap after that. She was as smart as the foxes, who are doomed. I've seen the paperwork on Geneva's desk; the Park Service plans to gas the dens in the spring.

I did catch one fox and managed to find him a home. The Bronx Zoo agreed to ship him down to the Great Smoky Mountains, where he can prey on wild pigs who threaten the delicate balance park officials strive to maintain.

When I learned the fate of other foxes that might wander into my traps, I made some changes. I quit scrubbing off the traces of fox blood. I neglected to remove my own scent from the cages. I even sprayed some of the trap doors with perfume I borrowed from Sallie's makeup bag. All this kept his brothers at a distance, safe from the ranger's pistol.

The zoo officials put my fox in a cage lined with the *New York Post*. They joked that he could read about Bill Clinton's sex life on his plane ride to Tennessee. And if that didn't interest him, he could look at the picture of the newborn baby found in a dumpster in Queens.

SOMETIMES WE RIDE THE PARK SERVICE HORSES around the island, and sometimes we take the jeep. We use the jeep when we have to carry fencing and equipment to build exclosures and barriers around the piping plover nests. We have forty-two nesting pairs here on the island, which is about a third of all the piping plovers left in the world.

Last year Geneva says they were able to hatch seventy-two chicks. Only four babies have fledged so far this summer.

Occasionally we find fox tracks around the empty nests. The cats and sea gulls take a toll, as do summer storms and high tides. But people are the worst. They drive across the bridge and crowd in here, walk over the nests, flop down on the beach with never a thought as to what they might be destroying.

Weekends we Bitches are out in force, hiding behind the dunes, guarding the nesting areas. It's getting so I like my nickname, because it means I'm doing my job.

I'M BUSY SLEDGE HAMMERING POSTS into the sand up on Kingman Beach when the old nude approaches me. "I've been watching you building these pens for days, deary. Why are you doing it?" He puts an arm around me, jostles me as if I were a child.

"The nests are hard to see, sir," I tell him, twisting away from him. "But they're here." I wipe an arm across my nose; he smells of coconut oil and something else I can't identify.

"I haven't seen a birdie all day, sweetie," he says. The shirt from that first day is gone. He wears three earrings. Nothing else. "Maybe they've gone somewhere else."

"They're shore birds," I tell him. "They have nowhere else to go. This is where they live. Once there were millions. All up and down the coast. Now there are a few hundred."

"Maybe I could help you," he says, and moves to take the hammer from me.

But I tell him to get himself back up to Gunnison where he belongs. I drum my fingers on the steel post and watch to make sure he goes in the right direction.

Some of the nudies like to be looked at. When they see our jeep approaching, they strut their stuff. As if we care about their appendages and pierces and wacko jewelry. Sallie, raised a Baptist, looks the other way. Nude is bad enough, she says. Nude and gay is over the edge.

Geneva says they think we spy on them, hide behind the dunes with our binoculars, hoping to gather evidence so we can close their beach. But who cares what they do down there? As long as they leave the birds alone.

"CHILL OUT, LADY," the fisherman says, kicking wet sand in my direction. "I'm not anywhere near your birds."

"You're in a restricted area," I tell him. "You'll have to leave."

"The nests are way up there on the hill," he argues. He takes a crab off his line and throws it to the waiting sea gulls. They scramble to grab their prize; the winners tear it to pieces.

"The plovers have to come down to the intertidal area to feed.

When the tide goes out, that's the richest feeding ground. That's why we rope it off down to the water. You'll have to go somewhere else."

He throws another crab to a gull who stands apart from the others. The bird gobbles it down, his beak twisting like a knife in the hands of a Jersey City gangster. Then I see that the gull has only one leg, and I wonder who to feel sorry for, bird or crab.

"Why don't you go get laid," the fisherman says, winding in his line, gathering up his equipment.

I stand very still, wondering what Geneva would do.

"You can't walk through this exclosure, sir," I tell him. I plant my legs wide and solid in the sand and jerk my radio off my belt.

"Just how am I supposed to get around your precious bird sanctuary?"

"Walk up to the road, sir. Walk along the road until you find a path down to an area that is not roped off." I tap a fingernail against the plastic on my radio.

He picks up his gear and moves off.

ONE MONTH ON THE JOB and I'm frustrated and angry. Geneva tells me to take a break. "Saddle up one of the horses and go for a ride," she says. "Hurricane needs a good workout. Take him over to Hidden Cove and look for fox dens and terns. Have a picnic on the beach."

I saddle up the chestnut gelding, and we race along the water's edge for most of the morning. We swim across to Skeleton Island, where I marvel at the blue herons and snowy egrets and oystercatchers.

There have never been piping plovers at Hidden Cove, but this year they're all over the beach. Hurricane and I round an outcropping of rock and I spot half a dozen nesting pairs. Babies and adult birds rush about helter-skelter, more of them than I can count.

I sit on my horse thinking that this is the way it used to be. Geneva is miles away, but I want to call out to her to come look. I want to slap my horse on the rump and fly up to the lighthouse and send her a signal, come quick, Geneva, come see what I found.

The tide is out and the birds are active. They scamper down to the water's edge, grab an insect or some interesting piece of flotsam, run back to the nest, or just zigzag around in bursts of energy. There are no predators, and the plovers are thriving.

I tether Hurricane to a piece of driftwood and settle down in the sand to document what I'm seeing. I make notes in my field book, map out the nests, estimate the number and ages of the babies. As the day advances, the heat, the lapping water, and the lovely sight of the peeping sand birds work magic on me. Nestled in the warm sand, I doze off.

I'm awakened by rap music booming from a portable radio, its insistent rhythm sending an electric shock through the air. The plovers have never heard such noise; they take cover wherever they can.

A group of boys comes dancing up the beach. They wear over-sized jeans that drag in the sand. I move behind a ridge of rocks.

One of the boys kicks an empty coke can into a tuft of sea grass, and three plovers run out, chirping fearfully. They're sand colored and orange, the black stripes between their eyes and around their necks not yet fully colored. They run about in melee, their hiding place discovered, the music reverberating between the water and the rock-strewn dunes.

"Let's catch 'em," one of the boys yells, and they swing into action. They herd the plovers away from the protective dunes, toward the sea. One plover is cut off from his nest mates, and he cries out. His pursuer falls on top of him. When the boy rises, he looks beneath him for the captured bird. It does not move.

I toss my notebook aside and come roaring out of my hiding place, yelling, racing down the incline. But the surf pounds and the boom box blares, and the boys pay me no mind.

They pick up pieces of driftwood and begin to beat the mounds of grass, looking for more birds, shooing the babies out from their shelters. They chase after them, driving them into the sea, up onto the rocks, striking them, killing them.

Then I'm on the beach, screaming, shaking my fists at them. "What are you doing? These birds are protected. Get out of here. Get away, get away. Get off the island."

They look at me as if I'm loony. I mash the button on my radio, yell at the dispatcher, my voice cracking, "Emergency, this is an emergency. This is Wheeler up at Hidden Cove. Send someone quick. Get the Park Police up here."

I'm still babbling when the police car roars up the road, blue lights flashing, siren screaming. Randy gets out and comes at a run.

"They're killing the babies," I shout at him, "deliberately chasing and killing them, smashing them with driftwood, I saw him, that ugly kid, where is he, where has he gone, he deliberately killed a baby plover."

But by then the boys have rounded the ridge of rocks and have disappeared. Their manhood proven, their joy taken, they've fled the beach. And the sea has conspired to save them; the tide washes away their footprints.

I walk out among the carnage and begin to count the dead plovers. There are five. Others may be injured and have hidden themselves away.

I look down the beach to where the boys have gone, and I think it's a good thing Geneva gave me only a radio.

ON THE BIGGEST WEEKEND OF THE YEAR, the July Fourth holiday, we get a report that a whale has washed up on the beach north of Gunnison. Geneva and I spin off in the jeep.

The whale rests partly in the sand, partly in the water. He is beyond our help, beyond anyone's help. His back is a mangled mess: a two-foot piece of spine is missing.

"Most likely hit by a boat," Geneva says. She identifies him as a minke, another endangered species; the bay used to be full of them. She walks around him, hand pressed tight against her mouth and nose. "The propeller nearly cut him in half. Bury him above high tide level." She turns and hurries away.

I watch her climb the dune and wonder if what Sallie says is true: that our boss is pregnant.

And how do I get this whale up to where we can bury him, I wonder. High tide is fifty feet away, up a steep bank.

The old nudie with the three earrings appears from nowhere. "We'll need to cut him in half," he says, shading his eyes from the sun as he looks around, calculating how best to get the job done. "Throw a rope around him and use your jeep to drag him up past that ledge of rocks. Dig a hole up there and bury him."

"Who is we?" I ask. "And if you want to roam wherever you want on this island, you'll have to put on some clothes." I end up shouting my final words to his retreating figure.

Ten minutes later he returns with a serrated butcher knife and begins cutting into the whale. "My friend brought it to cut a watermelon," he laughs. He's busy sawing through the rubber and the white fat and the torn innards of the minke when I notice he's put on bathing trunks.

It takes me two trips with the jeep and one ruined clutch before I get both pieces of whale up the hill. I radio for a clean-up crew to come dig the hole. It'll be morning, at the earliest, before they can come, Maintenance tells me. Maybe longer than that: they'll need a backhoe, and that'll have to come from the mainland.

By then the whale will have ruined many a New Yorker's holiday, I answer.

I wash off in the ocean, nurse the jeep down to the parking lot, and return to my job. I find a spot in the dunes where I have a wide view of the beach, lay my binoculars in the sand, lather on the sun block, spritz on some insect repellent.

The government is paying me thousands of dollars to roam the beaches and look for birds. Seek out and protect terns and skimmers, of which there are none. But I can guard the plovers. Keep people away from the exclosures. Keep the nudies within their boundaries. The Fed does not want them to offend the sensibilities of the majority.

The old man sits on a rock close by. I should chase him back to where I know he belongs, but I do not.

He leans back, looks up at the sky. "I've eaten many a plover egg in my day," he says.

"You've eaten these bird eggs?"

"Sorry, love," he says. "I have."

"My name is Kylie," I tell him.

He talks about ordering the dish in the finest restaurants in New York. They were considered a delicacy, he says, looking across the bay toward the city, which is shrouded in a mantle of pollution. "They served them on toast, covered with Hollandaise. They were mild tasting, kind of like..." and he looks up toward the sky, searching for a word to describe them.

"People used to come out here to the beaches and collect the eggs," he says. "Stick a needle in them, suck out the insides, and add them to their collections."

Like Geneva with the whale, my stomach has gone queasy.

"It was a long time ago," he says. "We didn't know. Things are so different now. Besides, I never knew I'd meet you."

"I'm really sorry, little girlie," he says. His eyes seem weary and his three earrings glint in the sun.

Sailors wore earrings in case they were lost at sea. If a sailor's body washed up on shore, the hope was that someone would remove the earring and sell it, then use the money to pay for a decent burial.

In the distance I can see the black hulk of the dead whale resting in two parts on top of the hill. Nearby, I see what I think is a fox den, but I choose not to investigate.

My nudie has put on bathing trunks. Things do not fit so neatly anymore.

He calls me "little girlie." I should object to that. Me, Kylie Wheeler. Phi Beta Kappa. Summa Cum Laude. The Bitch who dragged a whale up a hill and tore out a clutch on a tank of a vehicle.

But I'm touched. I lean back, close my eyes, scratch the poison ivy blisters on my leg, and think about the fox I rescued. Saved from certain death. Sent to Tennessee where he will prey on the feral pigs.

When I looked through the bars of the cage that day, into the eyes of the fox I'd captured, and he looked at me, I knew I did not want to be the cause of his death.

Now the old man looks at me, and I see that he is old, and gay, and his life has been hard. And there isn't much I can do. Except not make things worse for him. Maybe touch his arm when I leave.

From *Easy Travel to Other Planets*

TED MOONEY

It took Melissa nearly the full three weeks to grow used to sleeping in the bed that hung suspended from the ceiling of the flooded house, and even then, even after she had surrounded the bed with shower curtains to protect herself from water splashed or slapped, she would find herself awake in the night's stillest hour, listening to the pump's dull pulse as it circulated fresh seawater through the rooms, listening beyond that to the sea's slow suck as it entered the cove on which the house was built, and from the center of her insomnia she would gaze up through the skylight above her at the meteor showers that streaked the Caribbean sky, and she would think: I am going to die from the strangeness of this. By morning I will be dead of the aloneness and the strangeness.

But when the dawn did come, and with its first light the sound of Peter's speech—clicks and whistles and high-pitched creaks like an unoiled door as he swam into the elevator's harness and pushed the start button with his beak, leaving the deep pool on the first floor to greet Melissa on the second and demand his breakfast—when she was again in the knee-deep water with the dolphin, stroking him and preparing for the day's first lesson, all her despair slipped away from her like clothes shed, and she was glad of everything.

And the dolphin: the dolphin was patient, mainly: what else if not patient? His belly was scraped a bit from the rough spots on the floor, his back peeled a bit from the sunburned hours he and the woman had spent together on the flooded observation deck. In shallow water, a dolphin thinks about the danger to his skin, which is twenty times more sensitive than a man's and which dolphins feel to be the organ of dreams, though they do not sleep. Peter, under Melissa's daily tutelage, had learned to thrust his head out of the water and, with his blowhole, to approximate a few words of English, for which he was rewarded with kisses that created praise in his skin and a sad remembrance of the sagas handed down from the distant times of his dry ancestors. In shallow water, a dolphin will sometimes fall to dwelling on the shortness of life and will seek to make the best of it with amazing feats of attention.

Melissa awoke, on the last of the twenty-one mornings, in full moonlight. Without bothering to change her leotard, she flung back one of the shower curtains and stepped out of the bed into the warm and glittering water. Her breasts were swollen, slightly but painfully, with the approach of her period, and she explored them absently with the fingers of one hand while she listened for Peter. From the level below, faintly audible over the noise of the pump, came the creaking of his nighttime sonar as he moved about in the deep pool, unaware as yet that she was awake. Melissa drew the shower curtain shut, then splashed slowly across the room to where the plastic thermometer was tethered to the floor. She examined it and, on a clipboard hung high on the wall, noted a water temperature of 84°F.—normal for St. Thomas in April.

At the freshwater sink, Melissa felt a swell of apprehension pass over her as she drew the mildewed washcloth across her face, and she found herself thinking of Jeffrey, who was awaiting her in New York, at the other end of her day. He would hate the cut of her hair at first, short against the constant wetness and the salt, but later, in rooms made warm with appetite, he would savor the suggestion of danger skirted and of distance successfully traveled. Melissa believed that only she knew how to return to him, though there had been, and would be, others. She released the drain, and the water flowed out of the sink onto the bit of ocean which covered the floors.

Below, Peter briefly sonared a lizard fish that was feeding on the algae at the pool's bottom. Then he swam into the elevator and, punching the button with his beak, allowed it to hoist him up to the second story. He was still fascinated by the fact that electric lights were not fish, a discovery he had made by splashing water on

Melissa's desk lamp, and now he turned on his side to stare again at the floodlights as the elevator swung him out of its shaft and through the air over the flooded room. Once in the water, he looked for the woman. She had left her bed early. He made a noise like a human being with a cold and, when she did not appear, began slapping the water rhythmically with his flukes. Three slaps; Melissa appeared.

"Hello, Peter." She had been in the dry area in back and held a bowl of cereal.

"CCcccxxxxxx." He lifted his head out of the water and opened his beak to show he was hungry.

"Okay, okay, you greedy thing. Just a minute." She stepped down off the dry catwalk into the water and, reaching out her hand, offered a caress.

Peter swam rapidly toward her, then glided between her legs, forcing them apart with his body and striking her shins with the front edges of his bony flippers. Melissa tried to swat him, but he was already out of reach behind her.

"Goddamnit, dolphin! I've told you not to do that." Her shins were bruised purple from three weeks of this game. "One more time and I'll leave you alone the rest of the day."

Peter regarded her appraisingly. It is an attribute of the dolphin's eye that it is clear-sighted in both air and water.

Melissa fed Peter on the observation deck, taking freshly dead butterfish one by one from his plastic feed bucket and giving them each a short toss, not more than an inch, to indicate they were his. He caught them in jaws containing eighty-eight conical teeth of a sharpness and whiteness so imposing as to be hypnotic, and several times they had figured in Melissa's dreams: as mountains, as rows of prehistoric monuments, as a threat about to descend upon her leg. She looked out over the cove, listening to the faint reggae pulse coming from the radios of the fishing boats at anchor there. Dr. Ehrler had instructed her to make meals as dull as possible in order to avoid reward associations, so she never spoke to Peter during feeding. He nudged her leg and squawked, wanting another fish. She stared at the moon. On one of the fishing boats in the cove, a young down-islander discovered he had the wrong-size replacement batteries for his transistor and flung them angrily into the water; they sank forty feet and nearly hit a horseshoe crab. The moon traveled away, the sun rose.

"That's all there is," said Melissa, putting the empty feed bucket down in the water, letting it float aside like a toy. And she was halfway to sadness before she knew it.

Then Peter emitted a loud series of humanoid squawks, blats, and chuckles—the sound of English without the meaning—and when he knocked Melissa off her feet with a flip of his tail, soaking her, she, charmed, burst out laughing and said, "What do you know anyway, shithead? What do you think you know?"

Inside, beneath dangling microphones, Melissa and the dolphin labored fixedly at the lesson. Melissa said her name one hundred fifty times and Peter, absorbed in the strategies of human pronunciation, said it back. His vowels and *s*'s came easily in air now, and he had learned to shape an *m* sound by rolling over so his blowhole was just underwater; only the *l*'s were truly problematic. Melissa coached, gently touching his blowhole to indicate when he should listen to her. Both were drawn increasingly into the exchange, hearing the improvements, bearing down on them. She said his human name one hundred fifty times, and he said it back to her. They named his beach ball, his rubber rabbit, his brush. They counted to ten and back ten times.

In late morning, Melissa held up a diamond-shaped piece of plywood for him to identify. Peter rolled sideways to look at it, at her, then squirted the shape out of her hand with a blast of water and took off across the room at top speed, turning aside just before reaching the wall, so that close to a ton of water was thrown against it in a miniature tsunami. Without a pause, he swerved back toward her, trying, in the rub of water against his skin, to work up a vision of a place he knew in the deep ocean hundreds of thousands of body lengths away, a place free from the approach of shark yet decorously inhabited by all other manner of sea life: the rabbitfish, the butterfish, the spookfish; the croaker, the eelpout, the comb-toothed blenny; the starfish, sea horse, crab, and eel. He circled Melissa twice at high speed, then reared up on his flukes and stared at her. She had hair on her head and flexible lips.

"Peter, calm down," said Melissa, a little alarmed. "You're right: enough is enough." She picked the diamond out of the water and hung it on its wall hook.

Peter let himself back down into the water and swam to her. She leaned over, hugged him. "You did very well today, Peter, and on your last day, too." She could feel he was unusually tense. "Such a smart cookie," she crooned, kissing his back. He began to relax, then thought better of it and, slipping out of her arms, swam to a point a few meters away. With a heave of water, he reared up again, looking at her.

"Okay," she said to him. "If that's the way you want to be."

In the electronics room, she switched off the recorders and filed that morning's tapes next to the others. Out of the water, it seemed to her too easy to move now, as if the world below her knees had gone ridiculously insubstantial, and in response she had developed the tic of constantly wiggling her toes at the dryness. In certain parts of the island unfamiliar to Melissa, this tic, called obeah dance, is well-known and conclusive evidence of possession by jumbies, who may be banished only by the prompt and concentrated attentions of a red cloth dipped in goat's urine. Melissa sat on a high stool, lit a cigarette, and thought about her mother. There was a gecko perched atop the digital clock, drawn by the electric warmth even in the day's gathering heat, and it kept a lidless eye warily on her as she smoked. Each time it exhaled, Melissa could see its ribs, fine as thread. She stubbed out the cigarette and, reaching for the telephone, dialed her mother's number in Connecticut. The gecko fled; the phone rang once only.

"Hello?"

"Hi, Nona. It's me."

"You! But I thought you weren't back until tomorrow."

"I'm not back. I'm flying in tonight, but I wanted to talk to you now." She meant: I wanted to find out how bad it was before I got there.

"Well, it's good to hear you, Lissy. You don't even sound seriously waterlogged. I mean, I never thought I'd have a mermaid for a daughter, much less one who was an emissary of science, and you know what I—" She stopped.

"How is it, Nona? How are you feeling?"

A pause, blossoming into static, decaying back to silence.

"Pretty punk, Lissy," she said at last.

"Pain?"

"I have these pills."

"What happened at the hospital yesterday?"

"Bone scan okay, blood test okay, scarring of lungs from radiation treatment not too bad, and according to the X rays bronchial tumor shrunk by sixty-five percent. How does that sound?"

"It sounds wonderful."

"Doesn't it? But there's this other thing: I'm dying anyway."

"You are *not*."

"Don't treat me like a child. I know how I feel."

"But *I'm* the child around here," said Melissa, raising her voice. "*I'm* the fucking child around here." It seemed to Melissa that the tears came out of her skin, not her eyes. "I'm *your* child, Nona."

A pause.

"I love you, Lissy."

"Nona . . ." It seemed to be an appeal. They let it fade in to the hum of the wire.

"Well, have you taught that fish to sing yet?"

"Not a fish, a mammal," she said, wiping her eyes. "He can talk."

PETER SWAM RESTLESSLY around the rooms of the house, onto the deck, back into the house. Use of the telephone disturbed him; the faint cast of its electromagnetic patterns on his skin reminded him at up to fifteen body lengths of what he did not wish to know and caused dreams to flicker at terrible speeds along the length of him like shadow dapple. He swam to where his soft-bristled brush was anchored to the floor and rubbed against it, closing his eyes. It had come to him that the woman was leaving today. In some of his dreams, he was able to move about in the dry world, swimming freely through air and bearing without damage the full crush of gravity. In some of his dreams, the woman had grown cold to him and, with a variety of devices that resembled electric eels, would torture him, or remove his teeth, or prod him into metal boxes. He ceased rubbing and lifted his blowhole above the surface to breathe. Dolphins regard decisions made at the moment of respiration as more serious than those made underwater. Peter savored this luster of seriousness, then, using both eye and sonar, set off in methodical search for his yellow, plastic, melon-sized ball.

He found it slowly orbiting the outflow fixture in one corner. With his beak, he nudged it back along the surface until it floated beside the woman's desk in the opposite corner, then he took up position behind it, eye fixed on the door, mouth slightly open, and waited.

Melissa did not see him immediately. She was tying a kerchief over her head as she came in and was ticking off a mental list of drugs, treatments, and attitudes that Nona might yet be convinced to try. After she had hung up the phone, she had had an alarming vision of herself flying alone through a viscous, black outer space. In the vision, she had flown at first in a sitting position, as if in an imaginary chair, then, as she accelerated, she had tipped gradually forward until she was soaring along belly down, legs out, like a rocket, utterly without fear.

The yellow ball flew at her. She caught it in a defensive gesture, not comprehending immediately how it had arrived there, in front of her face. Twenty feet away Peter made a noise like a cocktail party heard through wax paper.

"You damn fish-that-sings! You're impossible!" she shouted, and threw the ball back at him hard.

He caught it in his teeth, then released it onto the water and butted it into the air with his forehead. It fell one body length short of Melissa, and was briefly, as it sat upon the surface between them, the object of their separate contemplations. Melissa splashed slowly forward to get it.

"God, how used to each other we've gotten! It's getting so the shape of my own body surprises me when I look in a mirror after watching you all day."

Melissa tossed the ball into the air in front of her and punched it over to Peter with her fist. He had to leap to catch it, water falling away from him on either side in great swashes.

"Sorry," said Melissa. "My fault."

They played catch with a concentration that mounted gradually, centering now on the ball, now on each other. Neither of them made noises beyond the small aquatic commotions involved in the game's toss and catch, and those sounds blended with the pulse of the pump downstairs, with the chirrups of the banana quits under the eaves, with the buzz and click of invisible insects at the window louvers, until Melissa's sense of the house itself became acute, as if it were clothes she was wearing—indeed, more than that, and she saw that she had come to regard the house, with its brothy blood of seawater, as a living thing in which she and the dolphin had come miraculously to take up residence.

She was surprised when there was no more room between them for catch. Each of Peter's return tosses had fallen short, and, dreamy with the heat, she had each time waded slowly forward to fetch the ball. Peter, at her knees, opened jaws that another time had bitten a six-foot barracuda in two. Melissa dropped the ball into them. In Connecticut, Nona dropped a cup of coffee onto the kitchen floor and, lacking the patience to clean it up, kicked the cup fragments under the table and left the room.

And when Peter did not release the ball, continuing instead to mouth it gently with his eyes shut, Melissa hesitated, but seeing that his jaws could not easily close on her hand while the ball acted as a prop, she reached into his mouth and massaged his gums gingerly until his grip relaxed and the ball rolled onto her palm.

She lifted it above her head, and as the dolphin turned on his side to peer at her with one bright, assessing eye, she heard herself say strange words. She said: "I've tried and tried and *tried.*"

She dropped the ball into his open mouth, and Peter this time let it roll farther back into his jaws, where it was less certain a prop. Her hand drifted in among his teeth like an unruly starfish, and she was reminded for an instant of the story Nona told about sitting once on Clark Gable's lap in the lobby of the Algonquin Hotel and counting his teeth.

Peter drew away from her. Her arm, in his jaws nearly to the elbow, came free. Without loosening his grip on the ball, he let himself sink on his side to the floor, and, underwater, took her ankle in his mouth.

She shuddered and, at the same time, so did he. Their eyes met, and held.

Moments began to topple.

Melissa tried to touch her shoulder-length hair, but it had been cut away.

She said: "I'm frightened, Peter."

Slowly, Peter began raking his teeth up and down her leg, opening his jaws gradually wider until her whole calf, knee, thigh moved through his mouth, and the yellow ball slipped out and away.

She reached a hand down and touched his back, the enormous muscle of it, the silken skin. In some of his dreams, the moon was again honored among dolphins and had come in full yellow light to settle slowly into the sea and be rubbed against in praiseful places by dolphins.

Melissa untied her kerchief and set it in the water behind her. She maneuvered the leotard off one shoulder, then the other. Her nipples were taut, and the sensation of Peter's teeth on her legs was like this tautness spread to the rest of her body. She rubbed his skin.

She began repeating his name.

When the dolphin's cock appeared, emerging erect from the slit on his underside, Melissa stepped away from his jaws and pulled the leotard past long red scratches and off her legs. Peter saw the hair. She moved toward him uncertainly, drawing the fingers of one slow hand upward through her cunt. She is very wet, and as she repeats the gesture her knees begin to quiver. She is surprised suddenly by the need to say something and can think of nothing.

She says: "Love?" And her legs buckle under her.

For two seconds, she is fully underwater. During that moment, she has the impression that she and Peter are moving at a speed so extreme that movement itself has subsided. When she lifts her head, spewing saltwater and gasping for air, the sensation vanishes at the same speed. Peter, his eyes half-closed, is ramming himself against her, and it comes to her that he does not know how or where to enter her.

On her knees, she pushes with both hands just behind his flipper until he understands he is to roll over on his right side. As she takes his cock into her hands, Peter makes faint quacking sounds, and she herself begins to murmur. He is concentrating utterly on the effort of keeping his movements to human scale; she, the fragile one, is aware of his restraint. Both hear with new intensity their quiet splashing as the sound of air and water mixed. Straddling him, she is entered.

They were making love in the shallow water.

WHEN JEFFREY RETURNED to the apartment after his day of teaching fifth-graders what was to be expected from them in life, his telephone was ringing. It was Nicole. She was going to California for a day and wanted to know if she could catch a ride to the airport with him when he went to meet Melissa's plane. Nicole's father worked for TWA, so she could and did fly anywhere for free—as long as she didn't get married.

As they sped up the ramp to the Cross Bronx Expressway, Nicole said, "How's Lissy taking it about Nona?"

In the air there were jet planes, helicopters, invisible particles. Jeffrey looked at Nicole through dark glasses. "I think she's doing okay," he said.

At the airport an Irishman with a bottle of Jameson's in his back pocket had climbed out on one of the hundred flagpoles overlooking the main lobby and was trying to pull down the South African flag. Melissa's plane was not due for an hour and Nicole's not for two. They had drinks.

"I forgot to ask what's in California this time," said Jeffrey.

"You know those costumes I've been working on?" Nicole began. "They're due at a studio in L.A. tomorrow, and since it's cheaper for me to fly out with them than to mail them, I thought I'd take a little jaunt." She smiled at him.

"Nikki," he said, "I admire your sense of proportion."

"I know you do," she answered. "It's what you like best about me."

This seemed indeed to be true, so Jeffrey finished his gimlet and ordered another. At the first taste of it, it occurred to him that Nicole, who was not taking her eyes off him even when sipping at her Dubonnet, might again be pregnant. She had had five abortions and her gynecologist was in L.A.

A sadness passed over him as he looked at her. "You know," he said, noticing it for what was easily the twentieth time, "you become absolutely beautiful in airports; you have no idea how radiant."

She gave a short laugh, finished her drink in a double swallow, and put the glass down in front of her. "I was born and raised at a ticket counter, Jeffrey, born and raised."

They played electronic ping-pong. Every time they hit the video ball with one of the video paddles, the machine produced a beep of deeply satisfying, quarter-inviting tenor, and after three such beeps, a child sitting nearby but out of sight began to accompany it loudly. Jeffrey won, then won again, then ran out of quarters.

"THERE'S SOME CHANGE IN MY BAG," said Nicole, who had decided on another Dubonnet and was on her way to the bar.

Melissa, in a stainless-steel bathroom twenty thousand feet above Washington, D.C., looked at herself in the mirror, then took a yellow pill to wake herself up. I look like shit, she thought. She wondered why there were never any windows in airplane bathrooms.

Jeffrey's hand, in Nicole's canvas carryall, touched a thing that was startlingly unlike quarters. He lifted it part way out of the bag, holding it by the barrel. He let it drop back down into the suddenly enhanced depths of the canvas darkness and lit a cigarette. The child was now beeping unaccompanied; its parents were trying to hush it.

When Nicole had safely installed her new drink on the console of the machine in front of them, Jeffrey inquired, in the calmest tones left to him, why she was carrying a loaded Walther automatic in her purse.

A commotion of what seemed to him to be genuine surprise passed over her. She reached into the carryall and, hauling the gun out by its barrel, dangled it in the air between them like a dead rat. "Why, this little thing? Is that what you mean?"

The bar's patrons were mostly gathered in one corner beneath a surpassingly large color television set and did not appear to notice this grossness.

"Nicole, put the gun back in the bag." She did so, then shrugged and, with lapidary attention, examined the ice cubes in her drink.

"It's Diego's," she said. "I'd forgotten all about it. We've been fighting a lot and he started waving it around at me a bit too often, so I took it out of his drawer when he wasn't looking." She had found Diego in Barcelona a year ago with the aid of her TWA pass.

"He still beating you up?"

"Nothing really unfriendly."

In his distaste for this arrangement, Jeffrey ate a handful of very salty peanuts and fed the hungry machine a quarter. Nicole's shoulder, touching his as they played, seemed to request tolerance, and he summoned it up—though with misgivings, since to whom was it directed?

"You know," he said, "you still have to get it through baggage search."

Nicole, who had failed to consider this, gave him a fond, infected look and won the game. When they left the bar, the beeping child was in noisy tears from the cuffing its father had administered, and Diego's gun had been transferred from Nicole's canvas bag to Jeffrey's leather one, where it was to remain for safekeeping until her return from California.

At a newsstand, as they leafed through a copy of *Curious Creature Magazine*, Nicole asked him if he thought they would ever have an affair.

"I don't know," he said, truthfully but elliptically. Melissa's imminence was making him a little anxious.

"I don't know either," she agreed.

Melissa's plane arrived on time. He and Nicole waited for her by the security gate, watching metal detectors detect belt buckles and sets of keys on the persons of those who wished to fly somewhere. In the seven years Jeffrey and Melissa had known each other, they had parted so many times, rejoined each other after so many absences, that knowledge of her physical approach had begun to invoke in him a ritual succession of conflicting feelings which, by their very opposition, ramified with blinding speed toward the erotic. He removed his dark glasses, the first passengers appeared, Melissa was among them.

"Tell me I smell like fish," she said as they embraced, "and that's the last time you'll ever get close enough to know."

"You smell like fish," he said. "I missed you. Welcome home."

Me Jane, You're Kidding

ELIZABETH ROYTE

IN MY SECOND TRIMESTER, I found myself waking before
dawn, sick. But I dragged myself down through the laboratory
clearing to meet Craig and run the spiny-rat trap lines anyway. The
rats, which were nocturnal, needed to be released from their traps
before the heat of the day. Together, we slogged the jungle trails,
uphill and down, weighing and sexing the creatures, reading off
their ID numbers—based on the pattern in which their toes had
been clipped—and noting the females' reproductive status.

Craig, a field assistant who had no knowledge of my own reproductive status, didn't eat in the morning. But I ate before going out,
and between each of the four rat-filled islands, and on the way home
to the lab. I drank water all day long, and I peed in the forest, off the
back of Boston Whalers, and in the laborers' filthy bathroom at the
Panama Canal Commission's dredging division in Gamboa.

I was living, for the time being, at a remote biological research
station, called Barro Colorado Island, in the middle of Panama. I
was here to write a book about the strange and wonderful world of
field biologists—what they did, what it was worth, and why. I had
arrived on the island in February and immediately began working
with botanists, primatologists, entomologists, and ecologists.

Every day, I woke at dawn, pulled on my boots, filled my water
bottles, and headed into the jungle that draped this six-square-mile
island. For two months, I measured seedlings, radio-tracked bats,
counted ants, captured moths, bagged the fecal samples of monkeys,
and hung flight interceptor traps in trees. And then I went home to

get married. Two weeks after this feat was accomplished, I was back on BCI, taking notes and scratching chigger bites.

I discovered I was pregnant in the usual way. I'd been feeling queasy since my trip home and strangely tired. One morning, it was near the end of June, I took the island launch to Gamboa, then a bus into Panama City. I walked purposively down the Avenida Central, shouldered my way into Machetazo, the Panamanian equivalent of K-Mart, and quietly asked the clerk for *una prueba de embarazo*.

I slept late the next day and, after ensuring that my roommate was nowhere in sight, cleared a small space in our bathroom. Then I set up my rudimentary hormonal assay and watched in wide wonder as the single yellow stripe turned to blue.

Just to see what it felt like, I kept the news to myself for a while. Besides, the only phone on which I could call my husband was in the mailroom, and it afforded zero privacy. I went for a hike. I sat on a rock and watched container ships steaming slowly over the continental divide. I thought about the creature growing inside me and acknowledged, okay, I'm not alone here. Instantly I felt more connected to the animal kingdom, in particular to the band of coatimundis I heard snuffling in the leaf litter at my back. But my thinking did not progress beyond this level.

Eventually, I broke the news to Peter. If he was excited, the emotion didn't survive the underground cables. We discussed our options, but we knew where we'd end up. In a week, a copy of *What to Expect When You're Expecting* arrived, in a plain brown wrapper.

The book stressed how "special" this time was for me. But I felt just the opposite. Everything on the island was busy procreating, and no one fussed about it. Pregnant monkeys leaped from branch to branch without a visible hitch. Birds sat on their eggs, larvae crawled from plant stems.

I went back to Panama City, to have the pregnancy confirmed and some blood drawn. Because I was thirty-eight, the obstetrician said I was "high risk," but he told me not to worry. "Biologically, you're younger than you are chronologically." His reassurance wasn't necessary. Miscarriage, pre-eclampsia, gestational diabetes, and premature labor had never crossed my mind. I began reading the pregnancy book before turning in at night, which was a bit like reading Steven King. The genre was horror—needles, incisions, stirrups— but somehow, it wasn't my horror. I suppose I was in denial.

My emotions during the first trimester ran amok. At times, I sat with my head on my desk and wept: What have I done? I felt no impulse to nest, as "the book" warned I might. My most consistent emotion was resentment, for my body was not my own.

Queasiness was a thing of the past, but now my digestive system had slowed dramatically. Eating wasn't any fun. I felt full after three tablespoons of corn niblets. Did this happen to other animals? No one on the island could say. Spider monkeys, I knew, defecated every four hours; howler monkeys every thirty. As with any isolated group of higher primates, the subject of how and when people shit was freely discussed at meal times. I got a lot of unsolicited advice on the subject of laxatives.

The food here was not ideal for pregnant people, especially if they didn't favor meat. The rice was white, the vegetables came from cans and were overcooked, then doused with margarine. I worried about getting enough protein. I popped *acido folico* and Tums, for the calcium.

For the mood swings, a confidante would have helped. But none of the female scientists had offspring, so I didn't even try for commiseration. Phone calls back home were prohibitively expensive. And so I kept my own counsel, surrounded by rationalists, adherents of logic and falsification who, paradoxically, had far greater experience with gravid placental mammals than I did.

Throughout its ontogeny, the fetus changed names. In the beginning, it was a fish. *Mi pescadito*. Sometimes, when I felt ambivalent about what was growing inside me, I called it F1, the first-generation offspring of its parent cross. For a while it was *la creatura*. For whatever reason, I was unimpressed by the "miracle of life" growing within me. The zygote was the size of a rice grain, then two rice grains. Its senses developed, my body changed. Everything about pregnancy was orderly, it seemed to me. I was warned to expect absentmindedness but spent more time pondering its adaptive advantage than wondering if I suffered from it. Nutrition and exercise were my only concerns. I played ultimate Frisbee with scientists in Gamboa a few times then gave it up. It was just too hot out there. Instead, I swam. A bat researcher named Bret and I would strike out for the first buoy in Lab Cove, then head toward the second. I knew there was a crocodile out there, but if Bret wasn't scared, then neither was I.

Bret tried to get me to jump off the tin roof of the boat dock. He showed me how to climb up, then he dove. I got onto the roof easily enough but lost my nerve when I looked at the water, twelve feet down. It took me fifteen minutes to get off the roof and onto a pylon, my arms and legs were shaking so much. Was the fish trying to tell me something?

Back on the dock, I lectured myself: fish do not talk. But what was I trying to prove? To the biologists, pregnancy was just another stage of life. No one was offering any special coddling, and I was determined not to want it.

In August, my Panamanian doctor remanded me to the States for amniocentesis. In New York, a nurse practitioner looked at my medical records, all in Spanish, and asked me a few questions.

"You're not digging around in the dirt, are you?"

"Yes, I am." She made a note.

"Well, you're not touching any animals, are you?"

"Yes, I am."

"What kind of animals?"

"I'm handling spiny rats, and sometimes bats." I thought for a few seconds and added, "I also go out with a monkey researcher and collect fecal samples."

The nurse practitioner shook her head and scowled. "You wear gloves, don't you?"

"I will," I said, soberly.

When I got back to Panama in September, I truly looked pregnant, and a few residents suddenly became solicitous toward me. Chrissy wouldn't let me haul beer crates between the lab and the boat dock anymore. Rafael, with whom I worked on a migratory butterfly census, wouldn't let me carry full fuel cans. I was ripping into a bag of pumpkin seeds I'd bought in Panama City when Bret reminded me that seeds are often heavily defended against herbivores with toxic chemical compounds. Among the alkaloids found in tropical leaves, seeds, roots, shoots, flowers, and fruits were cocaine, morphine, cannabinol, caffeine and nicotine—substances that may inhibit lactation and cause abortion or birth defects in mammals.

I went out on the *Urraca*, a fancy marine research vessel, but became so seasick in the Bay of Panama that I had to be let off the boat. I couldn't take scopolamine now. Nor could I use Deet to keep off the chiggers and ticks. Nor could I drink, enjoy the occasional cigarette, or stay up late. The island's narrow food choices bummed me out. Why couldn't we at least have brown rice? I wondered. Because it's more nutritive than white, I was told, and so more attractive to vermin.

Climbing a rope dangling from the branch of a Sterculia tree, forty feet up, my breath came in short gasps. I like to think I'd have made it to the top if I weren't pregnant, but the fetus was stealing my oxygen. There was a constant battle between my needs and F1's—for my blood supply, the nutrients I consumed and stored, for my air supply. The fetus was my own personal parasite, and I had few defenses against her. She would stay inside me until my placenta had enough of her, and then she would be expelled. When my mood was sunny, I imagined our relationship, from that point on, would be entirely mutualistic.

By my sixth month, I was doing field work for no longer than four or five hours a day. The island was nothing but ravines and ridges, and round-ligament pain often forced me to stop and rest. Now, I had to turn my head when Craig clipped rat toes, especially those of the more vascular pregnant females. I'd come in from the field, shower, and collapse on my bed. I read aloud to my little tadpole from *The Darwin Reader*. She flipped.

The tadpole turned, over the course of a few weeks, into a dolphin, and then rapidly into a chimp. She kicked and tumbled inside me. I began testing her, tapping on one side of my belly, then the other. She tapped back. Or was it the other way around? Was I reacting to her or was she reacting to me? I realized how difficult it was to design a controlled study.

Peter visited during my last month on the island, and I felt a palpable sense of relief. I began thinking about the genetic imperative to keep one's mate at hand during such a time. Was it because I was, theoretically, in a vulnerable condition? Or was this a way of ensuring that the offspring's father would make some parental investment after the blessed event was over?

I looked to the treetops for counsel. The four pregnant spider monkeys never strayed far from the troop. But once their babies were born, no single male attended them. After all, the monkeys copulated freely during estrus, and males presumably didn't know which baby was theirs.

I spent my final month doing minimal fieldwork—most of it from a boat. Peter and I walked the forest trails, we helped a flight physiologist capture migratory moths on the lake, and we read Jack Kerouac aloud to our chimp. By the time I left Panama, none of my field pants buttoned. It was November, and I was due in two months, having had exactly two prenatal exams during my entire pregnancy.

Back home, I slipped into the self-consciousness that characterized pregnancy in industrialized society. Here, pregnancy is something to which women apply themselves. They take exercise classes, birthing classes, breast-feeding classes. They take a lot of tests. The whole thing is very top-down and managed. It probably makes some people feel better, especially those who go to a lot of trouble to get pregnant. But there are still plenty of cultures where pregnancy and childbirth are a natural, unmedicalized event. And the animal kingdom is one of them.

I was, in retrospect, fairly calm about being pregnant in the jungle. But I had to be: in Panama, there was no one to indulge or feed my anxieties. I took my cues from the only females whose hormones were swinging as wildly as my own. The pregnant monkeys went about their business, the agoutis and coatis and anteaters and sloths did the same. In the back of my mind, I realized there was some risk to bearing a child, but I figured I'd take things as they came.

It was something I had learned from the animals.

Blood Lust: Why I Kill

THOMAS MCINTYRE

I WAS SIXTEEN WHEN I FIRST KILLED A LARGE ANIMAL. *The barren ground caribou was bedded on Alaska tundra under a lead sky. I bellied to the rim of the basin where he lay and shot him through the lungs with the rifle I had borrowed from my father. The caribou shuddered and rolled onto his side, his big-hoofed legs stiffening, his heavy antlered head sinking to the ground. The bull had pink froth around his nostrils, and as I walked to him he gasped, drowning in his own blood. While I watched, the big hooves began to kick and the round eye staring at me turned from deep, ice-water clarity to an opaque bottle green. The caribou stopped shuddering then. I still trembled.*

A woman asks me why I hunt.

"I like you so much," she says. "But it's hard. I just can't reconcile it. You *kill* things."

"Yes, I tell her. I do. What else, ultimately, is hunting about other than death? José Ortega y Gasset, the modern philosopher used by hunters desperate to sound literate once wrote: "The hunter is a death dealer." Ortega y Gasset was a hard-core existentialist who wrote the twentieth century's most influential work on hunting, *Meditations on Hunting*, and he pulls no punches on the dark side of the sport. Ortega y Gasset is important here because, at the end of the day, after the spotting and the pursuit and the stalking of the animal, killing is indeed what makes the hunter, animal and human, different from every other walker in the woods. Not that this always explains it to the satisfaction of my friends, especially environmentalists of a certain stripe, or to my own family. Sometimes not even to myself.

Killing seems incomprehensible because we have almost no

widespread experience of it anymore, no longer even slaughtering our own livestock. The writer Reynolds Price recently said in one of those plummy soliloquies broadcast by National Public Radio, "death has become almost the last obscenity, the single thing we're loathe to discuss in public." Mr. Price must eschew the watching of television. If he tuned in to the medium of the masses, he would discover that Americans are more steeped in a cult of death than Aztec priests. Millions tune in to fatal stockcar crashes, exploding space shuttles, and, perhaps grisliest of all, videotaped suicide. One click of a mouse brings you to an interactive sniper map on the Internet. In gigaplexes across the nation we watch Hollywood movies starring grunting heroes whose oversized muscles are overmatched by their even-more-oversized guns. Death chat surrounds us, from talk of "living wills" to "doctor-assisted suicide" to the "right to die."

Americans throw themselves on these canned altars of death, every day, while believing that it is wrong, even inhumane, to participate in the killing of the hunt. And yet that killing can never be genuinely understood or experienced without direct participation. This is what makes most writing about it, and almost all visual depictions —such as those obscene hunting shows found somewhere in the bowels of the cable listings—abysmal. Killing is the true unutterable, and as such it is what everyone, while seemingly repulsed, wants to glimpse. But only at a sanitized, plastic-wrapped distance.

For the record, hunting is not homicide, or the hunting of armed men in war, but the legal killing in the hunt of wild animals. It is not killing for the sake of killing. I can tell you that much. But hunters tend to be excruciatingly tongue-tied about what draws them to the hunt. Partly that's a matter of trying to tell a stranger about rock 'n' roll. But the taciturnity also comes about because, as Ortega y Gasset says, hunting means "accepting reason's insufficiencies." The desire to hunt, which must ultimately lead to killing, comes from a place well before consciousness and words, so that when it arises today it does so almost beyond articulation. Most hunters cannot even say when it began for them.

AT FOUR *I walked into the den in my father's best friend's house. Both men were employed in aerospace, but on the paneled walls were not valves or wiring diagrams but the mounted heads of a deer, an elk, and a wild boar. A black bear skin lay across the hardwood floor. Above these others hung a pair of perfect rose-ivory tusks, my father's friend having taken all his savings, cashed out his wife's life-insurance policy, and gone to French Equatorial Africa to kill an elephant at less than thirty paces in dense jungle. Even now, it is incomprehensible to me that these things would be found anywhere in tract housing in 1950s suburban Southern California.*

In later years there would be walking behind on desultory hunts for farm-raised pheasants set out by the state and fetching birds during the once-a-year San Joaquin Valley mourning-dove shoots. My father approached these outings as obligations; adventure a letting loose for which my mad parent was never prepared. I went on thinking, though, about horns and tusks and the kind of country in which they might be found until I was old enough to shoulder my own shotgun. Then I went on thinking about them some more.

The summer I convinced my father to let me go to the Talkeetna Mountains, taking the rifle he owned but never used, was the summer of '68. Chicago police in Lincoln Park and Soviet tanks in Wenceslaus Square were matters of minor note compared to my desire to hunt something "bigger than me." Looking at the caribou, the top of Denali beyond, and the sky above, I knew I had been right. Everything around me in the hunt was bigger than me; bigger than the caribou, too.

IS THERE SOMETHING SEXUAL ABOUT IT? she asks. Does it, you know? Bull, bed, belly, shudder, stiffen, gasp, tremble—what other conclusion could there be than that killing must be all about sex? When you think about it, aside from the Freudianization of all human behavior, hunting and sex can appear to be the last natural acts. For nearly all of us sex is our final bivouac in the wild, our only firsthand experience of it anymore. So sex becomes the template that we place over all wild experience, unable to recall that there was once for humans, and yet for animals, a little more to it than that. Sex in the wild is an intense, often perilous, but infrequent seasonal activity, and only one of many wild conditions, far more time taken up by gestation, birth, nurturing, feeding, gathering, divination, migrating, concealment, flight—and killing. It is a hangover from modernism to desire to see everything as sexual. But killing is not a division of sex. In the wild it is its own separate and discrete bureau.

I think I get what you're saying, the woman says. But I still don't understand why you feel the need to do it. I mean, is it fun? When it comes down to it, is it simply about having *fun?*

Sort of, I tell her. The correct response given by the more enlightened hunter of the day is that he takes no pleasure in killing. He does it solely in pious acknowledgement of the cost of his food, or as an anguished conservation measure ("thinning the herd"). Which is all, if you will forgive me, more than passing strange. Few people in the industrialized world are hunters for any other reason than personal choice. Far from bumming out its participants, hunting is, as Felipe Fernández-Armesto wrote in his history of food, "an attractive way of life, which still exercises a romantic appeal for some people in sedentary and even urban societies: thousands of years of civilization seem insufficient to scratch out the savage under the skin...."

It is a mistake to equate fun, with its implication of frivolousness, with pleasure, a fundamental element of life, and not necessarily just human life. You can see this in real "savages," those indigenous hunters for whom killing can be both arduous and risky. What experience I have had of such hunters is that they tend to display something akin to sacred delight when an animal is brought down. Why not, when a kill can provide food, clothing, craft material, even objects of veneration, all in a tidy bundle? Outside the human realm, watch the predators on the Discovery Channel. Even in close-up it's hard to detect much solemnity or remorse as the cheetah tumbles the Thomson's gazelle in a billow of ochre dust, or the croc rolls in the black river mud, the wildebeest calf in its toothsome grin. There aren't even crocodile tears.

The question should be whether one hunts for the joy of killing. I can say only that I hunt to hunt. I could find far less taxing means of satisfying an obsessive love of killing, had I one, than by hiking for miles through chaparral to shoot a plateful of quail. In fact, the too-easy, "lucky" kill can rob the hunt of much of its savor.

Killing, though, I must admit, does give me pleasure when I do it well. I believe this is the raw response to good killing by those who love to hunt. I know of nothing we do without coercion that is not finally rooted in pleasure, however postponed or sublimated or lofty. Denials of the pleasure inherent in the good kill are less heartfelt than they are hunters' politically correct means of throwing an increasingly denunciatory public off the scent.

Then does this make it wicked? She does not ask this; I do.

In his radio essay, Price, quoting a line from the Roman poet Horace—"*Feast, then, they heart*..."—counseled that unless "a heart craves blood and cruelty, its owner should feed it lavishly." What Price did not explain was how blood and cruelty are intrinsically linked, making it wrong to feed with blood—certain kinds, anyway. I was raised Catholic, and practice the religion still. Both metaphor and experience tell me that blood can be holy, sacrificial, celebratory, and yet not cruel. I know equally well that some of the most profound cruelties involve not the shedding of one drop of blood.

In our ever more denaturalized world, we can recognize nothing in spilled blood but heartlessness. This is not the fault of blood so much as of our stunted perception that makes us want to place our faith in a chimera like the one evoked by the phrase *cruelty free*. Never mind that it is most often employed as a marketing slogan for cosmetics or a goad for extorting donations for animal-rights causes; it represents a real desire. Yet to ignore the "savage under the skin," denies the inevitability of that inner and outer darkness Jung called the shadow and Freud relegated to the id. Denial leads to an incomplete rendering of the truth; it fails to account for each second of sentient existence that owes an irredeemable debt to an innate bow wave of cruelty from which we are powerless to extricate any living creature, ourselves included.

In true hunting, though, cruelty is never the goal and is either inadvertent or the result of inexperience. Good hunting means good killing. Good killing means possessing the skill, knowledge, and empathy to be able to inflict a wound that will end an animal's life in a matter of heartbeats, honorably, and with a minimum of sensation, let alone pain. When an animal is killed well, to use—who else?— Hemingway's words, all of him will race all the rest of him to the ground, leaving the hunter with almost no opportunity for regret.

Bad killing—fumbled, prolonged, obviously painful—can fill a hunter with physical unease, both for the unintended cruelty, and for the dishonor to the animal. Bad killing, though, to paraphrase Ortega y Gasset one last time, exists only at the expense of good killing.

There was a time when good killing mattered, when men were expected to be good killers. There is D. H. Lawrence's oft-repeated chestnut, referring to James Fenimore Cooper's *Deerslayer*, about how the "essential American soul is hard, isolate, stoic, and a killer." What never gets quoted is Lawrence's next sentence: "It has never yet melted." Maybe not in Lawrence's day; but since then the essential American soul, at least that of sensitized man, has turned into nothing less than a sump of goo. Killing has never been the exclusive route to manhood (or personhood), but neither has being abstractly repulsed by, or irrationally ignorant of it. To see a foreshadowing of the soul of today's American man, look at Woody Allen's nebbish Alvy Singer in *Annie Hall*, a character whose breathtakingly comprehensive catalog of passive-aggressive anxieties and puerility included an inability not only to drop a lobster in a pot, but to kill a spider, all these twitchy neuroses inexplicably meant to be endearing. It's endearing (barely so) only so long as it doesn't come down off the screen and end up being someone you have to live with or count on. It would then become apparent that it is not killing alone of which such a soul is incapable, but all too often trustworthiness, commitment, self-sacrifice, and courage, as well.

Debate over war often degenerates into a veiled yet passionate argument over these irreconcilable notions of what it means to be human. No example serves better than the US invasion of Iraq. The American Left was split between those who opposed the war because of their opposition to America's current president and, in some cases, to war itself, versus liberal adherents of realpolitik, who spoke of the suffering of the Iraqi people and supported the invasion of Iraq with the disclaimer that it was "the right war for the wrong reasons." But the right war, nonetheless. The very concept is foreign to many twenty-first-century Americans. Is that stance realistic? Is it even moral?

I kill, and try to kill well, because it is a difficult and complex physical act, involves moral and ethical reflection, compels me to look at death—and life—without an arbiter, and is an authentic thing in a grotesquely inauthentic world.

An end to good killing will not lead to a sounder environment, but will merely be evidence of one too weakened to sustain any longer the most ancient of nature's processes. Seeing a better world in the end of killing is like the conscious refusal of many of the environmental movement's leading intellects to bear children for the sake of a better planet. It may be humane to sever such an essential part of one's nature, but it strikes me as weirdly inhuman.

HOW LONG *had that Alaskan caribou been waiting for me? All of a caribou's life is a wait for the hunter, the killer, in whatever shape he may take. If not me, then the grizzly or the wolf pack or winter, no animal going gentle. And yet he was never afraid of dying, not even knowing that he was going to die.*

None of us goes gentle either, I thought. Or should want to. (Later in life I saw the hasty "gentle" of a .38 with one round fired, my father lying on the false green of a southern California lawn, having released himself, finally, from a life he could never fully live. Much later I watched my mother fall to the prolonged gentle of the arm-chair and the endless staring wait; both so very oddly rooted in an abject terror of death. Compared to those, I'd take the caribou's way any day.)

Standing beside the body of a dead caribou, I wondered why I had always been taught to fear death, or even be wary of it, because this wasn't what it was said to be like at all. If this was all it was, why even feel sorrow? It was too small for that, held up against the sweep of the tundra, against the snow of Denali, against the curtain of light flourishing in the night sky. All that I saw was bigger than killing, this kind of killing. It made death itself, even my own someday, small and barely significant, hardly worth mentioning. Killing gave me that.

Would I have learned this without first having killed? There is no way now that I will ever know.

Chicken 81

SARAH L. COURTEAU

MY MOTHER IS A KILLER.
She knows how to pull a chicken's head off under her size-ten shoe, but she prefers to lay it gently on a chopping block and lop off its head with a clean stroke of the ax. Then she swings the flapping body away from her so its red life spatters the yard.

She's grabbed up a shovel, an ax, a hoe, to hack the heads off copperheads and occasional rattlesnakes that have confused their territory with ours. Once she dispatched an unfortunate blacksnake with a knot in his middle. He'd swallowed the white stone we kept in the chicken coop to fool the hens into thinking we weren't taking all their eggs.

She has stood in the barn and dropped five of a litter of nine puppies with the blunt side of an ax head. We had nothing to feed them but a gruel my mother cooked each day on the stove. Her winsome sketches on handbills and the tearful calls my younger sister Darcy made to numbers in the phone book had failed to turn up any takers for the puppies. The guy at the animal pound said no one would adopt redbone-hound mix pups, and the pound would charge $5 a head to dispose of them.

My father kills with a gun, which my mother knew would terrify the puppies in their last moments. She did the killing because her weapon of choice is an ax wielded with a skill honed by many mornings of chopping kindling for the stove. In the end, he finished the job anyway. My mother had set down her ax after the pup with one blue eye sat down and looked frankly up at her instead of nosing the decoy food bowl like the other pups had done. When my father went out with the gun to deal with the three remaining puppies, he knew—though my mother didn't ask—to save that pup with the blue eye. We named her Annie.

Other killings I can't remember or she's lied to us about. Years after our mutt Brodie had run away and been replaced in short order with an Australian shepherd puppy, my mother let the truth slip at the dinner table. They went for a walk, and my mother shot Brodie in the head with a .22 pistol. I used to kiss little Brodie on the nose, but strangers made her nervous. When a friend's child bent to pet and coo, Brodie bit the girl in the face. On our farm, a dangerous bull might be tolerated, but not a dangerous pet.

Death is supposed to be matter-of-fact on a farm. A flick of the wrist, an arc of the ax, a squeeze of the trigger, and the wriggling animal becomes just another lump of flesh to be plucked, skinned, or buried.

Not for my mother.

This is a woman who has nursed along innumerable baby birds fallen from their nests, foundling rabbits quivering with the anxiety of existence, a hairless baby mouse she tucked away in an old sock, a wild fawn found by the roadside, goats heaving with the effort of holding in their own guts after a dog attack, a calf that lived in a corner of the front room after my father cut it from the womb of its dying mother, a small king snake with a broken back that lacked the prudence to stay out from underfoot. For weeks, as I remember, she carried bits of food out to him in a protected brush pile behind the house as he wasted slowly toward death.

I've asked her how she forced past that moment of hesitation when, ax in hand, she eyed the chicken and it eyed her back with the uneasy sideways look a chicken gets when it knows something bad is going to happen. The answer was always the same: It had to be done. We had to eat, she had to protect us, an animal's pain had to be extinguished.

When our neighbors gave us several white geese to butcher one fall, Darcy stood in the haymow while my mother and father killed them, wailing over and over, "Can't we keep just one?" The answer was as inevitable as the coming winter. Survival was not negotiable.

MY MOTHER DOESN'T KILL MUCH ANY MORE. Maybe it's because my grandmother died a few years ago and left my father a little nest egg. Maybe it's because the last of my six siblings is in school and my mother's job as a part-time sculptor has vaulted her into the ranks of moneymakers who buy their hamburger in plastic instead of on the hoof. The chief reason, I think, is her summer job three years ago at a chicken farm a mile up the road.

"I went into it with the same attitude of a Quaker going into the medical corps in Vietnam," she says. She wasn't there to send these chickens to the swift, steely deaths she had witnessed working at a Campbell Soup factory before she met my father. She was just there to care for them and make a little money at a job close to home.

The neighbors paid her twenty-five dollars a day to shepherd the chickens through six weeks of life, until their muscles were just the right consistency for Tyson chicken patties and nuggets. Then the chicken catchers would descend in big trucks, stuff the three-and-a-half-pound birds into crates, and haul them away to processing plants, from which they would emerge breaded and boxed.

My mother had charge of three chicken houses, forty-eight thousand chickens to a house, and several thousand Cornish hens besides. She had three main duties: feed them, water them, and kill any of the chicks that weren't uniform and spry.

She didn't discover that she would have to kill until her first day on the job, but she learned quickly enough. The man I'll call Alvin Smith, who owned the operation along with his wife, would scoop up a runty chicken. "He'd be talking but I'd be watching that chicken in his hand, small and soft as an egg yolk," she said. "Without looking down, he'd squeeze its head and it would loll limp in his hand, and all the while he'd be talking. Alvin was completely opaque."

It was easy to spot the deviants, the ones that weren't quite big enough or vigorous enough to reach the water line that was raised every two days in accordance with the growth plan plotted by Tyson, a company that has engineered the six-week lifespan of a chicken to the point where it considers its chicken feed formula a trade secret.

When Alvin or the woman who trained her was around, my mother killed, snapping the necks of as many as forty-five chickens a day. When I could picture the scene at all, I imagined her sweeping through the chicken houses like a cross between the Angel of Death and Little Bunny Foo Foo.

My mother has always been a sucker for the underdog, the slow starter, the runt. Now she was to cull any birds that didn't conform to the Tyson life plan. They wrecked the feed conversion ratio, wasting resources better consumed by chickens that would fit Tyson specs come collection day. If she put off killing them when they were young, she wasn't doing them any favors. The further they fell behind the other birds' growth, the harder their life of scavenging became. And, in the end, this was not a system that rewarded game survival. To put off the day of reckoning meant only that the mature chicken would be less easily and painlessly snuffed out.

I WAS LIVING IN ST. LOUIS THEN. When I called home, I started hearing little cheeps in the background. They were just a few at first, but they swelled to a chorus over the course of the summer. Within a few days of starting work, my mother had become an Oskar Schindler of the chicken farm. Once left alone to do the job, she started smuggling chickens home, a few at a time.

She couldn't save them all, but she chose the birds she called little champions, like the one that would leap up and peck a drop of moisture from the water line it wasn't tall enough to reach otherwise. One chick she brought home had a leg that stuck out sideways. She had lifted him up to the water line once, and he had the pluck to call to her the next time she made her rounds so she could help him again.

I started hearing scrappy tales of chicken survival during my calls home. She admired the way the misfits scratched for food on the chicken house floors or sought out condensed moisture on the door of the chicken house when they couldn't compete with the bigger birds at the feeders. In her enthusiasm, she held the chick with the sideways leg to the phone receiver so I could hear his reedy chirps, a triumph of life over science.

EVEN WITHOUT WHAT HAPPENED THAT SUMMER, I think my mother's association with big agribusiness would have been short-lived. Where before the force of necessity had borne her through each time she took an animal's life, now she was merely a hired killer.

It was a hot summer. Old folks who were too thrifty or poor to turn on their air conditioners were dying in their rocking chairs. Then one of the Tyson plants shut down to fix a wastewater problem, and the chicken catchers stopped coming to pick up birds for slaughter. The temperature controls where my mother worked were crude, and the chickens began to pant in the heat.

The birds passed the three-and-a-half-pound mark and the Tyson pickup date. As they closed in on four pounds, they began to run out of room. They started going lame, and my mother tracked down a Tyson field representative who diagnosed the problem as femur-head necrosis, a disease caused when bacteria fester in a chicken's equivalent of our hip joint. The birds lost even what little range of movement they'd had in the cramped houses. Everything from space allotment to bird weight was controlled by strict adherence to the Tyson schedule. Now that the schedule was disrupted, the precise equations began to jumble. The chickens started to die.

My mother made her rounds day after day, picking up the dead. The freezers in each chicken house that preserved the dead chickens before transport began to overflow, and then they gave out and the dead birds inside started to putrefy. The chickens that lived couldn't keep cool as they put on weight, and they panted miserably.

Chicken 81 clinched my mother's decision to leave. She was fastening chicken wire across a doorway so the chickens could get a little more air from outside while she did her chores. One chicken followed my mother as she moved from one side of the doorway to the other, and finally settled between her feet. She reached down and rubbed its head with her finger. All the other thousands of chickens that summer had run from her or avoided her. When she rubbed the head of this one, she could see the chicken enjoyed it.

My pathologically honest mother decided to commit seventeen cents' worth of larceny—the profit the Smiths made on each bird. She resolved to come back to collect this chicken and take it home after she'd finished her rounds in the house. Even among those tens of thousands of white birds, she knew she'd find it again. Most chickens confined themselves to a fairly small area, and this one had distinctive charcoal feathers on its neck and wing.

When she returned to the spot, she had collected eighty dead chickens. She counted and recorded the dead each time she passed through a house to track the attrition for Alvin. She searched all over for the affectionate chicken, convinced it couldn't have shuffled far. Finally, she gave up. She started to lift the makeshift screen she'd lashed across the door and discovered Chicken 81. In the half hour she was gone, her chicken had crawled partway beneath the screen and died.

My mother wept.

She gave her notice that afternoon but agreed to stay on until the Smiths could find someone else. Ten days past schedule, the Tyson trucks rolled in and the catchers hauled away the chickens in a flurry of feathers. Most of the chickens, anyway. In each house several hundred were left, those too small or too crippled to meet the Tyson specs. In the past, Alvin had orchestrated a chicken roundup, closing in on the rejects with a circle of chicken wire. Then he immobilized them any way he could—snapping their necks, stomping on them—to clean out the house for the next shipment of dandelion-puff chicks. This time, he was working at his job in town and the press was on, so my mother was left to clean house alone.

She went at night, when she knew the chickens would be sleeping. She left on her car's parking lights to shine into the house and silhouette the birds where they slept clustered in puddles of white. The water lines, the feeders, all the chicken house equipment, had been hoisted to the ceiling to clear the way for the chicken catchers earlier that day.

She started down the first cavernous house. The chickens had become accustomed to the occasional bump or nudge as part of life in close quarters. My mother would sidle up to one and try to grab it by the neck and give a quick twist before it could utter a sound to alert the others. A clean grab the first time was essential. Even if the chicken flapped afterwards, if it didn't squawk, its companions didn't suspect a death spasm. By the time my mother reached the end of the chicken house, though, the few birds that were left knew a predator was among them. She had to stalk them and chase them down as she pounced and twisted, pounced and twisted.

She stood in the dark to catch her breath, her hands and shoulders sore from her kills. And she started to feel that she wasn't alone anymore.

"It began to grow in me, this feeling that someone else was in this long, dark building. I shouted out loud, 'Who's there?' I felt for a moment as though a shark spirit was there, drawn by the blood itself."

My mother fought down her panic. She finished the job that night by promising herself she would never do it again. The few chickens she missed and discovered the next day she took home.

By mid-August she had trained a young man who lived near the Smiths to tend the chickens, and she was up to her elbows in clay at a local pottery and art studio where she'd been offered a sculpting job fashioning potpourri pigs and whimsical hound dogs. She'd stopped buying chicken in the stores. The chickens she had rescued grew and grew. With a little feed and the run of the place, their bantam-size bodies grew far beyond the three and a half pounds at which their brethren had perished, and they lumbered around the farm producing noises closer to a bellow than a cluck.

A brother of mine dubbed one of the roosters Boots, after its large, muscled legs. Boots had arrived nearly grown, one of the refugees from the final night of extermination. He strutted around the farm and, when he hit puberty, started a reign of terror. He lay in wait in the yard and jumped out at my little brothers. And he raped the hens so often and so viciously that one finally died, sealing Boots' own fate as surely as Brodie's snap at a child had sealed hers.

Whatever brutality Boots himself had suffered, he had transgressed outside the bounds of the life my mother was able to negotiate for him on the farm, requiring the raw life of his fellow chickens in order to sustain his own. As my mother had always done, she gathered herself up and did what she had to do. She put a kettle of water on to boil and brought out her ax.

"Boots, he had seen me killing the other chickens, and he never trusted me after that. In the end, he was fully justified."

From *In an Arid Land*

PAUL SCOTT MALONE

Prize Rope

W E'RE FIXING UP A MAJESTIC BREAKFAST for our
first morning. In my old black skillet, on my green Coleman
stove, sitting on green metal legs above a little sand dune, nine patties of Jimmy Dean's HOT sausage are sizzling. The sausage is my
job. I study it closely, turn each patty with the long blade on my
Swiss Army knife, sniff the wonderful greasy odor, take a sip of my
screwdriver in a plastic cup. Then I glance up looking for Eddie.

I find him out in the surf, still in its morning calm. He's fishing
again, his big head and his long black rod silhouetted against that
monster sunrise. He casts, turns his body to battle a low wave, reels
in his bait like some machine. Eddie doesn't much care for fishing;
he's doing it because that's what men do when they go to the beach,
and because he's heartbroken.

"What's on his mind?" Ed Senior wants to know, coming up
behind me. "I don't think he slept at all and he hasn't spoken a word
since we got up, just a grunt now and then, like an animal."

"Squaw problems," I say.

"That's what I figured," he says.

"So what's new, huh?"

"Dern women," says Ed Senior and he snorts a laugh to show
he's joking; he doesn't know the facts of the matter. I know the facts
and I know it's not Marcia's fault that Eddie's heartbroken; this is
No-Fault Heartbreak, you might say. She changed, he changed, they

changed, an old American story; and I happen to know she's in Albuquerque this week looking for a place to live.

We stand there worrying, wearing nothing but swim trunks, wriggling our toes in the sand, me with my knife, him with his Dutch oven full of biscuits, staring out to sea like wives of old. Eddie's my best friend, has been most of my life, and he's Ed Senior's only son. We've come here, to this lonely stretch of beach, because Eddie wanted us to. An empty house is a mean companion. So here we are, three white guys loose upon the earth.

"Dern women," the Old One says again, grinning at me as he turns away. He goes back to his fire pit, pokes the coals with a stick and replaces the Dutch oven on the blackened grate. The biscuits, the coffee, the fried potatoes with onions and some kind of private seasoning he brought along—these are Ed Senior's jobs, and he knows what he's doing. The eggs are Eddie's job.

"Is it time yet?"

"Pretty close," he says. "Better call him in."

We both look out to sea. Eddie casts again, reels it in like he's in a bad hurry, with an awkward but furious kind of precision, like it's a chore he's got to get through but never will.

It's unlikely he'll catch anything; we all know this. There's a fat old noisy dredge as big as a destroyer working in the shrimp boat channel just down the island from us and it's pumping the sludge over the jetties into the Gulf. Just our luck. The water all around is gray and gritty, the fish gone elsewhere.

I turn the sausage for the last time, slice off a juicy bite to be sure it's done, put down my knife and then I trudge through the sand to the water. I stand in the water, staring at Eddie, just watching him, still silent, until he turns and sees me.

AFTER BREAKFAST Ed Senior mixes up a new round of screwdrivers. He squeezes a lime wedge into each red cup and tells us it's his own personal recipe. We grin like conspirators, touch cups in a toast and then sit in folding chairs beneath the shelter we have erected with a blue plastic tarp and four crooked poles of driftwood.

Ed Senior slaps Eddie's knee and shows an enormous smile to be uplifting. He says, "Boys, this is the life, ain't it?"

The tarp flaps and complains overhead. We sip our drinks, smoke cigarettes we wouldn't smoke back in the city, breathe in the salty air, gaze at the roaring Gulf. Already it's ninety degrees and we're sweating, our pale bodies suffering.

It's an elaborate camp we have made. Our huge rented tent snaps and grumbles in the anxious breeze. Inside is all our personal gear, knapsacks and satchels and gimme caps, books that won't get read, two sleeping bags, Ed Senior's aluminum cot, a *Playboy* magazine, a .357 Ruger automatic, our wallets full of money and credit cards and fishing licenses purchased at a bait shop yesterday, along with tiny photos of loved ones. Round about are ice chests and old trunks, jugs of fresh water and big red gasoline cans, pairs of sneakers and tackle boxes already settling into the sand. A second spare tire, which the park rangers suggested we bring along when Eddie called last week, serves as the bar; it is covered with leaning liquor bottles and even, as a sort of joke by Ed Senior which we the young ones don't get, a metal martini mixer and a squat round decanter of expensive liqueur.

"Grace and style, boys," he explained when he emptied the "liquor store," one of the trunks, while we were setting up camp.

To put it straight, we overloaded. The roof of Eddie's big Jeep was weighted down so cruelly on our drive down here that the ceiling liner touched my head in the backseat. Better to have than to have not was our motto in packing. We are sixty-three miles from civilization. We are a long way from home. We are without supervision. This is how he wanted it; he wanted Remote. He has owned the Jeep for two years, put 64,000 miles on it, and yesterday, grinding through the deep soft sand in our search for Remote, was only the third time he has used the four-wheel drive.

Eddie rises, gulps the rest of his drink and without a word to either of us he picks up his rod and his bait can and then he walks like a man with a mission straight into the water.

WE FISH FOR A WHILE, catch nothing, but it feels good being in the warm surf, which is up now and fighting us. We're on the first sandbar. The water is groin deep. Ed Senior and I are working the trench between us and the beach. Eddie's still casting out, into the oncoming waves. He reaches way back with his brand-new surf rig and heaves with all his might, sending the sinker and the shrimp on its hook into a tremendous arc that ends with a tiny splash out among the breakers. Each time he looks somehow disappointed, as if he's trying to hit Florida or the Gulf Stream with every toss and intends to keep at it until he does.

Soon Ed Senior tires of the fight. I can see it in his drooping red face, his weary gray hair. He waves at me, points to the camp and smiles before he wades through the trench to the beach. He dries himself, changes into some baggy plaid shorts and a polo shirt, and I see him disappear into the tent for a nap.

Another hour of nothing. Now I'm tired too and I can feel the sting of the sun on my white-boy shoulders. Eddie the Machine is still working, casting out and reeling in, casting out and reeling in. I make my way down the sand bar to him, and he actually flinches and jumps when he senses me there beside him. He looks at me like I'm a Hammerhead come to eat him.

"Let's go in," I yell over the roar.

He shakes his head no, indicates with a nod that I should go ahead though if I want to. He reels in, turns to toss again and it's then that I notice there's no bait on his hook—nothing but curved steel. With that same look in his face he heaves and sends his naked hook flying toward Florida.

I yell, "Hey, man, they've stolen your bait."

Eddie glances at me with those cool blue eyes in his reddening face and he shrugs his reddening shoulders as if it doesn't matter, and he starts reeling in again. So I leave him there and slog it to the beach. In camp I find one of his tee shirts flapping from a pole of the shelter.

On the front of the tee shirt, in faded blue letters above and below a faded blue stencil of a big Texas gobbler, it says, *Thanksgiving Day Turkey Trot—A Marathon for Health—Greater Houston Heart Associa-*

tion. I remember that day. I remember a photograph of Eddie and Marcia, their faces worn out and drained of color but happy, their dark hair stringy and wild under their sweatbands, his hammy arm across her shoulders, and each of them wearing a Turkey Trot tee shirt. They're looking right into the camera and their eyes are the Lights of Expectation. Also in the picture are his mom and Ed Senior, who'd come in to town for the occasion, beaming like proud parents should. I took that picture, though I hadn't run in the race, to celebrate his return from the brink. He was healthy again after two years of struggling with it—the crud in his veins, the goo in his lungs, those murderous habits—and we were crazy with joy and love for what he'd done.

Back into the waves I go, carrying the tee shirt on a mission of mercy, and when I get to him I holler, "Hey, better put this on, you're roasting." He smiles at me and nods his head in thanks. I take his rod while he slips the shirt on and I very quickly bait his hook with a shrimp out of my own can.

He smiles again, nods again, takes the rod from me, turns, heaves, trying once again for Florida.

ABOUT MID-AFTERNOON Ed Senior emerges from the tent squinting and blinking in the blinding glare of sun and sand.

"Good God, Matt, is he still at it?"

"Yessir," I say.

"Has he caught anything?"

"Not that I've noticed."

We glance at each other with looks of wonder and concern, and then sit under the sagging shelter drinking beers. We sit there for quite a while, saying little, just watching Eddie out in the surf, the flight of an occasional pelican, a sand crab scampering about. The tarp above us is whooshing like a flag now.

Ed Senior is restless after his nap. He fidgets in his chair, scans the beach looking for entertainment. All of a sudden he says, "Hey, let's go do some scavenging, want to?"

"Well sure. Sounds fine with me."

"Wonder if he'll come along?" he says, looking out at Eddie.

"He's got to be tired."

"Gotta be."

"We'll coax him out with beer."

We take six cans from an ice chest and with two of them raised high I struggle through the water to the sandbar while Ed Senior starts the Jeep and drives down to the water's edge to wait. It's a reluctant Eddie who follows me out. He gets in the back seat and the Old One drives us up the beach in the direction we came from yesterday. The tide is out and so Ed Senior guns up the Jeep, races along the wet hard pack, splashing through pockets of water, and we're all grinning over it like riders on a roller coaster. Soon we're at the part of the island where the junk, the jetsam and flotsam, the debris, the detritus—whatever you want to call it—is the worst, the deepest, the ugliest.

It's a depressing sight—"like the Aftermath," as Eddie put it yesterday when we ground our way through here—but heartening, too, to scavengers like us. In the soft sand between the tide line and the high grassy dunes is all the stuff of modern life. Plastic laundry hampers, plastic milk crates, plastic jugs, half submerged in the sand. Huge chunks of lumber with rusty nails protruding dangerously. Hypodermic needles, little brown bottles, big green bottles, faded beer cans, lengths of oceangoing rope. Gifts from Mexico, New Jersey, Europe and all the ships at sea.

We wander through it, watching where we step, picking up this, picking up that, tossing it down. Soon we settle on rope as our objective—no telling what you might use it for. We drive a ways, spot a telltale yellow piece poking out of the sand, stop, get out, pull on it, and twenty feet surface in a long circular line. Two hours we stalk the beach, going five, maybe six miles, until there are two filthy laundry baskets full of coiled, stinking rope in the back of the Jeep. The Prize Piece is perhaps two inches in diameter, perhaps thirty feet long, with impressive loops woven into both ends. Eddie, smiling, says he'll use it as a clothesline, "or maybe to hang myself when the time comes."

Now we are disgusted with scavenging, hot and stinking and

exhausted, and headed back to camp. Eddie's driving. He's going fast, right at the water's edge—the roller coaster again, only faster, more erratic—up and down off low dunes, splashing through cuts in the beach at forty, fifty, sixty miles an hour. We're whizzing along, enjoying the cool breeze, the thrill.

Eddie, grinning ferociously, says, loud over the wind noise, "About time this Jeep started to look and act like a Jeep," and he takes us bounding over a little ridge. "Look at this," he says, pointing to a streak of beach tar on the pretty gray dashboard. "Now that's the way it ought to look." He guns it up, grins all around, his hair blowing, eyes bright. "Watch this," he says and this time all four tires come off the ground.

"Wahoo," I holler, caught up in the moment, his moment.

But I can tell Ed Senior is worried. The Old One is hanging on and frowning now with doubt. He wants to say something but won't, wants to be fatherly but can't. Eddie knows this. He glances over, returns his father's frown, and without warning he turns the Jeep into the surf, sending up spray like a motorboat, soaking us all, and then, stamping his foot on the brake pedal, he takes us to a rough tilting stop. The Jeep rocks up painfully on its side and hangs there for a tense moment before settling itself like a great wounded beast. Eddie smiles and looks around.

"Holy cow, boy, you trying to kill us?" says Ed Senior, and he lets out a nervous laugh. "This ain't a Pershing tank, you know."

Eddie opens his door and gets out. He runs, leaping through the waves, and dives in. Ed Senior and I sit there in the sweltering Jeep, wondering what he's doing.

He emerges, splashes back in, comes right up to the Jeep and leans his big head inside the window, dripping water.

"Y'all go ahead," he says, panting, his face blazing red. "I'll see you in a little while."

"We can wait," says Ed Senior. "Whatever you're doing."

"Naw, go on, I'm collecting sea shells."

"Sea shells!" says the Old One. "What for?"

Eddie backs away into the water, panting and smiling oddly,

bends at the waist like a runner to catch his breath, and looks at our wondering faces through the window.

"Because Marcia likes sea shells," he says.

He turns, runs away, jumping through the waves like a big old crazy dog, stretches out his body and dives in again.

THE SUNSET'S FULL ABOVE THE DUNES by the time Eddie appears in camp. Ed Senior, a martini in his hand, complete with olives, is moving fretfully around the fire pit. He has supper well under way—not the broiled snapper we'd planned on, but steaks and baked potatoes and even sweet corn, a fine meal.

"About goddamn time you showed up," he says to Eddie in a lilting, teasing voice. "Where're your sea shells?"

It's true; he walked in empty handed.

Giving the Old One a mean glare for bringing it up, Eddie says, "I'm not hungry, don't fix me anything," and Ed Senior returns the glare, his mouth hanging open in exaggerated shock.

"But you gotta make the salad, I'm no good with salad."

"I don't want anything, I tell you."

"Ah, for crying out loud," says Ed Senior. "You can't go without eating, son, you haven't had a bite since breakfast."

"I can go without anything I damn well want to go without," he says, and we're both a little hurt by his tone. We shuffle around in the sand, looking away, glancing back. Eddie seems to regret it but he's not apologizing. In haste he finds his rod and his bait can and he marches out to sea. He's lucky. The moon, about two slivers shy of full, is already up out there, hanging above the horizon like a great white eye giving off a big light.

"Well, I'll say this," the Old One grumbles after a long while. "If determination could feed the world, ole Eddie'd be the breadbasket, wouldn't he? Or maybe the fishing net."

"He'll get over it," I say, thinking hard. "I guess I did."

We glance at each other in the fading sunset, knowing I'm lying in the service of friendship, knowing these are not the facts of the matter, both of us wishing I hadn't said it.

"Let's eat," he mutters, turning toward the fire pit, and we are very quiet with each other all through the meal.

IT'S LATE NOW. The big eye of the moon has crawled well up into the starry sky, its bright light intruding on our privacy, even here, in Remote, Texas. Ed Senior and I have long since had our feast of steak and potatoes, long since concluded that we should leave Eddie's meal warming in the Dutch oven above the coals, long since passed between us the squat round decanter of expensive liqueur that tasted of orange peels and sugar water, long since given up our inebriated talk of nothing (that worthless drowsy kind of talk that always follows the lowering of the lantern's flame when the newly arrived gloom of night involves you in its promise of rest), long since had our sighs and our yawns and let our heads nod, long since offered our good-nights.

The Old One is in the tent, snoring. From my folding chair I can hear him over the night sounds of the surf, and it is somehow endearing to me and comforting.

"Better keep an eye on him," he mumbled before he went to bed, which is what I have done more or less, dozing and waking and watching. Long after midnight and he's still out there, on the first sandbar, casting out and reeling in, casting out and reeling in, trying to hit Florida, a dark irregularity in the triangular gloss of reflected moonlight, a human chink in a piece of finely wrought silver made beautiful by the imperfection.

At last I rouse myself and carry my folding chair out to the very edge of the water. I smoke cigarettes I shouldn't smoke, drink a beer I shouldn't drink, find the Big Dipper, imagine for a while, and then, growing bored with its simple design, I wish I were a smarter man who knew the positions and configurations of other constellations so that I could find them, too, and imagine even more. Off in the distance, beyond the jetties, the fat old dredge in the channel shines like a small city, its red and white lights speaking of other humans hereabout, rough working guys doing their jobs all through the night, reminding me that we are never, in the modern world as remote as we'd like to think.

I am, on the whole, terrified of dark water. There are wily sharks out there and jellyfish and stingrays and killer currents and no telling what else, and I am amazed, still, that my friend does not share this terror. Friendship, like love, I think, is one of the grand mysteries. Who knows what brings strangers together and drives comrades apart? Living with the mystery takes courage, I know, the courage to stand in dark water and to cast your line toward Florida, the courage to hope that, in spite of yourself, ignoring the odds, you just might catch something.

Back in camp I take our Prize Rope out of the Jeep and then I fumble around until I find my rod and my bait can. Dragging the rope, I walk out into the water until it's lapping at my thighs. A sneaky chill wriggles across my back and I have to stop. The trench is just before me, deep and hidden and fearful, and it takes me a moment to plunge in. When I do I go ahead quickly, kicking through the water, trailing the heavy rope behind, until I'm up safely on the sandbar and making my way toward Eddie.

When I'm close enough to hear, he calls out above the waves, "Been wondering when you'd show up." His voice is eerie-sounding, louder now and more distinct, out here in the watery void.

"Well I've never much cared for bathing with sharks."

I can see him smile in the moonlight, his teeth shining like phosphorescent gems. He's glad to see me, and I'm glad I came.

"What's that?" he says, noticing the rope.

"This, my friend, is our lifeline," I say. "Here, put this loop around your waist."

At first he laughs, says, "What?!" but when he sees I'm serious he does what he's told. We take turns holding our gear as the other one slips the rope over his head and slithers into it, a slow clumsy business. It's a heavy weight, but the water buoys the rope somewhat and when it's done I feel better.

"Why don't you take over for a while, I'm tired out."

"Have you caught anything?"

"Naw," he says. "Will though, I've had nibbles."

I dig into my can and pull out a shrimp, bait my hook, prick my finger in the process and worry that I'm bleeding, calling the sharks in for dinner. I cast out, let the sinker settle to the bottom, the way it ought to be done. My plan is to do it right, thinking if I catch something for him maybe he'll give it up, get some rest. Slowly I reel in, letting it settle, dragging it in, but I come up with nothing. So I cast out and try again.

As if it's the next line in a long conversation, he says, "You know what she told me the day she left for Albuquerque?" and he looks at me as if this is significant, something I need to know. "She said—I can still hear her voice like she was standing right there where you are—she said, 'It is possible I will miss you when I leave.'"

We give off looks full of injury and confusion, but I don't know what to say to him, don't know what to do, don't know why he told me that, so I reel in my bait and cast out again. Thinking about it, imagining his misery, I find myself reeling in without any thought of catching fish. I want to say something, I want to sound wise and brotherly, but I've never been any good at that sort of thing and when I open my mouth nothing comes out.

"It-is-*possible*," I hear him say again, emphasizing each word, trying to understand them, I guess, dwelling on it, "I-will-*miss*-you…" and he pauses here, "…*when-I leave*."

We are quiet for a while as the waves roll through us, holding our rods tightly in our hands, glancing at each other.

"I've been out here all day," he says. "And what I can't figure out is why anybody that once loved you, once shared everything with you, why she would ever say something like that to you." He looks over. He says, "You got any ideas?"

"No," I say, and it's the truth. I wish I did, I wish I had all kinds of ideas, but I don't and he knows I don't.

I cast out and reel it in, without method, without purpose, moving down the sandbar to get away from him since I don't want to hear any more. What good is such talk? When I'm out of hearing range, and the rope, our lifeline, is stretched to its fullest, I look back, keeping an eye on him as the Old One has asked me to. I can see his white Turkey Trot tee shirt glowing in the moonlight and his big head low against his chest and I think perhaps he is weeping. It would have been better, I think, if he hadn't said anything, hadn't mentioned Marcia's last words to him, words uttered in haste and anger and meant to hurt him, which they did, and then did again. But heartbreak is like that, I know.

I tug on the rope, gently, rhythmically, so he won't know it's not the waves doing the tugging, just enough to draw him off balance and away from his thoughts, and he seems to come out of the spell. Presently he lifts his rod and he turns and he heaves his sinker out into the dark churning waves, and, because this is why I have come, I do the same, and then we both reel in, quite deliberately, keeping our eyes on some invisible spot out there, and this goes on and on, on and on for a long time; we cast out and reel in, cast out and reel in, catching nothing, as the sharks and the stingrays and the jellyfish swim menacingly around us, as the killer currents conspire against us, as the moon ducks its big white eye below the dunes behind us, all through the blind mysterious hours, while the Prize Rope tugs at our waists, keeping us close, until, with the first pale sheen of sunrise, we can see once again just where we are, see once again the danger we have passed through together.

Searching for Mr. Watson

BILL BELLEVILLE

J UST MINUTES AFTER I LEAVE my home in northeastern
Florida to drive down to the Everglades to search for Mr. Watson, I zip past a wood stork. It is standing at the side of the entrance
ramp to the busy interstate, looking at once noble and woefully misplaced—like a lonely chess piece on a checkerboard.

The Glades with their vast subtropical wilderness are a good five
hours away at the other end of the state. But the stork is here anyway.
It is knee-deep in a drainage ditch—cars whizzing by on their way to
Disney World without a notion of *whatever can it be*—and it is doing
what wading birds like it have done in Florida before anything like a
human or a theme park arrived. It is sweeping its curved beak through
the cloudy water, hoping to connect with something alive there.

My friend Terry, an old college pal who will paddle the other
end of the canoe, misses the bird altogether, not because he is
obtuse, but because he lives on the opposite rim of the country and
his senses are already saturated with local exotica. It will take a
mighty dose of melodrama to jar him.

"Wood stork," I say, pointing with one hand and driving us
onto Interstate Four with the other.

"Is that a rare bird?" asks Terry earnestly, and I tell him that it is.
I say I am both heartened to see it, but disturbed it has ranged so far
outside its natural home. Not so long ago, this bird with the head that
seems fire charred—this "iron head"—was so integral to the Glades it
was considered a barometer of its health. But, the Everglades are on
the brink, have been for a while now. The wood stork is trying to roll
with this change, ranging far outside its historic territory.

Terry is from three decades worth of my past, a fraternity brother and ex-jock, a reformed party animal like myself seeking redemption in the solitude of distant natural places. Individually, we have struggled to unravel the jumble of civilized threads to get at the nugget of ourselves buried inside. From its discovery, we have come to learn this nature offered solace, living Whitmanesque lessons in the values of singularity and tolerance.

And so Terry hikes east of Los Angeles, back into places like Death Valley and Borrego Springs and camps there. I live in Florida and kayak on any wild body of water I can find—the St. Francis Dead River, the Blackwater Creek, the Mosquito Lagoon.

Now we are headed together to the Glades, to canoe deep into its distant western boundary in a hunt for the "Watson Place," a pre-Columbian Calusa midden mound. It is a forty-acre composite of shell and stunted tropical foliage, a thread between us and the time-wronged desperado who once lived here.

Like the Glades and the wood stork, we too are on the brink, aging jocks ranging beyond what is safe and known. In this way, we sweep through the experiences that still lay out before us, hoping to connect with something alive and vital. All we are sure of is we have come to appreciate wilderness for the way it lays itself down on the soul.

Unlike other men who seek solace in this way, we don't carry traditional props; we are not hunters or dapper L. L. Bean campers. I carry a set of old binoculars to watch for avi-fauna, but the truth is, beyond raptors and tropical wading birds, I'm lost unless a species appears clear and unobstructed in the scope. As for our gear, it is jerry-rigged and stuffed into duffels and garbage bags and pvc buckets.

Instead of giant foil pouches of official freeze-dried camp food, I have brought Noodles-in-a-Cup and tins of tuna and chicken. We have granola bars that look and taste like Oreos compressed into little rectangles. I imagine Jack Kerouac, when he went up on Desolation Peak out West, might have packed like this.

But I do place a lot of significance on a compass and the correct nautical map to lead me in and out of untamed places. Each tiny paper squiggle, each logarithmic degree corresponds to something tangible—an oxbow or bar or tiny islet. Once ground-truthed, these coordinates can sometimes nudge the senses, linking near meaningless geographic names to remarkable places on the landscape. Ahead in the Glades, my map promises Pavilion and Buzzard Keys, Chokoloskee and Rabbit Key Passes, Lostman's and Chatham Rivers.

I have tucked both compass and map inside a waterproof Seal-Lock Baggy I will carry on my lap when we finally reach our canoe. Also in the baggy is a paperback copy of Peter Matthiessen's novel *Killing Mr. Watson*. As I drive south on I-95, this idea amuses me, as if the immediacy of the adventure will require me to be ready at any time to understand direction, latitude, and literary metaphor. Nonetheless, this book and its sequels are the thread that has relinked Terry and myself after all these years, something real our adult selves respond to that goes far beyond the retelling of old locker room jokes and keg party stories.

After all, we twisted the party gauge to its edge, and then kept on pushing. When we quit playing sports midway through school, we developed a sort of restless enmity, a condition that could end in a fist fight, a brawl, a mindless round of punching holes in doors— the old kind, made of solid wood. The truth was, we were athletic, but we weren't typical monosyllabic jocks; nor did we fit the supercilious frat boy mold, either. Restless, without a real belonging or focus, we became known in the parlance as "bad actors." And, we did all we could to live up to that. Once established, our respective reputations had lives of their own, and they lasted long after the deeds were done.

Like me, Terry had read the three Matthiessen novels on Watson's life and demise. Like me, he felt a kinship with Watson—a complex soul who existed far outside the monotone of local myth. Matthiessen may have "reimagined" Ed Watson's life. But in doing so, he admits the retelling probably "contains much more of the truth of Mister Watson than the lurid and popularly accepted 'facts.'"

In *Watson*, *Lost Man's River*, and *Bone by Bone*, Matthiessen uses the real life and death of the renegade cane grower to re-create a wild place and a maverick culture special to southwest Florida. But if his books are about a vanished time, they are also about the social evolution of perception, about how the realities of a richly embroidered moment—or a mystifying personality—can be spun down into simpleminded slogans. Time has treated both the Glades and the strong, passionate man who was E. J. Watson this way, turning the magnificent Everglades into a swamp and the complex E. J. into "Bloody Watson."

But searching for Mr. Watson is not a walk in the woods. The Glades are a sprawling subtropical territory larger than the state of Delaware; ranger stations and interpretive boardwalks dot the outer edges, but inside, saw grass stretches to the east, and mud-rooted mangroves to the west, leaving little dry land in between. It is, as Matthiessen has observed, a "labyrinthal wilderness," and its sheer lack of accessibility has been the secret to keeping it so.

Or, as *Lostman* character Speck Daniel puts it: "what the hell kind of tourist would beat his way three to four miles back up a mangrove river to take a picture of some raggedy ol' lonesome place...."

Down we go on the notorious I-95 into Miami, the car-jacking, drug-shuttling, neon-rocker paneled, middle-finger-in-the-air conduit, finally turning west near the Latino bustle of Calle Ocho. From here, we drive through block after block of urban landscape that barely a half century ago used to be freshwater marl prairie, bristling with great fields of saw grass. Today it is colonized by espresso shops and *Santería botanicas*, 7-11's and Texacos hugging every available square inch.

"Man," says Terry, shaking his head. "Talk about sensory overload." I run this gauntlet for an hour until we are safely west of the city, headed out across the northern boundary of the Glades. Open space and dwarfed cypress and saw grass command the geography now, with great white cumulus billowing overhead, fed by the wet, feral terrain. There may be two more contrary realities this close to each other somewhere else in the world, but I'm not aware of them.

We are safely atop the Tamiami Trail now—a word squeeze of *Tampa to Miami*. It is the road that first splayed the Glades in two when it was built, water-spitting draglines and dredges crunching their way through the lime rock in the 1920s.

Water driven, the Glades are at the mercy of strangers upstream. And this Trail we are driving serves as a massive dam across it. The lazy but deliberate sheet flow of water that once swept down across southern Florida from just below Orlando is now squeezed under us through a series of mechanical gates, giant Erector-setlike devices built for flood control. Man plays God with the upland rainfall and water now, and as gods go, he has proved to be a baleful, selfish sort, a minor Old Testament deity with more ambition than wisdom.

Soon, we arrive at SR 29, the narrow southerly road that trails past "panther crossing" signs and dead ends six miles south in Everglades City, the fishing village now being transformed into an RV tourist mecca on the far western tip of the park. The freshwater sweeping down from the easterly saw grass meadows meets the coastal mangrove buffer a few miles inland from here. Everglades City is the jumping off point for our quest.

Clinging to shards of a hardscrabble pioneer culture still tended by a handful of stone crabbers and mullet fishermen, this little town on the edge of the park now teeters precariously toward a fun-house-mirror version of "ecotourism." Anything alive, it seems, is fair game: Airboat rides and canned "safaris" and "jungle boat tours" (Gators guaranteed!) are everywhere, as are boutiquelike souvenir shops painted peach and green, with incongruous names like Jungle Erv's. The nature rhythm—of place and people—has been squeezed and massaged and marketed in a heavy-handed attempt to catch up to the trendiness that has homogenized much of Florida's coast.

As I watch a gaggle of tourists board an air-conditioned park service pontoon boat for a guided excursion onto Chokoloskee Bay, my only thought is how white and spanking clean everyone is. The outlaw plume hunters and gator poachers, turtlers and contraband smugglers—the bona fide heirs to the Watson legend and time—have died, trickled away, tried to grow up. *Lostman's*, set in the past, foretells this gentrification: "...beaten flat, [it] would disappear beneath the tar and concrete, the tourist courts and house trailers, the noisy cars of vacationers with their red faces, sun hats, candy-colored clothes..."

We are eager to get to the former Watson homesite as soon as we can. But it is now late in the day. Faced with spending a night in a motel here or paying an outfitter to ferry us and our canoe back to the old Watson mound by motorboat, we choose the latter, planning to use the time saved to more thoroughly explore the creeks and sloughs of the backcountry on our five-day paddle back.

A SLIGHT YOUNG MAN named Justin wearing rubber white fisherman's boots has brought us to the threshold of the Watson site in his go-fast fiberglass outboard, expertly twisting and turning the wheel behind the center console to deliver us through the look-alike puzzle of mangrove islands and tidal rivers.

Justin's new girlfriend has come along for the ride, and on our trip here, I overhear her asking him who this Watson was. Either Justin had not read the Matthiessen books, or he didn't feel like re-creating the complexities of them. He gives her the shorthand folk version, the one locals have been giving to tourists for years. "He was a guy who lived back up here and grew cane . . . and when it came time to pay his hired help, he would kill them instead."

The "Watson Place" is one of several dozen primitive campsites in this odd park; most are docklike "chickees" built where there is simply no dry land to be found. But a few, like this one, are high mounds of shell and bone constructed first by the Calusas and later, colonized by farmers, fishermen, and assorted renegades. It arises from the dark tannin of the Chatham River like a high natural bluff, fringed at one edge with a thick cover of snake plants—a hardy, spiky ornamental that settlers cultivated in their yards in Florida a century and more ago. It is an odd relief, back here in this mud-driven monoculture of red and black mangrove, an exotic harbinger of other surprises yet to come.

It is 4:30 PM and the early spring sun is dipping down toward the top of the tall black mangroves just across the Chatham River and Justin is anxious to get back to the marina at Everglades City before dark. We quickly unload our canoe and supplies on a narrow wooden dock. The ferocious salt water marsh mosquitoes—"swamp angels" to the settlers—seem to be marshaling their forces for sun-down; their humming from back in the tangle of truncated tropical jungle at the edge of the clearing produces a low-grade static. It is early April, at the wane of an El Nino winter in which a few mildly colder months have barely kept a lid on the hatch of blood-sucking insects. We are as concerned about getting our mosquito-flapped tents set up as Justin is about getting home to his warm bed.

As Terry and I sort through our pile of gear, Justin cranks the motor, eases his boat away from the dock, and disappears in a meringuelike froth around the corner of Chatham Bend. I think of Ed Watson's old gasoline launch, the *Brave*, and how he puttered slowly down the Chatham to Chokoloskee Island in it one last time on October 24, 1910, the distinctive *pop-pop-pop* of the ancient motor announcing his arrival to a gathering mob of islanders who would murder him in broad daylight. Watson had scared them with his reputation one too many times, and he paid for it.

Finally alone now, we establish priorities: First, we douse ourselves with repellent, then we hurry to set up camp in the scant half acre or so of open, weedy land. At the clearing's edge, an entangled jungle has colonized the rest of the forty-acre mound, slender trunks and boughs of native gumbo-limbo and manchineel gridded together like spider webs, along with lime and guava and avocado left from the Watson era, all as feral and turned wild now.

After I work up a light sweat assembling my tent, I stop and look around, letting the reality of being atop the former Watson homestead settle in. The quiet back here is complete, so full it seems to have measurable weight. At the edge of the Chatham River, several large red mangroves, bowlike roots arching into the oyster shell mud, frame the water. The sun dips down below them to the west, and Terry asks, "you think ol' Ed trimmed back those mangroves to give him a good view of the sunset?" and I figure he probably did.

The old Watson place is the largest shell mound for miles in any direction. The Calusas shucked oysters and clams here, discarded bones from bear and panther, manatee and deer for at least two thousand years. Spiritually complex and savvy to nature, they understood its power—especially the water-thrashing energy of tropical hurricanes—and did all they could to literally rise above it.

In his time, Ed Watson painstakingly hauled timber in by boat to build a substantial two-story frame farm house, flanking it with flowering red royal poinciana trees. It was said to be the finest of its type inside the great uncivilized wash between Ft. Myers and Key West. Since Watson's death, the home was used by hunters and fishermen and squatters. Hurricane Donna damaged the house in 1960, and the park service—looking for any excuse to clear old private structures from public land—razed it soon afterward.

I ask Terry if he's ready to look for Ed's homesite in the jungle, and he says he is. It is a Friday night now, a weekend evening in the middle of the Everglades, darkness coming fast. A large, unseen gator bellows out a mating call from the edge of the Chatham—or perhaps it is a territorial warning. I can't imagine being in a place more removed from the superfluous collegiate atmosphere under which Terry and I met. He must think the same of me, for we both exist far outside the social convention that first bound us.

Off we go on a narrow trail back into the wall of stunted tropical foliage, ducking under low branches. Terry has on long pants and a T-shirt sporting an ET-like extraterrestrial, a large Bowie-type knife strapped to his belt. I am in jeans and T-shirt, wearing a baseball cap that reads "Jung." Under the thick canopy back here, the sun barely penetrates—by day, it is sepia tinted; in the early evening, it is downright gloomy. At the edge of the trail lies a skull and skeleton, a small mammal of some sort, about the size of a raccoon, like the wild-eyed coons I have been seeing clattering about on the bow roots, dark stripes bleached almost white by salt and sun.

We are in the midst of the insect static now, and despite our repellent, the swamp angels blanket us—hanging on for dear life, waiting for the chemical to wear off. Settlers, like Watson, virtually lived in the black smoke of smudge pots, which they kept burning day and night; when they had window screens, they rubbed crankcase oil on them to keep the insects from smothering the grid.

Just off the trail, I see what looks like knee-high concrete boundary markers, scattered haphazardly. I look closer and realize they are the original foundations Watson once built his fine house upon, raising it up a couple feet for ventilation. They are made of a tabby, crushed lime rock, and shells of the sort the Calusas left behind. From the elegant trunks of the gumbo-limbo trees, tissue-thin patches of red-amber bark curl like the skin of a sunburnt tourist, pineapplelike bromeliads tucked away in the crooks.

Just when the buzzing seems enough to drive us mad, I notice a mysterious structure peeking out from the thick jungle just ahead. It is made of the same tabby material as the foundations, except it is rectangular, as large as a room-sized funeral vault. The park service has built a wooden cap atop it to keep people and animals from falling in. "It's Ed's cistern," I say, "where he gathered rainwater." Weathered by a century of tropical heat and rain, the tabby walls look more like the sides of an ancient Spanish mission. A gumbo-limbo, far bigger than any of the others, grows from a corner of the cistern, happy for the fresh water still inside. Nearby, Ed and his family slept and dreamed, and I wonder, what of?

The swamp angels, perhaps a mutant breed, are starting to bite now, and we move as fast as we can back to our camp. I fire up my gas lantern, and as I do, an easy breeze picks up from the Chatham, enough to hold the insects at bay. We concoct a dinner swill over a one-burner stove, and as we eat, the scarlet sky turns gray, then full black. Fireflies, a rarity in Chemlawned Florida nowadays, dart the edge of the jungle with their green-blue light.

I look overhead to see Venus hanging itself just under the sliver of new moon; minutes later, the sky is as full of stars and constellations as any I have ever seen. I turn down the lantern and Terry and I sit in silence, watching meteors streak through the darkness like distant flares, as if underscoring our own sense of awe. From the Chatham, mullet leap and splash, joyous ghosts water-skipping in the night.

It is too warm for a sleeping bag so when I crawl into my tent, I lay on top of the bag, using it for a mattress. Above, the bright stars burn a soft glow through the thin fabric. From the river, I hear a deep humanlike exhalation, the sound of a bottlenose dolphin surfacing to blow. From back up the trail, a chuck-will's-widow calls its own name over and over, waiting for an answer that doesn't come. Everywhere, unseen critters rustle and gurgle in the isolation of the Everglades' darkness. Instead of distressing me, it has a remarkably calming effect, as if the mound itself is exuding the timeless exhalations of all who have come here before me, the Calusas, the renegades, Ed Watson. And now, into the collective dreams of the mound I also go.

The new morning is fresh, dew on the tent and the wild grass in the clearing. After a quick breakfast, we walk the edge of the jungle, find what must have been a farm plow in the weeds, metal wheels dark red with rust. Back in a few yards, we discover the frame of an old truck, rubber and wood long gone. Terry takes my photograph sitting on it. Out near the shell-encrusted shore of the river, we see the 150-gallon iron kettle where Watson rendered down his cane, still mounted inside a waist-high concrete and brick pedestal. Instead of cane syrup, the kettle holds stagnant rainwater, green now with algae, tadpoles swirling back and forth just under the surface. I run my hand on the concrete rimming the kettle; I realize someone once took the trouble to round and smooth the edges, a remarkable act of civilization in such a place.

Watson, as Matthiessen wisely guessed, was ambitious, a person who cared about how the world was ordered around him. He was, after all, the only white man to live on this mound more than a year or two—farming it for nearly two decades before he was killed in 1910. I reach down to the ground, pick up a piece of metal, maybe a ladle, iron corroded beyond recognition. Watson's presence here is nearly palpable: I think of him laying down this tool ninety years ago on the edge of the smooth concrete rim, going down to Chokoloskee to take care of business, just for the afternoon.

WE HAVE SPENT THREE DAYS HERE NOW, using the Watson mound as a base to explore local waters, segueing up into tight canopied creeks, including one that wasn't even on our map. Once back there, we paddled for almost a mile, until the tide ebbed finally out from under us, reshaping our path into an impassable slough of foliage and roots. Stoic, we rested, drank tepid water and ate granola bars, listened to the coon oysters spit, watched the mangrove crabs nervously scuttle over the mud like black mice. Terry, gracious, named the creek Belleville. From there, I saw my first swallowtail kite of the season, newly arrived from Brazil, joining the frigates soaring overhead like untethered origami. In three days, we encountered only five other boats, and all were fishermen hunkered down, coming or going to or from Florida Bay.

Each night on the mound, the chuck-will's-widow sang his sweet sad song, a four-note serenade of all he has ever seen and can't fully say. And the stars fell, inexorably marking mortal time. One evening, I slept next to the water and Venus rose under a crescent moon, laying down a trail of pale light that connected me to it, a planet too distant to imagine, yet able to touch me in these Everglades.

Now, with our canoe loaded to the gunnels, we are pushing away from the mound one last time for our two-day paddle back to Chokoloskee and Everglades City. Terry began to sketch and paint several years ago, waiting for each image to "push" its way out, allowing his unseen self to become less so on paper, healing old wounds. I try to do much of the same with words, a mechanism to remind me of what I have experienced. And now, in our coming back together after all this time, we grasp onto the tangible around us, discuss it with great joy, and then let it sink back into ourselves, waiting to see what it will finally reveal.

Upstream we go on this fine river, one eye on the tree line and the sky above, the other on the map and compass. Mangroves surround us on all sides and from a distance, they seem like a diminutive northern forest. Up close, though, the land under them is ephemeral, water and detritus-fueled mud, rich nursery grounds for the same critters—redfish, trout, snook, tarpon—the fishermen hunt. Neither fully land nor water, this place has long placed a hold on the imagination of visitors, spooking them with its mystique.

The early Spanish conquistadors, at once superstitious and brutal, first charted this territory as *La Laguna de la Espírtus Santus*, The Lagoon of the Sacred Spirit. As we bear down today against a building wind and outgoing tide, I think of this place in that way, a terrain with a pulse and a heart, able to breathe. Right now, its breath is sun-warmed mangrove leaves and sea purslane, a dusky perfume of salt and chlorophyll and sap.

Up the Chatham we go, following the narrow branch that meanders to the west, once almost running aground on a shoal that mysteriously appears in the middle of the river where eight and nine feet of water should be. Instead of working our way north through Last Huston and Huston Bays, we sneak around the lee sides of mangrove islands, crouching as close to shore as we can get to avoid the wind-driven thrash of the waves that will pile up in two-foot high white-caps. Sometimes the water is so clear we can see blue crabs scuttling across the seagrass bottom, needle fish flashing iridescent at the sur-face. Other times, it is soil brown, a moving organic soup.

As I paddle, I pay careful attention to direction, to the spin of a little sliver of metal locked inside glass, gauging how the world of mangrove and marl unfolds around us, curious how it matches up to my nautical chart.

Suddenly, the air is filled with scads of sulfur-wing butterflies, the color of pale planet light, fresh from a new spring hatch. We paddle through them for a mile until finally, they vanish as quickly as they appeared, a rain shower of butterflies. Up to the southerly forks of Huston Bay we go, and then down again into an unnamed branch leading to the Huston River. It empties us into House Hammock Bay, named for an old clan that once homesteaded here, collecting button-wood mangrove for charcoal like Watson did, fishing, and hunting.

House Hammock is barely two and three feet deep, and as I dip and draw my paddle it touches mud as often as not. Ospreys are nest-ing everywhere, young chicks just large enough to raise up and squawk now from their huge beds of twigs. Mother birds fly over us, small mullet in their talons, headed for home. In the distance, gators, bodies as black and corrugated as large truck tires, thrash in the water and mud to flee this odd apparition, a log with two moving heads.

Ahead, we will spend a night on the wooden dock chickee at Sunday Bay, and then surf rolling breakers back out of its broad lagoon. As we do, we will ride an easterly wind beyond Barnes and Crooked creeks, into the lee of the shoal-filled Cross Bays where we run aground, using our paddles as poles to finally push away. From there, we skim the conflux of Hurddles Creek and the Turner River, an intersection deep enough to hold giant half-ton manatees, up from Florida Bay to frolic like giant children, flukelike tails out of the water, bodies rolling and churning the water in some outsized mammalian ecstasy, safe at last from motorboat props. We sit at a distance and watch in quiet obeisance, then push on toward Chokoloskee under a bright tropical sun.

Once, just after a flock of white ibis fly low across the mangrove tops, I blunder somewhere off the map, getting lost as thoroughly as I have ever been. When I tell Terry of the mistake, I joke that we must be in such a state before we can ever truly be found, and he smiles and says gently, I know what you mean, bro.

Safely back on track, we finally enter Chokoloskee Bay, windswept and sparkling in the sun, the end game in sight now. I wonder what secrets are still hiding from us. But in the end, I decide it doesn't much matter, this lagoon of the sacred spirit and its ghosts will be here, whether I want them to be or not.

But then, there is this: I think one last time of Ed Watson and how Matthiessen treated him more generously than life ever did. I wish the same for the Glades. And I wish it in my heart for Terry, for me, for us all.

From *The Hidden West*

ROB SCHULTHEIS

SOUTH OF THE SAN JUAN AND ITS CANYONS, beyond
Navaho Mountain and Zuni, the Colorado River unfolds, on
and on, like a Chinese landscape scroll—rivers and mountains,
pocket deserts and tiny turquoise seas, playas, cuestas, basins—
unraveling to the very faded golden edges of the void . . .

If you followed the Colorado River far enough south—down
through the Mogollon Rim country, past the Little Colorado, the
Salt and the Gila, across the Sonoran Desert with its boneyard
mountains and surreal giant-cactus forests—if you traveled to the
very end, you would come to the Colorado Delta between Baja California, Sonora and the Sea of Cortez. After so many years, thousands of miles, of wandering the Colorado River country, it was no
wonder that one day I found myself dreaming of the river's end. I
saw it in my mind's eye: blue lagoons, golden sands and the heavy
water, the iron-red blood of the West, rolling at last into the sea. I
had to go there someday.

Looking through books and obscure maps, I found that the
delta of the Colorado lies at latitude 31°53′, longitude 115°. It is an
intricate place: choked on its own debris, the river fractures into
long shards of laguna, sloughs and oxbows. Before the dams upriver
cut off the flow of the Colorado and its tributaries, the delta was
really wild, a dangerous place. In the spring, when the entire Colorado Basin emptied its dead snows and spring rains down that single slender channel, the delta was a raging, placeless place, neither
earth nor sea. Whole islands drowned in a flood tide thick as library
paste; sand spits were whipped away like paper cutouts; whole

ranges of hills vanished. The map of the delta was one great blurry question mark: genesis, nameless.

In 1540, Hernando de Alarcon sailed up the Sea of Cortez and "discovered" the delta. The Cocopah Indians had lived there for centuries, and the Sand Papagos (more on them later) knew the place, but Indians never *discover* anything; they are just there, it seems, like the rocks, the ground water, the wild grass. Exploration of the delta went slowly. James Ohio Pattie, the intrepid trapper who had explored the depths of Glen Canyon in search of beaver, tried to cross the delta east to west in the 1820s, searching for a new route to California. He perished somewhere out there in the maze of creeks and marshes and salt dunes.

In 1857–58, Derby and Ives, two American naval officers, navigated the river all the way from the Sea of Cortez north to Callville, near the present location of Hoover Dam. For a time there was regular steamship service between Yuma and Callville and also in the delta itself: a Compania de Navigacion del Golfo de California S.A. operated between El Mayor and Santa Rosalie.

In 1922, Aldo Leopold, the American naturalist and writer, canoed the delta all the way from the American side of the border to the sea. He wrote of coyotes and bobcats prowling the riverbanks, and huge flocks of sandhill cranes falling like snow through the crisp indigo sky. Quail, deer, coons of thickets of mesquite and tornillo; everywhere the unseen presence of *el tigre*, the jaguar. It was like being back in the Pleistocene, Leopold wrote: "A hundred miles of lovely desolation, a vast flat bowl of wilderness rimmed by jagged peaks." It was a dangerous place, too. Leopold missed the forty-feet high tidal bore that rolled up through the delta on a full moon night that same year, wrecking the Mexican ship *Topolobampo* and drowning a hundred souls.

All of that happened before the dams. The Colorado River has an average flow of 13 to 17 million acre-feet a year. (An acre-foot is the amount of water it takes to cover an acre to the depth of a foot.) Today, only 1.5 million acre-feet make it as far as Mexico; the rest is siphoned off in the United States by an elaborate system of tunnels, dams and canals to water Los Angeles, the Imperial Valley, Denver, the desert cities of Arizona, etc., etc. The last 1.5 million acre-feet are used by Mexico to irrigate farmlands north of the delta, through a six-hundred-mile-long network of canals. The Colorado River no longer reaches the sea; it is no longer a river, and its delta is a dead carcass, inhabited by a restless, bitter ghost.

Still, I wanted to see the place, if only to exhume its remains, pay my respects. The maps of the delta I had showed such riddles as "Laguna Salada," "Volcano Lake," "Boat Slough"; phantom pieces of river such as the Paredones, the Abejos, the Nuevo, the Pescadero. There was a desert, el Desierto de los Chinos, where a party of Chinese immigrants had died of thirst. There would still be pockets of wildness here and there, I thought, and the ghosts of birds: silent song plumaged in a dry blue epidermis of air.

DURING WORLD WAR II, the U.S. Army, fearing that the Germans would use Mexico as a base for invading the American Southwest (which we stole from Mexico in the first place), somehow got the Mexican government to survey and draw up modern contour maps, suitable for military use. At least, that's the story I heard. Unfortunately, the project ran out of steam by the time the mapmakers were about a third of the way through the country, working north to south. There *were* maps of northern Mexico then, including the Colorado delta—but, of course, they were impossible to find. Finally I located a map store in Tucson, an appropriately strange little store that carried the maps. There was a master map on the wall; you picked out the maps you wanted from it, a clerk behind the counter called down to the basement, and a few minutes later a dumbwaiter ascended with your maps neatly rolled up inside.

With maps in hand, all I needed was a boat, a boat that could fit on or in my small car. I looked around and came up with a small inflatable boat of rubberized canvas, made in Europe. It rolled up into a canvas bag when deflated, and even the plastic oars collapsed like telescopes. You blew it up with a little foot pump. It was a quixotic craft, and I named it *Insh' Allah*, because when you got in it you were definitely entrusting yourself to God's mercy.

I left for the delta at dusk, in the middle of one of the worst winter storms in a decade. Snow was falling all the way from the Sierra Nevada to Ohio, and more sea storms were rolling in off the Pacific, crossing the northern California coast and becoming squall lines of snow when they reached the Sierra. The heater wasn't working in my car, and I had to drive wrapped in a sleeping bag and an old Army blanket, down mitts on my hands, a wool cap pulled down tight over my head: I looked like some kind of Andean space-man. My breath fogged the windshield, and every few minutes I had to scrape the thin onionskin layers of ice off with my knuckles.

Sunset on Lizard Head Pass: in a break in the storm, the peaks glowed nacreous in the bleak red light. Around Dolores it began to rain. I crossed the San Juan River. South of Shiprock it began to snow again, big flakes spiraling toward me like a billion soft, slow bullets, straining my eyes to focus through them on the dim highway.

Chili and fry bread in a Gallup café. Zuni Pueblo in the night, the sweet gray smell of piñon and cedar smoke in the air; no lights, a lone dog barking…At four in the morning I was crossing the high pine forests of the Fort and White River Apaches. Down through the Salt River Gorge. And then, as the first dawn light glowed on the eastern horizon, I saw the sprawling lights of Tucson ahead.

South. When you get to Tucson, you are south. I rolled down the car window, and already, at six-thirty on a winter morning, the air was lukewarm. Tucson is like a big chunk of Los Angeles dragged off into the Sonoran Desert and left there. The kids look like surfers with their blown-back white hair and Hawaiian shirts. Everybody has an ornate important car: a '46 Hudson painted electric blue, with three exhaust pipes; a silver pickup truck that sits eight feet high on oversized tires. I ordered breakfast in a drive-in restaurant where everything was square: square toast, square sausage and a square block of scrambled eggs that tasted like they had nothing to do with chickens.

I had crossed the heartland of the Colorado that night; I was in the lower Colorado Basin now, a country more akin to Mexico, southern California, than the high country of Colorado, Utah and the Navaho Nation.

THE NEXT DAY I drove west out of Tucson, across the Papago Indian Reservation. It drizzled at dawn, big drops of water sputtering in the dust, sending up an odor harshly sweet, as if a billion lighted matches were raining onto a field of dry incense. The damp earth shone like brown nylon.

Centuries ago—almost a thousand years, to be exact—the Papagos were one of the most highly civilized peoples on earth: the Hohokam, archeologists call their old culture. The Hohokam people had small cities, networks of irrigation canals, stone pyramids, a calendar; they were on a level with the pharaonic Egyptians, the Han Chinese. Then something happened—simply a few less inches of rain fell for a few years. Drought burned away the surplus food, and without it Hohokam society could not support pyramids, artists and calendar-keeping technocrat-priests.

Civilization is a luxury, really, a thin skin of gilt on human existence. Strip away the delicate surplus of energy and material that pays for it, and life becomes a matter of bare-bones survival again. The cities vanished; the priests, bards and artisans became extinct. The Hohokam, proud, imperial, gorgeous, became poor, plain, humble Papagos. The canals filled up with dust. What a difference an inch or two of rain makes; on what a frail mist of humidity ride all our dreams of power!

I passed through Papago villages, rancherias really, with such wonderful-sounding names as Ush Kug, Chaiwuli Tak, Wahak Hotrontk. Translated, they have prosaic meanings: "Not Much Water Here," "Lots of Dust," "Pretty Good Place to Grow Beans." Some of the Papago houses were typical Bureau of Indian Affairs constructions, shabby imitations of suburbia. Others, traditional, looked like someone had heaped up shards of dried mud and laid a sheet of rusted iron on top; but the outsides blazed with banks of flowering brush and cacti.

An interesting thing about the Papagos: for centuries, they have gone south on pilgrimages to the Sea of Cortez, where they gather sea salt on the beaches; the sea is their Mecca, their Lhasa. When Mexico and the United States drew their abstract border across the Papago Nation, the Papagos just kept going on their pilgrimages, sneaking past the border patrol on their ancient trails. The U.S. government accused them of "illegal importation of salt"! Finally, the government gave up; the salt pilgrimages still go on, they say, though the Papagos today have changed a lot since the white men came: they drive pickup trucks, raise cattle and dance to a queer, thumping kind of desert reggae polka called chicken scratch.

I crossed the border at the little town of Sonoyta. The road from Sonoyta west to the delta is a lonesome one, "connecting nothing with nothing." There were dry, deformed mountains on either side of the road, strata frozen in a series of violent epileptic seizures. I passed a crude roadside shrine, a gaudy *santo* staring from behind iron bars. Once in a while, a huge, ponderous Third World truck, painted with Virgins, whores, Orpheuses, angels, *banditos* and clowns, fancy as a mosque, came rolling down the road ...

About noon I came out of the mountains at San Luis del Colorado, population 63,644. San Luis is a typical small border city, with torn-up streets, tiny shops selling bicycle tires, false teeth, horror comics, fiery black slabs of meat, tiny cloying cakes. The men wore straw cowboy hats, and their faces were long and hard as rawhide. The music on my car radio was all brass and bombast, like a circus marching off to war, and the announcers so splenetic you half expected saliva to come sputtering out of the dashboard. They rolled their r's like castanets.

The whole style of the Frontera is adrenalized and, unsurprisingly, bitter. The Colorado delta area was once a place of Nilotic richness. The Mexican government relocated people from all over the country to live on big, irrigated *ejidos*. It could have been the Imperial Valley of Mexico. But the United States diverted more and more of the water upstream, leaving Mexico with only the flushings of American irrigation—saline, mineralized. This bad yanqui water poisoned the good Mexican bottomlands and withered the crops. Their own farms burnt out, the Sonorans were forced to cross the border into the United States to work on farms irrigated by the very water they themselves had once owned. Justice is never simple, but this seemed to me to be a particularly ugly piece of imperialism. Whan a lank, leathery man spat at my car on a back street of San

Luis and shouted "*Puta!*" I wanted to stop and get out and apologize to him. But my Spanish is bad, and he probably would not have understood and would have slid a thin, shining blade, the only bright thing in his life, between my ribs . . .

All that day I searched for the river and its delta, crossing and recrossing those dank alluvial plains scabbed with desert. No one I asked seemed to understand what I was looking for: some pointed north, some south, while one man gestured at the concrete canal at our feet with the air of a doctor pointing out the sky to an idiot. Once I came upon a ditch of stale septic water with a sign that said RIO COLORADO on its banks, but the water ended a hundred yards downstream, in an embankment.

The air was humid. The land looked like Bengal, patches green as malachite mingled with ashen hills; California fan palms sulked in the heat, villages of thatched adobe, hills of technicolor garbage, here a pig the size of a plow horse, egrets dozing in the trees, the whole scene compressed under a sky as slick and hot and heavy as volcanic mud. The back roads were muck and puddle. Beyond were the peaks of the Baja, the Sierra los Cocopas, Sierra de la Tinaja, de Juarez, San Pedro Martir, like crumpled, dusty brown-paper cutouts of mountains.

But where was the river? As the afternoon finally waned, I drove south, down through Riito, Recuperacion, El Doctor. There were the railroad tracks I had traveled years ago, paralleling the road and then veering off east into the Gran Desierto. Off to the west were swamps, marshes, shoals of mud. But where was the river Leopold had written about? I feared it had become nothing more than a spirit, an *espíritu;* and the jaguars had grown fat and lazy, and gone to the city to be mariachis, blowing bent horns in their gilded coats in the cantinas of San Luis and Mexicali.

That night I read by kerosene lamp in a concrete room in a closed-down hotel in the town of El Golfo de Santa Clara, on the Sea of Cortez. The surf boomed on the beach outside, and the lights of shrimp boats rocked on the black water. "The river does not run to the sea anymore," the old man at the hotel told me. "Isla Montague, Isla Pelican, Isla Gore—all gone now. Mud and sand." I looked over my maps by the sweet yellow light, listening to the winter sea and wondering where I might find a trace of the river—a splinter of metacarpal, a broken syllable of it.

THE RIVER I FINALLY FOUND the next afternoon was called the Rio Hardy; it ran along the western edge of the delta, under the dry peaks of the Baja. But it was, a Mexican youth at a roadside cantina assured me, the same as the Colorado. "Rio Hardy, Rio Colorado; Rio Colorado, Rio Hardy," he said, laughing, gesturing out across the brush and water. And so I inflated my little rubber boat, packed it full of gear and headed out onto the slow mulatto waters of the delta.

It was a strange place, acutely schizophrenic. The left bank was wild, impenetrable, with rushes twelve feet high. Leopold had called the delta Pleistocene, but this was Cretaceous, I thought. There were birds everywhere, egrets, cormorants, bitterns, blue herons, green herons striped like cats—feathered serpents, flying reptiles. The silence was broken by their dull croaking and the heavy flapping of their wings as they took off, like someone snapping a wet wool blanket in the mist. There was the silver clatter of coots running on the water on their parchment cymbal feet, flying away downriver low to the water. It was disquieting, all of those ancient plumed beings with their round, cryptic eyes staring at me as I labored down their river.

The right bank, on the other hand, looked like a third-class resort in a nightmare. The brush had been cleared to the ground, and there were vacation homes and cantinas, most of them shuttered down for the winter, bristling with television aerials, with big power boats moored along the shore. A woman in dark glasses and a red bathing suit, lying in a deck chair with a drink in one hand, watched me row past. The only person I met all day on the river was an enormous fat American man in a dinghy with an outboard motor, fishing out in mid-river. He was fishing for bass, and he had the saddest eyes I have ever seen.

"I worked for the Navy in San Diego for forty years," he said. "I own a little house down here, and I come down here to hunt and fish. These camps run way downriver, till the water runs out. They're almost all owned by Americans." He showed me a string of bass, their dead eyes as full of sorrow as his.

I camped that night in a vacant lot between two blocks of vacation homes; there was no place on the east bank I could even go ashore, the brush was so thick.

When I woke the next morning, mariachi music was blaring from a long, golden Buick parked fifty feet away, and a magnificent man in a glossy yellow suit—he was plump and looked as if he had been basted in corn oil—was walking toward me. I crawled out of my sleeping bag and stood up. "*Buenos días!*" he beamed. "I own all of this land. Actually, there are two hundred lots, and I own twenty nine and have option on the rest. Soon I will own all! I call this Campo Bebe One, after my daughter, and soon there will be Campo Bebe Two and Three!" I tried to look encouraging. "Pretty soon, big sign on highway, big light! Beer, everything. I no work, I plan!" He almost wriggled with joy. *El hombre dorado*, the gilded man, I thought, looking at him. "I can build you nice house in three days. I also own a construction company. Lotsa American friends living here now. They tell their friends, pretty soon *all* American friends living here!" As I repacked my boat and prepared to push off, he was still talking: "Plenty of time to pay, but you better buy fast. Pretty soon the whole river, *pht!,* sold!" As I rowed down the cold, misting river, he stood there on the bank, waving benevolently, the golden car booming like a giant jukebox.

INSTEAD OF GETTING WILDER, the river got worse the deeper I penetrated into the delta. The vacation homes were larger, gaudier. Power boats threshed up and down the river all day, nearly capsizing my little rubber dinghy with their wakes. Worst of all was a kind of skiff with a whole airplane engine and propeller mounted on the rear: you could hear it coming half an hour away, and it literally shook the banks of the river when it passed. Most of the boatsmen were duck hunters, and muffled shotgun volleys echoed constantly, as if there was a little war going on up and down the length of the Rio Colorado delta. "Got forty-four of 'em today," one red-hatted, red-faced thug called out to me as he cruised upriver, one hand on a beer and the other on the wheel of his electric-purple speedboat. I am no foe of hunting: I would rather eat elk than beef, beaver than lamb, rainbows than fish sticks. But the kind of loud, mechanized hunting these men were doing offended me. There was no class, no beauty to it.

By late afternoon I was sick and tired of the river I had dreamt of for so long. It was a long, long way still to the vast mud flats that were all that remained of the heart of the delta, and the way there was little better than a freeway for power boats. I could not see my way to traveling it: it was simply not worth it. The delta was dead and it had left an unbeautiful corpse. I decided to put in on the wild east bank, set up camp and push off into the bush on foot.

ONCE YOU PUSHED THROUGH the rushes and thicket that lined the banks, a green strip of jungle perhaps three feet thick, you were abruptly in the desert. Just like that. It was hard to believe you were in the same country at all. Desert stretched away to the jagged horizons.

I lashed my boat to a willow and set up camp in the ruins of a small *campesino* village that had once clung to the river's edge It was eerie. You could see all the energy, the ingenuity, that had once gone into the place, but it was all dead and gone now. Irrigation ditches crisscrossed the desert, full of nothing: there were fields furrowed, frosted with salt; dry cornstalks poked up, desolate. A brick-lined well went down twenty feet into the hard soil; there was black water at the bottom.

I tried to guess why the people had left. Were they squatters, driven off by some wealthy cattle rancher? Had the fields simply gone bad, scalded dead by the salt in the water? There were ruined houses—hutches, shanties—here and there, and some of them had been burned, the charred hulks of crude furniture still in them. A bed with its gutted mattress still in place sat in the middle of what had once been somebody's bedroom. Somehow this seemed saddest of all to me, thinking of the love that had been made there, the dreams dreamed, the children conceived. It seemed a symbol of the failure of everything most preciously human.

Tribes, villages, families, crack with time, spilling their loose clouds of people out into the world. The great cities inhale these lost people. The farmer who had slept in this slaughtered bed was probably driving a cab in Mexicali now or pushing a shovel in LA. The people were gone, gone forever, leaving this desert of ironwood and thorn, colored like a dried snakeskin or a moth's dusty wing.

I made a circle of crumbling red bricks from one of the houses and built a little fire of thorny sticks. Thunder rolled down out of the mountains of Baja; the air smelled of rain. I set up the tent while the stew simmered on the fire; as I ate, hunched by the smoky fire, the first rain began to flail in on the west wind. It was a strange rain: loud, hard, it didn't really seem to wet anything; the air drank it up even as it struck.

Sitting in the tent, listening to the rain by candlelight, I thought of something funny that had happened to me once on a trip to southern Mexico. I was talking to a thin little fisherman with a pure Indian face: there could hardly have been a drop of Spanish blood in his veins. We were talking about the history of his place, and he told me, very sincerely, "Oh, there used to be many Indians here a long time ago." "Where did they go?" I asked. "Oh, they went away somewhere, I guess," he said.

IT WAS THE INDIANS WHO KNEW the delta the best, of course: the Cocopahs and the Sand Papagos. As late as the 1930s, the Cocopahs lived in isolated camps in the vast flood plain of the delta, accessible only by foot or horseback in the dry season, dugout canoe in flood time. The Cocopahs hunted desert bighorn, deer, jackrabbits. They worshiped the mountain wildcat (*chimbica*, in the Cocopah tongue). They drank *toloache* (jimsonweed tea) for visions, and traded salt and clamshells to their relatives, the Ipai and Tipai of southern California, for sacred eagle feathers... According to the Mexican maps, there are still two Cocopah *ejidos*, cooperative farms, just north of the delta.

The Sand Papagos, then: They lived on the eastern verges of

the delta and in the volcanic wastelands of the Pinacates: impossible country. They lived on nothing, made sandals from sea lion hide, ate sand roots, made string from badger hair. According to Charles Bowden's fine book *Killing the Hidden Waters*, the Mexicans and Americans hunted the Sand Papagos to extermination; epidemics finished off the survivors. The last Sand Papago, a hermit named Carvajeles, died around 1912. The Sand Papagos were nomads, Bedouins without camels or tents. They left a few trails from the inland desert to the Sea of Cortez, and grinding stones in caves in the far mountains . . .

The next morning I walked out across that wide, barren plain. It was a chill, windy day, with a keen edge to it, and the sky was gray. An osprey sat in a dead tree holding a big, bloody fish in his claws. I walked and walked on mud roads that led nowhere.

Here and there I came upon more abandoned ranchos, burned huts, ghostly beds. A fancy white 1966 Ford Fairlane without an engine pointed due east, tires gone, parked there forever. I came upon a twisted knot of bobcat shit in the road. Six great, elegant pelicans rode south on the wind toward the sea. Leafless trees, like giant bundles of dead sticks; more burned-down houses, broken bottles, rusted cans. It looked like a war had been fought there and everyone had lost. The roads were heavy with mud; it dragged at my feet, as if it would drag me down under that hopeless country forever.

I felt fear; it stuck in the back of my throat like a numb quid of cocaine. I wanted to run, to run away from those failed farms, those sterile fields, and cross the river and drive north, north to where there were people, green things, red scarves, music; away from this place whose future was interred in salt: Deadland. I had seen enough. I turned and began to follow my steps back, slogging through my own footprints in the leaden mud. I looked up and saw the osprey again.

The osprey hung in the sky on crooked, stabbing wings, hovering over that dead, white country. If there was a message there, and there seemed to be, I did not like the way it read. The Aztecs built their great city of Mexico where an eagle hovered in the sky above the desert, a rattlesnake writhing in its talons. But no one would ever build anything beneath this dark bird; it was an omen of ending.

We live in the aftermath of the Pleistocene, on the dwindling rivulets left over from the Ice Age. Our lands are sore with salt, skinned by the wind, green hills turned on a lathe of drought till the grass and the humus peel away. Apocalypse slides in among us before we know it, quiet as a feeling on the air, a chill in the pit of the belly, a dry lack of dreaming, blue shadows between the ribs of a white horse.

"The rust of your silver, I say, shall eat your flesh as if it were fire," the medieval prophet said. It rang true as a snake's hiss in the silent graveyard of the Colorado.

OR PERHAPS I JUST DIDN'T GO FAR ENOUGH...

On full-moon nights, the Mexicans say, after the spring rains, when the ghost of the river is swollen and cold and the tides are running high, the river reaches the sea again.

The river and the sea rise, black and silver in the moon. A mountain of water rolls in off the Sea of Cortez, drowning the nameless islands, the barren continents of mud and sand: rolls up the channel of the old river in the moonlight. Green herons rise from their nests in the thickets, making music like dull wooden bells ...

And then the waters turn, and with a tremendous silver noise the river rushes out to sea again, streaming out into the Sea of Cortez.

If you had a boat, the Mexicans say (and I hope they are telling the truth), you could ride all the way from Campo Bebe out to the Sea of Cortez and to the Pacific itself on that black, lunar river.

From *Catfish and Mandala*

ANDREW X. PHAM

Wind

I KNOW THEY ARE UP TO NO GOOD when they pull along side me, giggling madly like three imps. That and their red faces. A red-faced Vietnamese is a drunk Vietnamese. And three drunk Vietnamese scooting along on one motorbike spells trouble. I tell myself Avoid. AVOID. But the road bowls straight into the horizon, banked on both sides by rice paddies as far as the eye can see. Few travelers. Oh, great.

For the umpteenth time, I wish I still had my pepper spray. I slow down, they slow down. I speed up, they speed up. They cut in front of me and slam on the brakes. I swerve, missing them by inches. They bark with mirth. Then they are behind me. As they pass, one of then kicks my rear pannier and sends me wobbling to the side of the road. As quickly as they came, they pull away. I heave a sigh of relief. A mile up ahead of me, they have stopped by the side of the road. I am thinking: Ambush. I slow down, considering my options. For once Highway 1 is deserted. I can't outrun them on a loaded bike. In any case, I am in no mood for retreat. Pedaling slowly, I unzip the bag mounted on the front rack, and loosen the eight-inch fillet knife.

They are standing on the side of the road. I jump on the pedals to pick up speed. Maybe I can ram them. Knock them down. But something isn't right with the picture. I choke on my laughter: they are pissing into the rice paddies. The driver of the motorbike shouts something unintelligible to me as I blow past. I look back and see them hastily tucking themselves in and piling on the motorbike. I ease off the pedals. There is no sense trying to outrun a motorbike, even one with three clowns on it. My old schoolmate, who had turned professional Vietnamese-American gangster, used to advise me, his bookish friend, "If trouble is coming, don't turn your back, because that's where it's gonna stab. Best to meet it with a grin. That way, you can see what's coming."

I pull over and wait for them, my hand next to the open bag with the knife. They stop a couple of yards from me.

I wear my biggest grin. "*Hello, Brothers!*"

"*Fuck, it's a Viet-kieu!*" yelps the round-faced driver as though he'd come across a rat.

"*I told you he looked like a Viet-kieu.*"

"*But he looks like a Japanese. I don't like Japanese. Maybe he's a half-and-half,*" argues a short man with a shoe-brush mustache. "*Oy, you. Are you a half-and-half?*"

"*Nope. Whole undiluted fishsauce, I am.*" I sniff my armpit, wrinkle my nose, and nod. "*Aiee! Pure concentrate.*"

They bellow at the joke, warming to me. We strike up a conversation. They want to know where I rode from. The skinny guy asks me,

"*Aren't you afraid?*"

"*No,*" I lie, grinning enthusiastically. "*In America, they have a saying: If you die, you die.*" I shrug.

"*Haven't people attacked you?*"

I nod.

"*What did you do?*"

I take out my knife, smiling, totally faking it.

"*Mean like a tiger,*" says the leader. He chuckles and the others follow suit.

I grin. "*Either that or stay home and watch TV.*"

They roar in appreciation. Sensing the shift in their mood, I slip the knife back into the bag. I tap cigarettes out of a pack of Marlboros I'd saved for occasions like these. I offer one to the leader. His eyes catch the logo. I almost sigh aloud when he puts it between his lips. His compatriots follow suit. I don't smoke but I light up with them to keep things going smoothly. Soon we are sitting on a dike, feet dangling over water, blowing smoke out over the young rice stalks, talking about how people live in America.

Their alcoholic buzz has subsided by the time we finish the pack of Marlboros. They invite me to join them on their next round. "*Bierom!*"—hugging beer—exclaims the leader. His chums hoot in agreement. Vietnamese men spend a great deal of money at these hostess-bars where pretty girls sit on a patron's lap as he drinks his beer. The "frisking" limits, if any, vary, depending on the depth of the patron's pocket. I decline and we part on handshakes.

I push on alone, feeling suddenly very tired and feverish. Just barely oozing down the road. I haven't eaten much all day. Breakfast was a lump of sweet rice and peanut crumbs wrapped in banana leaves. After chipping one of my molars on a pebble, I tossed the rice to the birds. Lunch was a bowl of beef noodle soup I couldn't eat because the meat, carved off a fly-encrusted lump, was rancid. I am exhausted. I've eaten nearly all my emergency rations: three Hershey chocolate bars, a snack-sized pack of Oreos, and six little cheese wedges. The last bar of chocolate in my bag is squishy like toothpaste, and my mouth is so cottony I can't bring myself to lick the chocolate from the wrapper. It is blistering hot and the sun is melting into the horizon like a scoop of orange sherbet. I am salivating. Haven't had ice cream since I arrived in Vietnam. Didn't dare. If I weren't already drier than a shingle of beef jerky, drool would be dripping down my chin. Funny, a scoop of orange sherbet was all I could wrap my mind around. Not even the faintest hankering for double cheeseburgers, French fries, chocolate milkshakes, apple pie à la mode, anchovy pizzas, Polish sausage, and fresh-baked croissants. I have no appetite and feel a bit dizzy. The fifteen miles to Ky Anh village seem like a hundred.

Up ahead a cattle-drawn cart—without a driver—labors along the side of the road, oblivious to the occasional truck thundering past. Closer, I see that the dark lump on top of the load of bricks is the sleeping driver, hat shading his face. He is sleeping at the reins, trusting his bovine to keep both of them from turning into roadkill. I have stumbled on the quintessential portrait of Vietnamese industry. In Saigon, a white American tourist had asked me, "Don't take this the wrong way, but why are so many Vietnamese men lounging around all day—don't they have to go to work or something?"

I could see tour buses passing this cart all day and foreign tourists shaking their heads at this evidence of Vietnamese work ethics. I burst out laughing, waking the napping driver. His startled face melts into delight when he sees I am a cyclist.

"Aa-LO! Ow arr you? Wherre you prrom?" he shouts, pushing his army pith helmet back on his head.

"*Viet-kieu, Brother,*" I reply. He looks a little crestfallen.

I grab onto the cart, giving the poor cow my extra weight. "*Brother, where are you going?*"

"*Home. Where did you bike from?*"

I ask him about his load of bricks. Couldn't sell them, he says. His family made bricks by hand. This is a poor batch the builders rejected, so he is taking them back home. Maybe farmers will buy them at a discount.

A cyclist draws up alongside us. I see his silver hair and bow in greeting, then looking down, I nearly fall out of my seat. He has only one leg. His right leg ends above the knee, the dark nub sticks out of his shorts like a big salami. A crutch hangs on the bike frame. His left leg churns the crank in a jerking rhythm, hard on the down-stroke, gliding with the momentum on the upstroke, a two-stroke engine running marvelously on one.

"*Uncle, that's amazing!*" I blubber. "*I've never seen a one-legged man ride a bike before.*"

He slows down and latches up to the cart next to me. "Oy!" he exclaims, very pleased for some reason. "*You speak Viet!*"

"*Yes, Uncle. I'm a Viet-kieu,*" I confess, and brace for his face to fall, but it doesn't. "*How far can you go on a bike?*"

"*Once I biked all the way to Ky Anh and back, twenty kilometers each way. But usually I only ride to the market, that's twelve kilometers round-trip.*"

His handlebar basket sags with packets of instant ramen, a bot-tle of what looks to be kerosene or rice wine, a can of condensed milk, and a tin of tea.

"*This Viet-kieu is going to Ky Anh,*" the ox driver tells the old man.

"*Ky Anh?*" repeats the old man in a tone I don't find encouraging.

"*There's nothing out there except a government-run motel. It's actually a bar-racks, but they'll overcharge you ten times for a bed.*"

"I'm overcharged all the time," I point out nonchalantly. "*How far is it?*"

"*An hour and a half. It'll be dark soon,*" the old man says, gauging the sky. He looks me over, apparently having come to a decision. "*Come with me, Nephew. I'll put you up for the night. I live by myself. There's plenty of room and you're welcome to hang your hammock.*"

Over two months in Vietnam, it's the first time someone's invited me home without his hands out. I accept the old man's generosity, bowing deeply.

"It is nothing." He waves off my thanks. "*Good, good. You'll like my beautiful villa.*"

Uncle Tu's home is a hut. In the burlap-textured dusk, it rises above the rambling vegetable garden like a big bale of hay. It sits near a lake, fifteen minutes from the road. He leads me into his plot of heaven, going down well-tended rows of vegetables, poking at this and that the way people open windows and turn on lights. He palms the tomatoes ripening on the vines, prods the earth with his crutch, clicks his tongue, squashes a snail, and fingers the fat string beans dripping off the vines. In the provinces, both hut and garden are required to make a home. Land is too precious to feed weeds.

The hut's thatched walls and roof are supported by four stout corner posts. The twelve-by-twelve-foot packed dirt floor is swept so clean it resembles hardened clay. The old man sits me down on a crude wooden stool and fusses with a coal stove to brew the tradi-tional welcoming-tea. First, he produces some twigs and wood shav-ings and arranges them carefully in the stove, which is essentially an eight-inch clay planting pot. He lights the starter pile with one match and places a block of coal, the shape of a chocolate cake, into the stove. We have our tea in no time. He hops over to the pantry cabinet, an end table with long legs, its feet set in bowls of water to keep the ants off. He takes out a clay pot and holds it up tenderly like a bottle of wine.

"*Clay-pot catfish, you like it?*"

"*Of course.*"

He glows with pleasure. It is impossible to travel in Vietnam without encountering clay-pot catfish. If Vietnam ever got around to declaring a national fish, the catfish would be it. Vietnam's rivers and lakes teem with this hardy creature. Peasants raise catfish in family ponds as they raise chicken in their yards.

"*Three days old, very, very tasty,*" he croons, smacking his lips as he sets it on the stove. He adds a bit of water and a dash of fishsauce. Then both of us settle down to watch it come to a boil. My mouth waters in anticipation.

That is the most wonderful thing about clay-pot catfish. It keeps well for weeks without refrigeration. The older the dish, the deeper the flavors, the more evenly the fish fat blends with the sauce of caramelized palm sugar, cracked pepper, and chili. In Uncle Tu's pot, I see he has splurged and added diced pork fat, whole red chilis, and scallions. The best thing about this dish is that even when all the fish is gone, the dredging is rich enough, especially if the fish head is saved, to be stewed again and poured over rice to make a poor man's meal—something I did many times when I was a boy.

"*Uncle, where is your family? I rarely see old folks living by themselves.*"

"*All gone, Nephew. Lost them in the War, wife and son.*"

"*Do you have relatives nearby?*"

"*No. I have my relatives-neighbors. That's plenty. They are good people, I'm a lucky man.*"

"*Where are they?*"

He hobbles to the door and bellows: "*Sonny! Sonny! Sonny!*"

A small boy materializes at the door. He sees me, glances at Uncle Tu, then, remembering his manners, he bows to us both. Uncle Tu tousles the boy's hair and gives him two packets of instant noodles.

"*Take this home to your mom, Sonny.*" The boy bows and runs home. Uncle Tu smiles after him. "*See,*" he says to me. "*I have family, my relatives-neighbors. Not so lonely.*"

He spreads the food on an end table, scoops out the rice into bowls for both of us. "*Nephew, please eat,*" he says, formally starting the meal.

"*Thank you, Uncle Tu. Please eat,*" I reply in kind.

We wolf down our plebeian meal of catfish, rice, pickled fire cracker eggplant with shrimp paste, and steamed string beans from his garden, polishing off every morsel. It is without a doubt one of the best meals I've had in Vietnam. For dessert, we drink more tea and nibble on my gooey Hershey bar. He strings up an extra hammock for me. Our fabric beds now crisscross the hut, making diagonals, mine above his since I am more limber. He blows out the oil lamp and we go to bed. Uncle Tu doesn't stop talking. He has an insatiable appetite for details about the rest of the world. How do they live? What do Americans do every day? Is driving a car scary? How do cellular phones work?

In the middle of the night, Uncle Tu makes a racket as he claws his way out of his hammock. I ask him where he is going. "*Going out for a piss,*" he moans. "*My worm isn't as strong as it used to be. Have to pee twice every night.*"

"*Wait. I'll come, too.*"

He urinates on the trunk of a tree. I go to the latrine down by the lake. Behind a clutch of brambles, a catwalk bridges out to the latrine platform built over the water, fifteen feet from shore. Since I came back to Vietnam, I have been able to avoid using these fishpond latrines. I mount the steps and take care of business. Through the latrine-hole cut into the planks, I see the dark water beginning to churn, coming alive, coiling on itself. It is unnerving. The catfish come to feed.

I WAKE UP, COTTON-MOUTHED, with a searing fever. Uncle Tu pours me a bowl of strong tea for breakfast, feels my forehead, and, without a word, starts hanging blankets over the door and the single window. I complain that it's too stuffy. Keep out the ill wind and evil spirits, he explains. He calls "Sonny" next door and sends him off to find the village's silver coin. The boy scours the area, following the trail of illness from farm to farm. The silver coin is part talisman, part medicinal tool, Uncle Tu says, an heirloom handed down from generation to generation. No one knows who it really belonged to, although everyone uses it when he takes ill. Most of the peasants are too poor to own a silver coin, and those who can afford one don't buy one, preferring the heirloom coin for its legendary healing power. In an hour, the boy returns with the coin. Uncle Tu sends him back out with some money to buy heat-oil, a mentholated herbal oil that makes one's skin feel hot.

I tell Uncle Tu I don't believe "scraping the bad wind" is an effective way to break my fever. He hands me the coin as though an inspection of it would clear my doubts. I unwrap a scrap of crimson velvet, worn smooth and slick with mentholated oil, and pick up the silver coin, which is larger than a silver dollar. Decades of extended use have worn the faces smooth, leaving just a telltale Chinese character.

"*It has healed many, many people. Very powerful,*" Uncle Tu says in a tone of benediction. He is very worried about me. "*You must have caught an ill wind out on the pond last night. That's very bad, water spirits are strongest at night.*" He starts rambling about folklore and superstitions, something about the land having power over things that come from it. I tell him that besides spooking me, he isn't doing me any favor by talking nonsense. "*It's not good,*" he repeats to himself. I give in, rationalizing that it doesn't hurt to be sure. When I was a child, my mother used this folk remedy on me and the worst thing I got was a dozen bruises that weren't as nasty as they looked.

Taking off my shirt, I sit hunched over on a stool. Uncle Tu rubs the ointment on my back. His hands are bony and rough like tree bark, but his touch is kind and gentle. I am embarrassed at this physical contact. My father and I have never shaken hands. We do not embrace. I cannot recall our skin ever touching. On rare occasions, we placed a hand on each other's shoulder in congratulations. But here is Uncle Tu, a stranger-once-enemy, drawing on all his skills to heal me with his hands, skin on skin. It is oddly comforting, and I am almost ashamed to admit that much to myself. When the oil is hot on my skin, he begins to coin-scrape my back with a vengeance, making crimson welts six inches long. Then he proceeds to do the same on my neck and chest. Half an hour later, my upper body is tattooed with bruises, my skin tingling with the heat oil. I roll back into my hammock, feeling strangely better. For good measure, I sneak a double dose of aspirin and doze off. When I wake up, Uncle Tu is hovering nearby. We slurp down a supper of rice porridge sprinkled with diced scallions and *ruoc ga,* shredded chicken jerky, and talk about the War.

"*No, I do not hate the American soldiers. Who are they? They were boys, as I was. They were themselves, but also part of a greater creature—the government. As was I. I can no more blame them than a fish I eat can be blamed for what I do.*

"You see, their pond is America. Here, in these hills, in this jungle, they are food.

"Me, I am in my land. I am in my water. These hills where I've killed Vietnamese and Americans. I see these hills every day. I can make my peace with them. For Americans, it was an alien place then as it is an alien place to them now. These hills were the land of their nightmares then as they are now. The land took their spirit. I eat what grows out of this land and someday I will return all that I have taken from it. Here is my home, my birthland and my grave.

"Tell your friend Tyle. There is nothing to forgive. There is no hate in this land. No hate in my heart. I am a poor man, my home is a hut with a dirt floor, but he is welcome here. Come and I shall drink tea with him, welcome him like a brother."

From *Team Rodent*

CARL HIAASEN

Jungle Book

A POLOGIES IN ADVANCE for the dead-rhinoceros story, but it must be told, mainly for what it says about my state of mind. Also, I've seen the pictures.

In the spring of 1998, over the protests of antizoo activists, Walt Disney World opened a theme park called Animal Kingdom. "From Dinos to Rhinos," promised the advance press release. "This newest and fourth major theme park at Walt Disney World Resorts sprawls across 500 acres reconfigured to look amazingly like animal reserves of Africa or Asia."

Typical Disney: Honey, I shrunk the Serengeti!

The new park offers the formulaic payload: fast-paced, telegenic, politically correct facsimiles of adventure. For instance, visitors are educated about threatened wildlife on a thrill ride called Countdown to Extinction. Meanwhile, a mock safari tracks ruthless elephant poachers through the bush.

But there's something different: "Celebrating man's enduring fascination with animals of all kinds, the new park provides natural habitats for more than 1,000 animals.... Rare and wonderful creatures, native to far-off lands, will include elephants, hippos, rhinos, antelope, lions, gorillas and much more, roaming freely. Natural barriers for safety are nearly invisible."

Incredible but true: Animal Kingdom is inhabited by real wild animals—not robots, not puppets, not holograms, not cartoons, but living and breathing creatures that (unless Disney starts tranking

women

immanence

connective - production
disjunctive - recording
conjunctive - consumption

them) will eat, sleep, drool, defecate, regurgitate, sniff each other's crotches, lick their own balls, and occasionally even copulate in full view of the tourists. *Unprecedented* is the word for it. Never before has Nature been granted an assigned role in any Disney kingdom; up until now, a fiberglass crocodile was the dream Disney crocodile.

Control has been the signature ingredient of all the company's phenomenally successful theme parks; every thrill, every gasp, every delightful "surprise" was the product of clockwork orchestration. Once you paid your money and walked through the turnstiles, there was virtually no chance (until you walked out again) that anything unrehearsed would occur in your presence. "Nothing can possibly go wrong here, because nothing can possibly happen," wrote Elayne Rapping in a superb essay in *The Progressive*. "The idea that nature might be 'red in tooth and claw' was utterly foreign to [Walt] Disney's world view. But even more than blood, he abhorred dirt. Indeed, it is no accident that Disney's central ambassador is a neutered, hairless, civilized rodent—by nature the filthy scourge of every slum in the developed world."

Real vermin weren't the only animals shunned by Disney theme parks. In 1988 the Orlando resort was infested by a squadron of black buzzards that roosted indecorously atop the Contemporary Resort and other photogenic landmarks. The birds are large, stoop-necked, foul-smelling carrion eaters, and their glowering presence was deemed disruptive of the Disney ambience. In particular, the vultures were drawn to Discovery Island, one of the few locations in the Disney domain where wild native birds were welcomed.

And the buzzards came on strong. They vomited and pooped copiously, with no regard for the sensibilities of tourists. Equally dismaying were graphic reports that the buzzards were hassling the imported flamingos and preying on the helpless chicks of herons and egrets. Various methods were employed to frighten the aggressive raptors—flares, fireworks, helicopters—but the buzzards never left for long. Scores were captured and relocated far away, but it scarcely put a dent in the ever-growing Discovery Island flock.

Then, mysteriously, the birds began turning up dead. Accusations flew, and suddenly Disney—squeaky-clean Disney—found itself charged with shooting, starving, and even clubbing them with sticks. Sixteen state and federal wildlife violations were filed against Walt Disney World and several "cast members."

Black buzzards are protected by U.S. law and are thus allowed to go pretty much wherever they choose. As odious as they might be to humans, the birds play a crucial ecological role as scavengers. A murdered buzzard was rotten PR for any socially conscious multinational corporation. As Peter Gallagher wrote in *Tropic* magazine: "From the carcasses arose one of the messiest scandals in the 19-year history of Disney in Florida." Although the company disputed most of the animal cruelty charges, the ugly publicity didn't abate until Disney made peace with the Audubon Society and donated $75,000 to a trust fund managed by Florida's game commission.

To Disney executives, the buzzard incident soberly reinforced the idea that Nature is nothing but trouble. Wild creatures don't get with the program. They've got their own agenda.

Yet ten years later, here's Animal Kingdom. What made Disney change its mind about the zoo business? Money, of course. Tons of it was being made in central Florida by Busch Gardens, Sea World, and a host of not-so-slick competitors offering one attraction that Disney World didn't: live exotic critters. After a week at the Magic Kingdom, tourists of all ages yearn to see something with real fur. How many embraces from six-foot prancing chipmunks can a kid be expected to endure?

So Team Rodent made the bold move. It began, typically, by recruiting some of the top zoological experts in the country. Then it started shopping for wild animals. One of the first to be acquired was a rare black rhinoceros, a five-year-old female. Only three thousand of the animals are left in the world. Disney said it had purchased this one from a wild-game ranch in Texas. If all went as planned, the rhino would soon be released in a man-made African-style habitat, where it would be fed, watered, and protected for the rest of its life.

Again from the press kit: "Disney Imagineers have created tropical forests and jungles, streams and waterfalls, and savannas and rocky ridges—fascinating lands filled with natural beauty, where animals and visitors will participate in the unrehearsed dramas of life in the wild."

Unrehearsed—finally! No more remote controlled crocs. Animal Kingdom would be the real deal, "unrehearsed dramas," meaning: If the critters decide to fight or fuck, we won't stop 'em.

Tragically, the young black rhinoceros never got a chance to test the limits of her Imagineered freedom. She died abruptly in the fall of 1997, months before the Disney zoo opened.

Discreetly the carcass was transported to the University of Florida in Gainesville, where a team of veterinarians performed a necropsy. It didn't take long to discover the cause of death, lodged deep in the animal's guts: a branchlike object, twenty-one inches long and three quarters of an inch in diameter. One end was sharp, having been cut with either a machete or a saw. The stick had punctured a lung and ignited a terrible infection. Disney's rhinoceros had died of pneumonia.

For doctors, the larger mystery was how the instrument of death had gotten inside the beast. Rhinos browse on grasses, leaves, twigs, and shrubs, and they're not always well-mannered eaters. It was conceivable that an exceptionally hungry animal could slurp down a twenty-one-inch branch without chewing it. And that would have been the working theory about Disney's dead black rhinoceros, that it had ingested the lethal stick from a pile of vegetation, cut for it as food by well-meaning handlers.

Except for one problem: The stick was found at the opposite end of the animal; specifically, in the last segment of the long intestine, within arm's reach of the rectum.

That strange and unsettling fact didn't fit the sloppy-eater scenario. A rhino's digestive tract is similar to that of a horse—twisting, lengthy, and convoluted. The doctors at the necropsy couldn't imagine how such a long sharp object could travel almost the entire circuit of a rhino's intestines before snagging. "Hard to believe," one of them stated flatly.

Yet the alternative seemed unthinkable: that a person or persons unknown had savagely inserted the stick via another orifice. But who? Why? And, for God's sake, *how*? Although the Disney rhino had been known as exceptionally docile, it was mind-boggling to suppose she might have stood still long enough for . . .

Back and forth went the sensitive discussion, and ultimately the veterinarians chose the circumspect approach: They declined to make an official conclusion about how the branchlike object might have entered the mammal, or from which end.

However, the doctors did agree on one important finding: The nearly ossified condition of the intruder proved it had been inside the rhino's intestines *before* Disney had taken delivery of the animal. The news must have been a huge relief to company executives, providing a strong defense against accusations of neglect or cruelty. There'd be no need for a delicate inquiry as to who, if anyone, had so viciously violated the young pachyderm whatever happened had taken place before the rhino arrived in Orlando. For added insurance, Disney botanists reclaimed the death stick and analyzed it. They reported that the tree it came from wasn't native to Florida.

Still, Team Rodent remained worried. No upbeat spin could be put on a story about an endangered creature expiring under mysterious circumstances on company property. With memories of the abused-buzzard fiasco still tender, a wall of secrecy went up. Anyone with knowledge of the rhino's demise was instructed to keep quiet, and to this day the attending veterinarians remain silent on the matter. Rumors about the rhino death have spread among employees throughout Disney's kingdoms; in one version the lethal instrument is said to be a two-by-four bristling with nails. A small story eventually did appear in the *Orlando Sentinel* and other newspapers, though with no mention of the possibility of foul play.

Upon learning how the rhinoceros had died, I assumed the worst: that the poor beast had been violated by a disgruntled or depraved Disney "cast member." It wasn't impossible. They had peepers and flashers, didn't they? Inside those stuffy costumes were real human beings with real human problems. What if Pooh had blown a gasket? What if Grumpy the Dwarf had no longer been able to suppress his darkest urges? Or maybe even one of the Mickeys? It was like something off the specialty video rack at Peep Land, this criminal debauchery of a rhinoceros; a rap verse off *The Great Milenko*. Sleaze lives!

Try to understand. For older, hard-core generations of Florida natives, no scandal is so delectable as a Disney scandal. This warped delight blooms out of deep resentment over the destruction of childhood haunts—an ongoing atrocity in which the Walt Disney Company remains gravely culpable, directly and indirectly.

Example: Peter Rummell, one of the hotshots behind Celebration and the ill-fated Civil War theme park in Virginia, was hired away from Team Rodent in 1997 by the St. Joe Corp. Rummell's stated mission is to turn St. Joe, once primarily a paper manufacturer, into a leading developer of commercial and residential real estate. St. Joe happens to be the biggest private landowner in Florida, holding 1.1 million acres, much of it unspoiled. The potential for an environmental holocaust is enormous, and there's no comfort to be taken in the knowledge that a Disney spawn sits in command.

For those of us who grew up here, the anti-Mickey burn is chronic and ulcerating. It manifests in behavior that's not always mature, well reasoned, or even comprehensible to outsiders. As ghastly as the rhinoceros story is, I admit it perked me up a little at first. In my imagination I saw the top-secret necropsy report landing with a slap on Michael Eisner's desk; pictured his expression cloud as he scanned the shocking medical description; watched the perspiration bead as he contemplated the dreadful ramifications of an endangered-mammal sodomization at a Disney attraction....

But no. Whatever happened to the poor beast wasn't Team Rodent's doing. And yes, I was disappointed at the news; crestfallen, if you want the unflattering truth. A rhino scandal would have been a dandy.

But why wish for such a perverse twist of events? After all, aren't the folks at Disney mostly good and decent and hardworking? And don't they honor, in spades, their pledge to bring fun and happiness to kids of all ages? Sure they do. Being dutiful parents, my wife and I made several pilgrimages to Walt Disney World when our son was small, and he always seemed to have a blast. How could such a mirth-giving enterprise and the people behind it possibly be regarded as evil? Even Insane Clown Michael—I know he's not really a puppy-killing, rhino-molesting, foulmouthed ghostwriter of third-rate misogynist rap songs. I know he's probably not even the Antichrist. He's just an exceptionally ambitious guy trying to do a job, a guy who somehow has come to believe his own gushing press releases, a guy who honestly doesn't see the whole picture.

Maybe that's the kind of person it takes, and maybe that's what is so scary. To do what Eisner's Team Rodent does, and do it on that scale, requires a degree of order that doesn't exist in the natural world. Not all birds sing sweetly. Not all lakes are blue. Not all islands have sandy beaches.

But they can be fixed, and that is Disney's fiendish specialty. What Team Rodent has "recreated" in Orlando—from an African savannah to an Atlantic reef, from a Mexican pyramid to a Chinese temple—has been engineered to fit the popular image and to hold that charm for tourist cameras. Under the Eisner reign, nothing in the real world cannot be copied and refined in the name of entertainment, and no place is safe.

Wet

JOE DONNELLY

EVERY NOW AND THEN, you are given an opportunity to face your demons. I'm talking about the aspects of your psyche that can reduce you to little more than a host organism for an aggressive colony of neuroses. My secret is that I don't like to share my water space. In fact, few things give me more fear of or contempt for my fellow man (or woman, but less so woman) than having one splashing in a small body of water next to me, and by *next to me* I mean anywhere on my side of the horizon line. Most of my adult life, which as a thirty-four-year-old I'd say began moments ago, if at all, I've avoided Jacuzzis, public pools, water parks, even bathtubs. My rule is that if the body of water isn't fed by pristine mountain springs the likes of which you see in Coors commercials, or if the other side remains visible on a clear day, I avoid it like a Jerry Bruck-heimer movie.

What am I afraid of? Is there any rational basis for why, when I look at a hot tub, all I see are naked bodies sloshing around in an oversized Petri dish that's been heated to ripe incubation temperature? Okay, if I put it like that, it's kind of rhetorical. But what's wrong with pools? Except for the fact that anything from one of *them* could end up washing off their bodies and splashing onto or into *mine*. *Oh, the humanity!* I may be a registered Democrat with liberal leanings, but this is more brotherhood than I'm prepared to sign up for. But, the questions I'd pay a shrink to answer are these: Is it really that bad in there? Or is it me? Am I going to start washing my hands every five minutes, progressing to compulsive rearrangement of my wife's underwear? Will I end up a grey-bearded man living on the top floor of the Sands Motel in Vegas? Is a weekend jaunt to Mexico already becoming too frightening to contemplate? It could be that I'm repressing something even more terrifying. If I gave up my compunctions (and compulsions) would I find myself sliding gratefully into the primeval ooze?

For years I was content to let these questions fester quietly, rather like one of those creeping, hard-to-shake diseases I was afraid to catch in a hot tub. (Psoriasis? Bilharzia?) Still, I worried there would be a day of reckoning. And there was.

It all came together for me on a recent Saturday as I stood seven stories above the huddled masses, waiting to take the plunge on Drop Out. Drop Out is one of the attractions at Raging Waters, where, knowing the issues I grapple with, a sadistic editor thought it would be fun to send me. Raging Waters may well be the last best hope for relief for hundreds of thousands of the Inland Empire's subjects, but for me, the name said it all.

So there I was atop Drop Out, "one of the tallest vertical drops in the country," waiting to pitch myself straight down at speeds approaching forty miles per hour into a catch basin for both customers and the fifteen hundred gallons of recirculated water employed to keep them sliding freely and landing softly. Far, far below was a viewing area where friends, family and chickens gathered to watch the Mountain Dew moment. If they only knew what I was thinking…because by then, it had all become so much clearer than the chlorinated pool at the bottom of the slide.

ON THE AFOREMENTIONED DAY of reckoning, my friend Kelly and I had climbed into my giant metallic blue pickup and made our way out of Hollywood and onto Interstate 10 East. That's troubling enough, but the really weird thing is, Kelly didn't have to go. She wanted to. Then again, Kelly's long been suspected of being an alien, and I figured she was going to replenish her juices, or take samples, or something.

The air over the San Gabriel Valley was festering like a scab on a dog's ass. Moving deeper into the heart of the haze, each mile pushing the thermometer toward the triple digits, I was struck by the notion that we were going the wrong way. We were driving away from coastal breezes and white, sandy beaches. Away from water that doesn't come from suspicious sources. Away from vendors competing for attention with endless and imaginative varieties of cool drinks and icy refreshments. Away from the dream and toward the hard reality that we are all prisoners of circumstance. Toward what happens when you are forced to make the most of a bad situation. Toward San Dimas, and its Raging Waters.

As we passed the roadside attractions of the 10—strip malls, auto complexes, chain restaurants—Kelly spoke of how she used to fantasize about being a mermaid in an aquarium and swimming up to the glass to smile at the happy onlookers. *Crazy alien bitch*, I thought to myself, and returned to my own haunted inward journey. The one that took me back through a long series of watery affronts, none more unspeakable than the Glenwood Springs Vapor Caves and Hot Springs incident.

Glenwood Springs is a little town in Colorado with a long history of hosting weary travelers, like Doc Holliday, who went there to treat his tuberculosis and ended up dying. But the town is perhaps most famous for its hot-springs pool and the Yampah Spa vapor caves. On New Year's Day 1994, both became permanently branded on my id.

Glenwood Springs is where me and my cousin Greg found ourselves after a New Year's Eve that ended badly, with allegations of wrongdoing on a lot of people's parts. The next morning, we gathered around the breakfast table of my folks' condo in silence, afraid to talk about how it had gone from beautiful to bad so quickly. That is, until Greg, the main instigator, pulled up to the table, grabbed a cigarette from my mom's pack—a bold move in and of itself—put his feet up on the table, lit up the heater, blew out a thick plume of smoke, waited a beat, and then said to my mom, "Sandy, where did we go wrong?"

Greg and I were instantly banished from the house. I decided it would be a good idea to sweat out our sins in the vapor caves and follow that with a relaxing dip in the hot-springs pool. My God, what was I thinking? As we climbed down into the bowels of the Earth, the dank, sulfuric air was suffocating. Waiting in every chamber for us to join them were Satan's rejects—asymmetrical limbs, contorted faces, strange protrusions, shorts that were way too short. And we were all seeping into each other along the brackish currents of the cave floor.

I kept my eyes down and tried to think of dry, cool places. But when I looked up to get my bearings, I saw my cousin Greg, red face tilted back in a hideous laugh. I swear he was twirling his tail. *Jesus,* I thought, *it's happening to us!* I ran out of the caves and sprinted the fifty yards to the hot-springs pool. Free at last! Free at last! But when my head popped out of the water all I saw were giant reptilian creatures clinging to the sides, thrusting their tongues into the air to catch the snowflakes that were falling from dark skies.

I jumped out of the pool, ran into the showers and let the cold water wash the whole nightmare off me. Just as I was sure that I had finally made it to a safe place, a glob of soap flew from the schlong of the guy who was lathering up across from me and nailed me between the eyes. I changed in the hallway.

In fact, the only good shared-water memory I have is of the little four-foot-deep raised pool we had in our back yard in Haddonfield, New Jersey. That was a long time ago, back when friends just came with the scenery. But, oh, the fun me and the neighborhood gang had jumping off the picnic table into the pool. . . .

"Hey, we should get a camera. One of those waterproof disposable kind," Kelly said as we exited onto the 210 West.

"Huh, what? Oh, yeah. A camera." Camera, sure. But what do they call it on your planet, *freak girl?*

We were getting close.

I had, of course, wanted to know what I'd be getting into before actually going. So I called the LA County Health Department, where Richard Kebabjian is chief of the recreational program for the Environmental Health Division. When I told him what I was up to, he laughed and said that a little information could be a dangerous thing. "I got an article I'll send you," he said. "I don't know if you're going to want to get in the water after that."

At the time we spoke, a large water park called White Water in Marietta, Georgia, was very much in the news due to an E. coli incident of epic and ultimately tragic proportions. According to reports in *The Atlanta Journal-Constitution*, between June 11 and June 18, twenty-six kids were infected with E. coli, usually benign bacteria residing in the intestines of humans and animals. Unfortunately, some E. coli have evolved into violent strains that produce a toxin that destroys red blood cells and platelets necessary for clotting. This causes cramping, diarrhea, and sometimes death. Actually, E. coli kills between two hundred and five hundred people each year. In most cases, however, an infection in a healthy adult will be self-limiting, meaning it generally works itself out after a period of flulike symptoms. In the White Water case, those infected were very young.

I asked Kebabjian where the E. coli in the Marietta incident might have come from. "That would have come from the rear end of a kid, probably," he said.

That's the other thing. Although most often associated with tainted meat, E. coli is ultimately a fecal matter, the unimpeachable evidence being that in the White Water case, the one child who died, two-year-old McCall Akin, was a vegetarian.

I actually read more about this, indulging in some kind of sick fascination. E. coli isn't the only potential enemy lurking in public pools, according to a document I unearthed called "Disinfection of Public Pools and Management of Fecal Accidents," by the same Kebabjian, published in the *Journal of Environmental Health*. Others include Pseudomonas aeruginosa, a "hardy thermophilic bacterium encapsulated with a slimy coating that makes it more resistant to disinfectants." This silent assassin is frequently responsible for folliculitis and dermatitis. Symptoms of folliculitis include malaise, fatigue, fever, and papulopustular rash. Personally, I live with most of these every day, but it's the last one that had me trembling. It sounded . . . unsightly.

Staphylococcus is another bacterium that has earned a place in the waterborne rogues' gallery. This one originates from the pool user's skin and oral and nasal tracts, and "can cause serious skin infections as well as conjunctivitis." Also wanted for liquid crimes against humanity are viruses such as adenovirus and enterovirus and hepatitis A. According to Kebabjian, viruses are more resistant to chlorine than their bacterial playmates and require higher levels to neutralize.

While viruses and oozy secretions are nothing to sneeze at, so to speak, the main concern at the intersection of environmental health and public pools remains fecal accidents. Riding shotgun with E. coli on the Hershey Highway are two other bad guys, *Giardia* and *Cryptosporidium*. "Both organisms are protozoans and are transmitted from person to person through [the] oral-fecal route," according to our intrepid health officer. "They can cause nausea, diarrhea and vomiting."

After repeated phone calls, I found myself becoming fond of Kebabjian, who was becoming something like my guide up the murky river into the heart of darkness. He seemed endlessly patient, and even rather amused. But all our conversations seemed to end the same way. In our last phone call, I remember asking: "What if someone has an open sore or something?"

"That's a touchy subject. There are laws, but it's pretty hard to keep someone out of a pool.... If someone has a birthmark or a genetic disorder that looks like something and you ask them to get out, you got a lawsuit on your hands."

"What if someone has a festering wound?"

"It would have to be self-policing. What else can they do? Put up a picture and say if you look like this, don't go in?" That sounded good to me.

"Besides," he continued, "pretty much the big danger here is a fecal accident."

I felt like I was back where I started. *Back* being the operative word.

I tried to calm myself. After all, a park like Raging Waters or Six Flags Hurricane Harbor in Valencia or Wild Rivers in Irvine can host more than six thousand customers a day. With that many people in the water, what are the chances someone's going to shit in *my* mouth? But, then again, with that many rear ends splashing around like loaded guns, I wondered what are the chances someone isn't going to let go with at least a muddy fart? Before Kelly and I braved the Drop Out, I wanted to know more about what they were doing to keep us safe from the forces of excremental darkness.

Easier said than done. It seems that any news concerning the pathogenic integrity of their operations is bad news, as far as Raging Waters and Hurricane Harbor are concerned. Fervent requests for a guided tour of the maintenance facilities, along with an explanation of how the pool water and chlorine levels are monitored, were repeatedly turned down.

My final plea to Andy Gallardo, spokesman for Hurricane Harbor, ended like this:

Me: "This is bullshit. You're giving me the runaround."

Andy: "I'm sorry you feel that way."

Me: "It's true, isn't it?"

Andy: "Isn't there somewhere else you can go?"

In Andy's defense, he did provide me with a couple of contacts, including the number of the World Waterpark Association, which is more than I can say for the mystifying firm of Lisa Carey Public Relations, which represents Raging Waters. After intense back-and-forth negotiations that would have given Richard Holbrooke fits, this was the final word from Lisa Carey:

"Hello, Joe, it's Lisa Carey getting back to you. . . . I want to pass along that Raging Waters will not be able to work with you on this project, and we wish you all the best. Thanks for thinking of us. Bye."

The first thing to catch your attention as you make your way down Raging Waters Drive toward the promise and threat of Raging Waters is a hapless reservoir that a stone could get maybe five skips on before reaching the other side. But that wasn't stopping about thirty boaters from looping around in tight circles with skiers attached. *Damn,* I thought, *these people are desperate for water.*

"That'll be $6," said the attendant when we pulled up to the outer reaches of the parking area. "Have a raging day."

"Have a raging day," said the shuttle bus driver as rear ends the size of cannons waddled out ahead of us.

"Have a raging day," said the cashier as she returned $1.02 from the $45 I handed her to gain admission for two.

"That'll be $6," said the locker girl. "Yours is locker 867, underneath the cotton-candy sign. Have a raging day!"

Right.

As you walk into Raging Waters on a Saturday with the temperature in the Hades zone, it becomes immediately clear that you aren't going to walk around Raging Waters. You are going to dodge. Dodge inner tubes. Dodge knee-high kids with haircuts they must have done something awful to deserve. Dodge the cigarette-huffing mothers chasing after them and then the packs of boys and girls chasing each other. In comparison to the walkways, the water, where the milling mass of humanity is somewhat contained, almost looks inviting.

Another quick revelation is that the park goers can be easily divided between the smart ones and the dumb ones. The smart ones are the ones wearing water slippers. You notice they are smart and you are dumb as soon as you find yourself actively seeking out stagnant walkway puddles to keep your feet from fusing to the cement.

After the initial shock of just being there wore off, Kelly and I stepped out of a puddle and headed for a children's play area with gentle slides, jungle gyms, shallow water, and laughing rug rats. I decided one of the kiddie slides would make for a friendly initiation into the Raging Waters. As soon as I splashed down, though, my body recoiled in horror. Had I forgotten everything I learned? The kiddie area is perhaps the most fecally suspect part of the entire park! Luckily, or so I thought at the time, there was a spot in the kiddie area where you could pull a rope and unleash a shower of water on top of you. I stood there pulling and rinsing, pulling and rinsing.

"What are you doing?" Kelly asked.

"I'm rinsing myself off."

"Where do you think that water is coming from?"

She had a point.

We hotfooted it over to Thunder Rapids, where the long, shady line looked like a safe haven. Boy, was I wrong. As the waves of humanity inched forward and the nature of Thunder Rapids became clearer, I started to panic. Not only were we going to be sent down a twisting, churning watery chute, but we were going to be forced to share a raft with several random denizens of the park.

I looked around my immediate vicinity at the likely candidates. I'm not sure anything would have been acceptable at this point, but I'm not exaggerating when I say the prospects were grim. It was like a Jerry Springer picnic. Buzz-cut blond dudes with bad White Pride tattoos. Black girls with too many rolls of fat seeking shelter under too little clothing. Prepubescent boys with girlie nipples. Chests with too little hair. Backs with too much. Bad teeth. Pimply skin. Thin upper bodies on top of fat lower bodies. And vice versa. Everything was just a little off, and I was afraid it was catching. All I could think, God help me, was that if everyone was beautiful like me, I'd be okay with this.

I tried to find a way out, but we were hemmed in by the mass of humanity. I would have climbed the fence around the park, but it was topped with barbed wire. There was no escape. At the moment of my greatest despair, a man emerged from behind a gate. He was wearing an official-looking outfit. Behind the gate were huge vats of what I assumed to be the chemicals that held the key to my fate.

"Everything okay?" I asked the guy.

"Yeah, everything's okay," he said, surprised at the question.

"No fecal accidents?"

"No, no fecal accidents," he said, closing the gate and scurrying off, not wanting to continue the conversation.

We moved closer to the point of embarking. Who would it be? Who were we going to be forced to absorb?

Just then, one of the lifeguards, the only other people within the park who seemed to have cracked the genetic code, called out for a party of less than three. I raised my hand and grabbed Kelly's and raised hers, too.

"Here, here!" I shouted. And like that we were brought to the front of the line and placed in a raft with a fine-looking fellow and his two healthy, but scared, young daughters.

"Don't worry, it's going to be okay," I told them. "Just keep your mouths closed."

Off we went, careening down the slide, flying up the sidewalls on the turns and then back down again. Water splashed over us, on us and into us. I held on in tight-lipped horror. Kelly, though, she was laughing a big, wide-mouthed laugh the whole way down. That alien freak, I thought, *she's feeding*. Apparently she got her fill, because when we got out of the water, she asked me if I was ready to go.

"Only one thing left to do," I said, nodding toward Drop Out, looming high above us. I was ready to meet my maker. "A little unfinished business."

On the way over, we passed one woman with a bleeding knee and one guy with a bleeding elbow.

At Drop Out, I fell in line behind a pint-size, skinny kid with short dreadlocks and innocent eyes.

"Hey, man, you scared?" he asked as we moved toward the launching deck. It was a brother-in-arms bonding moment.

"Yeah, I'm scared all right. . . ."

Only, I wasn't looking at the tiny people in the viewing area, or the pool at the bottom, which held the promise of a soft landing. I was staring in the other direction, at the Amazon Adventure, a quarter-mile-long, eighteen-foot-wide, three-foot-deep "tropical river" filled with five hundred thousand gallons of water. It can accommodate up to six hundred raft riders "who want to lazily bask in the sun while coasting down an endless waterway," and it was filled to the brim.

I watched the disturbing crush of people floating by in a parade of sizes, shapes, colors, and unfortunate outfits. They didn't seem to ask where they were going, or why. They just kept drifting, bumping into each other, splashing, mixing, sharing the same churning, recycling, undulating half a million gallons of water. I wondered what legacy each was leaving. What will one pick up from the next? From where I stood, seventy feet up, waiting to drop to a symbolic death, to violently dive feet first back into a metaphorical womb, it all looked so . . . free of will. So unconscious. Almost subhuman. I was immediately reminded of a Saturday-morning show I used to watch when I was a kid called *Land of the Lost*. In the show, a typical suburban family out rafting one day plunges over a waterfall during an earthquake and into a land time forgot. A land of dinosaurs and tropical vegetation. A land with a friendly but challenged prehistoric boy and his baby dinosaur pal named Dopey, both of whom inevitably cause problems that are solved by the resourceful (and extremely good-natured, considering all they've been through) family and the sexy cavegirl who looked like Pebbles would if she grew up and came to life. Along the way, viewers learn that the foibles and triumphs of human nature span the ages.

One of the show's mainstays was a gang of hissing, lizardlike creatures called Sleestaks. The Sleestaks constantly terrorized this ad hoc modern/prehistoric Brady Bunch. All my life, I've wondered why the clumsy, practically inert Sleestaks were so horrifying even to me, watching safely at home. But, looking down on the Amazon Adventure, it was beginning to make sense. As was my distaste for places like this.

The Sleestaks, and especially their rise to upright, human stature, only reminded me of the primordial pool from which we came. The threat of the Sleestak was the threat of being glommed with the ungodly ooze stewing beneath our skin and clothes. Things like phlegm, boogers, dandruff, loose toenails, pubic hair, psoriasis, seborrhea, earwax, scabs, blood, pathogens, parasites, secretions, viruses, urine, feces and ... goop, goddamnit, goop! We're made of slimy, fetid, fucking goop!!! And I don't want your goop! I don't want to commune with the rot from which we came and to which we'll return. I want to cling like an uncomprehending child to the illusion that we are divine. I don't want to be reminded that beneath the surface we're all just a bunch of Sleestaks, that evolution is a cruel deception. You bastards! You squirming tadpoles! When I look into your teeming depths, it's repulsion—and not love—I feel.

"... but not of this ride," I told my young friend. He looked at me like he understood, and slid into the chute.

I felt sorry for everyone who had been reduced to this state, and sorry that my secret misanthropy was floating down the lazy river into the primordial ooze like one of the bright-colored rafts. But I knew all the chlorine Raging Waters could bring to bear wouldn't neutralize that. So I stepped up and took the plunge.

Driving back to Hollywood, I realized that maybe it wasn't Sleestaks I was thinking of, but my friend Wilksey, who looks like a Sleestak and slobbers a lot when he drinks too much.

Later that day, safely home and showered, I called my mom.

"Mom, remember that raised pool in the back yard in New Jersey?"

"Sure."

"How did that work, just stick the hose in and fill 'er up?"

"Yep. That was it."

"Did you change the water?"

"Yep. I was too persnickety to leave it in there too long. The neighbor's Newfoundland used to come over and jump in. That wasn't too sanitary. And God knows how many kids peed in the pool. You know, Joey, you were the worst. I kept telling you...."

Oh, the humanity.

Island of the Damned

JACK HITT

"MILLIONS UPON MILLIONS OF YEARS AGO," goes some of the most profitable prose of the 1950s, "when the continents were already formed and the principal features of the earth had been decided, there existed, then as now, one aspect of the world that dwarfed all others." This is the portentous opener to a James Michener book, which…but you're probably wondering which dwarfing "aspect of the world" he was talking about, and who can blame you?

"It was a mighty ocean," Michener decrees, "a restless ever-changing, gigantic body of water that would later be described as pacific." This essential drama (restless yet pacific) drives page after geologic page. "Over its brooding surface immense winds swept back and forth." Reading this, one suspects that Michener wanted to give his readers a sense of tectonic formation by letting them experience it ("immense tides ripped across this tremendous ocean") in real time. Pages of inanimate drama occur before the first coral polyp appears, which livens up the action, at least for the invertebrates.

Deep into chapter one, Michener exhausts several pages of typing with a description of the ecological formation of a Pacific island. He takes you down below where volcanoes explode and cool into deep sea mountains on which coral coalesce over millions of years to form the underwater scaffolding that will one day support on the surface, like a cake on a stand, an island. In one watching-the-paint-dry riff, Michener actually describes how sand gets made. At last, his coral atoll gets filled in with this very sand, is fertilized by the droppings of wind-blown birds, and eventually bursts into a tropical island paradise. But just to show you how capricious the ocean is,

Michener wipes out his first island in a natural disaster and then, starting all over again, evolves yet another one. "Thus the ocean continued its alternate building and tearing down."

Which is the point, one suspects, of the entire book. But just in case we don't get it, Michener ends his inaugural pomposities with a scriptural flourish: "Master of life, guardian of the shorelines, regulator of temperatures and heaving sculptor of mountains, the great ocean existed."

In the decades since I was required to read it for an eighth-grade class called Geography of the Pacific, that story has stayed in my memory just like the author's ocean: Huge, immense, boring—the book *Hawaii* . . . existed. But not too long ago I returned from one of those tiny places conjured out of the ancient chaos of the sea. There I witnessed something rare and mysterious, even terrifying: The people have dug up and sold off the interior of their homeland in order to compete in the new global economy. What's left is so strange to see and elemental to visit that it's grudgingly led me back to the encyclopedist's eonic prose.

Called Nauru, the island is one of those tiny nations scattered like crumbs across the belly of the Pacific. It's just twenty-six miles south of the equator, twelve hundred miles northeast of Papua, New Guinea—in the center of an expanse of the world named, as if by Michener himself: Oceania.

This island may be as far away from everywhere as you can get and still be somewhere. In the months after the turn of the millennium, I had been sent there to look into money laundering. International finance experts charged that in the late 1990s Nauru, only a little bigger than Central Park, was literally responsible for bankrupting the former Soviet Union, which once occupied half of Asia. Cleaning dirty money in the new global economy, by the by, is quite easy. Banks of any standing are required to keep a record of each transaction—in the same way that one's personal checking account statement shows which checks were deposited and which funds were removed. Banks registered in Nauru are not burdened by a requirement for such paperwork. So money could come in and then go out to another bank with no dirty trail. Any international syndi-

cate could pay Nauru thousands of dollars to register its very own
bank, and in return the island nation gained a steady income stream
without the fuss of building a factory or putting its citizens to work.

When I visited Nauru, I went to the place where the Nauruan
government maintained all the "bank records." It was a one-room
joint; half of a small duplex. The only evidence of the global economy
was the number of humming air conditioners sticking out the windows, cooling the place to the operating temperature needed for
computers that contained little more than bank names and addresses.
I knocked on the door. A woman holding a broom answered. She
insisted that she knew nothing and nervously said she couldn't let me
in. The cleaning lady of the new global economy. I've met her.

"Upon its farthest reaches birds with enormous wings came to
rest, and then flew on."

After the article came out, I continued to check in on my little
Pacific island as if it were an old acquaintance whose self-destructive
ways made me perversely eager for fresh gossip. Nauru was my introduction to the harsh reality of the Pacific: The island paradise image
is now about as annihilating a cliché as, say, the icon of the noble savage was and still is to Native Americans. It's a postcard picture so
powerful and comforting it overwhelms the grim realities rampaging
behind it—as with Togo (plagued with the world's worst obesity) or
Tuvalu (international purveyor of porn) or Tahiti (wracked by
poverty). Nauru was once a lovely island place. Whalers in the nineteenth century referred to it on charts as "Pleasant Island." But like a
runaway innocent, she spent her beauty too easily and now she's lost
her only asset. The options are grim. In Nauru's case, the end is coming quickly, and it's impossible not to watch.

Some people collect porcelain elephants. Some wax their cars
on the weekends. I collect Nauru bits, which is not easy. The country's telephone service often shuts down completely, and the government now forbids anyone to visit. And yet, rumors leak out.

As I started to surf about online and check in on my favorite
topic, it quickly became clear that Nauru wasn't merely campy fun.
Among the collected episodes, I could find tales of heroism, such as
Nauru's bravery in the face of Japanese domination during World

War II; of dark chicanery, such as charges that the island sold pass-ports to Al Qaeda terrorists; of weird chicanery, such as the new charges that the island conspired with the CIA in "Operation Weasel" to help smuggle out North Korea's nuclear scientists; of sheer black comedy, such as the zany change of presidents due to death, intrigue, or corruption, like something more out of Woody Allen than Tom Clancy; of grim tragedy, such as the accounts now emerging of Iraqi and Afghan refugees marooned on the island; and, of course, the veiled horror secreted away in the very heart of the island.

"Winds from the north and south would howl across the empty seas and blast stupendous waves upon the shattering shore."

The country is actually in immense peril in part because it has chosen—as all of us have—to see its very own habitat, as well as its culture and identity, in purely economic terms. And now Nauru may simply have to go out of business. What's left of the tiny island after selling off various chunks of itself is imminently threatened by the rising levels of the ocean. ("How utterly vast it was! How its surges modified the very balance of the earth!") Just as immediate, the finances of the country are in such chaos that the entire popula-tion of twelve thousand might well have to declare bankruptcy, turn off the lights, and decamp for somewhere else.

Between the rock of ecology and the hard marketplace of the global economy, Nauru is not merely being squeezed, but is coming undone. Nauru is like the dreadful opening of *Hawaii*, only speeded-up and in reverse. And yet, the story is not about some small island, but something grander, something epic, something Michenerian. "Since no great amounts of sand had yet been built, the waters where they reached shore were universally dark, black as night and fearful."

WHEN I CALLED THE NAURUAN MISSION to the United Nations in New York to make arrangements to visit. The attache fobbed me off by saying that I would have to clear any visit with Nauru's publicity agent. How's that? An entire nation has a PR flack? This was my first, but not my last, encounter with the formidable

Helen Bogdan, spokesperson for nations, headquartered in Melbourne. A platinum blonde hipster who globe-trots in East Village black with rectangular eyeglasses, she appears to believe that all of the country's profound problems can be solved with a bit of rhetorical fluffing. She answers the phone by declaring her name as if it were a single sound or one of those long philosophical terms in German: Helenbogdan. I'll admit, when I rang her up I could sense her profound suspicion and so I was a little coy. I told her I just wanted to visit the island and I filled the phone call with words and more words that made some vague point about the virtues of a struggling nation and, you know, if you thought about it, going there would be a unique way to look directly in the face of the new global economy.

Helenbogdan didn't buy a word of it. Helenbogdan told me the seventh president in three years had been forced out and that while she would ask the new one, Bernard Dowiyogo, about my interest, Helenbogdan was fairly certain it wouldn't work out. On a subsequent transplanetary phone call, Helenbogdan told me that Helenbogdan was sad because Helenbogdan would not be able to help me in my quest to look into the face of the new global economy and that—Helenbogdan's voice deepened suddenly—under no circumstances would I be permitted on the island.

I booked a flight at once.

When I arrived at the airport in Brisbane, Australia, Nauru's link to the outside world, I started to get nervous and wasn't able to sleep. Truth is, I'm not much of a macho journalist and the place I had now signed on to visit was the preferred haunt of international mobsters. And a personage no less than the nation's PR lady, Helenbogdan herself, had specifically stated that I was barred from entering the country. I began to sweat when I read a paragraph in a visa application saying that people without stated business better have "sponsorship from a resident of Nauru." At the counter in Brisbane, I was asked to state my purpose. I said "tourism" and the lady fixed me with a gimlet eye as I struggled to keep my Adam's apple from dancing. I yammered about an adventurer's club that collected entry visas. It made a crazy sense and, I later learned, exists.

On board the plane to Nauru, I began to get a deeper sense of the country's desperation. Nauru Air Lines was down to one plane, and I was lucky to be on it. Last year, the plane was seized under a Philippine court order on behalf of a creditor. Apparently they worked something out. I was told by the two Aussies sitting beside me that a few presidents ago—that could mean weeks—the plane sometimes didn't fly at all because the country's leader would commandeer it to fly in party supplies.

The flight was full, mainly of Nauruans and Aussies. The back third of the plane's seats were taken over by huge crates of imports. Nothing is made in Nauru so everything must be flown or shipped in—which, given the failure rate of the island's desalination plant, includes water. Strapped in with bungee cords and lengthy customized seat belts, the enormous boxes shifted with the occasional turbulence and seemed to cause the plane to fishtail at thirty thousand feet. I brushed up on my rote mastery of the Lord's Prayer.

When the plane landed at 4 AM, I stepped off in a slow parade of locals and Australian engineers and in the dazed heat of this odd hour, I ambled without notice straight through customs and onto the shuttle bus to the country's only privately run hotel, the Menem.

My room looked like any old Holiday Inn room with its sagging bed, balsa-weight furniture, and tissue-bare curtains—except for the printed notice on the side table that asked guests to be considerate, water-wise, since the country was in its third year of a drought. The shower worked only once for me for about a minute. One afternoon I had to brush with what was handy, a Coca-Cola, and some minty toothpaste, so that I spent the rest of the day with a grin like Cameron Diaz's.

At 7 AM, I decided I would walk up the road about two miles to a knot of a dozen or so official buildings, which locals grandly call "the capital city of Yemen." It's as if everyone on the island has decided to play a child's game called "nation-state." The entire country is ringed by a single circular paved road; that's it. So nothing's hard to find. Even in the early morning, the equatorial heat reacted brutally with my freckled skin. About a quarter mile down the road sitting right on the beach I saw pocked graffiti-covered

Japanese pillboxes and World War II gunner nests still trained on the distant blue horizon. I wanted to crawl in one.

Along the way, I passed the Nauruan golf course, which must rank as one of the world's oddest. Because of the drought, there is no grass anywhere to be seen on the nine holes. The entire course is situated within an enormous rectangular sand trap, marked by a few struggling trees.

But then all the trees were struggling. The shore was lined with the usual image of tall palms that might have swayed in the breeze had there been one. But many of the palm trees were obviously moribund from drought—coconut-less, frondless, slightly obscene poles curving upward to a pale blister in a pale sky. I turned back, groggy and weepy from the exposure, hoping to refresh myself, maybe with some chemotherapy.

The hotel summoned a cab, which took fifteen minutes to arrive since it was the only cab on the island. As I waited, I read the remarks of former hotel guests, almost all of them scientists flown in for work: "No water, no booze, otherwise okay" and "Can't get lost here" and "Clearly nicest hotel in whole country" and—enigmatic engineer humor: "Great place to launch a rocket." Most of the talk in the lobby was about three Koreans who had been forcibly removed the hotel, screaming and kicking, by Nauru police and immediately deported. No one seemed to know any details.

In the heyday of colonialism in the late nineteenth century when every European nation with a boat charged open throttle to the Pacific to claim tiny islands, Germany was the first to put its jackboot on Nauru's shore. According to island legend, an early colonial officer took note of a big rock used as a door stop and noticed that it was made of pure phosphate. Right away the Germans built a small gauge railroad train into the island's interior and began carrying off, shipload by shipload, the island's soil.

Australia later seized the island, and in World War II, the Japanese conquered easily and moved the Nauruans to a Micronesian island north of New Guinea called Truk. It was the wartime Japanese who built the air strip I landed on, and throughout the island one can still see Japanese emplacements, cannons, even a crashed plane. At one point during the Truk exile, a Japanese commander asked the leader of Nauru to kindly send out some Nauruan girls to work as "tea mistresses" aboard his ship. The leader replied that the commander would have to cut his throat first. The Japanese found their tea mistresses elsewhere. This proud moment, when Nauru's leader defended his people's virtue, is a story that still gets told more than a half century later. Maybe because it's the last time it happened.

After the war, Australia restarted the mining and earned enormous profits before the island managed to achieve independence in 1968 and take over control of its financing. The Nauru Phosphate Royalties Trust raked in the cash over the subsequent decades. Health care and education were guaranteed. The quality of life, from a western perspective, soared. Cars, electrical appliances, air-conditioning, and imports of all kinds were available to nearly all. The Chinese arrived to provide backup labor. In the early nineties, the Trust had an estimated principal of $800 million, making Nauru, per capita, the richest country in the world. Nauru's leaders made a number of smart investments. Nauru is an absentee land-lord, to this day, for many living in luxury apartments in Melbourne, Australia, and Portland, Oregon, and Honolulu, Hawaii.

But, in that volatile decade, extremely bad investments were made, too. One of the country's London financial advisors, Adrian Powles, simply stole $60 million from Nauru. Other speculations were questionable and strange. Maybe you were in London in the early nineties and caught a musical based on the life of da Vinci called *Leonardo: A Portrait of Love*. It was a major flop and its primary backer was the entire country of Nauru. The Nauruan government flew itself, families, and friends to London first class to catch the show. They booked the front rows of the theater for opening night, which was smart since closing night was soon to follow. The entire fiasco cost $4 million.

In 1992, Nauru bought into a scheme of "prime bank notes." This was an early nineties scam that convinced naive investors that the super-rich secretly traded these notes for enormous, fast profits. It played into the idea, easily believed in those days, that the rich had formally set up a hidden finance system available only to those with special access. Nauru put up $30 million in the deal. But, of course, once the money was in hand, it was quickly laundered (ironically) through Antigua. The cash, and the investment counselors who conned Nauru into the scheme, were long gone.

Now that the scams are over and the bubble has burst, Nauru's entire national endowment is estimated (and exaggerated) to be $130 million. And there is no other economy in waiting. Unlike other tropical islands, tourism is an impossibility. The beaches are raked with small razorlike coral formations, making swimming dangerous. There is no natural harbor. Even the phosphate container ships are loaded via an impressively Rube Goldbergian cantilever piping system that reaches out into deep water. The work creates a huge DeLillo-like phosphate cloud that often hovers just off the island, a frightening industrial phantom.

Oh, and there is one other problem—the elephant sitting in the room of Nauru, and certainly the most profound explanation for Nauru's contemporary interest in money laundering: A century of phosphate mining has denuded roughly 80 percent of the island.

AT 5 AM ONE MORNING, my body clock wakes me up. I head outside my room to stand on the beach watching the starry darkness when suddenly it seems like a bucket of blood has been sloshed across the floor of the distant horizon. In the brightening crimson light, I decide to take a walk. Most of the houses on Nauru are made of unpainted cinderblocks. Everyone has a car. The yards are squares of talc. Trash, which is apparently too expensive to export, simply is collected in yards in piles. There is an Appalachian quality here. Few yards lack either a dog, pig, or some critter of unknown phylum, which chases me down the road.

It's not even 7 AM and the heat is once again slaying me. A car pulls over and the curious driver offers me a ride. He says a name, which I ask him to repeat three times because I can't quite understand the sounds. He has the same eyes as a childhood friend named Brian so that synapse takes command of his identity.

"What are you doing on Nauru?" Brian asks.

"Just visiting," I say.

"You're a tourist," Brian asks and chuckles.

"Um, yes. Always heard of the place."

Brian looks at me sideways for the longest two seconds I have ever suffered through.

"Let me ask you something," Brian says with sudden formality, "have you ever practiced the profession of journalism?"

"I. Have. Been. Known. To. Practice. Something. Like. Unto. Which. Journalism. Technically. Is," I say or mellifluous words to that effect.

"I would not want to talk to a journalist who would use my name," Brian says.

Rather sporting of him, I think.

I tell Brian that were I ever to find myself practicing some journalism somewhere, I would not use his real name. (To repeat, Brian is nowhere near his real name.) Then Brian offers to take me on a tour of the island. For twenty minutes we drive the circumference of Nauru, stopping once in a small store to buy the only thing it had for sale: white processed bread. The tour occurs in complete silence. Nothing is noted or pointed out. (The same thing happened later that day when I joined the hotel's official tour for visiting engineers. The tour guide, a woman, stood at the front of the bus, holding a microphone, but spoke into it no more than three or four introductory sentences.)

The eerie persistent silence of Nauru exists because there is only one thing anyone really wants to see. Brian drives all the way around the island and then pulls up beside the factory. "You want to see Topside, right?" he asks, using the local nickname for the interior of the island. At least he asks. The hotel tour never even mentioned the one truly distinctive thing about Nauru.

At the giant factory, where huge stony clumps are shipped in from the interior of the island before being roasted and processed into refined powdery phosphate, Brian turns up a dirt road. Right away, as we slip behind the outer scrim of trees, shrubs, and ground cover, all things green disappear to reveal a sight both terrible and spellbinding. The road itself becomes a kind of levee laid atop an expanse of pure ruination. On we drive to a place at the very center of what's left of the interior mound of the atoll where we can see in one sweeping view the belly of the island.

There are no words or pictures that can adequately capture what mining has wrought in Nauru. The small atoll has essentially been tonsured. The sickly collection of water-starved vegetation on the periphery—the dead palms, the pandanus trees with black crowns, the greenless golf course—is the good news. They mask the horror that lies just on the inside of that ring of trees and scrub: The entire interior has been cut down, and the underbed of phosphate strip-mined so deep that the only things remnant are the coral bones of the atoll as it might have existed a million years ago. It's a haunting landscape of dug-out stone channels. With all the topsoil and phosphate gone, what's left are sinuous canals marked by sun-bleached limestone towers and coral outcroppings. One would be hard-pressed to find a place that has been more wasted by the allures of the global economy. The winding channels among these coral spires are lined with an appallingly silky dirt. Old filthy trash blows around this blistering desert, the shredded plastic bags snagging on a bit of coral, the weightier garbage eventually sinking into the ruts where the rot manages to service the root system of a few brave weeds. If there is a speck of nutrient to found there, it is hunted by the feral dogs that long ago fled the domesticated life on the shore for a brutal Philip K. Dick existence in the coral channels.

One environmental theory that explains why Nauru's naturally periodic droughts have grown so much worse is called the "oven effect." Under the equatorial sun, the exposed, white-hot plate of Nauru's interior creates a column of scorched air that rises up fast enough to blow away rain clouds.

Brian points to a place—it seems almost hypothetical—out in the powdery distance and says it is his. I later found out that by tradition every Nauruan owns a discrete piece of the island. There are thousands of these tracts of land, some not much bigger than a double bed. I have seen a GIS map that breaks up the entire island into these microparcels. Despite the fact that most of the island has been exported to fertilize crops in the West, almost every Nauruan knows precisely where his designated splinter of homeland can be found in this coral boneyard.

Brian has almost nothing to say as we drive slowly with the windows down. Then he stops at another place. We get out and scan the skeletal landscape. He tells me how when he was a boy all this was dense tropical forest. He and his friends would hunt the black noddy bird, and then bring it home to prepare it in the traditional Nauruan style. The population of the country's signal bird has collapsed, as have those of the once populous frigate and tern. So Nauruans no longer ate the noddy bird. We sit in a hissing silence for a while. There is no breeze, just fine talc, airborne and stagnant like particulate suspended in the stillness of a laboratory vacuum. It seems to crackle and pop in the heavy birdless air. The emotional sensation of just standing there is one of intense, primal fear, like I could be murdered. Have you ever found yourself alone after hours in a cathedral, or a stadium, or a museum? There is an uneasy feeling of immense absence—of a congregation, of fifty thousand fans, or crowds. Here, on Topside, what's missing is the very life force of nature. Stripped clean, literally to the bone, all that's left is a rare silence that scares you in a way you haven't felt since childhood.

Brian sits still and stares ahead. Perhaps more unnerving than the landscape is his stoic face—absent of all affect, tensed by something unnameably sad. He holds himself immobile, as if his chiseled profile is part of the tour: an expression of shame I have never before seen.

He and his people, perhaps unknowingly, have sold off their motherland. It has been done gradually, perhaps unnoticed amid the joyful flush of sudden wealth. There are probably rationalizations and explanations, and yet it's an incomprehensible thing to see it and feel it. Imagine destroying the forty states from West Virginia to Nevada so the remaining ten could be temporarily wealthy. Imagine France paving Bordeaux; Israel salting Jerusalem.

Brian heads back to the post office. We don't speak, carrying away the interior's silence with us. As I lean down to shut the car door, he says that he hopes one day I'll get the chance to eat a noddy bird and then he drives off.

Since then, I can't say this foul-your-own-nest sensation has retained its rarefied feel. When a Canadian research institute reported that 90 percent of the largest marine species—including cod, tuna, and swordfish—had disappeared from the world's oceans because of overfishing, or when *Nature* magazine revealed that huge numbers of warm-climate animals had suddenly altered their migration patterns with some reaching as far north as Canada, it was unnerving and I recognized a common reaction among others. People would mention some new revelation to me, and then, since there really isn't anything to say, they'd drift away, slipping into a dreadful silence that I now recognize from the moment I first felt it myself amid the friable stillness of Topside.

AFTER I RETURNED FROM NAURU, I learned that the president would be visiting New York to address the United Nations during the millennium summit. Bernard Dowiyogo had served in this office four times in the last decade (and would serve a few more times in the new millennium). He had been tossed out of power in 1998 after telling his countrymen that they would have to rein in their lifestyle. His replacement, a phosphate mining executive named Rene Harris, accelerated the money laundering. The politics of Nauru essentially revolves around the notions of these two men. Harris tolerates the most brutal form of capitalism—sell anything and everything. Dowiyogo has tried to steer the country toward some sort of moral economic reform, hoping the West will reward him for his virtue. So far, he's been disappointed.

A courtly man, Dowiyogo invited me up to his Park Avenue hotel room for breakfast.

He and I sat together over a plate of sausage and eggs scrambled in that flawlessly yellow hotel style. We were joined by the country's ambassador and two other officials. Dowiyogo greeted me with the solemnity of a man whose acquaintance with smiling seemed as remote as Brian's.

"We cooperate with authorities when they come to the island with court orders," he said. He was trying to make the case that Nauru was no different from, say, Switzerland, which has in recent times begun to cooperate with foreign governments who come to investigate criminal indictments regarding its banks.

To some extent, that's true. In 1998, American authorities were investigating a Florida outfit called Greater Ministries International. GMI was affiliated with the Ku Klux Klan and was operating a Ponzi scheme that pumped Christians of their charitable dollars via something called the "Double Your Blessing Gift Program." When one of the organizers was arrested he claimed diplomatic immunity as an ambassador from the "Kingdom of Heaven." Apparently that crossed the line, and Nauru revoked GMI's banking charter.

According to the president, the current plan to rehabilitate the interior of the island will take twenty years and cost $300 million. It won't be easy. The bulk of the rehab plan is simply to knock over the limestone pinnacles to fill in the labyrinth of channels on the island, and that will require transporting to the island the biggest and most powerful land movers in the world. But since there is no topsoil left, their plan can't hope to regrow the island's forest.

"One of the things we have in mind," Dowiyogo said, "was that part of the dug-out area should be left as it is so that future generations can see what it was like." Like a museum, added the ambassador.

So maybe there is a new economy ahead. Eco-tourism, only in reverse. Instead of seeing the environment at its most lush, you'd see it at its most debauched. Which is why I keep up with Nauru. The details arrive like pathos and then quickly turn into bathos.

At breakfast, for instance, I asked President Dowiyogo what other ideas were kicking around Nauru to make money. He said they are "studying" one proposal. It is to slice the limestone pinnacles into cross-sections, polish them, and offer them for sale in the West as coffee tables.

I asked what other business opportunities his country was contemplating. President Dowiyogo took a bite of toast.

Another government official later told me in confidence that there had even been talk of permitting the country's phone code to be used for 1-900 sex phones. Vanuatu, another island a few thousand miles from Nauru has already gone this way. Nauru, perhaps recalling the invitation to become Japanese tea mistresses, is holding out for the coffee tables.

When I was on the island, I learned that the big Nauru holiday is called Angam Day. It celebrates the several occasions in the past when the island's total population has exceeded 1,500—the magic number always thought to be the perfect population for the island. With Nauruan natives now exceeding 10,000 and with the hope for the future balanced on coffee tables, I gingerly asked the president what might happen to the people on Nauru in the next ten years.

"That's not a problem," he said, explaining that there are at least two more years of full mining. Then the engineers are studying how to extract "residual phosphate" from the limestone pinnacles when they get knocked down. He explained that early estimates of the remining potential add another eight years of income for the island.

"What do you see as the future in twenty years?" I replied.

"That may be a problem," the president of Nauru said quietly. I had other questions, but I no longer had the guts to ask them. By now, the awkwardness of the breakfast had reduced the interview to little more than the sound of forks scratching plates.

A FEW WEEKS LATER I did have the chance to put my questions to the country's PR agent. Helenbogdan had flown to one of New York's more exclusive downtown clubs, Lot 51, to premiere a ten-minute publicity short, the kind of thing aired aboard a plane or in the waiting room of a travel agency. I attended the midnight Saturday night event where angel-headed hipsters waited outside a rope line for the chanee to sample the enticements within. There, clutching an obscure Bavarian ale, one wandered beneath a ceiling hung with rakishly tilted monitors displaying lush vignettes of swaying green palms, laughing brown children, and crashing turquoise waves. The few images of Topside were quick cuts, and the shots were so tightly focused on the pinnacles that you might be forgiven for mistaking them for Polynesian totems. I kept waiting for Jack Lord's face to show up followed by a horn section ripping into the staccato opener of *Hawaii 5-0.*

The film was said to be an attempt to restart a new tourism interest in the island, but immediately it ran across a pretty tough obstacle. Regular flights to the island had ceased a few months after I got out.

A year later, though, in late August, 2001—a week before September 11th—Nauru received two offers to make big money: one of them wicked, the other bizarre. Nauru entertained them both.

The first deal emerged during a crisis off the coast of Australia. A group of Iraqis and Afghan refugees were fleeing the oppressions of Saddam Hussein and the Taliban. They made their way to Indonesia where they contracted with the owner of a wooden boat named the *Palapa 1*. Crammed with 438 people, including children and pregnant women, the *Palapa 1* set sail for a one-day journey to Australia. In a grim replay of Gilligan's Island, the boat's motor died and it began to sink. To Australia's disgrace, helicopters from its coast guard service flew out over the course of three days to see the *Palapa 1* increasingly slipping below the water's surface. The refugees burnt bits of clothing to signal distress. The helicopters observed the scene beneath and then returned to the Australian mainland.

No help was dispatched.

During a storm that blew in the second day, according to one refugee I heard describe the situation, the refugees pressed their bodies up against cracks in the wood hull to keep the ship from going under immediately. On the third day of no food or water on board, the passengers prepared to die. The cries of starving infants, he said, were unrelenting.

Then the Australians figured out a solution. They noticed a Norwegian merchant vessel called the *Tampa* was on its way to Singapore. The Australian Maritime Safety Centre in Canberra radioed the captain, Arne Rinnan, and told him there was a ship nearby in distress. Observing centuries of maritime tradition, Rinnan responded at once to the SOS. The seas were choppy and it took hours to bring the 438 refugees aboard. The *Tampa*'s crew numbered only twelve. The on-board provisions were thin. Rinnan contacted officials in Australia, who told him to go to Indonesia.

Here, things get dicey. The *Tampa* was technically in Indonesian waters, but it was only 75 miles from Australia's Christmas Island and 250 miles away from the Indonesian port of Merak. On board the *Tampa*, the leaders of the refugees insisted that they be taken to Australia. Tensions were high on the bridge, according to Rinnan, so taking all things into consideration, he turned the ship toward Australia.

There it sat offshore for ten days. Australia refused to admit the refugees. Unbeknownst to Rinnan, as he moored there in the days leading up to September 11, 2001, he had also sailed into the foul weather of a bitter Australian election. Prime Minister John Howard was down in the polls by 40 percent. He took a tough stance with the *Tampa*, insisting that the ship "will not be given permission to land in Australia or any Australian territories." When pictures of the refugees thrashing about in the water with their children were shown on television, Howard said this was proof these foreigners were savages: They were willing to drown their children in order to blackmail Australia. Howard announced that his country would "not be held hostage by our own decency." (Later, when evidence emerged that Howard's interpretation of the "child-throwing incident"—as it's known in Australia—was knowingly and cravenly invented, the legislature launched an investigation into the prime minister's lies.)

In speeches at the time, Howard would shout, "We will decide who comes into this country." The crowds rose to their feet with thunderous applause.

While Norway, the ship's captain, and the United Nations condemned Australia, Howard quietly cobbled together a deal to dispose of the 438 unwanted people. Howard ordered his military to board the *Tampa* and move the refugees onto a barge. Named the *Manoora*, it departed for the three-thousand-mile ocean voyage to Nauru. In return, Australia offered the bankrupt nation $20 million, effectively upping Nauru's GDP by a third. Even though these refugees from Hussein's Iraq and the Taliban's Afghanistan were effectively allies of western countries such as the United States and Australia, they quickly became *desaparecidos* by being sent to an island that no longer permitted outside visitors. Prime Minister John Howard called the deal the Pacific Solution.

Maybe Australians didn't hear the Holocaust echoes in that

phrase. Judging from the polls, they also didn't catch the irony. Australians, themselves marooned on a distant island by unforgiving Brits only a century before, had managed to angrily carry out a primal re-enactment of their founding trauma.

Howard's approval numbers surged to 61 percent. He won re-election in a landslide.

What exactly has happened to the refugees since the *Manoora* dropped them off is one of the current great mysteries, and the latest twist in my nation-state hobby. Since there is no regular airline service and often no phone calling to Nauru, the fates of the *Tampa* refugees these last few years is cloudy. We do know that Nauru established two refugee settlements. A group largely dominated by the Iraqis was settled in an abandoned apartment building called State House. I remember it as a nothing more than a cement frame of a high rise. Brian had pointed it out to me as a monument to Nauru's unfinished works.

The other camp is ominously called the Topside Camp. These inmates, who are largely Afghans, are living at the edge of the hot white plate of Nauru's interior.

Emails from Nauru surfaced a few months ago, alleging a refugee death. Nauru refused to confirm or deny anything, dismissing the entire story as "Chinese whispers." These emails come mainly from refugee pen pals who live in Australia. If they are real—and to someone who's visited the island, they have a certain ring of truth—they speak to a ghastly existence reminiscent of some nineteenth-century Devil's Island:

> We are in camp now and situation in camp is very bad. There is no water sometimes they bring salty water from the ocean for us.... They build up fences around the camp just like zoo.

> I do not know what I have done that they punish me. Because of killing, cruelty, and injustice I abandoned my homeland and wanted to take shelter in your country.

> We don't deserve what is happening here.

We had a hope to come to Australia but now we are here in
Nauru Hell.

Since the emergence of these emails, another source has appeared
to confirm their message. Dr. Maarten Dormaar is a Dutch psychia-
trist who had been assigned the task of providing mental health care
to the refugees sent to Nauru. He has since fled the island himself.
He has admitted to me that, violating all protocol, he made videotapes of a few of these refugees explaining their new lives and had
them smuggled out in the suitcase of an acquaintance. I got in touch
with Dormaar and have seen these videotapes.

Dormaar says that many of the refugees have the symptoms of
people going slowly mad. They are all forbidden from working, even
the professionals such as doctors. So they are depressed, can't sleep,
and spend their days and nights reviewing the elements of their
nightmares. Many of them visit the doctor in the hopes of receiving
sleeping pills. Other complain of headaches and mysterious back
pain—all symptoms of severe depression. And there's one other
symptom: On a regular basis, Dormaar said, a refugee is rushed to
the hospital having slashed himself fifteen or twenty times in the
chest or arms.

It's something to do.

These refugees are all foes of Saddam Hussein in Iraq and the
Taliban in Afghanistan. Their enemies, the ones who fought for the
Taliban and for Hussein and were captured and taken to America's
concentration camp in Guantanamo Bay in Cuba, eat good meals
with fresh water. They each have an individual cell. They have calls
to prayer. They see an Imam. They have medical care and psychi-
atric counseling. Many critics point out that our enemies have it
hard on Gitmo, as it's known. They should direct their concern to
our allies on Nauru.

One Iraqi, Mohammed Sagar, is seen in one of Dormaar's
videos. He is sitting on a beach looking out at a flat unchanging sea.
Dormaar and Sagar had sneaked off one early morning to an isolated stretch of sand since video is forbidden. Sagar explained the
boredom and tedium of his daily life. His English is pretty good and

at one point, he quotes the immigration minister of Australia, who says that the refugees have so many options.

"But there are no options," Sagar says. And rather than even explain, he simply points—and the camera follows—to the vista of Michener's ocean. Endless, open, and equatorially hot—twelve hundred miles to the nearest smudge of land. Just as chilling is Sagar's description of the time when the architect of the Pacific Solution—Australia's Immigration Minister Philip Ruddock—came to visit the refugees. The moment being so critically important to everyone, the refugees all bathed and cleaned up. They stood in a line. The children were dressed in the most colorful clothes they could find. The women somehow found some flowers to hold. Smiling and at attention, they stood in a large auditorium, Sagar explains, as Ruddock at last entered the building.

"He did not even look at us," Sagar said. "He did not even turn his head in our direction. Instead he walked all the way across the room to speak to the Nauruan officials."

The only true advocate for the Nauruans is one helpless Australian senator named Andrew Bartlett. The island government tried to keep him off, but he used his power to bully his way into the camps. The government kept him out of the Iraqi camp at State House. The Nauruan officials said that they "feared for my safety," Bartlett told me in an interview. He did get to meet with the Afghans. Bartlett remembered one teenaged boy whose parents in Afghanistan had been killed. His family was condemned to die by the reigning warlord. So there is no returning. And there seems to be no departing Nauru. No one wants him. He literally has no place on earth to go.

"He spoke to me and tried to act tough," Barlett said. "They do not like to show emotion. But it only took a few minutes for him to break down and he started to cry like a little boy."

This summer, Amnesty International declared a global alert for the refugees on the island. So far, this means little more than that the organization is working with some thirty churches to launch a letter-writing campaign to John Howard, the man whose re-election was built on the deliberate isolation of these refugees.

By sheer coincidence, as concern about the refugees began to crescendo in 2003, Nauru fetishists like myself learned of another of the island's big money-generating deals. According to court papers filed by numerous members of Nauru's cabinet, the United States, through a number of CIA operatives, threatened the country with complete extinction if it didn't cooperate in a black-op scheme code-named—I am not making this up—Operation Weasel.

In a lengthy investigative report published in the Australian newspaper, the reporter Cameron Stewart wrote that the deal began with two shady operators in the Pacific who approached Nauru. One was Jack Sanders, a dodgy intelligence official from New Zealand. The other was an American named Steven Ray, whose reputation is discussed by Sanders in an email: "He is a buddy but beware that he co-ordinates black ops, too, so make sure you stay on his good side—he makes the IRS look like pussies."

These two met with Nauruan officials and eventually helped set up meetings with other, more establishment Republican figures in Washington, such as Michael Horowitz, a former Reagan official, and Jack Pinder, a congressional staffer on the House Finance Committee. Eventually, during the winter of early 2003, it was arranged for these men to meet with the president who, for the sixth time, was my old friend, Bernard Dowiyogo.

The offers made to Nauru were magnificent. The Americans promised to rebuild the island's entire interior and offered $250 million for the job. "The United States has many pockets," Michael Horowitz is reported to have said. There were promises of health care for the island's inhabitants, a working desalination plant, and other benefits. In return, Dowiyogo was to sign a few papers. He had to agree to be among the nations that would immunize the United States in the International Criminal Court—a particular obsession with the Bush administration. He also had to agree to stop all money laundering and passport sales. Finally, he had to agree to participate in Operation Weasel. This covert operation would have Nauru open an embassy in Beijing and permit it to be staffed by covert agents who would facilitate smuggling North Korean defectors and nuclear scientists out of China and into the West.

And yet, nothing happens with this island until every angle has been exploited. Once the Weasel deal had been cut, Nauru officials went to China's rival, Taiwan, to start a bidding war over who would get their embassy. Eventually the Chinese won the bidding, offering Nauru a windfall of $130 million in direct aid if they'd open their diplomatic offices in Beijing. At the time, a bitter member of Taiwan's parliament denounced Nauru as "a country that switches sides because of money." He wasn't far off. As practitioners of modern brute capitalism, you have to hand it to the Nauruans, they're good.

As the deal with the United States seemed to be moving forward without any hitches, Dowiyogo had a heart attack in Washington. While he recovered in a hospital bed in early March 2003, he was confronted by the four Americans and urged to sign all the papers. He did. But, according to the report, he neglected to get the Americans to put their guarantees in writing.

Then, somewhere in the summer of 2003, something went very wrong. It probably began with Nauru's zany presidential politics.

Not long after signing the papers on his hospital bed, Dowiyogo died. His replacement, Derog Gioura, attempted to get a "condolence motion" through the "parliament" but hostilities had grown so tense among the tiny band of men who run the country that the motion stalled.

Then, a few weeks later, Derog Gioura also had a heart attack. A third president came into power in the spring of 2003, but he only lasted another few weeks, before it went to Dowiyogo's old nemesis (and money-laundering abider) Rene Harris.

In the chaos that occurred during the six months between Dowiyogo's death and Harris's return to power, it seemed that Nauru was mostly cooperating with Operation Weasel. For instance, if you happened to call the Nauru embassy in Beijing that spring in 2003, the only person there, covert operative Jack Sanders, answered the telephone.

Then this happened: Cameron Armstrong, the reporter, called the US State Department to find out if Nauru was actually going to be redeemed by America's antiterrorism bankroll. Officials stated flatly that there was absolutely no deal with Nauru. In fact, Armstrong reports that the Export-Import Bank, at the encouragement of the US government, had moved in court to seize Nauru's only tangible asset, that damn plane. In hopes of saving the nation's only form of contact to the outside world, Nauru's cabinet flew to Melbourne and filed a lawsuit, hoping to embarrass the Americans into delivering.

Still, win or lose, the choices for Nauru have now dwindled to a very few. Try to think like a Nauruan president for a moment. (Hurry!) The phosphate is running out. Water must be either desalinated or imported. No food can be grown locally. There is no hint of paradise—birds are rare, trees are bare, 80 percent of the land is denuded: Tourism is not an option.

They only have one thing left to sell: Nauru's authority as a nation state. Its very sovereignty. The country's leaders have no choice but to root through the last valuable trinkets of their independence—a UN seat, a batch of "embassies," a passport stamp, bank regulations, a vote on certain international councils. And Nauru trades them with the same brutal, hard-core, used-car capitalist spirit that they learned at the knee of their teachers—the factory managers at the phosphate plant. This was Nauru's ultimate import from the West: an economic ethic that enriched one generation of Nauruans while finishing off the country.

From the outside, Nauru is seen as some kind of symbol. "Nauru is the tip of the iceberg," said Professor Carl McDaniel, a biologist with Rensselaer Polytechnic Institute whose book *Paradise for Sale* examines the nation's collapsing biosystems. "Nauru is what happens when you treat natural resources as economic resources. You can't sell off your own habitat for long, but this is what we're all doing, everywhere. Nauru is only the canary in the mineshaft."

Critics of Nauru in the American government have long held that Nauru's meaning is something else entirely. It's an example of what happens when a country steps too far outside the necessary banking and regulatory codes of the new global marketplace. In one of those Clancyspeak emails published in 2003, the covert agent who first approached Nauru warned: "If anyone wants to play fucking games, I'll end it all right now by making three phone calls and that shit-hole in the middle of the Pacific will be left high and dry by everyone concerned."

Could it really be that Nauru will become the first nation-state of the modern age to simply go out of business? Once, Australia offered to give the Nauruans a new island off the Great Barrier Reef. The Nauruans declined since it meant completely surrendering their sovereignty. But it does seem likely that some future leader will have to plan for such a contingency.

Should economics not finish off the country, it's almost certain that nature will. Maybe then we'll be able to understand just what *Nauru* means. While some argue the cause, no scientist disputes the inevitability of an increase in the ocean's water level. New environmental studies suggest that the rising waters will engulf the meager inhabitable ring of the island left by phosphate mining. Soon enough, we'll be out of the realm of metaphor and deep into the prose of Michener. Nauru will be delivered, again, to the mercy of our guardian of the shorelines, regulator of temperatures and heaving sculptor of mountains. Topside's bleached labyrinth, scarcely visible in the high water, will be the sole proof that people once lived there before it was abandoned to be a boneyard bare and alone at sea, available once again only to the birds for millions upon millions of years.

From *Last Car to Elysian Fields*

JAMES LEE BURKE

THAT EVENING the shy was as dark as I had ever seen it. Lightning rippled like quicksilver across the thunderheads in the south, and the sugarcane in the fields along the road to St. Martinville thrashed and flickered in the wind and rain, the oak canopy blowing leaves that stuck like leeches on my windshield. I went to Mass in the old French church on the square in St. Martinville, then when the church was empty put five dollars in the poor box and removed an unlit votive candle in a red glass receptacle and took it with me down to the cemetery on the bayou.

It was a foolish thing to do, I suspect, but I had long ago come to view the world as an unreasonable place, not to be contended with, better left to pragmatists and the mercantile who view the imagination and the unseen as their enemy. I parked under the streetlight, opened an umbrella, and walked between the crypts toward Bootsie's tomb. A generic compact car passed behind me, turned at the corner, and disappeared down a side street.

The bayou was high, dented with rain rings, yellow in the lights from the drawbridge. I placed the votive candle next to the marble tablet on Bootsie's tomb, wedged the umbrella so that it sheltered the candle from the rain and wind, then lit the wick.

The same compact car came out of the square and crossed the drawbridge, but I paid little attention to it. An event I had never seen in my life was taking place in front of me. Two huge brown pelicans drifted out from under the bridge, floating south on the tidal current, their wings folded tightly against the wind, their long yellow bills tucked down on their chests. I had never seen pelicans this far inland and had no explanation for their presence. Then I did something that made me wonder about my level of sanity.

I rose from the steel bench I was sitting on, pointing at the two birds, and said, "Take a look, Boots. These guys were almost extinct a few years ago. They're beautiful."

Then I sat down and folded my arms on my chest, the rain clicking on my coat.

That's when I saw the compact in plain relief against the streetlight at the corner. It was pulled into a careless position at the curb, steam rising from the hood, the driver moving around in silhouette, as though he were having trouble with his safety belt.

Dave! a voice said, as audibly as a voice speaking to you on the edge of sleep, as defined as a stick snapping inside the eardrum.

I rose from the bench just as the streetlight glinted on the lens of a telescopic sight and the muzzle flash of a rifle splintered from the passenger window of the compact car. The bullet whanged off the steel bench and blew pieces off a statue of Jesus's mother.

I ducked down between the crypts and pulled my .45 from my belt holster and sighted with two hands on the compact. But there were houses on the far side of the street and I couldn't fire. I started running toward the compact, the .45 held at an upward angle, zigzagging between the crypts, my eyes locked on the driver, who was fighting to straighten the car's wheels so he would not hit the curb.

He pulled around a parked pickup truck and floored the compact down the street. In seconds he would be beyond any safe angle of fire that I would have. I left the sidewalk and ran toward the corner of the cemetery, jumped on top of a crypt, and went over the chainlink fence into the street. The compact was twenty-five to thirty yards away, headed down the bayou in the direction of the church, the license plated patinaed with mud. I stood in the center of the street, both arms extended, and aimed low on the trunk.

I squeezed off three rounds, the recoil knocking my forearms upward, the muzzle throwing sparks into the darkness, the spent shells tinkling on the pavement. I don't know what I hit inside the compact, but I heard the hard slap of all three hollow-point rounds bite into metal.

The compact swerved around a corner and disappeared down a tree-lined side street that looked like an illustration clipped from a 1940 issue of *The Saturday Evening Post*.

I went back to my truck and used my cell phone to punch in a 911 on the compact, then walked to Bootsie's tomb, my ears still ringing from the explosions of the .45. The umbrella had not been disturbed by the wind and the candle was burning brightly inside its red receptacle, but the pelicans had flown or drifted southward on the current.

I heard your voice, I said.

But there was no reply.

I don't care who else knows it, either. That was your voice, Boots, I said.

Then I said a prayer for her and one for me and headed back for the truck, wishing the pelicans had not gone.

Don't worry, they'll be back. One of these days when you least expect it, you'll see them on Bayou Teche, she said.

I turned around, my jaw hanging, the clouds blooming with electricity that made no sound.

Edward Abbey was a novelist and essayist whose works include *Desert Solitaire, The Monkey Wrench Gang, The Fool's Progress*, and *Down the River*. He died in 1989.

Bill Belleville is a magazine writer, author, and Emmy-award-winning documentary filmmaker. His books include *River of Lakes: A Journey on Florida's St. Johns River, Deep Cuba*, and the forthcoming anthology *Sunken Cities, Sacred Cenotes and Golden Sharks*. Belleville has traveled on assignment to the Great Barrier Reef, the White Sea of Russia, the upper and lower Amazon, the Galapagos, and throughout Central America and the Caribbean. He lives in Florida.

Rita Welty Bourke's stories have appeared in numerous literary magazines, including *The North American Review, Shenandoah, Black Warrior Review, South Dakota Review*, and *Witness*. She has been nominated three times for the Pushcart Prize. She lives in Nashville, Tennessee, with her songwriter husband.

Charles Bowden's most recent book is *Down by the River*, a story of drugs, murder, and family on the US-Mexico border. He has written eleven previous nonfiction books, including *Blood Orchid, Trust Me, Desierto, The Sonoran Desert, Frog Mountain Blues*, and *Killing the Hidden Waters*. Bowden won the Lannan Literary Award for Nonfiction. He lives in Tucson, Arizona.

T. Coraghessan Boyle is the author of sixteen books of fiction, including, most recently, *After the Plague*, *Drop City*, and *The Inner Circle*. His book *A Friend of the Earth* is a futuristic satire of a ruined planet told from the point of view of a burned-out radical environmentalist employed as caretaker for a menagerie of predators by an over-the-hill rock star. Boyle's stories have appeared in most of the major American magazines, including *The New Yorker, Harper's, Esquire, The Atlantic Monthly, Playboy, The Paris Review, GQ, Antaeus, Granta,* and *McSweeney's*, and he has been the recipient of a number of literary awards. He posts diary listings on his website: www.tomboyle.com. He lives near Santa Barbara with his wife and three children.

John Gregory Brown is the author of *The Wrecked, Blessed Body of Sheldon Lafleur*, and *Decorations in a Ruined Cemetery*. He directs the creative writing program at Sweet Briar College in Virginia, where he lives with his wife, the writer Carrie Brown, and three children.

James Lee Burke has justly been called the Faulkner of the mystery novel. He was born in Houston, Texas, in 1936 and grew up on the Texas-Louisiana gulf coast. Over the years he worked as a landman for Sinclair Oil Company, pipeliner, land surveyor, newspaper reporter, college English professor, social worker on Skid Row in Los Angeles, and clerk for the Louisiana Employment Service. He published four novels while still in his twenties, including one dealing with pollution from a pulp mill in Montana. His novel *The Lost Get-Back Boogie* was rejected 111 times over a period of nine years, and upon publication by Louisiana State University press was nominated for a Pulitzer Prize. His books include *Sunset Limited, Heaven's Prisoners, Burning Angel, Purple Cane Road,* and *Last Car to Elysian Fields*. Today he and his wife live in Missoula, Montana, and New Iberia, Louisiana. People in New Iberia regard him as one of their own, even if he was born in Texas.

Bruce Chatwin was an art specialist at Sotheby's, a journalist with the Sunday *Times* in London, an archaeologist, and a restless, perennial traveler. He wrote seven books—including two novels and what has been called "a sui generis masterpiece," *The Songlines. The Songlines* is a mix of reportage and scrapbook musings on the central role of nomadism in the human character. *The Songlines* is not so much a book as an artifact, a battered stone inscribed with commandments, an object regarded with something akin to religious awe by desert rats. Chatwin's other books include *In Patagonia, The Viceroy of Ouidah, Utz,* and *On the Black Hill.* He died in 1989.

Sarah L. Courteau lives in Iowa City, where she is working on an MFA in nonfiction writing at the University of Iowa. The essay in this volume first appeared in *Witness* and was reprinted in *Harper's.* She was born and raised in the Ozark Mountains of northwest Arkansas and is currently working on a short story collection set there.

Joe Donnelly is deputy editor of *LA Weekly.* He has worked at *The Los Angeles Times, The Washington Post*, and *Vail Trail.* He was editor-in-chief of the much-loved and sorely missed *Bikini* magazine and prior to that he was the founding editor of *Stick*, a snowboarding magazine. His articles and essays have also appeared in *Detour* and *Black Book.*

Alexandra Fuller, the author of the memoir *Don't Let's Go to the Dogs Tonight*, was born in England in 1969. In 1972, she moved with her family to Rhodesia, which is now Zimbabwe. After that country's civil war in 1981, the Fullers moved to Malawi, and later to Zambia. Fuller's work acknowledges the dichotomies of whites living in Africa in a way that is both unapologetic and refreshingly unpretentious. Fuller now lives in Wyoming with her husband and two children.

Carl Hiaasen was born and raised in South Florida. His novels include *Tourist Season, Double Whammy, Skin Tight, Native Tongue, Striptease*, and *Basket Case*. *The London Observer* called him "America's finest satirical novelist." Hiaasen is also the author of *Team Rodent*, an unsparing essay about the Disney empire, part of which is excerpted in *Naked*, and two recent collections of newspaper columns, *Kick Ass* and *Paradise Screwed*. Oddly enough, a man who writes about tourists impaled on marlin spikes has recently won the prestigious Newberry Award for children's fiction.

Jack Hitt writes for *The New York Times Magazine, Harper's, Outside,* and many other publications. He is also a correspondent for *This American Life*. Hitt, who has slogged through the Cambodian jungle with mercenaries and former Khmer Rouge soldiers hired to protect endangered species, written about the importance of drinking to the socialization of college students, and described his revolting adventures in a cave full of bat guano, manages to combine a low-key but nonetheless solid sense of ethics with deep-seated irreverence. He is a former editor of *Harper's*. His book, *Off the Road: A Modern-Day Walk Down the Pilgrims Route into Spain*, was published in 1994 and will appear in paperback in 2004. Hitt lives in Connecticut with his wife, passel of children, and a large, carpeted van, which he insists gets good mileage when it's packed with kids.

Liz Jensen is the author of *Ark Baby* and *Egg Dancing*. Her most recent book, *The Paper Eater*, is a futuristic satire of consumerism that critics have likened to the work of George Orwell. She has worked in Britain and the Far East as a journalist and radio producer and in France as a sculptor. She lives in London.

Ryszard Kapuściński, who was born in 1932, has become a cult hero among fledgling foreign correspondents. Kapuściński has witnessed twenty-seven coups and revolutions and was sentenced to death four times. His books include *Shah of Shahs*,

The Emperor, and *The Soccer War*, as well as *The Shadow of the Sun*, the book about Africa from which this excerpt is drawn. He lives in New York City.

A. L. Kennedy is the author of numerous novels, plays, and short stories, including *The Life and Death of Colonel Blimp* and *Original Bliss*. Her most recent book is *Indelible Acts*. She has won numerous awards for her work. Her comments on the writing life, the publishing industry, and one reporter's characterizations of her teeth can be found on: http://www.a-l-kennedy.co.uk/index.htm. She lives in Scotland.

Klaus Kinski grew up in postwar Berlin. He became one of Europe's most celebrated actors, best known for his performances in the Werner Herzog films *Aguirre, Wrath of God, Nosferatu*, and *Fitzcarraldo*. He died in Northern California in 1991.

Paul Scott Malone is the author of the short story collections *In an Arid Land* and *Memorial Day and Other Stories*. His first novel, *This House of Women*, was published in 2001. A native of Texas, Malone now lives in Tucson, Arizona.

Thomas McIntyre writes for *Field and Stream* and *Sports Afield* magazines. He is the author of *Dreaming the Lion*, about hunting in Africa, and *Seasons and Days*, a collection of his essays in which a version of "Blood Lust" appeared. McIntyre was born and raised in Los Angeles and, although he rarely talks about it, is as familiar with the Rosalind Russell film version of *Auntie Mame* as he is with the writing of Ernest Hemingway. He now lives in Sheridan, Wyoming, with his wife and son.

Lydia Millet is the author of three novels, including *Omnivores* and *George Bush, Dark Prince of Love*. Her most recent novel, *My Happy Life*, won the 2003 PEN-USA Award for Fiction. She splits her time between Tucson, Arizona, and Los Angeles.

Ted Mooney's most recent book is *Singing into the Piano*. *Easy Travel to Other Planets*, his first novel, was published in 1981, when the scene excerpted here caught the attention of readers and reviewers. His hallucinatory fiction juxtaposes individual desires with political events: an obscure international conflict in Antarctica, people falling mysteriously ill from "information sickness," the deforestation of the Amazon basin. Mooney is senior editor of *Art in America*. He lives in New York City.

Andrew X. Pham was born in Vietnam and moved to California with his family after the war. *Catfish and Mandala*, which tells the story of Pham's solo bicycle trip around the Pacific Rim to Vietnam, won the Whiting Writers Award. He lives in Portland, Oregon.

Alan Rabinowitz is the author of *Beyond the Last Village: A Journey of Discovery in Asia's Forbidden Wilderness*, from which this chapter is excerpted. His two other books are *Jaguar: One Man's Struggle to Establish the World's First Jaguar Preserve* and *Chasing the Dragon's Tail: The Struggle to Save Thailand's Wild Cats*. He is director of the Science and Exploration Program at the Wildlife Conservation Society, based at the Bronx Zoo in New York. Rabinowitz has conducted surveys and led expeditions in diverse parts of the globe, often serving as the catalyst for the creation of new wildlife preserves. He lives in Mahopac, New York, with his wife and son.

Stacey Richter has been called an MTV-generation Eudora Welty. She has won three Pushcart Prizes and a National Magazine Award, and her fiction has been published in *GQ, Granta*, and elsewhere. She is the author of the story collection *My Date with Satan*. More of her work, including a short, animated film she wrote and conceived, can be found at www.staceyrichter.com.

Elizabeth Royte is the author of *The Tapir's Morning Bath: Mysteries of The Tropical Rain Forest and the Scientists Who Are Trying to Solve Them*.

Her work has appeared in *The New York Times Magazine, Harper's, The New Yorker, Outside, National Geographic, Smithsonian,* and other national magazines. She lives in New York City.

Rob Schultheis is the author of *The Hidden West, Bone Games, Fool's Gold,* and *Night Letters,* a book of his wartime experiences in Afghanistan that has been compared to Michael Herr's *Dispatches.* His newest book, *Bandit Country,* details travels in the Northwest Frontier Province of Pakistan, Mexico's Sierra Madre Occidental, the Golden Triangle of Southeast Asia, the outback of the Navajo Rez where the main "authority" are gangs like the Navajo Cobraz—lawless, stateless, quasi-nations that fall between the cracks of our twenty-first century "New World Order." Schultheis has covered Afghanistan for *Time, The Washington Post, The San Francisco Examiner,* and *The New York Times Magazine.* He lives in Telluride, Colorado.

Jeremy Seal has been called "Bruce Chatwin with a sense of humor." He is the author of *The Snakebite Survivors' Club: Travels Among Serpents* and *A Fez of the Heart: Travels around Turkey in Search of a Hat.* Seal contributes regularly to *The Times* of London, *The Daily Telegraph, London's Evening Standard, Conde Nast Traveller,* and other publications. He lives in Bath with his wife and daughter, where he is currently working on a book about North Cornwall.

Deanne Stillman is the author of *Twentynine Palms: A True Story of Murder, Marines, and the Mojave,* which was named one of the "Best Books of 2001" by *The Los Angeles Times Book Review.* "The Luckiest Horse in Reno" is excerpted from *Horse Latitudes,* her forthcoming history of the wild horse in America. Stillman is one of several writers who is finding new significance in the American West within the context of contemporary culture. She has written for *Rolling Stone, Slate, Tin House,* and *The Los Angeles Times Magazine.* Her plays have been performed and won prizes in festivals throughout the US and her satirical essays have been published in *The New York Times.* She lives in Los Angeles.

Joy Williams is the author of the novels *Breaking and Entering, State of Grace,* and of the short story collections *Taking Care* and *Escapes.* Williams's stories and essays frequently appear in such publications as *Esquire, Granta, The Paris Review,* and *The New Yorker.* She lives in Key West, Florida, and Tucson, Arizona, the setting for her most recent novel, *The Quick and the Dead.* Referring to an earlier interview, a reporter asked if she still preferred to write in remote, isolated parts of the country. "Tucson is hardly remote or isolated," Williams said. "It is quickly filling up with people who loathe the desert. They'd prefer to be anywhere else and are turning it into anywhere else."

Susan Zakin is the author of *Coyotes and Town Dogs: Earth First! and the Environmental Movement,* a cult history of the US environmental movement since Earth Day that one reviewer called "brilliant and irreverent, tough and funny... the most thorough and thoughtful survey of the American environmental movement." Zakin covered national environmental politics as a columnist for *Sports Afield.* Her articles and essays have appeared in *Salon, Vogue, Orion, The New York Times, Field and Stream, LA Weekly,* and many other publications. This excerpt is from her new book, *Tierra Incognita,* a story about the desert, death, love, and the evanescent nature of truth. She lives in Tucson, Arizona.